HARRISON FORD

Imperfect Hero

Also by Garry Jenkins

Daniel Day-Lewis: The Fire Within

Empire Building: The Remarkable Real-Life Story
of Star Wars

HARRISON FORD

Imperfect Hero

Garry Jenkins

A BIRCH LANE PRESS BOOK
Published by Carol Publishing Group

For Cilene

A Birch Lane Press Book
Published by Carol Publishing Group
Birch Lane Press is a registered trademark of Carol Communications, Inc.

Harrison Ford: Imperfect Hero was first published in Great Britain in 1996 in slightly different
form by Simon & Schuster Ltd.

Editorial, sales and distribution, and rights and permissions inquiries should be addressed to
Carol Publishing Group, 120 Enterprise Avenue, Secaucus, N.J. 07094

In Canada: Canadian Manda Group, One Atlantic Avenue, Suite 105, Toronto, Ontario
M6K 3E7

Carol Publishing Group books may be purchased in bulk at special discounts for sales
promotion, fund-raising, or educational purposes. Special editions can be created to
specifications. For details, contact: Special Sales Department, 120 Enterprise Avenue,
Secaucus, N.J. 07094.

MANUFACTURED IN THE UNITED STATES OF AMERICA
10 9 8 7 6 5 4 3 2

Library of Congress Cataloging-in-Publication Data

Jenkins, Garry.
    Harrison Ford : imperfect hero / Garry Jenkins.
        p.   cm.
    "A Birch Lane Press book."
    Originally published: London : Simon and Schuster, 1996.
    Includes bibliographical references and index.
    ISBN 1-55972-443-9 (hc)
    1. Ford, Harrison, 1942–   2. Motion picture actors and actresses—
United States—Biography.   I. Title.
PN2287.F59J47   1997
791.43´028´092—dc21
[B]   97-41446

Contents

HARRISON FORD

Imperfect Hero

Prologue

On March 9, 1994, a steady flow of Gulfstream jets dropped out of the Nevada Desert haze on to the griddle-hot tarmac at Las Vegas's McCarran International Airport, and taxied their way to a line of waiting limousines.

Even by the standards of the town some call Glitter Gulch, the planes' passenger lists made for impressive reading. They were carrying some of the most powerful individuals in the most potent industry on Earth—from Sumner Redstone, the billionaire head of Viacom and Paramount Pictures to Ted Turner, head of CNN; from Tom Cruise to Tom Hanks. The limousines dispatched each of them to Bally's Hotel, across the road from Caesar's Palace, where one of the key corporate events on the entertainment industry calendar was about to begin.

If the Academy Awards are for show, the annual convention organized by America's National Association of Theater Owners—NATO—is strictly for business. It is a place to shut out the world and defer to the deities of the box-office and the bottom line. It is where Hollywood oils the wheels of its billion-dollar trade.

Hollywood being what it is, such gatherings rarely end without a self-congratulatory slap on its collective back. In years gone by, NATO had, by tradition, brought events to a close with a series of awards, the most prestigious going to the outstanding box-office star of the year. With a particularly healthy year behind it—and the centennial of cinema only a year away—the organizers of the 1994 event decided to mint a rather more memorable honor. On March 9, they honored the "Box-Office Star of the Century."

To some it might have seemed a meaningless choice: Garbo or

Gable, Chaplin or Monroe, Hepburn or Tracy, Crosby or Cruise? How to choose? Impossible! To the delegates of NATO, however, the decision had proven remarkably simple. The words "box office" were the key.

And so it was that evening, in the ballroom at Bally's Hotel, the audience stood as one to applaud an actor whose films had grossed more than those of any other—$2 billion and still counting—a man whose credit had appeared on seven of the twenty most successful films of all time. As their ovation faded, the object of the adulation muttered wryly: "This confirms my worst fear—heaven is just like Las Vegas." As usual he did so in a spoon-bending bass and with a wry, dry downturn of his face's southern features.

Since his earliest days in suburban Chicago, irony had never been far from Harrison Ford's lips. His taste for the sardonic can never have been quite so richly indulged as it was at that moment in Las Vegas, however.

There, in the middle of a desert, Hollywood had come to acknowledge a man it had consistently cast into the wilderness. There, in the gambling capital of America, an outsider had beaten odds stacked so severely against him that, for a while, he was even refused a seat at the table.

When Harrison Ford first arrived on Hollywood's doorstep, all he was good for was fitting doors and fixing clocks, designing shelves and delivering pizza. Now, thirty years later, he was being given an award considered extraordinary even by Hollywood's insanely hyperbolic standards. Inside he felt a maelstrom of emotions. Outside all he could do was smile.

So how did this unknown actor overcome Hollywood's total indifference toward him, and subsequently evolve into the most successful performer in the first hundred years of cinema?

As usual, he wasn't giving anything away on that night in Nevada. Yet his desert-dry humor provided the odd clue. Casting his eye around at the other actors in the room, he said: "I look at them and think, 'Wow, what a talent.' They look at me and think, 'Wow, what a lucky bastard.' " As he brought his speech to a close he cut a deal with his hosts. "I'll keep people in the theater and you try to keep their shoes from sticking to the floor."

Persistence and luck have played a central role in the remarkable story of Harrison Ford. He had learned the value of both long, long before that glittering night in Las Vegas. . . .

PART ONE

*"I think being an actor developed from
not feeling part of society."*

Harrison Ford

1

STEERAGE TO SUBURBIA

In 1955 the winds of change sweeping through America blew nowhere more profoundly than in Chicago, the Windy City. With the United States experiencing the biggest consumer boom of the century, the metropolis on the shore of Lake Michigan was a ferment of ideas and innovations. Many would mold modern America.

In 1955 Chicago finished building itself a gleaming new airport— O'Hare—the nation's biggest. It was also in that year that its new Mayor, Richard J. Daley, ordered the most ambitious housing program the city had ever seen—an explosion of expressways and subways, skyscrapers and custom-made new suburbs. Enterprise was everywhere. In the Loop, the city's commercial heart, the advertising agency Leo Burnett launched the Philip Morris company's new cigarette campaign, the Marlboro Man. It was there too that Hugh Hefner saw *Playboy*, the magazine he had started a year earlier on a shoestring from his downtown apartment, pass the 100,000 sales a month mark. The pace of progress was dizzying. Yet at the Meltzer Junior High School in suburban Des Plaines, two things remained utterly immune to change. Each day in class, teachers would fight to be heard above the deafening roar of the planes leaving nearby O'Hare. And each day in the playground, the school's toughest gang would pick a fight with a skinny newcomer called Harry Ford.

The gang came from the town's blue-collar enclaves. They wore leather jackets and work boots, and greased their hair into the fashionable DA haircuts of the day. The girls who hung around with them copied the leather-jacketed look, chewed gum, and knotted scarves around their necks. Over in Hollywood that year, director Nicholas Ray was making a movie about alienated teenagers just like them— *Rebel Without a Cause* starring the young James Dean.

Harry Ford had moved into Morton Grove, a neighborhood of new, low-income homes spreading out across old farm land on the other side of the Des Plaines River, the previous summer. Just entering his teens—he would be thirteen that July—he was as different from the "hoods" as Dean was from his high school persecutors. The son of an Irish father and a Jewish mother, his hair was buzzcut short and he dressed Ivy League–style, in pressed shirts with button-down collars. He was something of a loner, a boy with a faintly sarcastic smile and a knack for making the girls laugh. This, and his air of quiet arrogance, was enough to incite the Meltzer bullies.

So it was that most days, usually during recess, the Des Plaines gang would seek out the boy from the wrong side of the river and beat him up in the school parking lot. After softening him up with a few punches, they would propel him over the edge of a steep slope, into dense weeds below.

At first, crowds of students came to watch, but the audience dropped off when Harry's beatings became a routine. Each time he would haul himself back up the incline, offer nothing stronger than another sardonic, lopsided smile and invite his torturers to try again. Most times they would, but it wasn't long before the thugs grew bored by his unwillingness to retaliate, and found a new boy to bait.

As Indiana Jones and Han Solo, John Book and Jack Ryan, Harry would cheat more intimidating odds, face down more formidable enemies. Yet in truth, there could have been few more valuable victories than those he won playing Sisyphus, doggedly climbing and reclimbing that grassy slope, turning the other fist-reddened cheek. If there is, as Graham Greene put it, "one moment in childhood when the door opens and lets the future in," then for Harry Ford it came in his moment of schoolyard triumph.

* * *

He was far from being the first of his family to show perseverance in the face of persecution. On a mist-shrouded morning in 1907, as his grandmother, Anna Lifschutz, stared out over the bow of the steamship carrying her into New York Harbor, the shadow of a more brutal bigotry had by then driven his ancestors halfway across the world.

The sight of the Statue of Liberty and its promise of refuge for those "yearning to breathe free," brought to an end an epic journey that had begun weeks earlier, deep inside Russia and a ramshackle Jewish *shtetl* in the city of Minsk.

At the age of nineteen, Anna Lifschutz had fled a world in which her people were being systematically murdered. Inside the "Pale of Settlement" along the western frontier of Russia, the four million Jews confined there by law were subjected to official persecution under Nicholas II. Between 1902 and 1906, thousands of Jewish men, women, and children died in pogroms—orchestrated episodes of looting, killing and rape. Minsk had suffered its greatest losses shortly before Anna left, in 1905. She was one of two million Russian Jews who fled the atrocities between 1880 and 1914.

Her voyage had begun as she gathered together her belongings—it was customary for young women to include a goose-feather pillow and a traditional lace petticoat as a dowry—wrapped them in a sheet, and boarded a train made up of linked box cars, segregated between men, women, and children. As the noisy train slowly picked its way through Poland and Eastern Europe, packing in more men and women like herself as it headed toward the main embarkation ports of Bremen and Antwerp, she may have been lucky enough to find a seat on one of the train's few benches. If not, she would have spent days sitting on a cramped carriage floor.

At the port she would have had to present the three vital requirements for her journey—exit papers, the price of her passage and a spare $25 as proof that she could support herself in America—then endured the ritual of being bathed and deloused and having her clothes and baggage fumigated before being allowed up the gangplank of the steamship.

The journey across the Atlantic would have taken between eight and fourteen days, depending on the size of her ship. Yet Anna's emotions would have been no different from those of the hundreds of other young women sharing her journey—a sense of loss at the friends and family she had left behind, and a growing excitement at the new life that lay ahead.

After passing through Ellis Island, Anna headed for the teeming streets of Brooklyn and Manhattan. It was there that she met another refugee from the Russian nightmare—Harry Nidelman, also from Minsk.

It was common for engaged men to head to America in advance to prepare a life ready for their fiancées to follow. Once established in a job and a home, they would send money for their wives-to-be to join them. It is not clear whether Anna Lifschutz had known Harry Nidelman before her journey to America. What is apparent is that they were soon married, and by the time their second daughter, Dora Nidelman, was born on October 5, 1917, they had settled in the town of Linden, in Union County, New Jersey. A first girl, Beatrice, had been born two years earlier in New York.

Harry Nidelman had succeeded in forging a new life for himself and his family. His given occupation on his second child's birth certificate was a machinist. Before that he had also worked as a tram driver in Brooklyn.

The Nidelman family's happiness was short-lived, however. Tragedy struck when Harry succumbed to the great flu epidemic that ravaged the country in 1918 and 1919. Sadly, he died while Dora was still a baby.

Left to raise her daughters alone and without a trade to fall back on, Anna moved her young family to Stratford Avenue in Brooklyn, a community of Jews from Galicia and Warsaw. It was there that Dora Nidelman grew up.

Like millions of other first-generation Americans, Dora's childhood and adolescence would have been defined by the conflict between the strictures of her Old World religion and the freedoms of the New World society in which she grew up. Many Jewish families were riven by arguments over their children's rejection of the Talmudic traditions of orthodox Jewish life.

While Anna Nidelman arrived in America only able to speak Yiddish, Dora grew up speaking English. An early, if modest, rebellion was her decision to change her name to the more English-sounding Dorothy. She moved further away from her roots when, toward the end of the 1930s, she left the East Coast for Chicago. By far her most dramatic break with the past came, however, when she met and fell in love with a Gentile, suave and dashingly handsome radio writer Christopher Ford.

Christopher Ford understood the pain of losing his father early, too. He had been born John William Ford in New York on November 20, 1906, the son of an Irish-Catholic father, John Fitzgerald Ford and a German-American mother, Florence Veronica Niehaus.

Like many a son of an Irishman in New York, John Fitzgerald Ford, born in the city in 1880, earned a living doing what came naturally. He sang on the vaudeville stages of New York and the East, specializing in one of the most popular entertainment forms of the day—blackface.

During the early decades of the century, the burlesque bars and halls were filled with such shoe-polished performers. Most were working-class Jewish, Irish, German, and Italian singers and comics singing songs and cracking racist jokes at the expense of one another's backgrounds.

"Maybe it was because a guy in blackface could get away with things he couldn't in whiteface. People figured you were an 'actor' when you had black on," wrote the vaudeville star turned historian Joe Laurie Jr. The life of a vaudevillian was a tough and unforgiving one—an endless cycle of, as Laurie put it: "Damp basement dressing rooms, layoffs, empty stomachs, long jumps for short dough (sometimes *no* dough), cancellations after the first show, terrible orchestras, amateur stagehands, lousy boarding houses with cold rooms in winter and hot ones in summer, greasy grub and, worse than all this, flopping."

For John Fitzgerald Ford, the bottle offered an escape from the soul-sapping routine. John William Ford was still a baby when his father drank himself to death, leaving his mother and a younger brother bereft.

After the loss of her husband, Florence Ford, age twenty-two when she first became a mother, seems to have been incapable of coping with the strain of raising a family. Her two sons were handed over to a sisterhood of nuns and entrusted to their care in an orphanage. Like so many orphans, the shadow of his rejection from his natural family would haunt Christopher Ford throughout his life. Many of its ghosts would color the upbringing of his own children. During his adolescence and early manhood, however, the trauma seems mainly to have instilled a rootlessness and an acute determination to succeed.

Undeterred by his father's tragic experience, he began by following him into show business. Blessed with a deep, resonant voice to complement his tall, strikingly handsome looks, he too began performing in music halls. By the 1930s, however, the itinerant world of the vaudevillians, imported largely by the immigrant influx of the first decades of the century, was in terminal decline. As a new medium began to dominate the world of mass entertainment, John switched his attention to radio drama, joining the new union, the American Federation of Radio Actors in Chicago in 1938. (It may well have been at this time that he first began to be known as Christopher rather than John Ford. That name had already been acquired by another Irish-American, one Sean O'Fearna, when he began making silent movies in 1917. By now the man known as John Ford the director was entering the golden age of his creativity with *Stagecoach*, *Young Mr. Lincoln*, and *The Grapes of Wrath*.)

Christopher Ford's move to Chicago coincided with the end of another painful period in his life. In New York he had been briefly—and, it seems, unhappily—married. A divorce had been granted there in October 1939. In Chicago Christopher joined an industry at its zenith. In the America of the 1930s and early 1940s, radio was king. Every home, no matter how impoverished by the Depression, had a cathedral-shaped Philco or Edison in its living room. And with soap operas filling the airwaves from dawn till dusk, radio was quickly employing more actors than the theater and movie business put together.

Within three years of joining AMFAR, Christopher had changed track once more, landing a job as a writer at WENR—a local Chicago station formed by the E. N. Rauland radio-tube manufacturing company, and one of the scores of small city stations making up the giant NBC "blue" network. The job was far from glamorous. It was not until the 1950s that stations loosened up their act sufficiently to allow improvisational DJs on to the airwaves. From the jokes on the variety shows to the lead-ins spoken by the announcers, everything was scripted and scrupulously monitored. Writers' duties could be as brain-numbingly boring as giving birth to the "Good evening and welcome," lines announcers delivered in their perfect English tones. In a Chicago still recovering from the ravages of the Depression, however, radio remained the most vibrant and sociable industry the city had to offer.

Christopher lived in an apartment at 713 North Rush Street, in the city's liveliest area. It seems likely that it was through work that he met Dorothy Nidelman, who, after arriving in Chicago, worked briefly as a radio actress. If there is uncertainty over the circumstances of their meeting, there can be no doubt about the course of events that followed. The part-time actress and the handsome radio writer quickly fell in love.

In the 1940s, a romance between an Irish-Catholic divorcé and a Jewess would have been the cause of much hand-wringing anguish, even within the multiethnic melting pot that was Chicago. No matter how strong the stigma of a mixed-religion relationship, it seemed far better than the prospect that faced Dorothy by the end of 1941, when she discovered she was pregnant.

Dorothy Nidelman and Christopher Ford were hastily married in a civil ceremony on February 3, 1942. At twenty-four Dorothy was eleven years her new husband's junior.

Almost six months after the marriage, at around 11 A.M. on the morning of Wednesday, July 13, Dorothy Ford gave birth to a baby boy at Chicago's Swedish Covenant Hospital. Days later he was registered with a name derived from that of his maternal grandfather: Harrison Ford.

"I think it's Yiddish for 'son of Harry.' Even though I wasn't son of Harry," the son smiled later in his life. By then, through his own extraordinary exploits, the name had acquired a certain sturdy heroism. During his childhood, though, it bestowed on him all the disadvantages of a distinctive Christian name. It stuck out so much that for most of his young life he preferred it if people called him by his grandfather's name, Harry.

The new family spent its early years at an apartment next door to Dorothy's previous address on Irving Park Boulevard. They later moved to a more spacious apartment on West Sunnyside, on the edge of the Loop.

The sight of commuting workers may well have been the first images of the outside world to make an impression on Harrison Ford. As a toddler he loved nothing more than standing at the apartment window, waving at the passersby as they made their way to and from their work-places. During the early years of his childhood he would have wit-nessed a Chicago living up to its reputation as America's "city of big shoulders."

Harrison had been born in the first summer of America's World War II, almost eight months after Pearl Harbor. By then Chicago had already become one of the crucibles of the nation's war effort. Its steel mills and smelting plants fired at full capacity, thousands of laborers arrived from the southern states to work in the munitions factories, and some of the finest brains in the world came to the University of Chicago where a team led by Enrico Fermi was taking the first tenta-tive steps toward the bomb they would explode at Los Alamos. The lion's share of the Government's $1 billion national armaments budget was spent in Chicago. By the time it had been used up, Chicago had helped the Allies win the war and had dug itself out of the Depression.

By the end of the war, Dorothy had given birth to another boy—Terence. The moment when his monopoly of his mother's affections came to an end marks the beginning of what Harrison Ford can recall of his childhood. His first memory, he confessed once, was being awak-ened in the dark and "being told that I had a little brother."

Terence and Harrison, or Terry and Harry as most remember them, grew up in the center of Chicago, attending the Graeme Stewart Ele-mentary School. Terence, born with darker, curlier hair, bore little resemblance to his older brother. "The family joke is that there were different milkmen," he said once. But there seems to have been little sibling tension. "Our three-year age difference prevented any rivalry." Over the years both brothers have described their early childhood with words like "stable" and "normal." Young Harry's early ideas of life bor-dered on the distinctly *ab*normal, however.

One of his earliest hobbies was breeding rats, for instance. Asked once who his boyhood heroes were, he cited Abraham Lincoln, Hank Sauer, the tobacco-chewing slugger with the Chicago Cubs, and George Washington Carver. "Carver invented one hundred and one uses for peanuts. I guess that is kind of unusual," he conceded.

His earliest ambition was to be a coalman. Every week, from a window, he would watch the local delivery man unloading the family's supply. Compared to the backstabbing world his father described at the dinner table, this seemed, to the innocent Harry at least, a worthy life. "My dad would get all dressed up, go to work, come home, sit at the dinner table and bitch like crazy about those bastards at work," he recalled. In comparison, the life of the coalman seemed somehow more sensible. "He didn't go home at night and tell his wife how uncooperative the coal was." It was a view he would soon come to change; one day he would want nothing more than to be like his father.

Harry grew up knowing only one of his grandparents. Even then he only saw Anna Nidelman occasionally when she visited from her home in Flatbush. His abiding memory of the family's matriarch, he recalled once, was a rather frightening one—of her false teeth, lying in a glass! Without a grandfather to offer alternative role models, the young Harry found his most powerful childhood influence in his father. Given the family's Jewish roots, the bond between mother and son—Dorothy was, by now, committed to homemaking, listing "housework" as her occupation on her first son's birth certificate—remained an unbreakable one. Yet much of young Harrison's personality appears to have developed in response to Christopher's influence.

Later in life, for instance, he would come to admit that his childhood was spent feeling displaced from the rest of society; he viewed himself as an outcast, a skeptic. Much of this view seems to have been an inheritance from Christopher, whose early life—it is safe to guess—must have fueled similar emotions.

Certainly, from an early age, his father encouraged Harry to question the world around him. On weekends, for instance, Harry was exposed to the diversity of Chicago's religious traditions. The family would attend services at Protestant and Catholic churches, or synagogues—even the city's splendid Bahai House of Worship. The view that nothing should be taken at face value was reinforced over the dinner table and whenever Harry accompanied his father to work.

One childhood experience would remain lodged in Harry's mind forever. Christopher had remained a member of the radio actors' union, eventually becoming an active member of the board of the Chicago branch, and was friendly with some of the best-known actors of the day. During one trip into the Loop with his father, Harry was introduced to the star of one of the American Broadcasting Corporation's most popular children's shows, *Sky King*. Between 1947 and 1954, the adventures of the quiet rancher who fought evil at the controls of his plane hooked children across America. The heroic voice of Sky King was supplied by Earl Nightingale, one of the busiest radio actors of the time. In the fertile young minds of a million American children, Sky King was a square-jawed farmer, an American avenger in the mold of Gary Cooper or John Wayne. His father showed Harry different. "He turned out to be short and unconventional-looking."

The experience seems to have had a profound effect on Harrison, deepening a mature and mistrustful nature he would display through his childhood and beyond. "It intrigued me, how different show business was from what people thought," he said, recalling it decades later.

His father's worldly cynicism may, of course, have been a reflection of his own sense of betrayal as a rejected child. Given his early experiences, Christopher could have had faith in little that represented his past. Yet if it was his way of warning his child of the coldness of the world outside, he seems to have done so in the tones of Father Knows Best. He shared little of his own experience with his son, steadfastly refusing to discuss his years in the orphanage and on the vaudeville stage.

"It was a rough life and my father is unwilling to talk about it," Harrison said once, when asked about his father's past. It seems more than a coincidence that, as one of the most familiar faces in the world, Harrison was by then demonstrating the same intensely private, painfully secretive nature himself.

While Harrison remained close to his mother, his father's domineering nature eventually provoked a predictable counterreaction. "A lot of what he did was in opposition to his father," one of his closest friends said years later. "He was much closer to his Jewish mother."

As Harrison edged his way through his early childhood, however, his father's shadow grew even more overpowering. His influence seems to have increased with it.

Christopher's belated rise to prosperity coincided with the decline of America's radio days. As the establishment of the first national television network in 1948 ushered in a new age, he once more moved with the times, on this occasion joining a burgeoning advertising agency, Needham, Louis & Brorby.

The creation of Maurice H. Needham in 1935, the company had a single room for an office and three modest accounts billing $270,000. During the boom years of radio, the bespectacled, bow-tied Needham had one of the fastest-growing agencies in Chicago and America. It was during the 1950s that the agency achieved their greatest success. Freed from the economic constraints of the Depression and the war, American families embarked on one of the greatest spending sprees of all time.

"Never has a whole people spent so much money on so many expensive things in such a way as Americans are doing today," *Fortune* magazine reported in October 1956.

It was the advertising men who fed the insatiable appetite for newer, bigger, better products. And it was the new, coast-to-coast TV networks that literally drove the message home. From frozen peas to fridges, TV could sell products better than any radio ad ever did. Characters like the Jolly Green Giant, the Pillsbury Doughboy and the Marlboro Man gave even the most humdrum household item a new-found allure. If there was new science to be demonstrated, then the adman's mantra was simple: "Show what the product can do." So a Remington razor was seen shaving fuzz off a peach, while a Band-Aid demonstrated its strength by lifting up an egg. It was Christopher Ford's job to sell the new science, to "show what the product can do."

By the mid-1950s, Needham, Louis & Brorby represented seventeen of America's national advertisers, and billed more than $30 million a year. Their clients included Lever Brothers and Kraft, State Farm Insurance, Hotpoint, Campbell Soups and Quaker Oats. Maurice Needham's tiny acorn had grown into a mighty oak now rooted in Chicago's newest and tallest structure, the Prudential Building on Michigan Avenue. "It was an exciting time. In those days we were buying entire programs, a half hour of TV time. State Farm Insurance had *The Jack Benny Show* and S.E. Johnson had *Johnny Ringo*," recalled one of his colleagues, Dorothy Densler.

Advertising men became a force in American life, leading flamboyant creative lives that defied the nine-to-five norm. Even within this stylish environment, Christopher Ford stood out. "He was dashing, very handsome; he cut quite a figure," recalled Dorothy Densler. As noticeable as his looks was his sense of humor—a quality his staff enjoyed. "On one occasion, when he got back from vacation, his staff had moved all his furniture out of the office," said Dorothy Densler. "He appreciated it; he was very dry."

Not all Americans welcomed the new consumerism of the mid-1950s. Some saw the spend-spend ethos as a betrayal of the solid principles of American life, with the advertising men as high-tech hucksters, little better than the quack medicine men of the old Wild West. To Harrison Ford, however, his father was far from a villain. The more he saw of Christopher's world, the more he wanted to be as detached and untouched by convention as him.

"He seemed to have a more interesting career than most other guys' dads," he recalled once. "It encouraged me not to want a 'real' job."

By Harry's twelfth birthday, the family had moved out of central Chicago. As the 1950s boom continued apace, so the new breed of Americans emigrated to homes in the suburbs, custom-built with garages and enlarged kitchens to accommodate them and the material trappings of their success. Here they raised the children of the postwar "baby-boom."

Second time around, Christopher Ford had built a marriage and a family life. In the late summer of 1954, his success at Needham, Louis & Brorby enabled him to buy a property in Morton Grove—a new suburb named after the construction boss Morton Robbins. Predominantly split-level homes, they were home to the young professional classes. The Fords moved to a new house at 7318 Davis Street in July that year.

"Even the streets were not paved, that's how new Morton Grove was; it was like the country then. There were only a couple of policemen and not that many families with children," recalled Dennis Zetek, whose family had moved in around the corner from the Fords, on Clark Street. He and Harry Ford struck up an instant friendship and began to spend time at each other's homes.

Life in the embryonic new suburb seemed straight out of one of Norman Rockwell's idealized portraits of all-American life in the *Saturday Evening Post*. It was a tight-knit neighborhood of tight-knit families, enjoying the bountiful new life of the 1950s in whitewashed, clapboard houses. For early-generation Americans like the Fords, it represented the fulfilment of the dreams that had brought their fore-fathers across the Atlantic—the end of the journey from, as the writer John Gregory Dunne put it, "steerage to suburbia."

The Ford household seemed no different from that of *Leave It to Beaver*, the most popular TV series of the late 1950s. Dorothy would invariably be buzzing around the home in denim culottes, cooking, cleaning, ironing, and often singing a song. "They were handsome people, his mom and dad," Dennis Zetek said. "She had silver hair and was a real homemaker, always ironing. I remember she used to sing a song on the radio: 'That's the Trouble With Harry.'" Harry and Dennis played baseball together and supported the Chicago Cubs. "Harry's mom liked baseball, too; she used to like watching the World Series."

Harry Ford had inherited his parents' love of singing, his friend recalled. Using tapes Chris Ford had obtained through work and a cumbersome old Webcor tape recorder, Harry and Dennis would croon their way through the standard hits of the day, mimicking Perry Como and Pat Boone. "We used to play them at stupid speeds," Dennis Zetek grinned.

The ethos of the new neighborhoods spilling out into the Illinois countryside was togetherness. As Morton Grove slowly took shape, its youngsters were among the most devoted adherents of this community spirit. "At that point in our lives we all traveled in larger groups. I just remember the group of us gravitating together because it was such a new area and so small we were all looking for companionship. There were a couple of people who had boyfriends or girlfriends but they had very short lives," recalled Nancy Rottner, now Nancy Moses, one of twins who lived on Oleander. She and her sister were so alike they were able to switch classes in eighth grade so that no one noticed. Harry, Dennis, and the Rottner twins spent much of their time together.

Harry Ford seemed different, however. His reticence was an inher-itance from his parents, his father in particular. "Though even my par-ents are a little bit more voluble than I am," he admitted once. Yet when it came to offering opinions, no one was quicker off the mark or more caustic. It was a duality he would carry into adulthood.

"I remember him as a very tall, slender boy who quite frankly had an answer for everything. When I first saw him as Han Solo I thought he was playing himself. He was always very quick-witted—*too* smart on occasions. He was more mature than the rest of us," recalled another of the Morton Grove gang, Marilyn Fox, now Spiegel.

"He wasn't boastful but he did have an inner sense of self. He was not the kind of kid who cowered in the corner, afraid to speak out for himself or be himself. He always *was* himself. He was a strong enough personality so he had a sense of self-esteem. A lot of kids don't have that," Nancy Moses said.

Harry and Dennis, the Rottners, and others rode around on bicycles, hung out at Stan's Snackshop on the corner of Dempster and Holland, spent Saturday afternoons at the Rand Park swimming pool or inside the Pickwick Cinema in Park Ridge when the weather turned cooler.

Christopher had shared his passion for entertainment with his boys from an early age. "He would spend a lot of time taking us to the films and theater," Terence Ford remembered. *Bambi*, Harrison recalled once, was the first film he ever saw. But in the darkness of the Pickwick, the adolescent Harry failed to form an abiding love for the movies or the icons of Hollywood, John Wayne and Cary Grant, Marilyn Monroe and Doris Day. If there were any stirrings, they were of the more pubescent variety.

He seems to have been unhindered by hang-ups about the opposite sex. One of the occasions when his tongue proved too quick came when he made a reference about Nancy Rottner's emerging figure. "My sister and I had developed earlier than others and lots of remarks were in reference to that. I can remember flattening him once after he made some smart comment to me," she said. As punishment the twins called him Farry Hord.

His humor made him popular with the girls in general, however. "He sort of knew that he had good looks, wit, charisma, and personality and that he could be the center of attention. He was attractive enough and witty enough that the girls were attracted to him," Nancy Moses said.

There were blemishes to the Norman Rockwell perfection of life in Morton Grove, however. Harry's dry, diffident wit and ability to charm the girls soon caused problems when the Morton Grove children began attending the local grade school, MS Meltzer Junior High on Ballard Street. The school's location also took in the less salubrious suburbs of Des Plaines, on the rim of O'Hare Airport.

Dennis Zetek and Harry Ford stood out instantly. And they were dealt with just as quickly. A gang of hoods ruled the roost. Cheered on by gum-chewing girlfriends dressed à la Natalie Wood, they meted out punishment to anyone to whom they took a dislike. "It was their school and we were outsiders," recalled Dennis Zetek. "We were not dressed like them. My first day, this guy stamped on my foot with these work boots. They were tough guys that went there."

Harry Ford was a natural target. He stood out as being different even among a group of outsiders. "They might have sensed an underlying arrogance that they didn't want to blossom. That probably came from the distance at which I held myself from people. And still do," he admitted once.

To the grade school girls, Harry was an amusing oddity. "He was sort of a prankster. I can remember him as a kid who did not take things too seriously, especially schoolwork. He liked to have fun, a bit of a wisecracker," said Nancy Moses.

He capitalized on his popularity when he and Dennis Zetek went to dances and parties together. "He liked girls, I liked girls. We were always hanging around with girls," recalled his partner in crime. "If there were two girls at a party, he would be the one to go up and ask them to dance. He was a leader in that way."

One girl, a voluptuous siren called Sharon, became the object of their twin desires. According to some, she may also have been the provider of one of the most important parts of their education . . . "Sharon was the first girl that got breasts. She was very sexy for a seventh grader," recalled Marilyn Spiegel. "She was the neighborhood tart, as I recall. They used to go to her house a lot. I think boys learned what boys learn with her!"

2

BOY LEAST LIKELY TO SUCCEED

In September 1956, Harry enrolled at Maine East High School, a few miles from Morton Grove, on Dempster Avenue in Des Plaines. "Maine is like a great drama with each one of you a leading character," the school's magazine the *Lens* pledged its new arrival in its welcoming edition. "From the first scene as freshman until the final curtain at graduation, Maine is your stage."

The words may well have inspired many of the 1,350 pupils who arrived on the sprawling campus that autumn, but they left little impression on Harrison Ford. He picked up where he had left off at Meltzer, playing the role of outsider, oddball, Boy Least Likely to Succeed. And he played it far from the glare of the school's spotlighted center stage.

The task of remaining invisible was not a difficult one. Meltzer's smallness had made him conspicuous. At Maine East the student body was growing even more quickly than its reputation as one of the most academically successful schools, not just in Chicago but in America. As the suburbs continued to swell, a record intake arrived in Harry's year. A new school, Maine West, was already being built to accommodate the invasion, but in the meantime, school days were being divided into an early-morning and an afternoon "shift" system. Later in life he would have to work hard at the art of blending into the background. At Maine East it was easy.

The staples of high school life were no different from those at any other school in America: homecoming, hops, and devotion to the school sports team—at that time the all-conquering Blue Demons gridiron team. Despite his beanpole height, Harry was distinctly unathletic. As a result he had little or no interest in football, wrestling, or basketball, the mainstays of Maine's sports program. His sole contribution to the sporting life of the school was a brief membership on the gymnastics team during his freshman year.

Instead, his lack of impact was characterized by a list of his other activities: the model railroad club, the social science club, and the audiovisual club. The latter carried a particularly unalluring stigma, at least when it came to the girls. "He was one of those guys who would bring the TVs round to the classrooms for the teachers. They were kind of geeky guys, although he was never really geeky," recalled Marilyn Spiegel.

His self-sufficient nature was even more apparent by now. "He was always his own person," Spiegel added. "Everybody else wanted to be in the right groups. He had a very wry, sarcastic sense of humor; he always got to the bottom of things. I used to hang out with the cheerleaders and school council people and he used to say in a teasing way, 'What's so great about them?' "

When Marilyn affected airs and graces, Harry would tease her that she was "not from Park Ridge," the most exclusive suburb served by Maine East, and one of the most well-to-do in Chicago. He would soon have to drop that particular line of invective, however.

The teenage Harry did follow in his father's footsteps by becoming involved in the school's fledgling radio station, WMTH, but his only contribution was as a technical helper. Still seeing himself as an outsider, he had no interest in becoming the Alan Freed of Des Plaines. Even the school's vibrant drama society, under Joseph Stilp, saw nothing of him. It was only when he took on the role of occasional class clown that there were glimpses of untapped talents.

"Harry was in my English class and sat directly behind me. We had a teacher whose name was Adie Hockstrasser, an old spinster who was uglier than a back barn door," recalled a classmate, Jim Coomer. "She had a habit of pursing and smacking her lips, so a lot of us called her 'old liver lips.' I remember that Harry had a way of imitating her when she turned round to write on the board. He was kind of a class clown, but it came out at the back of the class. He was quite prone to getting attention directed toward himself. He was a fun kid, although he was rather quiet."

Academically, Harry maintained a low profile too. His SAT marks, he admitted once, were "not great." If the young Harry harbored any sense of being a disappointment, his insecurity could only have been heightened by the continued successes his father described over the meatloaf and mashed potatoes at home. By 1957, Christopher's accounts at Needham, Louis & Brorby, included "ALL"—Lever Brothers' mass-market washing detergent. With the edict "Show what the product can do" in mind, Christopher came up with the idea of opening a window into the workings of the washing machine. Through the miracle of television, American housewives saw how hard ALL's suds worked on washday. This revolutionary idea helped pave the way for the windowed, front-loading washing machines of the future. It was a huge hit.

Another triumph was the rose symbol of Parkay, Kraft's bestselling household margarine. Christopher came up with the idea of using the relatively untried technique of stop-motion photography to show the elegant blooming of a rose. It remained Parkay's symbol for years to come.

In the summer he was able to buy a three-bedroom, "English-style" house at the end of North Washington Avenue in Park Ridge. Ivy-clad and imperious, it stood out among a row of impressive-looking houses built as Park Ridge blossomed in 1930. The center of town was a short walk away.

"It was a beautiful house," recalled Dennis Zetek, who traveled over from Morton Grove to visit his upwardly mobile friend. "There was lots of polished wood and spindles on the stairs. It was very Early American in style."

His father's success in gaining them a foothold in Park Ridge was the most striking example of a force Harry was already recognizing—the Midwestern work ethic. He saw its values at home, at school, even at the new hamburger stand where the kids of Des Plaines spent their money. There, each morning, a dour but inexhaustibly driven young businessman called Ray Kroc was the first to arrive at the stand he had opened in April 1955. He was there again at night, cleaning and cash-ing-out after a hard day. While Harry and his friends dreamed of being Hank Sauer or Abraham Lincoln, Kroc lay awake dreaming of seeing a model of his humble eatery on every American Main Street. By 1992 there were 8,600 of them in America, another 12,000 around the world, each of them modeled on the golden-arched restaurant in Des Plaines, McDonald's.

The teenage Harrison Ford may not have felt a part of his adolescent world; he may not yet have understood where his place was within it. But it was during his childhood that he was imbued with the principles of the Midwestern way. Years later he would repeatedly echo Ray Kroc's famously straightforward philosophy: "Nothing in this world can take the place of persistence."

"I was taught the work ethic in its most fundamental form," he would say. "And I admire people who work hard."

Respect for the value of money was a central pillar of that ethic. His parents taught Harry that wealth was to be earned, not expected. "My parents came through the Depression and we were taught to believe that we were not entitled to comfort," he explained years later. "So when I was poor I didn't really mind, because I didn't have a lot of ambition for stuff."

The teenage Harry had little trouble earning pocket money. Polite, intelligent-looking, well-spoken, and from a decent part of town, he found a string of weekend and holiday jobs in and around Park Ridge and the Chicago suburbs. As he did so, his spirit of enterprise blossomed.

Harry briefly worked on a yacht on Lake Michigan, helping cook for the heirs to Chicago's powerful Swift meat-packing company. He rustled up meals from a copy of *The Joy of Cooking* which his mother had given him, and by bombarding the *Chicago Tribune*'s reader service line with inane questions: "This is Harrison again. I know you told me yesterday, but how long do you have to bake a potato?" He joked once that his performance on a very choppy lake, where he was deeply seasick, was "probably the most heroic thing I've ever done."

His longest-running job was at the Evening Pipe Shop in Vine Avenue, Park Ridge, a tiny store run by Bob Rowe, an elderly businessman specializing in smoking pipes and mixing special blends of tobacco. It was there Harry started smoking himself, a bad habit he has manifestly failed to rid himself of since. "Harry really enjoyed that. It was something a bit different and more mature than the rest of us would think of doing," said an old schoolfriend, Bill Russell.

Russell, also from Park Ridge, became Harry's closest high school friend, along with another member of his year, Stuart Shakman.

Within the well-tended confines of Park Ridge, Harry's background was highly unusual. "Back then, Park Ridge was medium wealthy, pretty much upper-class WASPS. It was pretty homogenized. Harry's family being of mixed religion was very rare," said Russell.

The latter recalled Christopher Ford as an impressive figure. "He was a sophisticated, suave-looking guy with gray hair and a mustache. A real good-looking guy. He was kind of ironic and sardonic and not a strict figure. He would wink at you, and never lecture us—a real man about the world," said Russell.

Thanks in large part to Christopher's influence, or so it seemed to Russell, his eldest son was a step above his peers in terms of his personal development. "It could have come from his father. He had a maturity that others of us at the time did not have; he knew more about the arts, literature, Irish literature. He was a little bit more worldly than the rest of us," said his friend.

Physically, however, he lacked that maturity. Despite his emerging physique and height, his face had yet to lose its baby fat. Even when he reached drinking age, he looked a sophomore. "When I was twenty-one, everyone thought I was seventeen," he admitted once. Often it was sheer *chutzpah* that overcame his deficiencies. Once with Bill Russell, Harry talked his way into a downtown Chicago bar by claiming he was a visiting Indian dignitary. "We were underage. It probably just occurred to him on the way through the door. He convinced them he was from India and moreover that he was of age," said Russell. "Harry was an amazing actor. He could pull things like that off. It was extraordinary. He was always bold about things."

Around the world, women would learn to love his air of dangerous detachment, his hard-edged humor, but it was clear what most members of Maine East's female population thought about the spindly, unathletic, and faintly unusual Harry Ford. "At that time in high school he really was *not* a catch," Marilyn Spiegel decided.

Many people found his sly sense of humor difficult to take. His far more popular friend Bill Russell often had to find him dates. "He was probably self-conscious and it came out as smart-alecky," said Russell. "He would put people down and I'm sure it was defensive. We would have to fix him up frequently because he couldn't find a date."

In their senior year at Maine East, Harry's date to the prom was a dark-haired student council leader from Des Plaines called Jane Lewis. He and she had dated off and on throughout the year. Her friends found Harry a difficult person to get to know, as in unfamiliar company he could clam up completely.

"Harry was not a real outgoing person. He was really shy," recalled a friend of Jane's, Trudie Swanson, who double dated with Harrison and Jane and her then-boyfriend Ron Martin. "He could have been considered nerdy. He wore dark-rimmed glasses, and he didn't look like the way he does today. He hadn't developed yet, either personality-wise or physique-wise."

With Harry and Jane, Trudie and her date went to the movies and ate at Romano's, the most popular young people's hangout in Des Plaines. It is an indication of how casual both couples were that Jane and Ron Martin eventually married each other rather than their high school dates.

"Jane was a real nice girl. He dated her on and off for a long period of time, but he also dated other girls; there was never any exclusivity," said Bill Russell. In their search for sexual experience, Harry and his friends could expect little beyond the exploratory fumblings in the back rows of cinemas or the back seats of their fathers' cars. Unchaperoned high school hops or house parties were scarce, and opportunities to share a bed with a date or a steady girlfriend even thinner on the ground. "We didn't have intercourse; it was very rare. It did not happen in high school for me and my friends," said Russell. "The most was heavy petting."

None of the trio was in search of serious girlfriends, according to Russell. "We weren't looking for a long attachment."

By their senior year at Maine East, Russell and his friends regarded themselves as among the most popular young men on the campus. "We thought of ourselves as 'top shits,' " said Russell. A family of sisters, the

Jacobs girls, were frequent companions. In the summers on the shores of Lake Michigan, Harry, Russell and Shakman—all aspiring musicians—would serenade them with their imitations of the balladeers of the day.

"We would take our guitars and the women to the beach on Lake Michigan. We used to walk through people's gardens on to the beach. They were nice to us if we played songs," said Russell. Rock-n-roll music, drifting up to Chicago from the Deep South, had no place in their repertoire. "We looked more like the Kingston Trio than Elvis Presley. They were a real, clean-cut group of the time. And so were we," said Bill Russell.

In the decades that have followed, no period in the life of young Americans has been mythologized with quite the same saccharine sentimentality that has been lavished on the 1950s. TV series like *Happy Days* would pay homage to a time for grease-haired heroes and endless evenings in jukebox cafes, and Harrison Ford himself would contribute to the legend-making in *American Graffiti*.

For the Class of 1960 at Maine East High School, however, life had little to do with this idyll. "We didn't own cars. We were bumming from parents or our friends. We knew drag racers but we weren't into that. That wasn't our schtick," said Bill Russell.

With the legal drinking age fixed at twenty-one for boys—bizarrely, it was eighteen for girls—alcohol was rare and there was no equivalent of Arnold's Drive-In malt shop. "It was almost a dry town. We weren't going into cocktail bars," said Russell. "In fact, there weren't many places to hang out in Park Ridge—it was school and people's houses."

Maine East's values belonged to an earlier era. "Some guy whose main claim to fame was that he was fixing up a '47 Ford and combed his hair a lot was not a star in the class. The heroes were the ones who accomplished things academically, athletically, politically, or socially. If a guy was 6 foot 2 inches, weighed 210 lbs, and could sprint and carry a football he could be a hero," recalled another member of the same Maine East vintage, Larry Clapper.

Harrison Ford was not a hero in anyone's book. He did not excel on the sports fields or in the classroom. When, in the wake of the technological Pearl Harbor that was the launch of Sputnik in 1957, "accelerated" science classes were introduced at East Maine, his sense of failure was only intensified. The fact that his high school was among the most highly regarded in America offered little solace. "In that school we had more mathematics and science than anybody in an American high school. There were a handful of suburban Chicago schools that in that kind of thing were among the top ten in the nation. Maine East was one of those," said Larry Clapper. "But Harry was not a star of the school that way. I don't think he was a star of the school in any way."

On March 3, 1960, around 1,500 parents and pupils squeezed themselves into the school's cavernous auditorium for the opening night of the annual variety show, *Mainspring*. For the Class of 1960, the curtain was ready to come down on the "great drama" that had been their high school life.

The program for the show, traditionally staged each year by the school's senior students, was filled with more than thirty acts, from acrobats to ballet dancers, jazz bands to folk groups. There were the Snowgirls, the Red Red Robins, the Two Hawaiian Maids, and a ballet troupe called the Springtime Beauties.

Over the course of three nights, more than 4,500 people watched the Class of 1960 take its curtain call. It is safe to assume that none of them, not even Christopher, Dorothy, or Terence Ford, saw anything to indicate that the awkward, slightly stagestruck member of a dance troupe called the Tower Trotters was one day destined to become the most successful actor in the first century of cinema.

Harry, in theory, took part in two acts. Along with Stu Shakman, Bill Russell, and Dick Sandberg, he performed in a parody of the *Banana Boat Song*. Shakman, Russell and Sandberg saw the song as a chance to "ham it up. . . . We couldn't figure out what else Ford could do, so we let him carry the instruments on to the stage," recalled Shakman. The plan was that, as their "Day-O"-chorus corroded the patience of its audience, tomatoes would be hurled at the crooners. Shakman recalled that the throwing started prematurely—and that, one way or another, Harry was the cause. "I can't remember if he was doing the throwing or if he tried to sing!"

Harry's only serious attempt at stealing the limelight came as he joined Shakman and Russell in the Tower Trotters, a dance troupe made up of seven girls in black leotards and chiffon skirts, chaperoned by seven white-tuxedoed males. Judging by the look of thinly concealed surliness on the face of the crew-cut figure almost at the end of the line, he did not much enjoy his first exposure to the performing arts. "It was not the kind of dancing we were used to; it was more like ballroom dancing," recalled Russell, who had been more used to twisting and jiving nights away with his friends at Maine East's Friday night hops.

Despite the leaden-footed contribution of Messrs. Ford, Shakman, and Russell, *Mainspring* was a rousing success. "Each night the final curtain fell to thunderous applause and the cast was forced to take repeated curtain calls," school yearbook the *Lens* reported.

As the end of his final term approached, the giddy gratification of a life on the stage was far from Harry Ford's mind. Bereft of ideas about the direction he should take, he did what most aimless teenagers do, and turned his mind to landing a place at college. Yale and Harvard were hardly beckoning, with his SAT averages. However, Maine East's career guidance counselor was friendly with the director of admissions at Ripon College, a respectable, liberal arts college up in the neighboring state of Wisconsin. Its entry standards were not too punishing, and his father was now more than able to afford the tuition fees. To his surprise, Harry was offered a place.

On June 9, the *Park Ridge Advocate* was devoted to the Class of 1960's graduation. Photographs of 464 seniors were spread through the community's main newspaper. Wearing a collar and tie and a look of fitting seriousness, Harrison Ford was among them. He was there too that night, at the school fieldhouse at the junction of Potter and Dempster Roads, where he joined 726 other pupils in collecting his diploma from Bert Ball, president of the Maine Board of Education.

One or two of his friends emerged as stars of the school. Dick Sandberg picked up the top English prize and was among the top dozen or so students of the year, while Stu Shakman collected a "good will" honor. Harry Ford simply left as he had arrived, without drama. As the ceremony came to an end and graduates milled around, signing each other's yearbooks, and wishing each other well, some wondered where he would fit into an America entering a new and uncertain decade.

Pipe-shop attendant, advertising executive . . . cook? "Actor" was on no one's list.

"I never thought of him as an actor; you think of actors as being very outgoing," said Larry Clapper, who left Maine East expecting little of the classmate who had scribbled his signature rather curiously that night. "He signed my yearbook. It's kind of weird. 'Larry, you a wonderful guy, you swell, you great, good luck Harry Ford.'"

Others simply assumed he would, like the rest of them, slot into the Midwestern way: no fuss, no frills, an honest day's work for an honest day's pay. As Marilyn Spiegel put it: "No one would ever have believed that he would be a movie star. You just would never, ever have guessed it."

Those who knew him best felt that he would surprise them somehow, however. "He had a very independent streak and didn't give a damn what other people thought about him," said Bill Russell. "Harry didn't do things to look good, or to make somebody else happy. He did the things he liked and he knew his own mind about things. In that sense he probably had a better game plan for life than the rest of us."

Years later it would be Harrison Ford himself who compared the psychological stages that form every young adult to carpentry: "You know what they say. The first planks of personality are nailed down at the age of two, the next at around seven, the final ones around seventeen."

By his own definition, in that case, the seventeen-year-old who left Maine East that summer was the owner of an identity at odds with the world he had so far inhabited. "All of my fantasy life as a child was about *not* being a child," he said once. Now at last that childhood was over.

3

FISH OUT OF WATER

In the autumn of 1960, Ripon College's proudest boast remained that it had been responsible for the education of a lantern-jawed young Irish-American from Milwaukee, who arrived on the campus from Naval Academy and the Great War in 1920.

The pugnacious science student shone more brightly in the debating and drama societies than he did in the laboratory. It had been while in New York, representing Ripon at a public-speaking competition, that he landed himself a place at the American Academy of Dramatic Arts and left Wisconsin for New York before graduating, with the blessing of his tutors.

Their faith was rewarded when he returned in 1940 to collect an honorary degree, an award to complement the pair of Oscars already perched on his Hollywood mantelpiece, and his growing reputation as the leading actor of his generation. Late in life he pleased his alma mater even more by narrating an official history of the college and writing in his memoirs: "I owe whatever success I had to the start I got at Ripon."

In time, comparisons would be made between Spencer Tracy and the gangly freshman who loped through the college's doors forty years after him. He too would get a start at Ripon. He too would leave without a degree to his name. He too would evolve into American cinema's most enduring Everyman. There, however, the comparisons come to an abrupt end. Harrison Ford would leave Ripon in disgrace, and he would never pass through its portals again.

Picturesque and picket-fenced, Ripon was the sort of community in which Frank Capra would have set a movie. The city's sole claim to a place in American history is the white clapboarded house that stands on Blackburn Street. Inside the "Little White House," on March 20, 1854, a group of disgruntled citizens formed a new political alliance dedicated to the cause of opposing slavery; they called themselves the Republican Party. Other American towns also lay claim to this distinction, but it somehow seems right that the Grand Old Party should have its roots in a town as conservative as Ripon.

Ripon was only a three-hour drive from Park Ridge, but to Harry Ford it must have seemed light-years away. Life moved to a different beat. Park Ridge people commuted into Chicago, held down high-flying jobs in the Loop. In Ripon folk worked for Speed Queen, a washer and dryer manufacturer established since the turn of the century, or Rippin' Good Cookies, supplier of "the finest biscuits in the Midwest." Either that or they worked the land dairy-farming or supplying peas to the Jolly Green Giant. A handful of shops lined the Main Street. There was a cinema, a few bars, and a pizza restaurant— and that was it. In Ripon people lived a quiet, uneventful life in a quiet, uneventful town.

The college had been established in January 1851, on a hill overlooking the rest of the community. Ripon regarded itself as a liberal arts college and remained proud of its enlightened approach to education. Yet to the teenage Harrison Ford it seemed a far from liberal environment.

He arrived to discover a world of petty rules and regulations. Sports jackets and ties were still a requirement for evening meals. He also learned that each Monday afternoon he would have to don the starched gray uniform of the Reserve Officer Training Corps, ROTC. For two hours he and his fellow pupils were drilled with the precision of West Point recruits.

For all its formality, however, many Ripon students thought the place one of the more pleasant spots to acquire an education in that corner of America. "It was not a diverse community; the greatest diversity were Italian-extraction people from Cicero, Illinois, who we were convinced were connected to the Mob. But Ripon was a terrific place to go to school," recalled another 1960 freshman, Bill Haljum. "It was a wonderful campus because it was so small, and you ate together whether you were in living groups or not. You could not avoid meeting lots of different people."

Haljum, from Los Angeles, had not set his high school alight academically. "Ripon was the only out-of-state college that would accept me," he admitted. "After we got in, they started looking at grade points and scores on college boards. The standards got higher, and we were convinced the people got duller in each class behind us."

Arriving in sleepy Ripon in June, he found an instant soulmate in another underachieving, metropolitan fish-out-of-water, Harry Ford. He, like Haljum, had relied on some string-pulling to get there. "I think a personal favor may have been called in," he would surmise. Unlike Haljum, however, Harry was less enamored of Ripon. "I didn't fit in—nor did I want to," he said, looking back later in his life.

During his first month at Ripon, a month packed with infantile hazing events like wearing "beanies," taking part in greasepole fights, and playing in the "Toilet Bowl" gridiron match, Harry was accepted as a member of the Sigma Nu fraternity. He spent the next four years in the fraternity house, South Hall, where forty or so students shared dormitories watched over by a housemother. Haljum too became a member of the hall, eventually sharing a room with Harry Ford.

The fraternity houses at least offered some room for individuality. There were "jock" houses, academic houses and fun houses. Then there was Sigma Nu. The earliest rumblings of campus discontent were years away, particularly at isolated colleges like Ripon, but the seeds of the dissatisfaction were sown in fraternities like Sigma Nu.

"It was a conservative school, but we were a real diverse group. We did things that were considered wrong, like having a Hawaiian member, a nonwhite, which we were not allowed to do," recalled Irv Ott, two years Harry's senior. "We had the editor of the student paper, the producer of the college radio station, a real mix of people."

As the 1960s came of age so too did Harry Ford. Nearing the end of his teens, he was already a complex mixture; he could be sociable and entertaining, but he remained standoffish and serious. "He could be sullen, withdrawn at times. He was not a very warm guy, quite a closed individual," recalled Ott.

"Harry was really quiet, very reserved," said Haljum. "He had a terrific sense of humor, but it was not the kind of thing where he was constantly the cutup." He deflected intimacy with an eccentric, ironic humor. "Because of his height he did a lot of physical humor. The way he would leave a room was always spectacular. He would almost dash out like an ostrich, straight-legged, with his long neck and square jaw," Haljum chuckled.

Younger, less cosmopolitan students saw Harry Ford as something of a bohemian. "I can see that it might have been far too conservative for him. When I think back about him, I think of him as being ahead of all the rest of us. He wore sandals and blue jeans; back then in a Midwest town that was not what everyone wore," recalled Nancy Prellwitz, then Hohnbach, another new arrival in 1960.

His quiet, cocksure manner had been the cause of his beatings in junior high school. Once more there were those who took exception to the kid with the crooked smile and the knack for snappy dialogue. Particularly when he was acting in cahoots with Haljum.

"Ford or Haljum would always be trying to make it appear as if the rest of the class were following them, that one of them was the leader," recalled John Hibbard, a 1960 freshman from the town of Eau Claire, Wisconsin. "When someone acted that way in a group without having been elected, the group didn't think much of them. I felt that way, and that's the way most people I talked to felt. 'What a jerk.' 'Who is this guy who comes up here from Des Plaines and thinks he's God's gift?' Nobody thought he was. By the end of the first year they had backed off."

Undeterred, the twosome imposed themselves elsewhere. As at every college in America, social life revolved around drinking, dancing, and dating. The Spot, in the center of Ripon, was the most popular venue. The owners had converted the cellar into a beer and pizza parlor. Under Wisconsin's strict drinking laws, under-twenty-ones were not allowed to drink the hard liquor on sale upstairs. Instead, beer bashes were the backbone of undergraduate life. "It was a hard-drinking college," recalled Irv Ott. Haljum and Harry made themselves even more conspicuous by forming a band that played at the bashes—the Brothers Gross.

"Harry played guitar, I played nothing; so we made a gutbucket, a one-string instrument with a large, galvanized steel washtub for the base and an arm that holds the other end of the string. You rest on the arm and it tightens the string. I played that," recalled Haljum. "Jeff Thomson was the real musician; he played twelve-string guitar and a banjo. There was also Don Schober and Pete Powers, who would join in and sing sometimes."

The Brothers Gross knew their limitations. "It was not memorable music, quite frankly. No one was calling us to recording studios saying, 'You gotta get that one down,' " said Haljum. "Folk music was big in those days, so we were ripping off the Brothers Four, who were a popular group at the time. None of us were gifted. We made up in enthusiasm what we lacked in talent. And we had a blast."

On more than one occasion Harry, Haljum, Schober, and Jeff Thomson performed impromptu songs beneath the windows of the sorority halls. "We did silly things like serenading the ladies until two o'clock in the morning. It usually ended with them throwing rolls at us," Don Schober recalled.

Even at the dawn of what was to be the most promiscuous of decades, the mating rituals of Ripon remained a throwback to a more chivalrous, straitlaced time. If two students were serious about each other they would become "pinned," the girl wearing her boyfriend's fraternity pin. It was one small step removed from an engagement to be married.

Officially, having sex was unthinkable. It was only as Harry arrived that students were even being allowed to visit members of the opposite gender in their dormitories. The issue had been the subject of heated debate. Should doors be kept open while students entertained their visitors—and if so, how? One faculty member had facetiously suggested an ice cube. If it melted, it was time the visit was curtailed.

"The rule had just come in that you could have a lady in your room, but the joke was that she had to have one foot on the floor at all times," noted Bill Haljum.

"People were different then. You were twenty-one, and it was time to settle down and get married and have a family. You were coming out of a very conservative era," explained Irv Ott.

His friends did not have Harry Ford down as a man on that particular mission, however. He seems to have played the field with gusto. "He was popular among the ladies," recalled his Brothers Gross colleague Don Schober. And: "Back then, people went to college to find a mate. Harry was never like that," laughed Bill Haljum.

By the time he reached his junior year, halfway point of his time at Ripon, Harry had been freewheeling socially and academically for two years. The second half of his studies would be a more serious matter. His first task was to choose his major subject.

Harry had studied a little philosophy in his freshman year under one of Ripon's most charismatic faculty members, William Tyree. Harry approached him for a place as a major in his department.

"I was quite surprised when he suggested he would become a philosophy major. I said, 'Certainly, Harry,' but I couldn't help thinking privately, 'I hope you gain in interest and work,' " recalled Tyree. "He was a very casual student. I thought he was talented but I also thought he wasn't terribly interested in anything."

The reputation for high living and high jinks that he had formed with Bill Haljum did little to dispel this view. By now the duo had taken over a room on the second floor. With the eccentric Haljum, nicknamed "Topper" because of his habit of wearing a top hat, Harry had a riot.

"It was a little larger because it was a corner room; there was a single bed against either wall and we had a window that looked out on to Scott Hall, the freshman hall," Haljum remembered. "So we could stand at the windows and dump water on people, stuff like that."

Their room was badly placed for smuggling in girls. "I don't think we ever had any female visitors. If we were chasing ladies, we found other places to go," said Haljum.

For all the fraternity fun they shared, Haljum found Harry difficult to get to know. To the student from breezy, bare-it-all California, the Midwesterner was a curiously closed book. "He never talked about his family," he said. If the subject of Park Ridge came up, it inevitably concerned the pipe shop where he still worked during vacations. With pipe smoking *de rigueur* at Ripon, Harrison was able to open up a thriving business. "For a time he would supply us all with pipes for cost. You could almost design them yourselves. He would call the guy at the pipe shop and he would deliver them to us," said Haljum. "At college you had to smoke a pipe. Harry loved to smoke a Calabash, like Sherlock Holmes. He would sit at his desk with this sucker in his mouth. It took a giant jaw to keep the thing from falling out because it was so heavy. I once tried a smaller one, and it was more than I could bear." Harry often told Haljum and other friends that he wanted to open a pipe shop of his own.

There was no mistaking the earnestness with which Harry was taking his studies by now. As a philosophy major he could be crushingly serious. Haljum found his roommate's intensity in turns peculiar and boring. "We spent lots of evenings wondering where the hell life was leading, but he was much more serious about philosophy than any of the rest of us," he said. "To be serious about philosophy in central Wisconsin in a small school—that was unusual. He'd get really excited about Kierkegaard and I would say, 'Excuse me, Harry, the Green Bay Packers are playing.' I majored in history—a nice, simple subject," he added.

Harry turned to his philosophy teacher for the stimulating conversation he seemed to need. He and Professor Tyree became close friends and confidants. Ripon demanded a certain formality between its students and faculty members. "He called me by my surname—no student ever called me by my Christian name," said Tyree. But over the coming years, he became as close to Harry Ford as any other Riponite. Student and teacher shared glasses of sherry at Tyree's house in Ripon. Often they would have supper together at favorite haunts, wolfing down pan-fried local pike and lobster tails at the Republican House restaurant in Ripon, or traveling out toward Green Lake and the Tuscombia Country Club, taking turns picking up the bill. Conversation was always as lively as it was serious. "They were conversations between friends. We talked about everything, as friends do," said Tyree.

Tyree was most likely to get an invitation to dinner after Harry had received a check from his parents. Money was tight, particularly to a pair of city boys with a habit of living beyond their means. Both he and

Haljum were forced to take up jobs to supplement their free-spending ways. Harry worked at the Spot and in Vieth's, Ripon's main clothes shop. He had alternative incomes as well as his pipe-ordering service. "He used to play nine ball pool for money. He was pretty good at it," recalled Haljum.

The money raised by his impersonations of Fast Eddie Felson made little impression on the debt he had run up by early 1963, however. By now both roommates had got into the habit of obtaining credit at Ripon's stores. As they arrived back at college after Christmas, each discovered the collective debt was around $5,000—roughly $2,500 each.

"It was clothes, dry cleaning, wherever we could get credit," said Haljum. "It was a daunting debt. I was dreading to have to go back to cook at the Colonial Inn in Green Lake and Harry was saying, 'Shit, I don't want to go back to Vieth's.'" Together the roommates came up with the idea of a humor magazine. "Harry did terrific pen and ink drawings, so he drew a lot of cartoons and did a lot of the layouts. We purloined a few other articles that we could fill in, then we both ran around and sold ads in town."

For the next few weeks, their corner room was a hive of creativity. As far as the good burghers of Ripon were concerned, the magazine—the *Mug*—was an official college publication, although: "It was free enterprise. We gave advertisers the impression that it was an official publication of the school but it was an official publication of Bill and Harry," Haljum confessed.

A glance at the magazine reveals as much about the Ripon College of the early 1960s as it does about its resourceful founders. The *Mug* centerspread represented the closest conservative Ripon had come to its own edition of *Playboy*. The spread, called "*Mug* Shots," presented what Harry and Haljum considered a dozen of the most glamorous "specimens of feminine pulchritude" on the campus. Harry, a keen photographer throughout his life, was, in all likelihood, the final arbiter of the selection. Supplemented by lewd cartoons and ads and homages to drunken nights in the Spot, the magazine was a subversive shot across the bows of the Ripon Establishment. Yet when the official *College Days* newspaper worried that the *Mug* might "weaken" the moral fiber of the college and its more serious publications, Harry and Haljum could not have cared less.

"We made about ten grand on the deal. We got all our bills paid off, paid for all of the printing," explained Haljum. "It was quite a success as far as we were concerned because we didn't have to do any real work."

Perhaps encouraged by his success in using his wits to avert one crisis, Harry soon adopted the same approach to avoid another, potentially greater disaster. As his junior year had worn on, Harry's performance in class had confirmed Professor Tyree's worst fears. There was a huge gulf between beer and midnight-oil-fueled discourses with Bill Haljum and the practical requirements of a philosophy major. "He was a pretty good solid student. He did strong B work always, and he didn't fake it," said Professor Robert "Spud" Hannaford, by now his main philosophy teacher. "If he hadn't read an assignment, he would say as much whereas another kid might try and wing it. He was very upfront like that, and in general he was a very upfront kind of guy."

It was obvious to both Hannaford and Tyree that, by now, Harry's interest had begun to wane. "My recollection was that it was history of philosophy and we were getting into some heavy-duty figures and German idealism and that none of it took," said Hannaford. "It was Hegel, I think."

Realizing he was not making the grade, Harry began fishing around for ways of averting failing his degree—a possibility that would have been viewed as a catastrophe back in Chicago, where Christopher Ford was shelling out $2,000 a year in college fees alone.

He approached Lester Schwartz, one of Ripon's most colorful characters. Trained in Paris, where he had known Picasso, Schwartz ran Ripon's most avant garde course, Elements of Art. On his farm overlooking Green Lake, Schwartz was trying to create the same sort of environment as the great Chicago architect Frank Lloyd Wright had at nearby Taliesin. Schwartz encouraged students to work on the land, to appreciate the landscape before beginning to study how to place buildings within it. Disappointingly for Schwartz, his dreams were most passionately appreciated by Ripon's sports stars. By planting trees, pulling up fence posts, and rolling barbed wire, they could get the good grades that eluded them in class. "The athletes were happy to be involved with physical challenge, along with the beer at the end of each session," Schwartz recalled.

Harry had spent time on the farm earlier during his time at Ripon. He wondered whether he might be able to achieve a major under Schwartz. When the professor explained the work required, however, the student thought again. "Harry's eyes squinted and his face screwed up. No way would he participate," he recalled.

In years to come he may have regretted this decision as the life of an architect briefly became his. Schwartz's loss was, however, Philip Bergstrom's—and acting's—gain. Bergstrom oversaw Ripon's theater society with the musical director Ed Willson.

Acting may have been the last refuge of the floundering philosopher, but it soon proved a subject in which he seemed to be able to excel naturally. By now Harry had begun to fill out. He had grown his hair longer, lost the facial puffiness of his freshman photographs, and grown into a fine physical specimen. (Willson, as open a homosexual as Wisconsin could comprehend in those distant days, had already noticed Harry Ford on campus. "Have you seen Harry Ford? He is rather cute," he asked another member of faculty early on during Harry's freshman year.) The sonorous bass voice he had inherited from his father was also developing into an impressive instrument. Under Bergstrom and Willson's tutelage, he began to flourish.

In his junior year, Willson cast Harry as "Mack the Knife"— the lead in *The Threepenny Opera*, Brecht's adaptation of John Gay's eighteenth-century *Beggar's Opera*. The show had been a huge hit on Broadway, where its catchiest song, "Mack the Knife," had become a hit for Bobby Darin and others.

At around 8:15 P.M., on Saturday, May 3, 1963, Harry took his first tentative steps on to the stage at the college theater, the Red Barn. The experience left his knees knocking and his heart racing, he admitted later. "It scared the bejesus out of me." Around the campus and at the party afterward at North Hall, Ripon cast its verdict on the new performer. "He wasn't bad as an actor, although you would not have looked at him and said, 'There's a great talent.' But he was intelligent; he did very workmanlike work," judged Professor Hannaford. "I thought the guy was terrific," recalled his roommate Haljum. "He wasn't Bobby Darin, but he had something."

Others were not so sure. It was soon apparent that his performance in *The Threepenny Opera* scared the bejesus out of many in Ripon as well. The local newspaper, the *Commonwealth*, complained that while "enjoying naughty plays as much as the next person," it felt Mack the Knife's exploits did not set the right example. "Sex on the campus is already flaunted, and a play of this type where the hero is no more than just a big ladykiller does little to improve this situation," it editorialized.

For Harry, the controversy only added to the appeal of his dangerous new discovery. That weekend he became the third-generation Ford to find himself intoxicated by the strange world of the theater.

As he put it years later: "I had never thought about what I was going to do when I grew up. I didn't realize that there was an option to *not* grow up, and when I realized that, I knew I had a profession right there."

4

LADYKILLER

The handsome twenty-year-old who had brought Mack the Knife to life at the Red Barn quickly discovered that the stage provided other perks too. Rather pretty ones.

Bergstrom and Willson had been sufficiently impressed with Harry's debut to ask him to take the lead in their next show—a production of the popular musical *The Fantasticks*. The same invitation had been extended to Mary Lee Franke, another junior, who had taken the female lead Polly Peachum in *The Threepenny Opera*.

Franke was unsure of her leading man's maverick, un-Wisconsin ways. "He almost seems more likable now than he was back then. Back then, everyone did the same things and tried not to stick out, but Harry did different things," she said. "He was not run of the mill, he did not follow the crowd. He was very Ivy League, sharp dressing, very neat. He walked around campus smoking a pipe. He was smart-alecky sometimes." Inexorably, however, she found herself drawn to him.

Mary Lee was "pinned" to another boy—Bill Kuehl. She knew that Harry had been seeing a girl called Jan Stevenson but that the romance had cooled. She and Harry began to engineer clandestine trysts together.

"We had a little romance going between the two musicals but it was secret because I was pinned to another guy," she recalled. "So we met on the sly. I remember meeting him in the music building after hours. I had a key because I was Mr. Willson's assistant. He was over in Oxford teaching."

The Wisconsin girl soon realized that Chicago boys expected matters to progress more speedily than their country cousins. "He was kind of fast, as we called it back then. It was only a couple of times that I met with him after the production was over and realized that he was not my type." As far as Philip Larkin, the English poet, was concerned, "Sexual intercourse began in nineteen sixty-three." His words were lost on Mary Lee Franke, however. "Harry was too fast," she blushed. "It was just not the kind of thing I was looking for."

Harry and Mary Lee did not allow the ending of their brief fling to spoil preparations for *The Fantasticks*. As Willson and Bergstrom began molding the young couple, Franke, a music major, recalled being underwhelmed by her leading man's vocal abilities. "You wouldn't call Harry a singer," she recalled. "I was training operatically. I was not real impressed with his singing voice. He did not have a very melodic voice, he had no vibrato, he just kind of spoke to the music. But he carried it off and he was a lot of fun."

It was during rehearsals that Professor William Tyree first noticed that his young friend might have found a niche for himself. Tyree had only visited the Red Barn to recover from the shock of almost having killed him.

Harry had called Tyree one afternoon. "He said, 'Are you busy early tonight? How would you like to go out and have a steak, I just got a check from my parents.' He said he had to be back for a rehearsal at 7:30 P.M." The pair made the six-mile trip to the Tuscombia Country Club. "On the way home, my foot went way down on the accelerator. I was driving a DeSoto, and the speedometer had broken the day before," Tyree recalled. "We came to the top of the hill and suddenly it dawned on me how fast we were going. Had a car been coming, it would have turned us over; we would have gone down the hill and probably have been killed. In the infinite mercy of God, nothing was coming. I pulled the car over as far as I could, and thanks to the balance it stayed upright."

The experience left the philosophy professor shaken for days. "I was never so frightened in my life. Periodically I had nightmares about it." His relief was all the greater when he saw his student friend on stage.

"I discovered his talent at *The Fantasticks*," said Tyree. "One night I went over and I was sitting back in the dark on my own. I remember clearly that I was watching a virtuosic talent. His philosophy studies continued, but he had discovered the theater. He undoubtedly ought to have made drama his major from the beginning." By now, however, Harry was committed to philosophy. Soon that choice looked more and more like a serious error.

As Harry headed toward the crucial final year of his study, it was Tyree who detected the first signs of a looming crisis. Harry had called him one afternoon asking for a lift to a picnic organized by the theater. Tyree arranged to pick Harry up outside his hall at 4 P.M. but was surprised not to find him waiting. He went into the hall and up to the room Harry shared with Bill Haljum.

"Harry was lying on the bed, virtually naked, facedown," said Tyree, who recalls then making his presence felt. Suddenly Harry unleashed a torrent of abuse. "He was cursing, using all sorts of profanities and obscenities. I think he was semiconscious," said Tyree. Harry apologized, threw on some clothes and drove off to the picnic with Tyree. His mentor's opinion of him slid even further when Harry proceeded to get drunk. "He drank a lot of beer and was belching a lot. I was not pleased with his performance," said Tyree, who told Harry to get a ride home with someone else.

In hindsight, Tyree recognized that Harry was becoming increasingly troubled by his academic failure. But the incident strained their relationship.

By his senior year, Harry was conspicuously missing from virtually all of his classes. "We were somewhat concerned during his senior year; we were thinking that there had been some kind of crisis. The basis for our concern was that we never saw him at all. He just wasn't doing any of the work. There were papers that were course requirements and he just did not do them at all," said Professor Hannaford. "And he had no plan to do them, it seemed."

Years later, his student described the struggle he passed through during that time at Ripon as "a clinical depression." He was unable to hand in work and found the pressure to do so piling up on him. Rather than confronting the problem, he retreated to his room, living off delivered pizza and sleeping "sometimes for days." He described the depths he descended to, to Pulitzer Prize–winning author David Halberstam in 1994: "I would sleep for four or five days at a time. There was one class that I never went to. I remember once when I slept for several days and finally roused myself, got myself out of bed, managed to get dressed—this seemed to be taking an intense effort—and actually made it to class. All of this seemed to be happening in slow motion. I even put my hand on the door of the classroom, but I seemed unable to turn the doorknob. So I let it go and went back to sleep."

In October 1963, Harry returned to the stage of the Red Barn, taking the lead in *The Fantasticks*. His hair colored boot-polish black for the part of El Gallo, with an Errol Flynn mustache stuck in place, he exuded a dark, debonair charm. He and Mary Lee Franke stole the plaudits. "To bring this play to life requires not just work but talent, and talent there was," wrote Dr. J. R. Bowditch in the newspaper *College Days*. "Harrison Ford as the narrator El Gallo sang, talked and moved with a grace and conviction which were delightful. His voice had remarkable tone and expressiveness. He seemed equally at home as a dashing clown and mellow man of the world."

Harry and Mary Lee had succeeded in keeping their short-lived romance a secret within the tight-knit college community. By now both had moved on to relationships that would blossom into something far more serious than their clandestine meetings in Ed Willson's music room. While Mary Lee's relationship with Clip Matthis, whom she later married, would raise few eyebrows, Harry's would become the talk of the campus.

Mary Louise Marquardt had arrived at Ripon in her junior year, in 1962. Her solitary, slightly somber nature was understandable, given the tragedies that had already befallen her. Mary Louise's early life had been a series of losses.

She had been raised in Milwaukee, the daughter of one of the city's most eminent doctors, Dr. Charles R. Marquardt. A member of a respected Wisconsin family dating back to immigrants from Walachia,

Dr. Marquardt had graduated from Marquette University in 1930. He had gone on to become a fellow of the American College of Surgeons and a specialist in urology. He married Hortense Wallschlaeger, a graduate of Milwaukee County Hospital's school of nursing, with whom he had two daughters, first Charlene and then Mary Louise. The family lived in a stylish house at 2737 North Grant Boulevard, in the well-to-do Sherman Park area of Milwaukee, where they were regarded as pillars of the community. Dr. Marquardt was a prominent campaigner against reforms to the socialized medicine system while Mrs. Marquardt was an energetic member of the nearby Kingsley Methodist Church.

Mary was only sixteen when her mother died suddenly, in February 1958, aged just forty-eight. Mary's upbringing was entrusted to an aunt, Emily Knebes, wife of Dr. Marquardt's brother Erwin. Friends at Washington High School still remember Mary: "She was a quiet, withdrawn girl, understandable given her loss," said Nancy Prellwitz, who went on from Washington High to Ripon College.

Mary left Washington High School to study at Stephens College in Columbia, Missouri. Only three years after her mother's death, in December 1961, in her sophomore year, her father, who had been working in the X-ray department at the Deaconess Hospital, collapsed suddenly and died of emphysema. He was only fifty-six.

After her father's funeral, Mary transferred back from Missouri to Ripon College, in her home state and a popular destination for old high school friends. As a late arrival, unattached to a sorority house, she was apart from the main social life of the college. "The sorority and fraternity houses were very active; there were lots of comings and goings involved with them—that's where most of the action was. Mary lived alone and was an independent so she was out of the mainstream," recalled her old high school friend Nancy Hohnbach.

Despite her shyness, she quickly attracted suitors. Bill Per Lee was one of the first. "She was very much her own person," he recalled. Per Lee introduced Mary to his mother one weekend. "My mother's favorite anecdote was that Mary could skin animals. I remember catching these mice and I remember her skinning them," he recalled.

Her musical taste was eclectic, but serious-minded—Purcell rather than Presley. "I don't remember her having any interest in popular music," said Per Lee.

When her relationship with Per Lee cooled, Mary had to look no further than his roommate for a new boyfriend. John Hibbard was another Wisconsin boy, a bright, ambitious law student. Their romance was serious enough for them to spend much of the summer together. And when, at the end of his junior year, Hibbard transferred to the University of Wisconsin in Madison, ninety miles away, they carried on their relationship. Hibbard returned to Ripon as often as he could, often hitchhiking along the rural roads to see Mary. On the campus the relationship was one of those expected to grow into engagement and marriage. And sooner rather than later.

It was after spending Thanksgiving with Mary and her Aunt Emily in November 1963 that Mary broke the news to him. The campus had huddled around TV sets, absorbing the shock of the Kennedy assassination. None of that generation of Americans will ever forget where they were when they heard that newsflash. For John Hibbard it was a doubly unforgettable moment in his life. It was then that Mary told him she had started a romance with Harry Ford.

"She told me they were seeing each other. I really didn't know, except what Mary had told me, what sort of relationship they had. I felt very bad at the time. I was very smitten with Mary," he recalled. Hibbard knew of Harry's popularity with girls. "My recollection is of often seeing Harry in the company of a girl, but that did not necessarily mean she would be in his company next week." He could not disguise a sense of jealousy—"because he was always flashy about it."

Inside, John Hibbard was angry. It was only out of respect for Mary that he did not confront his former philosophy classmate. "It does not do any good to challenge the third party. When people make a romantic decision, it is their own, not somebody else's," he explained. "Certainly I felt that way with Mary. I had limitless respect for her brains. I did not think she would get fooled, jerked around, defrauded. It was sad for me, but it was her decision."

The romance caught almost everyone at Ripon by surprise. It was left for others to voice the thoughts that John Hibbard kept to himself. On the face of it, Mary seemed an unlikely conquest for the dashing leading man of the Red Barn.

"It took everyone very much by surprise. Harry always seemed to have lots of friends and lots of girlfriends. He had always been seen with girls who were prominent on campus and very, very attractive. And Mary was very quiet and quite plain," recalled his old flame, Mary Lee Matthis. Bill Per Lee thought it an odd match too. "She was a pretty, self-contained person. He was more outgoing; he had that sub-urban style and panache that did not go too well in a Midwestern social structure," he recalled.

His philosophy professor too had heard talk of Harry having a rep-utation with girls. "I remember people reporting that he was making out with women. It is my impression that he really was having a pretty good time," Hannaford recalled. He felt aggrieved for Hibbard. "Mary's connection with John Hibbard was a serious connection. She had been dating him for a long time. Mary was not a superficial girl at all; she was a serious, thoughtful girl, and John was a very bright, conscientious guy—a guy I really respected a lot." He heard of the breakup "with some surprise. I really felt badly about John's loss. But Harry swept her off her feet."

"She was very down to earth, hardworking, she didn't wear makeup. Maybe opposites attract," said Nancy Prellwitz.

Time would prove them all wrong. Despite outward appearances, Mary shared many of Harry's inner qualities. As events would prove, they fitted together perfectly.

The happiness Harry was finding in his romance with Mary was becom-ingly increasingly overshadowed by the pressures building toward grad-uation and getting a job. For a while there was talk among Ed Willson and Richard Bergstrom of taking *The Fantasticks* on the road, but it faded as quickly as the newspaper reviews. Alongside the eulogy to his performance at the Red Barn the paper ran a list of visiting head-hunters, from graduate schools and commerce, the military and the church. Where was Harry headed? He didn't have a clue.

The crisis reached breaking point when Harry was summoned to see Spud Hannaford. It had only been his interest in acting that had stopped his philosophy professor from raising the alarm sooner. "It was with some relief that we noticed he really did seem to be interested in the work in the theater. He was involved in the plays, and he did his job there seriously. It was some indication that he hadn't just come apart at the seams."

By now, it was clear that Harry had no intention of meeting the requirements of his course. "He just wasn't doing any of the work at all," recalled Hannaford. "Papers had to be written and none were, so there was no alternative but for me to give him an F."

The decision meant that he would not be able to graduate at the end of his senior year. Hannaford had been left with no option. "At that point in a kid's career, if they have finished everything up to that time you are willing to give a little slack, and give them a minimum passing grade if they do any of the work in a satisfactory way, but there wasn't any question of it. There was just nothing there at all."

Harry's failure left Professor Tyree feeling terrible for his friend. "It was not a good period for him. Harry was really mad at himself. He had a passion for excellence and he wasn't delivering," says Tyree. There is no doubt in his mind that the moment was a turning point in Harry's young life. "Since then I think he has been highly responsible as an actor," he said simply. "I think he has wanted to prove himself."

Mary joined the rest of the audience at the Red Barn Theater on Saturday, March 7, 1964, to watch her boyfriend's most ambitious theatrical effort, playing Dr. Antrobus in Thornton Wilder's *Skin of Our Teeth*.

As the white-haired, wide-berthed Antrobus, Harrison waddled on stage with a cushion up his sweater, "a fake mustache and a half pound of talcum powder" in his hair. Of his three college stage performances, it was the one he would cherish the most. "That's when I caught the illness," he said once.

This time, J. R. Bowditch was even more grand in his praise. "Harrison Ford as the indefatigable inventor-writer-optimist-visionary George Antrobus showed that his fine performance in *The Fantasticks* was no fluke," he wrote. "He looked, acted, and spoke the part of a man of fifty who one minute is ecstatic over his invention of the alphabet and the next is bashfully eager over the prospect of a tête-à-tête with a peroxide-blond beauty queen. Harrison possesses, in gesture and delivery, the indispensable sense of pace."

Whatever euphoria Harry may have felt at this success was short-lived. As the news that Mary had graduated was being confirmed, her boyfriend was facing up to the fact that his delinquent behavior meant he would not get his degree. His only option would have been to go to summer school and retake his exams. "He would have had to repeat the course. He could have done that," said Spud Hannaford. By now, however, he only wanted to get away from Ripon altogether.

Harry left Ripon only days before graduation, with his parents already provisionally booked into a local hotel in readiness for their son's moment of glory. Having dipped into his own pocket, to the tune of $8,000 at least, Christopher did not hide his anger. "My parents had paid for four years of education, and at the end of it there was no degree," Harrison explained years later. "It was not taken lightly."

As the inquest into his failure got underway back in Park Ridge, however, Harrison gave his parents some even more shocking news. First, he announced, he had decided he was going to follow his father and his grandfather and risk a life on the stage. Second, he and Mary Louise Marquardt were engaged to be married.

5

THE BATHTUB BARITONE

Harrison Ford was faced with the first real crisis in his life. He had left the rarefied atmosphere of Ripon without a degree or a clear notion of where he was headed. He had delivered the news that he was going to become an actor, partly out of the feeling that he had to "announce to people what I was going to do with my life," and partly looking for a rebuke from his parents. "Discouragement was always something I was happy to have."

None had come, however, and now he was an actor faced with the instant reality of an actor's life. He was out of work.

Enter Lady Luck.

In May 1964, another Ripon student had arrived in Williams Bay on the shores of Lake Geneva, Wisconsin. The Bay was a summertime retreat for the affluent city dwellers of Milwaukee and Chicago, a sanctuary for families like the Wrigleys, the chewing-gum millionaires and owners of the Cubs. A friend of this student, Mary Case, asked her whether she knew of any talented actors up at her college, as the Williams Bay theater company—the Belfry Players—had lost one of its leading actors and needed a replacement. Fast.

The Riponite had seen Harry Ford shine in *The Fantasticks*. "Why not try him?" she asked Mary.

Within days, Harry and Mary Louise were sitting on the porch of

52

Mary Case's house on the edge of the lake talking to the director of the coming season, William Fucik. Fucik, a tough but respected director from California, had taken on three promising youngsters as "resident actors." A live-wire New Yorker called Fred DiMaio and Raymond Sager, a product of the highly regarded Goodman Theater in Chicago, were in Wisconsin, ready to begin rehearsals. The third actor, unfortunately, had let them down.

"I remember Mary Case calling and saying, 'Well, we have another possibility, if you would like to come over,'" Fucik recalled.

Over a drink on the porch, Harry and Mary—who was equally unsure of her future direction—talked about Ripon and their experiences at the Red Barn. Fucik listened and weighed up the solemn-looking twenty-one-year-old and his fiancée. "My first impression was that he was a good physical type; he could play a variety of parts. I could see intelligence, alertness . . . he was not in any way a braggart. This young girl that was with him was very intelligent and I felt they would be a good couple," he recalled.

Fucik knew that compared to DiMaio and Sager, who had worked at the Belfry the previous summer, Harry's experience was limited in the extreme. But he saw a raw and malleable actor, someone with promise. Fucik was a natural with amateurs. "I knew that I could always reach people. In working with amateurs, I felt that in the time that I had, I could train them in the necessities of a role—if they followed my program of rehearsals," he said.

Normally the choice would have had to pass through a committee, but with time against him, Fucik took a chance and offered Harry the third "residency." "We were desperate in a way. But that was not desperation," he said. Fucik explained that the work schedule would be punishing and his wages minimal. Bed, board, and an acting apprenticeship were the rewards offered. Fortune and fame, beyond this corner of Wisconsin at least, would have to wait.

For Harry, the decision could not have been easier. What were the alternatives? Another summer in a Park Ridge pipe shop, another spell as an improvisational chef, or military service? Here was a heaven-sent opportunity—and he grabbed it.

* * *

Since 1934, the Belfry's home—a disused Mormon church with pews for seating and a working bell to summon the audience to performances—had satisfied the lakeside set's appetite for civilized entertainment. At the same time it formed part of the bedrock of American theater, serving, like the English repertory theater, as a training ground for new and emerging talent. In 1949, Fucik had been in Williams Bay when a young, undisciplined actor called Paul Newman had, according to the town's theater critic, shown "too much comic exaggeration" in, among other productions, *The Glass Menagerie*.

In the summer of 1964 the company had set itself one of the most ambitious programs in its history, consisting of a half dozen plays: *Take Her, She's Mine; Little Mary Sunshine; Night of the Iguana; Dark of the Moon; Damn Yankees;* and *Sunday in New York*. As the company's only "professionals," the resident actors would be needed in all six. Harry was in at the deep end. He got down to work.

Rehearsals began in mid-June. Fucik, a product of one of California's most innovative theaters, the Pasadena Playhouse, already had a reputation as a brilliant coach, working inside Hollywood. His directorial style was minimalist, no-nonsense, and brusque. It was only late in his career that someone summoned the courage to suggest he should consider using the carrot as well as the stick. "Put some money in the bank before you take it out," was the precise expression, as Fucik recalls it. "When I was on a tight schedule, it was not my tendency to go round praising a lot," he admitted. He cast Harry in a minor part in the opening play *Take Her, She's Mine*, saving his debut as a leading actor for *Little Mary Sunshine*. He would give him four weeks' rehearsal for it, two weeks for his smaller part in *Take Her, She's Mine*.

Harry's first major problem was that there were two musicals, *Little Mary Sunshine* and *Damn Yankees*. Mike Cuthbert, a graduate of the University of Wisconsin, was given the job of polishing the new recruit's vocal performance. No easy task. "His voice was absolutely raw, bathtub tenor baritone. He did not know where it was. Definitely the sort of voice that sounds best in the middle of a lake," Cuthbert recalled.

Little Mary Sunshine, Rick Besoyan's delightful spoof of the sentimental, nostalgic 1920s musicals of Friml and Romberg, provided the toughest challenge. "You have got to be able to sing in *Little Mary Sun-*

shine. But he was just dying; it was really tough on him," said Cuthbert. "In *Damn Yankees* he could speak-sing a bit, like Rex Harrison, and, because he was such a good actor, bring it off."

The two men worked hard at overcoming the problems. "He was very creative and quick-minded, and he did it with less schtick than lesser actors," said Cuthbert. The voice coach was helped by his pupil's utter lack of vanity. "He worked extraordinarily hard to make it, and I never saw any temperament. He made it easy because he knew he was not talented vocally. He said: 'I've gotta learn this stuff if I want to do this business. I've gotta learn this stuff, so let's get at it.' "

The most eventful and nerve-racking weekend of Harrison Ford's young life began at around 8 P.M. on the night of Friday, June 26, 1964.

It was then that the sound of a solitary church bell began drifting through the streets of Williams Bay and out across the peaceful waters of Lake Geneva. In keeping with quaint tradition, the audience for the first night of the new season took the tolling of the bell as their cue to begin filing respectfully into the old church and taking their pews for the first performance of the opening production, *Take Her, She's Mine*.

As the curtain came up, there were those in the audience who detected a touch of anxiety in the young "resident" making his professional acting debut, but after a hesitant start in the supporting role of the fiancé of the unpredictable Mollie, played by Harvard graduate Eleanor Ferris, the tall, handsome newcomer soon found his feet.

By the time the audience set off into the warm Wisconsin night, his assured performance was already being talked of as one of the play's highlights. One can only wonder how much more forgiving the Belfry audience might have been, had they known the real-life worries on the mind of young Mollie's fiancé that night. The next morning Harrison Ford was to be married himself!

Harrison and Mary's marriage license had been issued in Milwaukee the previous Thursday by the Milwaukee County clerk, Clemens Michalski. Harold Martin, an old friend of Mary's family, had agreed to marry them at St. James's Church in the little town of Mequon north of Milwaukee where he was rector. They had one frantic week in which to arrange the wedding.

To many of Harrison's friends, the news came as a complete shock. He had simply not seemed the marrying kind. Bill Russell was certainly taken aback by the phone call he got from his old high school friend the week before the ceremony. Russell, home in Park Ridge on vacation from Cornell University, had hardly exchanged "How are yous?" before Harry issued an apology for the lack of notice and a formal invitation asking him to travel up to Milwaukee on the weekend.

"I had met Mary a couple of times, but it was out of the blue to me," Bill said.

On the Saturday morning Russell, Stu Shakman, and their two dates of the moment made the ninety mile or so drive north along the shore of Lake Michigan. Harry and Mary were married in a simple Catholic service. Terence Ford and Mary's sister, Charlene, acted as the witnesses. On the marriage certificate Harrison listed his profession as actor, while Mary left the box marked *Usual Occupation* blank.

"The wedding was very small and informal. There weren't many of us there, only Stu and I from high school," Russell recalled.

If the guests were in any doubt as to the lack of planning Harry and Mary had put into their nuptials, the groom confirmed it after the few formalities were completed. "Any chance of a ride back to Williams Bay?" he asked Bill Russell as the congregation drifted off.

"Mary and Harry, Stu, I, and our dates drove back together. That was their honeymoon as far as I could see," said Russell.

There were not many faces from Ripon at the ceremony. Only a few Riponites seem to have been told about it. Some who had known the newlyweds at college reacted with concern. Those who had been friends with Mary during her Milwaukee childhood knew that she had been a lonely young woman. Harrison had offered a security she had been lacking since her parents' death, and she had embraced it without hesitation. "There was no family structure there for her, probably no one to say anything," Nancy Hohnbach recalled.

"I thought, 'Gee, Mary's taking a rash move here,' " said Hannaford. "Here's a young man who doesn't know exactly what he's doing. He thinks he wants to be a movie star, for God's sake! What more foolhardy venture can you think of than that? He was okay as an actor, but he wasn't dazzlingly handsome, he wasn't dazzlingly talented. And it's a very risky business."

Others put their feelings about the match, and the breakup of Mary's romance with John Hibbard, to one side. "I sent them a collection of Beethoven by von Karajan as a wedding present," recollected Mary's old flame, Bill Per Lee. "I wished them well."

Mary spent the early part of her wedding night watching Harry's second performance in *Take Her, She's Mine*. After the final curtain call, they headed back to their temporary new home, Crane Hall—a grand old residence next door to the theater. The newlyweds spent their honeymoon settling into the theatrical life together, an experience both seemed to relish.

Mary had formed a close friendship with Fucik and his mother, who lived in Williams Bay. As the season wore on, she became a vital cog in the Belfry wheel. Mary ran the box office, painted sets, and cooked for the cast. Her new husband's duties expanded for a while too. When the technical director left after two productions, Harry turned his hand to building and erecting the sets. He found he had a knack with hammer and nails.

The two became the most popular couple within the theatrical community that summer. "They were both quiet and self-confident; they seemed like a couple who were completely in tune with each other," recalled Michael Wilmington, a Williams Bay resident who took on several minor roles during the season and helped Fucik write the programs and publicity notes for the productions. "He was a small-town hero, the natural quarterback who is modest and not full of himself. I was seventeen at the time and looked up to him, like he was my mentor. And Mary was the kind of person that you really liked. She was not a knockout, ravishing beauty, she was a lovely, blond, blue-eyed, earth-mother type. She wore these long earth-mother dresses, lavender, old-fashioned, and funky at the same time. Her look was Mary in Peter, Paul, and Mary—the intellectual, bohemian, college-girl look. Everyone called her 'the queen in the kitchen.' "

Harry had had his share of wild times at Ripon; now he had a wife and a career. He and Mary confined their nights to candlelit suppers with friends like Mike Cuthbert and his wife and Fucik and his mother at their house on the edge of the lake. "Mary had a French pen pal. She and my mother spent time writing letters in French," recalled Fucik.

On the stage of the Belfry, Harrison was winning good reviews. Critic Herb Moering of the *Williams Bay Independent*, in his column, "Moering's Musings," had spotted his first-night nerves, but he wrote: "Harrison Ford seemed to grow in stature throughout the play." By the end of the evening he was "utterly believable."

If he didn't already know it, Harrison's early appearances confirmed that he possessed something priceless. DiMaio may have had the chutzpah, and Sager the gravitas, but Harry had the charisma. "Harry in his early twenties was one of the best-looking guys I have ever seen. He was the kind of guy that people just looked at," Michael Wilmington has said. "He was not incandescent; he could be quite stiff. But people just liked to look at him."

As the season wore on, he proved he had application to go with the physical gifts nature had bestowed on him. Fucik demanded nothing less, but he saw there was an extra determination and intelligence that others did not have. He knew too that he had a wife who was behind him. Everyone was struck by Mary's strength and her warmth. Together the young couple seemed capable of conquering the world.

Thanks to Cuthbert's hard work, Harry shone in the second production of the season, *Little Mary Sunshine*, though his voice was showing signs of wear by the penultimate show, Adler and Ross's *Damn Yankees*. Harrison took on the lead of Joe Hardy, the handsome, athletic alter ego of fat, middle-aged Joe Boyd, the dyed-in-the-wool Washington Senators fan who—prepared to do anything to prevent the "damn Yankees" of New York winning the baseball pennant— enters into a Faustian deal with the Devil. To the ear of the town critic, Adler and Ross's showstoppers, "Heart" and "Whatever Lola Wants" were less impressive than "You're the Fairest Flower" and the rest of Besoyan's breezy musical.

"Harrison Ford as the young ballplayer Joe Hardy . . . provides some fine acting, such as how to escape the temptress Lola, who usually gets what she wants. Ford can sing too, although not as well in this show as in *Mary Sunshine*," Moering mused.

As a scorchingly hot summer wore on, a dramatic persona was being formed. Harry may have been something of an accidental actor, yet the more he discovered about his abilities, the more comfortable he felt in his new life. It was at Ripon that he had first begun to relish the kick of the collaborative process. It was, he said later, "the first time I ever felt comfortable working with people." Yet here too was a world where he could keep his distance, remain the outsider. "It was an opportunity to live other lives and experience things that I would not be able to experience in my own life," he would come to reflect.

Inspired by his discovery, driven by a desire to put the failure of Ripon behind him, encouraged by the soft yet steely support of Mary and, above all, pushed onward by the formidable Fucik, the apprentice eagerly and determinedly acquired the tools of his trade. "I can look at him now and see a lot of what he learned then," Fucik declared. Nowhere were there more fruitful lessons to be absorbed than in *Little Mary Sunshine*. "He learned to spoof there. Later on, in the Indiana Jones series, possibly some of the spoofing he did there came from some of the stuff he did in *Little Mary Sunshine*. He was a very intelligent actor."

Fucik did all he could to give Harrison as broad a range of experience as possible. "When we did *Dark of the Moon*, I said we must give him a character part, as he has not done one throughout the season. I felt that the final show, *Sunday in New York*, was important because it was high-class, sophisticated comedy and this would be another style that he could attempt. I worked a lot with him on that light comedy. I think he could do that very well."

Fucik found his last-minute student hungry to learn. "If a person has it in them to take it, then I give it to them. And Harry always did. He might have got the impression that I was always correcting him rather than praising him, but he took my directions well. Harry always knew I wanted to help him."

Fucik worried little about damaging egos. He had no time for prima-donna-ish behavior, even from himself. When Newman publicly paid tribute to him as the greatest coach he had ever had, Fucik called him to pass on the order: "Never mention my name again. . . . Newman? I've never heard of him," he would scramble if the subject was raised. He left the plaudit hunting to the guru of the Method School, Lee Strasberg. "Some years I had more actors up for nomination than he did. But I don't want it or need it." Here too was a philosophy which found a willing disciple in the down-to-earth Chicagoan. His repayment to Fucik for the enormous help he gave him has been to never mention his name, not even once.

Beneath the solid, hardworking, eager-to-learn exterior, however, Fucik did detect a fragile ego. Only once did the director feel he might have hurt the feelings of his star pupil that summer. "Somebody missed a line and he came in with something and it threw the show off a little. I said, 'Harry, that was an awfully dumb thing to do.'" The pained expression he picked up on Harrison's face made the director wish he had bitten his tongue. "I wished that I had never said it. He was *not* dumb. I should have considered my words more—it was a good try."

During the summer, Christopher and Dorothy traveled up from Chicago to watch their son's progress. They knew Harry well enough to suppress any doubts they had about his career choice, for any hint of negativity on their part would have made him dig his heels in further. By now Christopher had left advertising. He had sold the house in Park Ridge and with Dorothy begun a new line of business, trading in fine antiques. To their delight, there was much to admire in the workmanship their son was displaying on stage at the Belfry. In *Night of the Iguana*, Fucik allowed Sager and Harry to alternate in the lead. The Method of Sager met its match in Harry's naturalistic Tom Jones. "He was infinitely better."

As the season drew to a close, Harry and Fucik's conversations turned more and more to whether he might have a future in the profession. His father also contributed to the debate. "His parents were very supportive. His father would talk to me about how he was developing and everything," recalled Fucik. "At the end of the season he asked me, 'Now, should I encourage him to head to Hollywood or Broadway?' I said, 'Hollywood. He is a personality with excellent adjustability; theater in New York takes too much at this point of his training. He would have a better opportunity to get some experience in Hollywood.' I knew Jim Arness, who was producing at the time. I felt I could give him some entries."

Years later, Harry would spin a tale about tossing a coin to decide whether he went to New York or California to ply his trade. "It was easier to be poor in California," he joked, sensing a line that might make good copy. But it was during afternoons and evenings spent sitting on the edge of the lake with his acting coach that he grew to realize his chances were better on the West rather than the East Coast. The decision seems to have been far more calculated than a random flip of a dime. When Fucik offered to put him and Mary up at his home in Newport Beach until they got on their feet, his mind was made up.

Over dinner with Mike Cuthbert and his wife he began to speak openly of his ambitions. "He said he was off to Hollywood—in fact, I kidded him about it because I thought he was going to be a stage actor, dedicated to the art," Cuthbert recalled. "He said, 'not at all—I want to make money.' There was sort of laughter, but the way he worked, he had a lot to do. He worked hard at it, and he did it well. I didn't have any doubts that he would be rich and famous."

And so it was to be Hollywood. After the final performance of *Sunday in New York*, Harry and Mary loaded up the beaten-up Volkswagen bus they had bought during the summer. The vehicle groaned under the weight of their belongings and wedding presents. The young couple were hitting the road with everything literally staked on a future in the film business. As a small crowd of friends gathered to wish them well on their adventure, someone realized they had not packed the cat they had befriended at Crane Hall. As he climbed into the bus, Harry joked: "If it has any kittens on the way to California there won't be any room for them in here."

Word of Harry and Mary's decision to head west found its way back to Ripon College. To the rational minds of the faculty it seemed a reckless, even a hopeless gamble. The mild, forgiving, Midwestern audiences of the Red Barn and the Belfry were one thing—but Hollywood? As Mary and Harry picked their way across the country, skeptics like Spud Hannaford shook their heads slowly. Publicly they articulated thoughts that others, maybe even Mr. and Mrs. Harrison Ford themselves, kept under wraps. As the young newlyweds headed across the Mississippi, toward the Rockies, the desert and the Golden State: "We all thought, Gee, what a shame. What chance has that kid got?"

6

CALIFORNIA DREAMING

I n the autumn of 1964, William Fucik could monitor the progress of his most gifted protégés from the comfort of his living room, overlooking the endless azure of the Pacific Ocean on Newport Beach in southern California.

On television he could tune into reruns of *The Untouchables*, the phenomenally successful series that had, between 1959 and 1962, turned the cold-eyed Robert Modini into a star the world knew better as Robert Stack. Or he could switch on *Gunsmoke*, in which the sturdily heroic James Arness was, for the tenth season in succession, casting his giant, 6 feet 6 inch shadow over the Wild West. Easiest of all, he could flick through almost any show business magazine and find the taut features of Paul Newman staring out at him. At the Belfry Fucik had found Newman "undisciplined, loose, having fun." By now he had tightened up his act enough to have racked up two Best Actor nominations at the Academy Awards for *The Hustler* and *Hud*.

For three months or so that autumn, however, the most noticeable example of young talent in bloom was actually sitting in his living room with him. It was there that Harrison Ford readied himself for his assault on Hollywood. "We tried to prepare for everything and anything," Fucik remembered. "Right down to practicing being on the *Tonight Show*."

Harry and Mary spent their first few months in California living with Fucik. All along the Pacific Coast, youngsters like them were arriving on the edge of America. Endorsed by TV shows like *The Beverly Hillbillies* and pop paeans like the Mamas and the Papas' *California Dreaming*, the Golden State offered a vision of endless sunshine and limitless wealth. Young Americans headed west in such numbers that, by the mid-1960s, California overtook New York as America's most populous state.

Compared to a Midwest still to shake off the shackles of the innocent, optimistic 1950s, California offered Harrison and Mary a taste of a more daring, yet somehow stranger society. They would embrace many of its values, yet neither would quite fit in there. For Harrison it would always remain "the silly state."

In their first few weeks, Harry and Mary relied heavily on Fucik and his connections in the sleepy but chic community, on the beautiful Orange County coast, an hour or so from Los Angeles. The director tapped his contacts to get the young couple jobs. Mary's know-how—and specifically her ability to fill in the complicated new Medicare forms—made her an asset in any doctor's office, and she was quickly snapped up for such work.

Fucik also introduced Harry to Jerry Robinson, a friend from his time at the Pasadena Playhouse then working in the yachting business. Impressed by his pupil's work backstage at the Belfry, Fucik suggested that Harry could be useful around Robinson's boatyard. "I have just the job for him," Robinson told him. The three-masted America's Cup yacht *Columbia* had just returned from a long voyage via the Panama Canal and was in need of refurbishment. By day Harry worked in the harbor. By night, under Fucik's watchful eye, he continued to learn his other trade.

Master and pupil picked up where they had left off in Wisconsin. "We would sit here in my living room and work in the evenings. If we were watching a show on TV, I would automatically say, 'Well, now—suppose that was you?'" Fucik recalls. On weekends he even taught Harry to surf, readying him for any offers of a role in the Jan and Dean beach movies that were filling cinemas back in an East suddenly obsessed with life, California style. "I suggested that he get busy with his surfing because beach-party pictures were so popular at the time," said Fucik. "We went surfing a few times here. He liked the water and was a fine swimmer."

While many new Californians sank into the laid-back, easy-living ways of the West Coast, Harry and Mary remained hardworking and serious-minded Midwesterners. "Mary had the discipline from her medical family, possibly. There was certainly a great discipline there," said Fucik. "Harry was very disciplined too; he had wonderful control of himself. He had wonderful physicality and coordination. He moved well, and he looked well, photographed well. And he had his fine voice."

The young couple charmed all who met them. Robinson and his wife became close friends and spent weekends sailing out to Catalina Island. The technicalities of yachting remained a mystery to Harrison, however. Throughout his life it remained a skill he promised to teach himself one day.

Within a few months of his arrival, Fucik suggested Harry return to the stage. It had been six months since he had taken his final bow at the Belfry; he was turning rusty in his living room. His tutor suggested he enroll at a drama class that a friend, Bob Wentz, ran at the nearby Orange Coast College. By now Mary and Harry had moved to an apartment in nearby Laguna Beach. Wentz's course was full, but—trusting Fucik's judgment—he found a way around the problem. "I'll make him my assistant," he told his friend. As he studied, Harry landed himself a job at the Santa Ana branch of Bullock's, the department store. His knowledge of antiques and clock repair, picked up from his father, was invaluable, as was his Chicago-hewn knack of being appealing in interviews.

Harry also worked nights as a pizza deliveryman, an experience he valued simply for the opportunity it gave him to keep his own counsel. "Nobody knew who I was or what I was doing and nobody said any more to me than 'A large pie with cheese and pepperoni.' And that gave me a lot of time for looking around and thinking," he said.

In February 1965, Harry drove down to the Laguna Beach Playhouse, a thriving community theater on the beachfront where a friend of Wentz, a young director-actor, Doug Rowe, was planning a production of Stephen Vincent Benét's epic Civil War poem, *John Brown's Body*. Rowe had agreed to give him an audition.

"He just showed up at rehearsals after the play had been pretty much cast," recalled Rowe. Rowe liked what he saw, however. "He was always very comfortable on stage. We could tell right away that he was blessed with a wonderful voice." The production was the most ambitious attempted at the playhouse in years. The stirring text of Benét's poem, a chronicle of the Civil War from the slave ships to the surrender of General Lee, had been combined with a powerful score and a Greek-style chorus.

During rehearsals, Rowe, along with Wentz, Marthella Randall, Denise Ulm, and Ed Brown, had agreed to divide characters from the Yankee and Southern sides among themselves. Rowe was to play both Jack Ellyatt, a Union soldier on the run, and Clay Wingate, a Southern plantation owner's son. Impressed by Harry's brief rehearsal, Rowe handed the part of Wingate over to the newcomer. His only condition was that Wingate's opening speech be transferred to his character Ellyatt; Rowe explained that he was rather fond of the lines.

The director soon discovered that what he lacked in experience, Harrison Ford more than made up for in determination. "The thing that originally attracted me to it was the Southern soldier's speech. When I decided to cut it and keep that speech to myself, both he and Mary were not pleased," he said. "Mary to this day still kids me that I wanted to take away her husband's lines." The young couple's protests were vehement enough to force Rowe to back down and return the speeches he had annexed for himself.

To Rowe, Mary's influence was unmistakable. Ever-present, ever-supportive, she seemed to be the driving force behind the quiet, self-assured newcomer. She would sit in on rehearsals, reserved but ready to make suggestions that might help her husband. "Mary is one of the most remarkable women I have met in my life," said Rowe. "To have someone who is that strong as a partner makes it a lot easier. She was just an amazing woman."

His lines restored, and small cameos as a Yankee soldier and a mate aboard a slave ship added, Harrison offered nothing other than application and charm during the remainder of rehearsals. "Some of our youngsters are as bold as brass; they come down with all the self-assurance in the world and they think they are great," recalled

Marthella Randall, a stalwart of the theater and a director herself. "But I remember Harrison being very shy and retiring. He was unpolished but he had a great voice and a very natural way of moving; there was a natural grace about him. At that time he was uncoached and it didn't matter."

Offstage, as usual, he gave little away. "I was very taken with him. I had the feeling that he was not the partying type as some of our actors were. I am not very outgoing myself and it was hard to talk to him to draw him out in any way. Knowing him then, I would never have imagined that he would have turned out in the roles he did; they were very foreign to his nature. I saw him as a quiet college professor."

"He was a charmer, quiet and strong, not one to flip around back-stage," recalled Doris Shields. It was his voice that most impressed her too. "It had a stunning timbre."

Rowe formed a friendship with the young Midwesterners that was to become a lasting one. "I can't believe that over the years he hasn't done another play, because it is a medium in which he can thrive," he said.

The play was performed in the then-fashionable "rehearsal" style. As it opened at the beginning of March that year, Doug Rowe's equanimity was mirrored in the reviews. Praise was divided equally between the Yankee and the Southerner. Ellen Torgerson from the *South Coast News* found Rowe "thoughtful, eloquent" and "often brilliant." "Harry Ford," she added, "makes a startlingly good debut . . . He speaks his part with the seemingly casual correctness and rich passion of the naturally talented actor. Handsome, debonair, arrogant and elegant, Ford's Wingate is a neat pleasure to see and hear." Arnold Hando in the *Laguna News/Post* hailed the performance as "perhaps the most memorable in the history of the Laguna theater . . . Harry Ford," he went on, "may be the best young actor in the area—and this is his area debut."

The car accident he suffered one morning on the corkscrew roads above Laguna may have temporarily impaired the handsome, debonair exterior of Harry Ford. Ultimately, however, it provided him with a trademark as identifiable as Marilyn Monroe's mole or Clark Gable's mustache.

He was driving to Bullock's one morning, at the wheel of the Volvo that had replaced the venerable old Volkswagen. The car was one of the first to have seat belts, a fiddly arrangement on a small peg behind the driver's shoulder. As he took one of the sharp curves on the hilly road, he realized that the seat belt was undone and reached over to fix it. Before he knew it, the Volvo had hit a high curb, gone up on two wheels, and careered into a telephone pole. Dazed and bleeding profusely, he staggered out into the middle of the road. When cars began creeping their way around him rather than stopping, he acted with typical sto-icism. "It pissed me off so much that no one would stop that I refused to gesture to ask them," he explained later in his life. "So I just stood there until somebody finally stopped and took me to the hospital."

The bleeding outpatient was treated by a resident doctor rather than a specialist. Simultaneously symbolic of bloody machismo and pain that will never be healed, the jagged scar his impromptu needlework left would prove the perfect accessory for a career in tough but sensi-tive roles. At the time, though, Harrison cursed the amateurish-looking job the doctor did of stitching the livid wound. For a start it proved almost impossible to shave around.

His wound, however, did little to damage the growing confidence with which he acquitted himself on the stage of the Laguna Beach Play-house. As the show's brief run came to an end, it was Ian Bernard, the musical director, who first voiced the idea that he should think about trying for a place up at Columbia Pictures. Bernard, an actor turned screenwriter and musician, had a good connection at the Gower Street studio, where *Synanon*, a script of his, set in a drug-rehab unit, was about to go before the cameras under the direction of Richard Quine, with Eartha Kitt, Stella Stevens, and Edmond O'Brien in its cast. "We talked a lot during rehearsals, and I enjoyed his company," Bernard recalled. "There was an honesty about his acting that caught my eye. And I thought he was mature, good-looking, and sincere enough."

When Harrison showed interest in talking to a friend at Columbia, Bernard set the wheels in motion. "I had never done that for anyone before, nor have I done it for anyone since. You meet so many actors, but there was something about him that made me stick my neck out. I would not have sent a dingbat," said Bernard.

All actors carry a sneaking respect for the forces of serendipity. Few have not had cause to wonder what force compelled them to be in the most unlikely of places at the most unlikely of times. It may be the profession's one true faith. Fortune had already smiled on Harrison Ford in Williams Bay. Now it would shine on him again—although he would curse it for doing so soon enough.

His interview confirmed show business's "don't call us, we'll call you" cliché. He has enjoyed telling and retelling the tale over the years, usually in heavily ironic, Mickey Spillane sentences. "It turned out to be just like the movies. I walked into this small, heated, walnut-paneled office. Little bald-headed man with a stub of a cigar, white-on-white shirt, white-on-white tie, sitting behind a desk. Two telephones. Behind him, a man who looked like a racetrack tout on two more phones. I sat in the only chair available, right in front of the desk and listened to them discussing big names and big money," he told *Cinema* magazine, trying the story out when fame finally arrived years later. "Then the bald guy looked over to me as if he'd discovered a snake in his soup. 'What's ya name? How tall? How much do you weigh? Any special hobbies, talents, capacities? Speak any foreign languages? Okay, fine. If we find anything for you, we'll let you know.' "

Harrison left the room, pressed for the elevator and waited to head back down to earth. When no elevator appeared, he decided to pay a visit to a toilet he had spotted back down the corridor. He never discovered what happened between the two men and their four telephones in the time it took him to relieve himself. But as he reemerged, the "racetrack tout" was galloping toward him, beckoning him to come back into his office. "If I had gone down in the elevator, it wouldn't have been worth his while to chase me."

Back in the room, the bald man continued to treat him with thinly disguised contempt. "You're not the type we're usually interested in, but howdya like to be under contract?" he asked the young actor. "Sure, absolutely," Harrison replied, too embarrassed to explain he had little idea what that meant. By the time he had once more headed for the elevator, he had been told to report to the head of Columbia's New Talent Program, Walter Beakel, a few weeks later.

That day, as he drove back toward Laguna Beach, weeks away from his twenty-third birthday, the possibilities must have seemed as endless as the gleaming Pacific, stretching beyond the horizon.

"When I was very young I thought myself a maverick," he would say, reflecting back on his youth. "But by the time I reached twenty-three I realized I was just a stubborn son of a bitch who didn't want to do things the way everyone else wanted me to do them."

Self-awareness would be one of the few positives to emerge when the irresistible force that was Harrison Ford came into collision with the immovable object that was Old Hollywood.

PART TWO

*"If you're going to define
me properly, you must think
in terms of my failures as well
as my successes."*

Harrison Ford

7

"YOU AIN'T GOT IT, KID"

alter Beakel would have given anything to have been
perched on the rails of the corral at the Columbia Studios
ranch in Burbank one morning in the mid-1960s. Under
the wise, watchful eyes of the wranglers and rodeo veterans, new young
actors were being screen-tested for their suitability in what Hollywood
then called "oaters"—westerns. The performance of one troublesome
rookie had, apparently, put broad, knowing smiles on the leathery features of the Columbia cowboys.

Beakel, the coach in charge of molding the studio's raw recruits,
could not suppress a grin either as he watched the newcomer at work
in the screening room afterward. The image still lives with him. It was
the only time he saw Harrison Ford scared to death.

"If you could have seen the look of stark terror in his eyes as he
bumped along, hanging on for dear life, you would have died laughing,"
Beakel recalled. "All you could see on his face was him thinking, 'What
am I doing here?'" It was a question Harrison would come to ask himself more and more frequently.

The optimism of the Belfry and Laguna Beach dissipated within
days of his arrival on the famous Columbia set on Gower Street. Harrison had walked into an era—and a system—in its death throes.

Columbia's despotic founder, Harry Cohn, had overseen the studio's glory days, from Capra to Sinatra, when, as he put it, "Every Friday the front door opens on Gower Street and I spit a picture out." King Cohn may have been dead seven years when Harrison walked on to his lot, but the unsubtle cynicism of the man who said he could turn "your mother or your aunt" into a star was alive and well. So too was the nepotism that had earned Columbia the nickname "the Pine Tree Studio." (Because it's full of Cohns!) The "bald-headed guy" who had given Harrison his first taste of Hollywood could have been King Cohn's grandson, Bruce.

Thanks in no small part to Cohn's cruelty to his actors, the studio system that had helped create Hollywood had been all but broken by the mid-1960s. Harrison Ford was not alone in suspecting that his heirs were extracting their final, sadistic twist of pleasure from the last of the so-called contract players.

Harrison was entrusted to Beakel, a founder of Chicago's innovative Compass Theater. At Compass, the classically trained Beakel had nurtured a diversity of talents, most notably Elaine May and the thirty-five-year-old Mike Nichols, whose directorial debut *Who's Afraid of Virginia Woolf?* with Richard Burton and Elizabeth Taylor had just established him as Hollywood's flavor of the moment.

In his classroom at Cohn's old screening room, Beakel drove his actors through a rigorous training program, an A to Z of the acting life. Stars of the Columbia lot supplemented his classes: George Segal taught the art of auditioning, Richard Brooks offered a director's-eye view, Jerry Lewis passed on pearls of comic wisdom. There were also improvisational workshops run by another star of the Compass, Severn Darden, and a course on the Method run by Lee Strasberg's son, Johnny.

Beakel thought Harrison among the best of a crop that ranged from the progeny of the powerful, like Nat Cole's daughter Carol, to inexperienced unknowns like Cathy Walsh from Kentucky who arrived with no background in theater at all. "I loved Harrison. He was the brightest kid in the whole program, most articulate, best read, best educated," said Beakel. "His problem was that he was very unlike the studio type."

For all the earnest good intentions of Beakel's acting academy, survival in the studio system still required skills that were not taught in any classroom. While executives remained in no rush to drape the dust covers over their casting couches, the willing way and the sycophantic smile would always carry newcomers farther than their naked talent. "It was very political, like the French court during the revolution," Beakel admitted. "You didn't dare turn your back, or you'd get stabbed. If you were a contract player you had to play to one of the executives to get him to favor you and support your career."

The art of ingratiating himself did not come easily to Harrison Ford. "The politics did not go down well—he was very antipolitical," said Beakel. "And his attitude demonstrated that he did not approve of their game."

To the powers at Columbia, Harrison Ford seemed the reverse of what was expected of the lowliest form of studio life. The rebuffs of childhood and early adulthood had, if anything, deepened his reserve. But while he remained almost unknowable as a person—"He had no intimate dealings with people; he was very protective, very guarded in terms of what he did," said Beakel—he left few in the dark about his opinions. "He was very iconoclastic. He didn't like anything or anybody," said his coach. There was no shortage of those who were unimpressed by the self-protective slyness of his humor and the defiance of his nature.

Since the Oscar-laden success of David Lean's *Lawrence of Arabia* in 1962, Columbia's focus had increasingly fixed itself on European-flavored movies and British actors. Studio chief Mike Frankovich had based himself on the other side of the Atlantic, from where he had lined up a raft of new productions, including *A Man for All Seasons* with Paul Scofield, *Georgy Girl* with Lynn Redgrave, *Night of the Generals* with Peter O'Toole, and *Oliver!* with Ron Moody. With Frankovich in Europe, much of the power within Columbia rested with his right-hand man—a tough, uncompromising agent-turned producer named Jerry Tokovsky.

While Tokovsky occupied the most powerful seat at the studio, Harrison Ford never escaped the shadow of Madame Guillotine. "He and Harrison just clashed. They were from two different planets. Tokovsky really thought Harrison was worthless," said Beakel. Tokovsky repeatedly told the talent coach his new boy was "stiff," "unappealing" and—worst of all—"not a good actor."

Beakel acted as a buffer, but no sooner had Harrison signed his contract—"for 150 bucks a week, and all the respect that implies"—than the insults began to drip down as if by Chinese water torture.

First he was told by the Screen Actors Guild that he couldn't use the name Harrison Ford. Only one actor was permitted to use the same name, and this one remained the property of the silent movie star of such hits as *Up in Mabel's Room* and *The Mysterious Mrs. M*. The fact that no one in Los Angeles even knew Ford had died in obscurity in 1957 somehow summed up the industry.

Worse was to follow. No sooner had Harrison adopted the initial J. into his screen credit, than he was summoned to be told that Harrison was "too pretentious." Asked whether he had any suggestions for a new name, he proposed Kurt Affair—"the most ridiculous name I could think of."

The final insult came when he was told that his standard, short-back-and-sides haircut lacked personality. He was ordered to visit the studio hairdresser, from where he emerged brilliantined, bouffant, and boiling with rage. "They thought it would be a good idea to make me look like the new Elvis Presley," he said through clenched teeth later, still struggling to see the joke.

At the time, his treatment at Columbia was no laughing matter.

His new world could not have presented a starker contrast to the civilized, cerebral surroundings of the Belfry and the Laguna Beach Playhouse. There he had been allowed to assert his own personality, at least. To Harrison the Columbia routine was as anachronistic and ridiculous as Ripon with its ROTC drill and dress codes. Contract players were required to wear jacket and ties each day in the Columbia dining room. Elsewhere they were groomed in what he regarded as "bullshit" but Columbia considered the arts of Hollywood. He had to endure everything from escorting starlets to the Academy Awards to posing in swimming trunks on the beach for popular magazines like *Argosy* and appearing at the showcase evenings where new talent was wheeled out before their lords, masters, and mistresses. The latter experience, where a quick dance, song, or scene was followed by an evening of glad-handing, went against the grain more than anything.

"It was horrible, like dressing up meat for the market, not what you would call the best environment for Harrison. But he did not shame himself; he'd just smile his crooked smile and shake the hands," Beakel recalled.

"It was 1964–65 and Columbia were still playing 1920–30. Horrible, worse than any factory," Harrison said once. "Nobody knew your name or cared a damn about you. I went nuts!"

In some ways Harrison should have been perfect fodder for the studio system. "I don't want to be a movie star. I want to be in movies that are stars," he volunteered once. But at the age of twenty-three and possessed of that combination of opinionatedness and stubbornness that would later become known as *attitude*, it was obvious pretty quickly that he was never going to fit in at Columbia.

The experience of feeling unsuited to the world he was inhabiting was not a new one. He had been a fish out of water before, at Ripon, in Morton Grove, even, to a lesser extent, in high school. At least this time he could take some kind of solace from the knowledge that it was not entirely his fault. As he once succinctly put it: "I arrived in an industry that was completely fucked up."

Early in 1966, thanks mainly to Beakel's efforts, Harrison was cast in his first movie, a spy-caper vehicle for James Coburn, called *Dead Heat on a Merry-Go-Round*. His role was hardly challenging—a hotel bellboy required to appear on screen for some forty-five seconds while he delivered a message to Coburn. He walked on to the soundstage at Columbia where Bernard Girard was directing prepared and word-perfect. Not that that meant much.

The first words Harrison ever delivered on celluloid were: "Paging Mr. Jones. Paging Mr. Jones." If it had been up to Jerry Tokovsky, they would also have been his last.

He was hauled into Tokovsky's office and read the riot act. Time has turned the confrontation into a defining moment.

"He calls me into his office after that film," Harrison told the respected British film journalist Tony Crawley in *Cinema* magazine, beginning one of his more colorful renditions of his favorite story in 1978. "Now remember, all I had to do was deliver a lousy telegram, right? 'Kid,' he said. They always called me 'Kid,' probably because they didn't know who the hell I was. 'Kid, siddown. Lemme tellya a story. First time Tony Curtis ever appeared in a movie, he delivered a bag of groceries. A bag of groceries! You took one look at that person and you knew that was a star. You ain't got it, kid. You ain't got it! Get back to class because you ain't gonna work again in this studio for six months, maybe a year. Go get your shit together!' "

Typically, however, rather than nodding and accepting his master's verdict, Harrison fought back. "I thought the point was that you were supposed to look at him and think that this is a grocery clerk," he shot back.

Tokovsky's reply was equally characteristic: "Get the fuck out of my office."

"He was on the shit list after that, I can tell you," recalled Beakel, who didn't agree with his bosses' view of Harrison. "He had his own mind. It was on the distaff side, very tangential—a person who doesn't buy that stuff, who looks at you skeptically, questions and challenges you. . . . But I liked that," said Beakel. "It was rare to find it in an actor at that time."

His skills were not yet polished enough for him to lace his acting with the qualities Beakel found so interesting, however. Given his diffident nature, Harrison had difficulty in displaying his inner complexity in Johnny Strasberg's Method classes. Denuding himself à la Brando did not come naturally. "No, it didn't. But that didn't mean that he didn't try, because he did, he really made an effort. But that would have been the most distant thing for him at that time," said Beakel.

Instead, Harrison was more at home using his quick wits in the improvisational work he did with character actor Severn Darden. "It takes a person who is very cerebral, very bright, who can make up dialogue while they are acting," said Beakel. "I think the improvs he did with Severn were the best thing he did. That was the last thing the studio was interested in, though."

His intelligence worked against him in more ways than one. As it intimidated his bosses, it also built self-doubt within himself. Criticism that washed over some of Beakel's students were arrows to Harrison's heart. He questioned his own abilities more and more. "He was hurt a lot at that time; after all, the ego hasn't really formed at that age. His intelligence was a disadvantage, because it brought self-criticism, which can be self-defeating," said Beakel, who increasingly became Harrison's main source of support.

In the troubled crucible of his developing self-image, Harrison was certain of only one thing: he was *not* another version of someone else. "I was sure that the most important thing for an actor to do was to hold on to what was individual about himself," he said. As each day at Columbia became a battle of wills, Harrison could at least take solace in the familiarity of the situation. He might not have been willing to play Elvis Presley, but he was quite prepared to once more play Sisyphus.

Tokovsky was true to his promise. It was not until the autumn of 1966 that Harrison was considered for another role, this time in a western tentatively titled *The Long Ride Home*. Oaters were still playing well at Columbia. *Cat Ballou* with the Oscar-winning Lee Marvin had been the unexpected hit of the previous year and the rising Sam Peckinpah had cut his teeth with *Major Dundee* starring Charlton Heston. Harrison, his horse-riding skills patiently polished by the horsemen of the Columbia ranch, was given the role of Lieutenant Shaffer.

The experience offered a new, even more depressing insight into the realities of his profession.

The day shooting began in Kanab, Utah, the more experienced members of the set saw the writing on the wall. Paul Petersen, a child TV star struggling to make the transition to adult leading man and a veteran on the Columbia lot, instantly recognized a film that had been organized to meet the pay-or-play conditions of its stars' contracts. "They dragged out a script that was almost thirty years old that had the requisite number of parts to pay us all off," he recalled. The result was a film that did nothing but harm to all associated with it.

"This was one of the worst pieces-of-shit movies you ever saw. It was an unpleasant experience. Roger Corman was fired as the director within five days, Glenn Ford, George Hamilton, and Inger Stevens thought it was a great piece of art and were constantly fiddling with the script, people were getting injured left and right because it seemed as if they did not have the money for stuntmen. Harrison, myself and the rest collected our checks and kept our mouths shut," said Petersen.

Petersen found Harrison intense but likable. "I was still famous from the *Donna Reed Show*. Getting drunk and getting laid was my primary objective after hours. In that era, music was memorable and sex wouldn't kill you," he said. "Harrison was pretty quiet. He did his work and went home."

Harrison and Mary had rented an apartment on Hudson Avenue. With $75, half his weekly wage, going on the monthly rent, their life was hardly high-on-the-hog. "We were both poor," recalled Walter Beakel, whose wife Nancy befriended Mary. The Fords and the Beakels spent Christmases together. "We couldn't afford fancy gifts. Nancy and Mary used to make these clever stained-glass presents."

Apart from Beakel, Harrison formed few lasting friendships with his Columbia colleagues. Afro-American actor Paul Winfield, one year older than Harrison, but another conscripted to the New Talent Program, was one of the rare souls with whom he found anything in common. Victimized more for his color than his cockiness, Winfield nevertheless identified a kindred spirit.

"Harrison was my only friend, the only man who took me at face value," Winfield said years later. "He was a breath of fresh air, very nonjudgmental in his dealings with people. I don't think he's changed very much as a human being since."

Generally, however, Harrison fell back on friendships away from the Hollywood scene. Bill Haljum got a phone call soon after his former roommate moved up to Los Angeles. He was taken aback by his invitation to meet Mr. and Mrs. Harry Ford. "When he showed up married in Los Angeles, I was really surprised, because he had not been serious about any of the women he had dated. It did not seem like he was looking for a mate," recalled Haljum.

And Mary Marquardt had seemed a particularly unlikely candidate. "I knew Mary, but not as Harry's mate. At college she was strange: her parents were dead and there was always this distance. She was aloof but not cold. Sad, I suppose," he said. As Haljum got to know the young couple more, however, he responded to Mary's intelligence. "She had terrific character."

If Harrison had little time for the politics of the studio, Mary had even less. "She was not interested in the Hollywood scene at all," Walter Beakel recalled. With the ferment of the anti-Vietnam movement rising on the campuses of California, the petty Machiavellianism of Columbia and Hollywood seemed even more infantile.

Nancy Beakel had enrolled at UCLA and had joined the marches organized by the mushrooming peace movement. Inspired by her example, Mary, Harry and her husband did all they could to mobilize antiwar opinion. "Most of the people we knew were like that. Mary and Harrison at the time were very socially aware. They were those kind of people, anti-gun law, antiwar. We set up petitions, that sort of stuff," said Walter Beakel.

It was no fault of Walter Beakel's that Harrison remained lower than the kids in the mail room at Columbia. He continued to push him for roles that might have changed the tide, even landing him auditions for the most coveted jobs in town.

In 1967, there was no hotter property than *The Graduate*, Calder Willingham and Buck Henry's acidly funny script about a college graduate's struggle to assimilate into the outside world. With Mike Nichols signed up to direct, every agent in Hollywood was pushing their men forward for the role of Benjamin Braddock, a role guaranteed to launch a major career. Beakel saw that the edgy, intelligent young man Willingham and Henry had created in their original script was as well suited to his friend Harry Ford as Columbia was ill suited to his talents. He drew on his friendship with Nichols and landed him an audition.

"The role as it was originally written was more Harrison Ford in life than anybody else I knew," he recalled. Beakel helped Harrison prepare for his meeting with his old Compass colleague.

Harrison auditioned twice, but ultimately failed. His inability to emote the edginess that was his offscreen trademark let him down. "He didn't do too well. He was young and he did not quite have the confidence to execute an audition," said Beakel, who had to watch as the role went to the older, more experienced Dustin Hoffman.

As Hollywood wrestled with itself in the mid-1960s, Harrison was, in reality, handicapped by something more profound than the deficiencies that failed him in his *Graduate* audition. Work would rid him of his lack of experience. Time would rid him of the baby-faced complexion that still made him look like a teenager. He could not, however, lose his look of intelligent, intense masculinity, a commodity seriously out of fashion in the movies of the time.

"His type was out of style. Harrison was a young leading man; while the guys who were coming up like Dustin and Pacino, Hopper and Fonda were antiheroes. The problem was that he was not off the wall," said Beakel. "And he was not short and homely."

Even when Harrison was thought suitable for roles, his unpopularity at the studio could be guaranteed to derail his prospects. No period summed up the hopelessness of his position more than his brief involvement with a movie called *The Model Shop*.

Apart from Walter, Beakel, Harrison's sole supporter was Gerry Ayres, one of the more cultivated producers at work on the lot. During the spring of 1965, Ayres had befriended the innovative French director Jacques Demy, who was in Los Angeles for the Oscars. His extraordinary screen operetta, *Les Parapluies de Cherbourg*, had been nominated for three awards.

Ayres had offered the thirty-four-year-old Demy the opportunity to fulfill his dream by making a movie for Columbia in Hollywood. Turning his outsider's eye on the California of the day, Demy, with his writer-director wife, Agnes Varda, developed a story set in one of the risqué sex parlors, or "Model Shops," springing up in Los Angeles.

When Ayres and Columbia gave the project the green light, Demy invited the beautiful French actress Anouk Aimée to join him across the Atlantic. For the lead role, however, he wanted a fresh, new American face. "Jacques believed in the old Hollywood dream that you could cast the unknown, who would become a star," Gerry Ayres later recalled to Agnes Varda. Harrison J. Ford certainly fell into the "unknown" category.

Demy and Agnes Varda were introduced to Harrison by Ayres and Walter Beakel. "Jacques did tests with him and Anouk Aimée, and loved him. He thought he was the best man for the part," recalled Agnes Varda.

Strangers in Los Angeles, Demy and Varda were befriended by Ayres and Harrison. With Mary and Ayres's wife, the French filmmakers immersed themselves in the peace-loving spirit of the 1960s. In 1967, with the Summer of Love in full swing, life in Los Angeles seemed a succession of "happenings," concerts and renaissance fairs. Since his Ripon days, Harrison had always been a natural candidate for the counterculture. By now he wore his hair long, often sported a shaggy beard, and had adopted jeans and a working shirt as his uniform.

He was a less extreme version of the Haight-Ashbury hippie that his brother Terence seemed to have been modeling himself on. Terence had drifted into Los Angeles, where he had taken up the apartment below Harry and Mary. Diffident by nature, even more bohemian in his lifestyle, and lacking, at twenty-three, the direction his brother had found, Terry embraced Timothy Leary's invitation to "Tune in, turn on, and drop out" with evangelical zeal. "Any substance that altered my mind, I took," he confessed once. "It was probably an effort to overcome my basically shy attitude. Harrison was always more confident and outgoing." (En route to spells in Morocco, Nepal, and a Tibetan monastery in Scotland, he eventually gravitated to one of the most colorful hippie communes, the Hog Farm in Sun Land, California. It would not be until 1987 that he rid himself of his problems, a transformation in his life "like night and day.")

To Demy and Varda, Harrison was less a subversive, more a free-thinking young man in tune with extraordinary times. "Harry was not a hippie; he was more in the mood of the flower children. It gave a grace to everybody in the way they behaved, the way they shared at that time," Varda recalled.

Sundays would be spent listening to the Doors and the Mamas and the Papas around Demy and Varda's rented Beverly Hills swimming pool, or attending the "happenings" that were, by now, as common as acceptance of the Maharishi and marijuana. "They were going to these renaissance fairs; everybody would go with their dogs and kids and share their food and sing. Endless picnics with half of the town there. The togetherness was there. It was very nice, very simple, very happy," Varda recalled.

As he got to know Harrison better, Demy grew more and more convinced he was right to star in his film. Having promised his friend the lead, Demy even went so far as to start researching the film with him. Together the two men trawled Santa Monica Boulevard and its "Model Shops," where men paid to make their own amateur films of loosely clothed models.

"We had to rent those little cameras and buy some films, four exposures of film, I think it must have been thirty-five dollars," Harrison recalled years later in a documentary made by Agnes Varda, *L'Univers de Jacques Demy*. "We were both very shy. Neither of us knew what to do, so the girl sort of said, well, you know, 'I pose like this and I pose like this.' "

When he got wind of the work being put into the film, it was Walter Beakel who had the unpleasant duty of bringing Harrison and Demy back down to earth.

Beakel took Demy to one side and told him Tokovsky would not allow it. "I said please don't tell anyone, but you are not going to get Harrison for this film because the executive does not like him," recalled Beakel.

Demy, however, was determined to cast his young American friend. "Jacques fought like a tiger to get him," said Varda. Beakel soon found himself in the middle of a humiliating scene. "I got to my office the next morning and the red phone was ringing. I answered. It was Tokovsky: 'Get down, the fucking office now.' "

Angry at the influence his boss was exerting over the fate of his actors, Beakel defended his actions: "You wouldn't tell Mike Nichols how to cast, would you?"

Despite the fact Demy was sitting in his office, Tokovsky replied: "This is no fucking Mike Nichols!"

"Jacques Demy was sitting right there . . . That's studio," Beakel shrugged.

Eventually Demy and Varda were forced to look elsewhere and cast Gary Lockwood, star of Stanley Kubrick's space epic *2001: A Space Odyssey*.

Harrison took the news philosophically. The reason for Columbia's blocking of his casting boiled down to something that he was, by now, tired of hearing. "I was told that the head of the studio had said to forget about me," he informed Agnes Varda later. "That I had no future in this business."

8

UNIVERSAL SOLDIER

If William Tyree's memory serves him correctly, he was in his office at Ripon College when a telephone call came through long-distance from California some time around 1967. He was pleased to hear from one of his former students, but faintly amused by his request.

"Dr. Tyree, the draft board is breathing down my neck," Harry Ford explained, politeness personified. "I wonder if you'd be willing to write and certify that I am a conscientious objector."

Tyree's mind couldn't help rewinding itself to the events of four years earlier and Harry's headlong slide into academic disgrace. "For about a semisecond I chuckled, because Harry had not been particularly conscientious about anything," recalled Tyree. "That chuckle was probably fatal."

Tyree went on to assure his old pupil that he would do his "very best." "I said: 'By all means have them write to me, Harry.' But I never heard from them—or him again."

If drugs, free love, and the hippie movement represented the 1960s at its dippiest and dreamiest, the war in Vietnam was its nightmarish flip side. As more and more troops were being sent to Southeast Asia, it had become inevitable that Harrison would find himself in line for military service.

As a college student he had been eligible for a deferment from serving in the military. If he had been a teacher, engineer, scientist, or even an apprentice plumber, he could have been eligible for another deferment. As an actor, however, he had to account for himself before the draft board.

Millions of young Americans faced the same prospect. Some left the country, some used money and influence to escape, some—like Bill Haljum—joined the National Guard. Others enlisted the specialist "draft counselors," whose notoriety extended to faking psychological illness or homosexuality. "The Vietnam draft cast the entire generation into a contest for individual survival . . . the fittest—those with the background, wit, or money—managed to escape," wrote the historians William Strauss and Lawrence Baskir.

Harrison, however, became one of the half-million young Americans who took the rather nobler—but potentially disastrous—course of declaring themselves conscientious objectors.

Discouraged by Tyree's response to the seriousness of his situation, Harrison wrote his own justification for his pacifism. "All my philosophy education from college went into the support of this position. I did it on the basis of a moral conviction which I still have," he said in a rare confessional years later. "I would have been willing to do alternative service, but I didn't want to kill people."

After a few uncomfortable months dreading the morning mail, his fears began to fade. The man who would become one of cinema's most resilient fighting men never discovered why he was not called up to serve his country. He did not even get a reply to his lengthy letter to Washington. "I don't know what they thought about it," he wondered years later. "But I didn't get drafted."

In any event, by the end of 1967, his prospects of being drafted had slipped even further from view. As it picked its way through America's fittest and finest, the draft board did what it could to protect family men from conscription. Late that year Mary broke the news that she was expecting their first child.

By then, Harrison had achieved the seemingly impossible at Columbia. His stock had, if anything, fallen even lower on the Gower Street lot. Predictably, no one had found a kind word for *The Long*

Ride Home when it was released. *Variety* flayed it roundly, if a little xenophobically, damning "the kind of graceless action and low comedy routines which indicate that . . . it is aimed primarily at the European market."

Two actors named Ford did provide *A Time for Killing* with its only hope of being remembered by the Hollywood historian, although only one seemed noteworthy at the time: it was Glenn Ford's hundredth film, and the first in which Harrison Ford died on screen.

He had barely recovered from the experience when he was cast in the film version of Murray Schisgal's hit Broadway play *Luv*, starring Jack Lemmon, Elaine May, and Peter Falk. After four months of shooting in New York, British director Clive Donner had brought his production to California to wrap up. As if to prove to Harrison that conformity brought its rewards, both Severn Darden and Nina Wayne from *Dead Heat on a Merry-Go-Round* had been given expanded roles. He, however, had not. Donner's only requirement of Harrison was a scene in which he played a hippie whose car is involved in a light traffic scrape with Lemmon and May's characters, Harry and Ellen. As Ellen reverses into Harrison's Ford convertible, he leaps out to confront her. When he sees a woman at the wheel he turns his anger on Harry, who is sitting behind her. After landing a full-blooded punch on Jack Lemmon's nose, Harrison the hippie drives off never to be glimpsed again.

It was hardly surprising that by the time he had finished his third film as a member of the New Talent Program, Columbia had reached the conclusion that he and the studio had best part company. Tokovsky told Beakel that he intended to let him go. When Beakel told his boss Mary was pregnant, his only concession was to offer to extend Harrison's contract by a few weeks.

By then, however, Harrison was in no mood to accept charity. Tokovsky called him into his office and delivered his verdict in typically brusque style, according to the account his least favorite apprentice gave us years later. "Kid, you're not worth a bunch of shit to us." Muttering something about Harrison's forthcoming fatherhood, he went on to offer a few extra weeks if Harrison signed a piece of paper his secretary had ready for him. According to Harrison's version of events, he told him precisely where he could stick his paper.

On this occasion his timing was terrible. Their first boy, Benjamin, was born that autumn. Money was too tight for a major celebration. Mary made some clever announcement cards, and they were dispatched to friends and family with the good news.

With an extra mouth to feed, Harrison needed to find work—and fast. Walter Beakel knew his friend could be a monumental pain in the ass compared to other, more cooperative actors. But he believed "the kid" had talent; it simply needed nurturing. "Everybody could tell very early that the kid had potential. But he did not have enough confidence and enough technique to cut it, because he was very young. He hadn't matured enough to go into creative, emotional, leading-man roles," he said.

Aware of the dire financial consequences about to be unleashed on the new family, Beakel fixed Harrison up with an agent, Dick Clayton. Clayton knew Universal Studios was running a similar program to Columbia's and was close to Monique James, its head. She agreed to see Harrison Ford. James and Universal needed young actors—no matter how much trouble they were. And if anyone was going to knock "the kid" into shape, it was Monique James.

The short, matronly daughter of a former managing editor of the *New York Times*, James had a reputation as Hollywood's finest shaper of talent. As an agent she had helped mold Grace Kelly; as a talent spotter she had given Paul Newman his first acting job in New York. She regarded her thirty-strong group of young actors as an extension of her family. In return her charges regarded her with a kind of awe. "She was psychologist, mother, chauffeur, and camp counselor to us all," recalled Susan Clark, one of the promising youngsters under her wing when Harrison Ford arrived at Universal.

Beakel spent time with Harrison preparing him for his interview. James personally interviewed the Columbia reject and accepted him into her program. To his amazement, Harrison was back under contract within three days of walking out of Columbia.

Television's stranglehold on the entertainment business was even more evident at the once-great movie lot, where the TV production giants MCA had acquired the reins in 1962. Universal, home of Valentino and Von Stroheim, Boris Karloff and Lon Chaney, was now the residence of *Run for Your Life* and *The Road West*, *Pistols 'n' Petti-coats*, and *Dragnet*.

To serious actors like Harrison Ford, television remained inferior, ignoble work, an activity justifiable only to fill in time and bank balances and then to be ridiculed, apologized for, or, if necessary, denied altogether. Even the worst movie was still considered infinitely more worthy than the very best television work. At Universal, however, he discovered that there was no room for such elitism. "Their television department was going great guns. Movies of the Week were the new thing," recalled Paul Petersen, one of the few familiar faces Harrison found on the Universal lot; Petersen too had transferred there from Columbia.

Just as at Columbia, there were compulsory acting classes—even for those who already had film experience under their belt. When television roles came up, casting calls were held inside the six-story "Black Tower" on Lancashire Boulevard, in which Universal's legendary boss Lew Wasserman ruled with an iron fist in an iron glove.

Harrison and the other studio players underwent the same daily grind.

"Harrison, like me, was bottom of the barrel," recalled Don Stroud, a Hawaiian lifeguard being converted into an actor by the studio at the time. "They had a little acting school there with Vincent Chase. We worked on those TV shows and you had to know your lines, you had to do your stuff, and we all took it seriously."

"I was late one morning because my girlfriend had had a miscarriage. It was noticed. You could be Forrest Tucker and David Janssen and be drunk by lunchtime, but if you were at the level Harrison and I were at, you made sure you showed up," said Paul Petersen.

As a Universal foot soldier, Harrison gave no one any reason to doubt his dedication or his professionalism. With a family to support and the trauma of Columbia still fresh in his mind, he kept his head down for the next two years. Compatibility was another matter, however. His increasingly hippie-ish dress sense and often eccentric behavior once more made him a square peg at the dream factory.

"He would always wear a buckskin coat, jeans, and boots. He was sort of a rebel, different—pretty much of a loner," recalled Don Stroud.

Harrison's habits raised eyebrows. Often he would be seen sniffing from a small case he carried in his jeans. "We were all kind of square; it was the days before cocaine. We weren't sure what it was, whether it was drugs. People would say: 'He's doing drugs.'" Curiosity eventually got the better of Stroud and his colleagues. "Turned out he was sniffing snuff."

Harrison began his television career back in the saddle. In February 1967 he popped up alongside Doug McClure in an episode of *The Virginian* called "The Modoc Kid." After that he appeared in "The Past is Prologue"—an early episode of *Ironside*, the new legal drama with Raymond Burr of *Perry Mason* fame.

In March 1967, he was cast for his first movie under the Universal colors, a western called *Journey to Shiloh*. Based on a novel by Will Henry, it told the tale of seven young Texans in search of glory alongside the flamboyant Confederate Civil War General Hood. Harrison's character was Willie Bill Bearden. Completing the seven with Harrison, Paul Petersen, and Don Stroud were Michael Burns, Jan Michael Vincent, Michael Sarrazin, and—in the lead—James Caan.

Once again Paul Petersen found Harrison the most concentrated man on the set. "He was there and he was paying attention. Even in rehearsals he was intense," Petersen noted. "Harrison would practice throwing a knife until he was perfect each time," agreed Don Stroud.

Unlike *The Long Ride Home*, the film turned out to be a passable success when released in June 1968. *Film and Television Daily* thought the movie in itself "commonplace" but "redeemed in a measure by the vibrant performances of its young cast." Harrison was one of those "noteworthy among them."

Its reviews were good enough to win him an audition for a movie being planned by John Schlesinger in New York. "Michael Sarazin, Harrison, and I flew to New York to audition for *Midnight Cowboy*," Don Stroud recalled. Harrison may have used the trip to catch up with his little brother, Terence, who was working at the famous Max's Kansas City nightspot. If he did, it would have been the only worthwhile benefit from his trip to the other side of the country. Once more, Harrison failed to catch the eye at his audition. In the end the role of Joe Buck, and the international acclaim that was to greet it, went to the tall, blond Jon Voight.

The rejections hurt. At home, Harrison could be dark and difficult to live with. The frustration foamed into rage. "I have a constant level of stress that is neither necessary nor completely healthy," he confessed later in life. "The symptoms are that intimate bystanders will be lightly abused for things that have nothing to do with them."

There was plenty to stress him out at the studio. "It was a difficult time at Universal, in particular for young people. Monique James was really tough. She had a very particular idea of the look and the behavior she wanted. Harrison was so quiet, and unless you have the right part no one is going to see what is going on in your face," said Paul Petersen. "The studio system that people talk about was the grand days of MGM, but there was a whole B group, and a C group whose opinion did not count. They look you right in the eye and tell you what is true: 'Shut up, you know nothing.' "

Some actors were simply grateful to be there at all. "To me they were wonderful days," said Don Stroud. "We would go to the commissary and watch the stars having lunch. We were driving around in limousines going to the Academy Awards and we had five dollars in our pockets. A lot of people knocked being a contract actor. I was a guy who worked in Hawaii as a lifeguard, and Troy Donahue wanted someone to surf for him on *Hawaiian Eye*, so I became a movie star and made a ton of money."

Harrison's aspirations were somewhat different, and he was offended by what he saw as the hack sloppiness of Universal. Years later he still fumed about the time he played a biology teacher in a show whose name he had long since forgotten. His opportunities were few, but given ten days to prepare for the part he was determined to make the most of them. One of his scenes required him to give a lecture on spiders. "I went and bought a tarantula," he told the writer Georgina Howell. "And I worked with it, tamed it, and brought it with me. I put it in a coffee can and I said to the director, 'Look what I got.' And he said, 'Get that goddamn thing outta here.' I explained that this was a scene about sexual attraction and danger and he said: 'I don't wanna hear about it. Put that thing back in the can and take this knotted-up ball of black twine and go stand there and say the lines.' "

At times he could only laugh at the lunacy of the world he was inhabiting. In 1969, shortly after he had appeared in an episode of the deeply forgettable comedy *My Friend Tony*, with James Whitmore and Enzo Cerusico, he was cast in an episode of the schmaltzy, but somehow highly popular, *Love American Style*. He was cast as a hippie in an episode called *Love and the Former Marriage*—the story of an ex-husband comforting his ex-wife as they wait for their daughter to arrive home from a date. The role required, he remembered, a brief but meaningful speech in which he passed on "some hippie wisdom."

By now, his hair was still shoulder length and his beard as Jerry Garcia-like as he could get away with. Over the weekend before shooting began he joked that he had finally found a role for which he was suitable. "Monday morning, I went into makeup . . . and the first thing they did was ask me to cut my hair and shave," he recounted once. "I tried to explain that I was playing a hippie, but they mumbled something about 'America inviting me into its living room' and how we wouldn't want to 'offend.' And I thought, 'Oh shit, I'm in trouble here.' "

In wardrobe he was given "a navy-blue shirt with this high collar with contrasting white stitching on it and a pair of Burgundy jeans made out of some plastic material with a wide white belt. They even had a scarf with a little ring to put around my neck."

Convinced there had been a mistake, he headed off in search of the show's producer. All fell into place when he tapped the executive on the shoulder. "When he turned around I saw he was wearing the same thing I was. He was a hippie producer, I guess," he said. "At least the check went through when I got paid."

Such was his frustration that he moonlighted as a cameraman. He had become friendly with the colorful Earl McGrath, former manager of the Rolling Stones and now the owner of an art gallery in Los Angeles. The connection brought him into contact with a wide circle of musicians working in Los Angeles, from Don Everly of the Everly Brothers to the country and western singer Jimmy Buffett.

When Jim Morrison and the Doors, at the apogee of their fame on the West Coast, commissioned the director Paul Ferrara to make a documentary, Harrison was hired as a member of the camera crew. His lack of experience dovetailed perfectly with Morrison's philosophy about filmmaking. "There aren't any experts; theoretically any student knows as much as any professor," he said during filming of the movie, called *Feast of Friends*. After a week on the road with rock'n'roll's Lizard King, however, Harrison had his doubts. "I don't think any of it was in focus, not a bit of it," he said of the footage he shot as second cameraman. Morrison's legendarily excessive behavior may have had something to do with the fuzziness of his lens work. "I couldn't keep up with those guys. It was too much."

The last straw came when he was hired back to the studio at which he had spent his unhappiest times, Columbia, in 1969. *Easy Rider*, Dennis Hopper's drug-drenched drive into the dark side of 1960s America, had become the surprise hit of the year. *Getting Straight*, the story of a postgraduate returning to university for his master's degree amid campus violence, was Columbia's effort to tap into the same jaundiced vein. Again, it was hardly a role to get excited about—Jake, a sideburned student.

Once more the experience was an unhappy one. On location Harrison saw director Richard Rush reduce his role to blink-or-you'll-miss-me minimalism. And by the time his performance was released the following April, it mattered little that the film went on to be something of a cause célèbre. By then Monique James and Universal had told Harrison he was surplus to requirement. For the second time in Hollywood he had been given the bum's rush.

"Young Harrison was very fragile. I think he was hurt a lot," said Walter Beakel, whose connections were this time unable to offer immediate help. Harrison's unwillingness to play the political game had been the cause of his dismissal. If James had regarded herself as the Universal earth mother, Harrison Ford was her errant child.

"I don't think Harrison was included as part of the family. He was not the kind of kid who toes the mark. His ambivalence came through, and Monique could not stand that," said Beakel. "You had to suck up to her or you were out. Harrison would never do that unless he really, really, really respected you."

Years later, Harry was able to draw solace from the fact that Hollywood did not know what to do with itself, let alone an intense, dangerous young actor with a chip on his shoulder. He may not have appreciated it at the time, but he was in good company. Among the other stars-in-waiting on the TV carousel at the time were the likes of Michael Douglas, Martin Sheen, and Diane Keaton. "An odd time, the 1960s," Harrison mused years later. "All the studios were making their biggest films in Europe. Everybody in Hollywood was taking acid and smoking dope and here I was acting like a baby actor getting nowhere."

As the 1960s drew to a close, there was no more astute judge of acting talent in Hollywood than a deceptively polite, soft-spoken producer and casting director called Fred Roos. Roos's philosophy was fiendishly simple when it came to casting. If actors were interesting offscreen they would be interesting on-screen. Conversely, if they were dull in life, they would be duller still on celluloid.

It was a principle that had served him well enough so far. At the turn of the 1960s he had, through his friend Don Devlin, got to know a raw, ferociously high-living young actor from New Jersey called Jack Nicholson. While cutting his production teeth at Roger Lippert Productions, an idiosyncratic, low-budget production company based at Fox, Roos had cast the actor in two inexpensive action movies he had shot in the Philippines, *Back Door to Hell* and *Flight to Fury*. Back then Roos was one of the few people in Hollywood who believed Nicholson had something special.

It was not long after his friend Walter Beakel introduced him to his former Columbia protégé that Roos began to develop the same instinct about Harrison Ford. "Walter called and said, 'Here's an interesting guy. He doesn't go down well here at the studio but I think you'd get him,' " he recalled. Harrison met Roos at the offices of Compass Management, a sideline business he was running with his friend Garry Marshall.

Roos found Harrison to be all Beakel had promised: truculent, tight-lipped, and, probably, trouble. "When actors come in to see you, they are eager to please. They want to be liked and loved and given parts. He did not give an inch. I was able to draw him out, but there was no effort at all to ingratiate himself, which is unusual," said Roos.

Intrigued, Roos spent an hour talking to the young man. "I responded right away to him," he said warmly. "He was never an effusive hail-fellow-well-met kind of guy. He was always a bit standoffish and surly and sarcastic. He was very suspicious and cynical of the industry. We just hit it off."

By 1969, after his brief flirtation with producing, Roos had begun to concentrate on what he acknowledged was his greatest strength, casting. From finding fodder for TV shows like *I Spy*, *Guns of Will Sonnet*, and *Mayberry RFD* at Universal he had graduated to casting feature films. His first success had been rescuing Richard Chamberlain from the TV hell of *Dr. Kildare* and relaunching his career in *Petulia*. Now he had been asked to help on one of the most prestigious projects in town, Michelangelo Antonioni's first American movie, *Zabriskie Point*.

Depending on which side of the fence you sat on at the end of the 1960s, Antonioni was either an artist deserving of a seat at the same celestial table as his Renaissance namesake or a left-wing intellectual turned filmmaker responsible for some of the most tediously pretentious piffle in recent cinematic memory. MGM were in no doubt he was the former and had given him a three-picture deal to prove it. His first picture, *Blow Up*, made in England with David Hemmings, had justified their faith. Now Antonioni was ready to turn his eye on America, and more specifically California in all its kaleidoscopic color.

Given that Antonioni's directorial style owed everything to improvisation, the script was an unreliable guide to what might emerge at the end of filming. In theory, *Zabriskie Point* centered on the experience of a young man who, disillusioned with the mindless materialism of his life, steals a plane and joins an alternative community in the California desert.

Roos saw enough dangerous intensity in Harrison to recommend him for the lead: "He was on-the-money perfect for that part; he was born to play it." Harrison met Antonioni, who had been shown the brief "highlights" of his career to date. Once more, alas, Harrison failed to make the right impression.

Roos had been sure he was what the Italian needed: "He was not a leading man in the way they thought of leading men at the time. The strongest quality I saw was his great sense of masculinity. There was a kind of dangerous intensity that he had, and combined with all that was this droll sense of humor. And then he had extreme confidence, but nothing braggadocio, just an air of confidence. I was so bitterly disappointed when I couldn't convince Michelangelo."

As minor recompense, Roos found Harrison a place in an airport scene in the movie. "I slipped him in for two or three days' work. Harrison always needed the money," he recalled. In the meantime Antonioni's film degenerated into as vacuous a piece of moviemaking as Hollywood had seen in years. Despite its promise to "blow your mind," *Zabriskie Point* only succeeded in blowing the reputations of almost everyone connected with it. "A huge, jerry-built, crumbling ruin of a movie," Pauline Kael called it.

In 1970, few films summed up Hollywood's lack of direction more profoundly. Yet Harrison Ford may have been the only person who walked away from the disaster that was *Zabriskie Point* absolutely sure where he was headed. His young ego bruised, his confidence weakened, he had made the decision to fall back on his greatest strength.

Having talked the decision over with Mary he put the word around that he had decided to give acting a break. He would only consider worthwhile roles. Television producers need not apply. Attrition rather than attitude was to be his hallmark from now on.

Looking back on it, he later offered as explanation for his decision the kind of warped logic that might have found its way into an Antonioni film. It certainly summed up the drug-hazed Hollywood he was about to disown: "If you think you're going nowhere and you stop, then you're not going nowhere any more."

9

MISFIT, OUTCAST, ORPHAN

L ate in the 1960s, Earl McGrath was shopping for furniture to fill
his new Los Angeles home. He enlisted the help of the former
assistant buyer of the knickknack and antique department of
Bullock's department store. He admired the man's fastidiousness; his
trained eye would help distinguish the fake from the authentic.

During a visit to one particularly grand emporium, McGrath spotted a pair of period tables and suggested to his adviser that he might
buy them. When the man heard they cost $1,100 each, he couldn't dis-
guise his disgust. "That's outrageous," he protested, his face wreathed
in a look of belligerence with which McGrath was familiar by now.
"I'll build you two tables for $200."

Thus was born the career of Harrison Ford, carpenter.

As it happened, he never built Earl McGrath's tables, although the
latter spent $400 on equipment with which Harrison was to have made
them. By the dawn of the 1970s, these tools had become his lifeline.
Zabriskie Point and the ending of his Universal contract had delivered
him to a painful crossroads in his career. Carpentry would prove his salvation—financially and psychologically.

Friends like McGrath had been among those who had actively encouraged Harry to give acting a break. "You've got to get out of the posse,"

the art collector had told him. As ever, Mary was supportive of his decision, although even she had to admit her husband's timing was bad.

Toward the end of his time at Universal, Harrison and Mary had
bought their first home. They had paid $18,500 for a tumbledown
house on Woodrow Wilson Drive, a meandering hillside street near
the Hollywood Bowl and within a short drive of Wasserman's "Black
Tower." In the years since he had banged away backstage at the Belfry,
Harrison had developed his building and decorating skills. His plan
was to gut the house, then rebuild and redesign it himself, using his
salary as an actor to buy the timber and other essential materials. Suddenly faced with a mortgage and the loss of his job, he was forced to
work on the homes of others instead. He had often heard friends
bemoan the lack of skilled craftsmen in Hollywood, so, with the tools
McGrath had bought him, he set up a workshop in the garage at
Woodrow Wilson Drive and bought a battered pickup truck.

Soon afterward, a friend mentioned that the Brazilian musician Sergio
Mendes needed a recording studio built at his home in Encino. Harrison summoned up the *chutzpah* that had won him underage entry into
Chicago bars and advertising in the *Mug*, and drove off to see the composer. Mendes was so impressed with the grandiose blueprint Harrison
described that he offered him the job—a $100,000 contract. "Luckily
Sergio forgot to ask if I had ever built anything before," Ford grinned.

Soon carpentry was allowing Harrison to once more improvise his
way out of a tight corner. Mendes's house was within three blocks of the
Encino public library. Harrison would turn up for work with a couple
of experienced hired hands and books on master carpentry and archi-
tecture. Petrified Mendes would wander out with his early morning
coffee and catch him cramming up ahead of the next day's work, Harrison went to elaborate lengths to avoid being found out. "I'd be standing on Mendes's roof with a textbook in my hand," he recalled once.

The care he lavished on the rehearsal room and studio set word of
his excellence spreading. As his embryonic business found its feet, he
did work for the director Richard Fleischer and actress Sally Kellerman.
Then Fred Roos asked him to do some work at his house in Benedict
Canyon.

In the time since *Zabriskie Point*, Roos had gotten to know Harrison
well, discovering in the young actor a combination of danger and droll-

ness, presence and perfectionism. "He was prickly but not a prick," said Roos. Carpentry somehow seemed a metaphor for his approach to acting—and life.

"He was so tasteful and caring about the way he did the carpentry, he wouldn't accept anything that wasn't perfect. If I would suggest I wanted something he thought was in bad taste or I was making a mistake, he would refuse to do it," said Roos.

Harrison designed for Roos a grand platform bed and two bedside tables to match. "He built me another bedside table that gave me all the things I wanted in it. I could control the lights from it. It had compartments to keep things in. It was a custom-made, *perfect* bedside table that accomplished everything I wanted. And it's still by my bed right now," announced Roos.

Soon Harrison's skills were in demand, even though his prices were far from inexpensive. "He did not come cheap. Anything that he did in carpentry had to be not only a work of art but an incredible piece of craftsmanship. He wouldn't compromise by doing it cheap or with lesser materials. He absolutely would browbeat you. I wasn't rolling in money—a difference in cost meant a lot to me," said Fred Roos. "But he would just push you. He'd say, 'Spend the bucks, spend the bucks.' "

In Hollywood he knew the correlation was simple: money meant respect. As a result of the success of his second line of business, that respect walked with him when he took his rare steps into the audition rooms.

Systematically stripped of his pride within the studios, he had, in reality, been ill equipped to deal with the humiliation of casting calls and screen tests. "An actress is slightly more than a woman, an actor is slightly less than a man" ran an old show business saw. It haunted Harrison more than most. The constant rejection left him somehow emasculated. By turning up in his carpentry overalls, as he frequently did at the time, he redressed the balance, at least in his own mind. "I wasn't there as a person who needed the job to put bread on the table. I had, for once, a real life behind me," he explained later. "When you're an out-of-work actor and you walk into an audition, you're an empty vessel." On another occasion he put it even more bluntly. "It gave me my balls back."

The fact remained that he badly needed the income from his carpentry. Even his old ally Walter Beakel found it impossible to find him the break he needed. His former Columbia teacher, by now an agent, realized how tough times were when he passed him on Cahuenga Boulevard in his rundown old pickup truck. Beakel asked after the family, then enquired about life on the acting front. Harrison replied in one-word answers.

"What are you working on?"

"Nothing."

"What's coming up?"

"Nothing."

Compared to the histrionics of the more highly strung out-of-work actors in Los Angeles, it was an unremarkable admission. But Beakel knew Harrison well enough to realize that his frustration was simply boiling away inside.

"He did not go out to bars and moan and cry, 'Nobody's noticing me, nobody's hiring me,' or anything like that," said Beakel. "I knew the Fords were short of money, but he would not say anything. He went to work. And somehow he always took care of himself. He was from the Midwest. He knew how to work. And that kept his head straight too . . . But that was the lowest I ever saw him. He was very, very down; nothing was going for him," he recalled.

Soon after seeing him, Beakel switched agencies, from Gersh to Kumin-Olenick. Harrison had been dropped from Gersh's books. "They let him go because he wasn't making money. As an actor under contract to the Gersh Agency you had to make at least $10,000 a year in commissions, which meant you had to make $100,000. Well, a young actor couldn't make that then," said Beakel.

As soon as he was installed at Kumin-Olenick, Beakel suggested putting Harrison on their books. "They wouldn't permit me. I wanted to keep on working with Harrison. I had faith in him. But they didn't think he was an actor; they didn't respect his talents at all," he recalled.

"The question was, 'What do we do with him? Where do we cast him? As what?' If you were looking at Harrison then, he was a misfit, an outcast, an orphan. Quite honestly, at that stage it was as if he wasn't even in the industry."

The fact that his reputation spread so quickly in his carpentry when it was moving so slowly in his acting career was an irony devoid of any humor, so far as Harrison was concerned. Soon Kellerman was calling him "Carpenter to the Stars"—only semi-jokingly. Carpentry opened new and unexpected doors, including those of the golden couple of L.A. letters, John Gregory Dunne and Joan Didion.

Dunne and Didion befriended their handyman after he fitted shelves at their Malibu home. At Dunne and Didion's parties, Harrison met and mingled with an eclectic band of stars and strugglers, a beachside Bloomsbury. He thanked them by turning his sardonic smile on the egos that landed there.

Dunne's favorite moment came at a party for Tom Wolfe, an epic, even by the hedonistic standards of the drug-drenched 1960s. Even Julia Phillips, author of the coruscating *You'll Never Eat Lunch in This Town Again*, admitted she was impressed by the contents of the couple's drug cabinet. According to one account of the Wolfe party: "A record number of roaches filled an ashtray."

Wolfe turned up in his by now *de rigueur* combination of white suit, blue shirt, and white tie. Harrison, sensing a need to deflate the famous wordsmith, dashed back to Earl McGrath's house and changed into a mirror-image of the author's outfit—a blue suit, white shirt and blue tie—adding a construction helmet for good measure. For most of the night he shadowed the author, adroitly leaning to his left when Wolfe leaned to the right, drinking with his right hand if Wolfe sipped with his left. "Marcel Marceau could not have done better," the host said later.

Even in the bitchiest of circles, no one wrote off the unknown actor with a gift for wielding a claw hammer. "You could always tell he was going to be a star. There was something different about him, and he had a special quality for a young actor—something powerful and force-ful," Didion pronounced years afterward. Almost no one in Hollywood shared her optimism at the time, however.

In 1970, Fred Roos suggested Harrison meet a manager friend of his. Patricia McQueeney readily admits her first thoughts on seeing the dishevelled figure slumped on a sofa in her office were not along the lines of *Eureka!* As she remembers, they were: "What in the world am I going to do with *him?*" Harrison showed up wearing a pair of his oldest jeans and one of his wariest expressions. McQueeney recalls him sit-ting with "his hands clasped between his knees and his head down looking up at me, lowering at me like he's inclined to do if he's not comfortable." However, she agreed to take him on.

McQueeney, a genteel and elegantly attractive import to Los Angeles from a cut-glass Connecticut background, had worked her way into the management business after spells as a model and a television presenter in New York. She had worked for Roos and Gary Marshall when they ran Compass, but had taken over their client list when they moved on to producing and casting. In 1970 McQueeney's clients included Teri Garr and Frederick Forrest, Cindy Williams and Martin Sheen. (It was Williams and another client, Candy Clark, who persuaded their agent to call the company Pat McQueeney Management rather than her preference, The Muckluck Agency!)

Despite her relative lack of experience, Pat was able to drum up interest in work for Harrison. Soon, however, she was winning insights into why the actor-cum-carpenter had been struggling. A quarter of a century later she was still getting the same treatment.

"He was always careful in the roles he chose even when he was stone broke," said McQueeney. "I can never change his mind to do or not do something. I can jump up and down and beg and do a little dance, but it never does any good." His pernickity behavior impressed some, but not all, of his friends. Friendships could be strained by his stubbornness.

In 1970, CBS Television and producer Norman Lear were putting together an American version of the BBC's hugely successful *Till Death Do Us Part*. The role of the rabid American cousin of Warren Mitchell's Alf Garnett, Archie Bunker, had been given to the Irish Broadway star Carroll O'Connor. Harrison was offered an opportunity to play Archie's liberal, unemployed, sociology student son-in-law, Mike Stivic, or "Meathead" as his foulmouthed father-in-law preferred to call him. The part would have been by far the most high-profile of his career—CBS was planning to launch the show in January 1971 in its prime-time, Tuesday night, 9:30 P.M. slot. No matter how tempting the promise of such precious coast-to-coast exposure, however, nothing could rid Harrison of his distaste for the ranting, racist Archie and his tirades against "jungle bunnies, spades, spics, and chinks."

Over a coffee in the kitchen at Woodrow Wilson Drive, Harrison explained his decision to Doug Rowe, who had returned to California after a spell back east.

"He had an extremely strong conscience. He didn't want to do it because of the way the lead characters spoke, in that bigoted way," he recalled. "That was diametrically opposed to Harrison. He was always a man with a strong social conscience." When the show became one of the biggest hits of the new season, turning O'Connor and the young Rob Reiner, who took on the role of "Meathead," into household names, Harrison had no qualms.

Rowe understood his decision. "The end result is that you are out there in a piece forever, so you have got to take care in making selections."

His old roommate Bill Haljum found it harder to comprehend his principled stand. Now a rising account executive at the advertising agency Leo Burnett in Chicago, Haljum offered him an advertising role that would have transformed his fortunes—financially at least. "I was working on a mouthwash brand at Leo Burnett and we were shooting commercials. A couple of them Harry would have been terrific for. So I tracked him down and called him up and said, 'Hey, come on out. You'll make some money. You've only done these little TV shows.' *That's* when I found out how serious he was," Haljum admitted wryly. "He said, 'No, they won't take me seriously if I do commercials. I have got to stay orthodox and pure and only do acting stuff.' So he never showed up for them."

Haljum had witnessed his friend's earnest side before. Given that money was obviously tight, he found his attitude hard to fathom. "These things would have given him anything from $12,000 to $30,000 easily. He'd say: 'No, I'm not interested, I gotta stay legitimate.' After that we kinda lost track of each other."

His friend's frustration paled in comparison with Pat McQueeney's: "He had a young family and a mortgage and I would say, 'Harrison, this is $30,000 they're offering you,' which in 1970 was a lot of money, and he'd use a four-letter word and say, 'I'll go build a cabinet.'"

Even when he did agree to talk about a role, sycophancy was not on the menu. Harrison would turn up for auditions in his carpentry gear, jeans, and invariably a denim shirt. Often he wore a snarl too. "There were a number of times when I would send him on interviews to read for something and the casting person would call up and say, 'Why did you send that hostile guy? I thought he was going to punch me in the nose!' "

It took the news that Mary was pregnant again to make Harrison put his high-principled stand on hold. Behind with his health insurance payments since he had started his carpentry business, he was forced to look around for ways to make up the money.

He accepted a role in a Universal movie of the week, *The Intruders*—another cowboy yarn, this time about a band of frontier townsmen threatened by the Jesse James gang. The film premiered in November 1970, a few months after he had cropped up opposite Burt Reynolds in "The Manufactured Man," an episode in the first season of *Dan August*, the detective series that preceded Reynolds's leap to superstardom.

Another spell lost in episodic television hell was averted by the sudden reappearance of Lady Luck—this time in the avuncular form of Fred Roos. By the turn of the 1970s, Roos, a graduate of the film school at UCLA in the 1960s, had renewed his friendship with the star of the university's film department—a big, brash, bearded New Yorker named Francis Coppola. Coppola, the son of the composer Carmine Coppola, had caught Hollywood's eye when his master's thesis movie, *You're a Big Boy Now* was turned into a well-received general release movie by Warner Brothers.

It had taken five years for his maverick genius to translate itself into box office gold, but by late 1971 his almost complete adaptation of Mario Puzo's bestseller *The Godfather* was the talk of Hollywood. While he waited for Marlon Brando's Don Corleone and the "smell the spaghetti" realism of his Mafiosi to transform his career, Coppola agreed to produce *American Graffiti*. This was the second feature made by a former assistant of his—a diffident twenty-eight-year-old from Modesto, in northern California, George Lucas.

While Coppola had been starring at UCLA, Lucas had been the leader of a gifted group of young filmmakers at its great rival, the University of Southern California. USC's "miracle group" included directors John Carpenter, John Milius, Randal Kleiser, and Robert Zemeckis and writer Dan O'Bannon. Over at Long Beach State yet another circle had been forming around its film school's most gifted youngster, Steven Spielberg.

If there was a uniting spirit among these youngsters, it was one the young Harrison Ford had shared over at Columbia and Universal— contempt for the studio establishment. Roos, whose knowledge of LA's pool of untapped acting talent had proved useful to many of the emerging stars, put the phenomenal success that would follow down to a belief that "stems from the basic thing back in film school of not liking the way the system ran . . . The key was having your own setup, not being answerable. That's what it all comes down to," he said.

By 1972, Coppola was almost in a position to make himself unanswerable to anyone—briefly, at least. Now his friend Lucas was attempting to attain the same power. Soon they would be in the vanguard of a movement that would sweep away the Old Hollywood. In the final analysis, of all the members of what came to be known as the New Hollywood, none would contribute to that downfall as significantly as Lucas.

Lucas had written the movie *American Graffiti* with former USC friends Willard Huyck and Gloria Katz. Set in a small California town in 1962, it was a rock-n-roll–soaked elegy to a time when teenagers spent Saturday nights cruising in their hot rods and dreaming of romance. The story centered on one long, eventful night as the Class of '62 prepare to leave their backwater high school for the wider world beyond.

Lucas, whose first film, a darkly mechanical, science-fiction piece called *THX 1138* had been the victim of the kind of studio interference his film-school set despised, had found finance at Twentieth Century–Fox after hawking the idea all over Hollywood. Roos had helped Coppola on *The Godfather*, unearthing new talents, like Al Pacino, and rescuing others, like Diane Keaton and *Journey to Shiloh*'s James Caan, from television oblivion. His brief was to perform the same miracle on *American Graffiti*. Lucas, determined to blend a believable chemistry between a group of young actors, insisted that Roos find him five options for each of the main characters he had written.

Roos's tastes did not always accord with the rock-ribbed conservatism of the old Hollywood order. The TV producer Aaron Spelling once hauled him into his office, furious at his casting of Jack Nicholson in the cowboy drama *Guns of Will Sonnet*. "He yelled at me after seeing his work, like I was bringing some weirdo into his midst," said Roos. Harrison, sharing Nicholson's lack of humility but lacking his all-forgiving smile, put producers even more on edge.

Yet Roos's belief in his friend's abilities had, if anything, strengthened as he got to know him through his carpentry. Despite the fact that he was pushing thirty, he asked Harrison to test for the part of a young buck—a drag racer called Bob Falfa.

It was instantly obvious that there was something different about Lucas. Harrison went to audition at the commercial production studio in Hollywood, run by Lucas's friend and collaborator, cameraman Haskell Wexler. Lucas already had a reputation as something of a technocrat. This was to be one of the first films ever auditioned on videotape. In addition, Harrison was told, the director would be there in person. Lucas was looking at every single performer called to audition.

Harrison arrived at the studio to discover Roos in charge. In a corner sat the small, bearded figure of Lucas. Soon he had discovered something else about this new director—he was chronically shy. In contrast with virtually every other director he had met, Lucas preferred to stay in the shadows. If any of the actors asked him whether they were okay, he would mutter, "Great! Terrific." Always that.

Lucas put hundreds of young unknowns through his "cattle call." Thanks in great part to Roos, Harrison heard days later that the part of Falfa was his. After a brief argument over money, he accepted.

Only one of the actors chosen—Ron Howard, an eighteen-year-old who had been cast by Roos years back for TV's popular *Andy Griffith Show*—had any sort of reputation in Hollywood. Along with the young New Yorker Richard Dreyfuss, a former professional boxer called Paul Le Mat, Suzanne Sommers—a model with no acting experience whatsoever—and several members of Pat McQueeney's growing "family" of actors, there was no argument that Harrison Ford sat comfortably in the "unknown" category.

In June 1972, on the eve of his thirtieth birthday, Harrison joined the set of *American Graffiti* in the sleepy California outpost of Petaluma. Few who witnessed his behavior over the next four weeks would have guessed he was by far the most mature of the film's fledgling players. His maverick streak still stood out a mile.

The month-long shoot was carried out almost entirely after dark, between 9 P.M. and dawn. Universal was so determined to ensure Lucas stuck to his minuscule $750,000 budget, it had a representative there to switch the generators off on the dot at six each morning.

Lucas may have picked his cast for their compatibility on-screen, but offscreen they proved a high-combustion mixture.

Petaluma had been chosen to recreate the nights of Lucas's own auto-obsessed adolescence because of its long, well-lit strip. The cars would cruise up and down each night, watched over by a few locals. Harrison's character Falfa was at the wheel of a souped-up Chevrolet that had been used in Monte Hellman's four-wheeled *Easy Rider* imitation, *Two-Lane Blacktop*, the previous year. When he began roaring up and down the strip between takes after a few beers, he attracted some unwanted attention.

"The police who were on the picture threatened to impound the car and take him downtown," said Lucas. "We shot all night. It was pretty boring. Because he had the whole run of the picture, but he didn't have to work every day, he did have a tendency to drink a lot of beer."

Harrison and Paul Le Mat were the wildest of the crew, roaring around the film's headquarters at the city's Holiday Inn like novice rock-n-roll stars. They raced their cars up and down the strip, urinated in the hotel soft-drink machine and tried to set fire to Lucas's room.

Their behavior terrorized some of the film's female contingent. "Harrison and Paul were pretty wild. They were drinking a lot of beer in those days. I found them very intimidating, like Hell's Angel types," recalled Candy Clark, the film's ditzy blonde, Debbie, one of several Pat McQueeney clients cast by Fred Roos. "Harrison was really intimidating. He had quite a glare at that time."

Cindy Williams, cast as Laurie, the film's feistiest female character, was one of the few who had known Harrison beforehand; their friendship stretched back toward the end of his time at Universal. She had been working as a receptionist when they met at a Melrose Avenue health food store, "in the vegetable aisle," as she recalls. By now they were both managed by Pat McQueeney and had formed a lasting friendship.

Far from being frightened by his intensity, Williams looked on Harrison as a delinquent older brother. "I had girlfriends who would meet him and they would say, 'Wow, who is that?' He is very attractive and extremely appealing and a great guy. But to me he was always like my brother. I would be thinking, 'So what kind of trouble are you going to get into today?' " she said.

On the *Graffiti* set, Williams and the rest would hear of a new outrage almost every night. "Every day we would arrive and someone would say: 'Have you heard what's happened now?' One scandal was when they were racing each other to the top of the revolving Holiday Inn sign and putting beer bottles on the top," Candy Clark recalled.

The high jinks reached a climax one night when a bored and beered-up Harrison and Le Mat were messing around at the Holiday Inn. "They were crashing beer bottles from their balcony into the parking lot," said Candy Clark. After a flying beer bottle smashed into the windshield of a Cadillac, the film's bad boys got into an argument with the more serious, withdrawn Dreyfuss.

"There was this huge commotion down the hall from me," Cindy Williams recalled. "Harrison ended up chucking Richard into the swimming pool from the second-story window."

Dreyfuss, who was due to do close-ups that night, climbed from the pool bleeding. Candy Clark was the first to see the damage inflicted on him. "Richard was supposed to come over to my room and we were supposed to be going out to do something," Clark recalled. "Finally, thirty or forty minutes had passed since he was supposed to be there, when a knock came on the door and he was standing there leaning on it, soaking wet, with a great big knot on his forehead. Those pranksters had tossed him into the shallow end of the pool headfirst."

"I remember I had to give him my pancake makeup, as there wasn't makeup on *American Graffiti* because they couldn't afford it," Cindy Williams recalled.

Lucas, under intense pressure to finish the film, simply shrugged his shoulders. "Richard got cut right across his forehead, which made him get a little upset," he said. Lucas may have been prepared to let Harrison's behavior slide—but the hotel was not. "He was always in trouble with the management," said Clark.

After Petaluma's own version of the "Dreyfuss Affair," Harrison was asked to leave and was relegated to the smaller Howard Johnson hotel nearby. "The next thing I knew was that Harrison is in the Howard Johnson, segregated from the rest of us," said Williams.

"I was a bit of a carouser in those days. And I was in the company of other hell-raisers," Harrison confessed later. "If I'd been in the company of priests, I would have behaved differently."

For all the offscreen drama, working with Lucas was a revelation. Methodical, undramatic, he seemed the antithesis of the egotistical Hollywood helmsmen he had worked with. He also listened to his actors—a trait Harrison in particular found almost unbelievable. Lucas suggested that Harrison cut his hair short so as to accentuate the difference between the outsider Falfa and the rest of the story's small-town teenagers.

"How about me wearing a white cowboy hat?" he countered, unhappy about the prospect of shearing the remnants of his mane.

Luckily, Lucas had known kids at his Modesto High School who wore cowboy hats. "Yeah, that's a good idea, let's try it," he replied.

Later Lucas asked Harrison to further define Falfa by singing a song. Friendly with Don Everly, Harrison suggested one of his hits, which he then proceeded to crucify in his worst bathtub baritone. When the effort was rejected he switched to an impersonation of Ezio Pinza from *South Pacific*, crooning "Some Enchanted Evening." Again Lucas liked his inventiveness. After considerable haggling—Harrison had to suffer the pain of overhearing a voice in a trailer shouting, "He doesn't even know the words!"—the song stayed in.

It was only later that Harrison realized the full significance of those two moments. It was the first time anyone had bothered to acknowledge that he might be capable of making a contribution on a film set.

His contribution to the *Graffiti* team spirit was never in question, as far as some members of the cast were concerned.

On the final day of filming, he, Cindy Williams, Ron Howard, and Charlie Martin-Smith were waiting for a lift back to their hotels. Throughout the shoot they had been growing increasingly incensed by the behavior of one of the film's drivers. "He had an attitude problem. He did not like the fact that actors got driven to the set," said Williams. As shooting progressed, the driver's behavior worsened. "He was mean and he had no sense of humor. If we weren't ready to leave the Holiday Inn for the set on time he would just leave without us. It was like he had no respect for human beings."

On the final day of shooting, after filming the climactic drag race in which Falfa's car overturns, the driver arrived to deliver Harrison, Ron Howard, Charlie Martin-Smith, and Williams back to their hotels for the last time. "He pulled up and stopped a hundred feet from us," Williams recalled. "It was like a Mexican standoff. He wanted us to walk over to him and get into the car."

Tired and unwilling to argue, Howard, Smith, and Williams began walking toward the car. They were soon stopped in their tracks. "Harrison very gently pushed us all back and said: 'No, he's coming to us,'" Williams recalled. For a minute or so Harrison simply stared at the driver. Eventually he got the message and pulled up in front of the quartet. The lesson was not quite over, however.

"We started to get into the car, and Harrison pushed us back again," said Williams. This time Harrison's instructions were to the driver. "Now get out and open the doors," he told him.

As the driver dutifully did as he had been instructed, Howard and Martin-Smith became aware of something that Cindy Williams was to see many times afterward. "Harrison's like a good King Solomon. It was big to us because the guy was demoralizing us on a daily basis," she said. "On a real personal level, Harrison is an advocate of Everyman. He'll go to bat for the little guy, he's been the little guy and always has that part of him. He will speak up and that's why every now and then he'd have a bad boy reputation. He is very generous with himself and his sense of justice. He does have that streak in him of a real hero."

Lucas squeezed enough money out of the budget for a party to mark the end of filming. He also put together a twenty-minute showreel for his cast. Harrison was one of the loudest voices at the end of the screening: "This is a fucking hit!" On May 15, 1973, at the Writer's Guild Theater in Beverly Hills, Harrison joined the rest of the cast for a preview of the finished film. This time he crept out of the cinema, apparently shamed by his performance.

There was no cause for embarrassment. From its opening night, when long lines snaked around the Avco Theater in Westwood for the Los Angeles premiere, *American Graffiti* was a hit. And it remained that way throughout the summer and beyond. Steadily, stealthily, it became the most profitable film investment a Hollywood studio had ever made. A film that eventually cost $1.275 million delivered $55.886 million into the pockets of Universal, a ratio of $50 for every $1 invested. George Lucas, who had overcome bitter Fox protests that the film did not work in its original form, was a step nearer his dream of autonomy. His dream of becoming a millionaire by thirty had been fulfilled two years early.

Harrison Ford had his ambitions too. At last he had made some sort of progress toward achieving them. More significantly, he had found a group of people who seemed to care as much as he did. He would look back at the moment with a grateful smile. "It was as if the whole world had changed."

It was soon obvious that the world had not changed that much. Bob Falfa was not one of *Graffiti's* headline roles. The critics concentrated on the jaunty intensity of Dreyfuss and the well-scrubbed sincerity of Ron Howard. While Dreyfuss moved on to *Jaws*, the first of a series of films he would make with the emerging Steven Spielberg, Howard reprised his role in the TV series inspired by the hit, *Happy Days*. For Harrison Ford, it was back to full-time carpentry and the confidence-sapping cycle of rejections that came with being a part-time actor.

Among those he did woodwork for was Talia Shire, Francis Coppola's sister. Coppola then turned out to be the first director to offer him a worthwhile role since Bob Falfa. Again it was Fred Roos who had fixed it.

The film was *The Conversation*, a dark and unsettling Kafkaesque story centering on a surveillance expert. Harrison traveled up to San Francisco to audition for one of the lead roles opposite the film's star, Gene Hackman, but was beaten to it by another of Pat McQueeney's "family," Frederic Forrest. There was another role going, a thin one admittedly, defined in the script in no more detail than the phrase "Young Man."

When Coppola offered him the part, he once more discovered a director who listened. Excited by the script, Harrison came up with the idea of making his character "the Homosexual Young Man." The key to the character, as he saw it, was a suit he had noticed in a San Francisco store. Made of garish green silk, similar in color to a billiard table, it cost an outrageous $900. Friends like Cindy Williams were, by now, well used to his idiosyncrasies, but they were unsure how Coppola would react when Harrison persuaded the production staff to buy it. "They didn't have it in the budget," Williams recalled.

Sure enough, at the read-through, Coppola's first question was how much the suit had cost. "Jesus Christ—$900 for that? What the hell are you?"

Undeterred, Harrison went into an extended explanation of the character he wanted to create on screen. Such details would not have mattered so much to Lucas. To the operatically inclined Coppola, however, passion was all-important. Gay roles were still regarded as risky, but to Coppola the smell of danger was an aphrodisiac.

"Hey, that's really good," he told Harrison.

Set designer Dean Tavoularis was called in and asked to design the character's room in a way that complemented the characterization. The Homosexual Young Man—and his suit—was in.

When Cindy Williams and other cast members met in the lobby of the St. Francis Hotel in San Francisco, Harrison signaled his triumph with a flourish. "Nobody knew he'd won the battle of the suit. And when I came down he was sitting in the lobby smoking a long cigar, reading the *Wall Street Journal*—in his silk suit," she recalled. "Now there's a picture."

Once again, someone had credited him with the intelligence and the ability to make a contribution. Martin Stett, the most striking cameo of his career, was born as a result.

The Conversation reinforced Coppola's status within Hollywood; it picked up Oscar nominations for Best Picture and Best Screenplay. Harrison's performance had little immediate effect on his precarious finances, unfortunately. His fellow graduate of the William Fucik acting academy, Jim Arness, offered the next slice of emergency funding.

During Arness's eighteenth season as Matt Dillon, Harrison starred in two episodes of *Gunsmoke*. In "The Sodbusters" (November 1972), he played Print, a cattleman caught up in a dispute over water rights. In "Whelan's Men," shown in February the following year, he turned up as Hobey, a member of an outlaw gang. The television history books recall little of his contribution. It seems his return to the range did come at a high price; during filming he was thrown from a horse. "I lost all my front teeth," he confessed once.

As the barren times dragged on from one year to the next, visitors to Woodrow Wilson Drive would be shocked by the scene that greeted them. A tarpaulin hung over one bare wall; there was a blanket instead of a bathroom door. "There was even a hole in the living-room floor," Fred Roos recalled. Whenever he asked his friend when he was going to finish the house for his family, by now augmented by a second son, Willard, "he'd say, 'I'm gonna get to it. I'm gonna get to it.' "

"He had bought the house to fix it up. Times were tough for them, they really were. It was not an easy situation. They were hard-pressed to make ends meet, but they always did," recalled Doug Rowe, who became a frequent visitor, spending afternoons drinking coffee. With money tight, hospitality was often confined to a peanut-butter sandwich. Rowe sympathized with Harrison's frustration at the progress of other actors. "It was hard seeing work being done by inept actors who were stars. But I never saw him going around slamming fists into doors."

It was not in his makeup to vent his anger in public. When darkness descended, even Mary was locked out. "When I cry, I cry alone," he admitted once. "That is my nature. I turn inward, and even my wife cannot reach me."

Mary, so often his soothing savior, began to find herself cut adrift. Often she would call friends, worried at the depth of her husband's despair.

"Mary would call me and say: 'Harrison is depressed. Would you talk to him?' " Cindy Williams recalled. Money was often at the root of her friend's depression. "They were as poor as church mice and it broke your heart that he wasn't working all the time," she said. Williams realized the extent of her friends' difficulties when she saw them struggling to get together enough cash to take Ben and Willard on a family trip. It was not as if they were planning a trip beyond their limited means. Harrison and Mary simply wanted to drive back to the Midwest. "They were trying to get $70 together to take the whole family back to Wisconsin for a vacation," she said.

Williams lost count of the number of times she comforted her friend over the telephone, often with a joke for which she would cross herself afterward. "I used to say: 'You're like Cary Grant and Fred Astaire. Some day, Harrison, you'll see.'" She cannot recall the last time she said it, only what happened afterward. "And lo and behold, *from my lips to God's ear . . .*"

10

A COWBOY IN A STARSHIP

In the late winter of 1975, it was difficult to judge which of his two friends Fred Roos was irritating most—George Lucas or Harrison Ford.

In an office at the Samuel Goldwyn building in Hollywood, Lucas was conducting another epic cattle call. For six months, new actors and actresses had been flashing by, as he recalls, "every five to ten minutes." Almost as often, it seemed, Roos had been appearing at his door, shaking his head sagely and sighing: "George, why are you bothering when the guy you need is right under your nose?"

Lucas was hardly likely to forget the actor Roos was lobbying for even if he had wanted to. He was venting his anger outside Roos's office at the Zoetrope office, next door. Furious at being forced to do carpentry work under Lucas's nose while the casting went on around him, he was "banging on things" as loudly as possible.

If there was a single turning point in Harrison Ford's life and career, it finally arrived as he labored away on George Lucas's doorstep. This time Lady Luck had little to do with it. This time it owed more to conspiracy than serendipity.

For more than two years Lucas had been working on the outline for a space fantasy, an epic and more accessible journey to the universe of Stanley Kubrick's masterpiece, *2001: A Space Odyssey*. By now he had

115

pumped $1 million of the personal fortune he had earned from *American Graffiti* into developing the mythic storyline he had written himself, inspired by influences as diverse as Carlos Castenada's *Tales of Power* and Tolkien's *Lord of the Rings*, *Flash Gordon*, and *The Forbidden Planet*. By August 1975, it had been distilled into the outline for a series of three stories, known collectively as *The Adventures of Luke Starkiller*. With the support of Fox's Alan Ladd Jr., he was ready to film the first, tentatively called *The Star Wars*—the story of the young farmboy Luke and his quest to acquire "The Force"—the superhuman, quasi-religious powers of an extinct order of knights, the Jedi.

Lucas had calmed complaints that the film lacked "star power" by casting Alec Guinness in one of the supporting roles. He played Luke's mentor—an elderly Jedi knight named Obi-Wan Kenobi. At the Goldwyn Building, Lucas's objective was to cast the three main characters in a story that, for all its mysticism and sense of deep-space derring-do, boiled down to that old Hollywood staple, the love triangle. The principals in his intergalactic *Gone With the Wind* were Luke, soon to have his name softened to Skywalker, a teenage princess, Leia, and Han Solo, a character described in Lucas's script as: "a tough James Dean–style starpilot, a cowboy in a starship: simple, sentimental, and cocksure."

With his friend Brian De Palma, who was searching for young actors to star in his new horror movie *Carrie*, Lucas began the laborious process of interviewing in the autumn of 1975. Roos, as ever, was willing to help Lucas with advice on young, up-and-coming talent; he was sure early on that the part of Han Solo was perfect for Harrison Ford.

Lucas, however, had a clear idea of what he wanted. "And generally I wanted to stay away from people from *American Graffiti*," he added.

It was at this moment that Roos chose to ask Harrison to come into the Zoetrope offices to build an elaborate new doorway for the company he was running with Francis Coppola. Harrison knew Lucas was casting his new film at the office and blew his top. "Harrison told Fred: 'Lucas is coming in here; I don't want him to see me working on a fucking door,'" recalled their old friend Walter Beakel. "But Fred insisted that he do it."

The experience turned out to be every bit as embarrassing as Har-

rison had feared. At one point Richard Dreyfuss arrived, having bad-
gered Lucas into giving him an audition. The sight of the guy who had
hurled him out of a second-floor window now brought low himself was
irresistible. Dreyfuss launched into a routine about being the carpenter's assistant, an act that sunk Harrison's spirits even lower. "Harrison
was really pissed off about that," laughed Beakel. "I felt about as big as
a pea," the victim recalled later.

Given the "shit-kicker" scrapes Harrison had landed himself in on
the *Graffiti* set, and the sporadic curriculum vitae he had assembled
since, Lucas's decision to ignore him seemed eminently understandable.

The American television schedules of the time are peppered with
evidence to prove that Harrison Ford remained a small-screen jour-
neyman well beyond the mid-1970s. In the wake of *The Conversation*
there had been the two appearances on *Gunsmoke*. Then, in February
1974, he popped up in "Crossties"—an episode of ABC's martial arts
western series *Kung Fu*, with David Carradine. Harrison played the
member of a marauding gang of ex-farmers, the Youngbloods, driven
off their land by a ruthless railroad company. (Even allowing for the
mystic appeal of the offbeat western, then into the second of three
series, writer Robert Schlitt's claims of parallels between the Youngbloods and the dispossessed of Vietnam were lost on all but the most
pretentious fans of Carradine and his hero, Kwai Chang Caine.)

Months later, Harrison appeared in "Edge of Evil," an episode of the
first series of *Petrocelli*—a flashy legal drama starring Barry Newman as
the eponymous hero Tony Petrocelli. William Shatner, then another
piece of Hollywood flotsam after the cancellation of his sci-fi series,
Star Trek, was among his costars.

Even as Lucas had begun casting *Star Wars*, Harrison had been working on a glossy pioneer saga that could easily have damned him to
serial television stardom. The two-hour epic, originally called *The
Americans* but then altered to the grander-sounding James A. Michener's *Dynasty*, charted the fortunes of Ohio frontiersfolk, the Blackwood family between the 1820s and 1850s, and starred the eccentric
English star Sarah Miles as the matriarch. Harrison, along with Amy
Irving, Gerrit Graham, and Tony Swartz, played Miles's conniving,
ungrateful offspring in the lavish-looking melodrama. Fortunately, as

it turned out for Harrison at least, *Dynasty* proved a dry run for Michener's more successful *Centennial* two years later. By the time the film was shown in NBC's *Saturday Night at the Movies* slot in March 1976, he was quietly grateful for the lukewarm reception he and *Dynasty* received.

Not all his television work was as woeful, however. In between stints back in episodic TV, in 1974, he had impressed the distinguished producer-director Stanley Kramer and landed himself a part in his ABC television series, *Judgment*. Kramer, his movie career in terminal decline, had returned to the courtroom genre that had served him so well in earlier successes like *The Caine Mutiny* and *Judgment at Nuremburg*. Each episode staged a reconstruction of a high-profile trial, with the narrating Kramer loftily offering an alternative piece of advocacy.

Harrison was called in to try for the lead in what was to be the most high-profile of the series, a dramatization of the court martial of Lieutenant William Calley, the American soldier tried for the atrocities at My Lai in Vietnam.

"Calley's taken. See what role you want," Kramer told Harrison as he handed him a copy of the script. Harrison was drawn to the part of the young enlisted soldier who becomes the principal witness against his superior officer. Worried by Harrison's inexperience, Kramer asked: "That's the hardest role in the movie. Are you sure you can do it?"

When Harrison assured him he could, the director of *High Noon* and *Guess Who's Coming to Dinner* extended his trust. On set with a distinguished cast including Richard Basehart as the defending attorney, Tony Musante as Calley, and his *Graffiti* chum Bo Hopkins as the prosecutor, Harrison rewarded Kramer's generosity with a five-star performance. When the *Judgment* episode was aired in January, 1975, he was—for the first time in his television career—singled out for praise, albeit brief. He "stood out" *Daily Variety*'s reviewer wrote. Of all his performances, *Judgment* would remain one of Harrison's personal favorites. Yet the truth of the matter remained that in 1975 Harrison Ford was hardly an automatic first choice for a role in anyone's movie—let alone one that marked the long-awaited return of the genius behind *American Graffiti*.

By the end of 1975, however, George Lucas was becoming desperate. Of the hundreds of actors he had auditioned for the part of Han

Solo, only a handful had even come close to the sardonic cockiness he needed. He had, for a while, toyed with the idea of casting a black actor and had almost chosen the little-known Glynn Turman, a minor success in *Peyton Place* and star of only one vaguely noticeably movie, *Cooley High*, the screen version of the television hit *What's Happening*. "I didn't want to make *Guess Who's Coming to Dinner* at that point, so I backed off," he said later.

As his frustration grew, he would each day see Harrison, a caustic grimace on his face, a carpenter's belt hung gunslinger-style around his waist, and wonder. Eventually he cracked. "Harrison was there outside working all the time. I just said at lunchtime or sometime, 'Would you like to read some of these things, because I need somebody to read against all these characters?' And he said he would do it," he recalled. Harrison read through the part at Cindy Williams's home. (After being turned down for the part of Leia, she had heard the most dreaded phrase in Hollywood. They were looking for "a young Cindy Williams.")

When he saw the results of Harrison's screen tests, Lucas realized the wisdom of what Fred Roos had been saying. Han Solo *had* been under his nose, all the time. "He was by far the best," said Lucas. "Even in the beginning, whether it's Bob Falfa in *American Graffiti* or Han Solo, within a minute or two of him being on the screen you got a whole sense of a lot of backstory with him. Part of it is just his physical ruggedness, but part of it is also the sly intelligence he keeps projecting."

Harrison worked particularly well with two other actors—Carrie Fisher, daughter of Debbie Reynolds and Eddie Fisher, and Mark Hamill, a fresh-faced graduate of TV shows like *The Partridge Family*. Lucas's final choice came down to two groups of three for the roles of Solo, Leia, and Luke. One triumvirate consisted of the thirty-two-year-old New York stage actor Christopher Walken, as Han, Will Selzer, star of a misfire ABC sitcom called *Karen* earlier in 1975, as Luke, and former Penthouse pet Terri Nunn as Leia. Harrison, Fisher, and Hamill formed the other. Only Walken recovered from the rejection when Lucas broke the bad news that he had opted for the Ford-Fisher-Hamill combination.

As far as Harrison was concerned, it was simply another case of right-place-right-timing. But their friend Walter Beakel suspected otherwise. "It was a complete setup by Fred Roos, a clever scheme to expose Harrison to Lucas in another light. It did the trick; it worked," he said. "I had a sneaking suspicion, then Fred told me years later. But I don't know if Harrison knows to this day that it was an entire plan on Fred's part. I am almost certain he didn't know."

Fred Roos smiles inscrutably at the suggestion. "I can't recall exactly how it happened," he said. "Print the legend."

Filming was due to begin at Elstree Studios in England in the spring of 1976. Harrison's greatest concern was leaving Mary and the children, not to mention his carpentry business, for a shoot expected to last three months or more. Hard as he pushed Lucas and Roos over his fee, his biggest problem remained that weeks in England would leave him grievously out of pocket. "I got paid less for the role of Han Solo than I was earning as a carpenter," he confided later.

Mary, however, was convinced that he could not pass up the chance. Whatever obstacles Harrison erected, she tore them down. "I would never have accepted the role in *Star Wars* if Mary hadn't been right behind me all the way," he admitted. "She goaded me on by dealing with all the problems connected with getting back into acting and was a tremendous support all along."

By March, Harrison had heeded his wife's advice and agreed to gamble on a ride aboard Lucas's rocket ship. The bet would not pay off for both of them, however.

It did not take Harrison Ford long to formulate his opinion of the London suburb of Borehamwood, home of the once-illustrious Elstree Studios. "Boring Wood," he was calling it within days of first setting foot there. Over the course of the next decade, however, events at the studios would rewrite the history of Hollywood and his own life. "Boring" would hardly be the appropriate word.

Harrison arrived in London to discover George Lucas in an already frazzled state. The monosyllabic, monkish figure had become even more withdrawn as he committed himself to a gamble many believed was misguided. With a budget of $10 million, a storyline few understood and a cast of virtual unknowns, the unease was summed up by the refusal of some Fox board members to call the film anything other than "that science movie."

From the earliest days of filming in March in Tunisia—the earthly landscape most similar to the desert planet Tattoine, home of Luke Skywalker—the omens were unpromising. The first delays came on the second day of shooting as the Sahara Desert suffered its first winter rainfall in fifty years!

Back at Elstree, Lucas's high-speed, high-tech approach and his reliance on "blue screen" sequences to which the special effects would be added later was unintelligible. Britain's hottest summer of the century, and Lucas's clinical manner, withdrawn one moment, manic the next, made life even harder.

"We had no idea what was going on," said Peter Mayhew, a seven-foot two-inch bit-part actor hired to play Han Solo's sidekick, an eight-foot hairy bear, or "Wookie," called Chewbacca. "They were telling us that special effects would be going on afterward. When they said the spaceship is going through asteroid belts, nobody knew what an asteroid field visualized like. We were told to do this, stand there. It was difficult to realize what it all meant . . . George was so uptight, superenthusiastic, he wanted everything done exactly as he said. Everybody more or less bowed down. It was a meeting of the old-fashioned and the modern, and the results were inevitable."

Harrison, as one of the very few who had worked with Lucas before, had an understanding of the man and his methods. He also knew that he was open to ideas—and the occasional joke. Almost everyone found difficulties with his stilted, sci-fi psychobabble. Carrie Fisher's least favorite line was: "I thought I recognized your foul stench when I was brought aboard, Governor Tarkin." At one point Han Solo shot from the hip. "You can type this shit, George, but you sure can't say it."

At least, if Harrison, Hamill, and Fisher thought there were problems with a scene, Lucas would take note. His relationship with many of the Elstree crew was far less collaborative.

To say that the British filmmakers did not get on with their American cousins would be something of an understatement. "We thought they were strange people, and I suspect they thought us a bunch of idiots. But it was a new way of making movies, and we were just not used to that sort of thing," explained a Brit called Tony Way, at that time an assistant cameraman.

Lucas's major confrontation was with the cameraman Gil Taylor, a veteran of *Doctor Strangelove* and the Beatles' *A Hard Day's Night*. Taylor refused to use the soft-focus lenses Lucas wanted in order to give the film the muted look he had in his mind. The director retaliated by moving lights, the ultimate insult to a cinematographer. In the end the two reached a standoff, with Lucas terrified that if he sacked the cameraman the entire crew would walk off the set.

The occasional high jinks of the cast did not help transatlantic relations. A running gag between Harrison and Fisher involved substituting the word *Jew* for *You* in well-known song lyrics. So they burst into renditions of "Jew Light Up My Life," "Jew Made Me Love You," etc. Unaware that both of them were half-Jewish, an assistant director complained that they were being anti-Semitic. Cut off from Mary and the boys, marooned amid the elegance of White's Hotel in Mayfair, Harrison gravitated toward his fellow Americans. He and Carrie Fisher became bosom buddies—and maybe more.

Fisher made no secret of the fact that she was almost overwhelmed when she first set eyes on Harrison Ford. "You look at Harrison and you listen; he looks like he's carrying a gun even if he isn't. He's this incredibly attractive male animal, in every sense of the word. This carpenter stud . . ." she said. And: "I've never had that same impression of anyone else in my life. I knew he was going to be a star—someone on the order of Tracy or Bogart."

Harrison and Fisher became inseparable on the set. Fisher, already on the verge of a drug problem that would drive her to the edge of self-destruction, smoked marijuana openly. Harrison, according to some, joined her. "They had a nice little relationship going there. Whenever anyone couldn't find Harrison, you'd say, 'Have you tried Carrie Fisher's changing room?'" recalled Dave Prowse, a former bodybuilder cast as the body of Darth Vader, the sinister, black-helmeted leader of the evil Empire's war machine. (Vader was voiced by James Earl Jones.)

Fisher's sense of humor, even at nineteen, made her a bone-dry doppelgänger for her leading man. ("A Texas chain-saw survivor," she called her twice-divorced mother.) "Those two were always going to get on," said Fred Roos. "They have the same cynical, jaded view of the world."

George Lucas was all too familiar with Harrison's maverick manner, but as the shoot progressed, the director saw a new maturity in him. If there was one single element on the *Star Wars* set responsible for this new attitude, it was Alec Guinness.

Guinness wouldn't condone his fellow Brits' disrespect for Lucas, spending time trying to understand what seemed to him in particular a baffling new way of making films. In many respects, the master class Guinness gave his young American colleague mirrored the metaphysical events in Lucas's *Star Wars* story. Harrison, like Luke Skywalker, was the eager apprentice. Guinness, like Obi-Wan Kenobi, was the font of wisdom.

Guinness was warm and charming toward Harrison from the moment they met. He surprised Harrison immediately by spending two hours trying to find him an apartment in London. It was not the kind of behavior he had been used to in Hollywood, not even from stars of considerably less magnitude. "He was delightfully down to earth and absolutely did not insist on deference. Although you couldn't but grant it," Harrison recalled later.

The results would transform his career. On the Elstree set the chemistry was finally right. Released from the day-to-day pressures of putting bread on his family's table, inspired by the company of Guinness yet encouraged to improvise by Lucas, the *Star Wars* shoot marked the moment Harrison emerged as an effective and innovative actor.

"I think the experience of the *Star Wars* films, especially the first one, and working with a lot of British actors, mellowed him out as an actor," said George Lucas. "He began to see how it was a real profession—in terms of how you act professionally on the set. American actors are quite a bit different than European actors, and they approach it very differently. I think being around a lot of very professional actors who did their job and didn't cause a lot of difficulties and didn't take a lot of time and did their homework before they came on the set—all the kind of professional things you expect caught him at the right moment. When he was doing *Graffiti* he was a little bit on the wild side. And I think that made him realize how important the job of an actor is. He became a very good professional actor from that point on. He disciplined his talent in a much different way."

Unlike Lucas, a comic-book freak from an early age, Harrison had scant interest in science fiction. Even as a little boy in Chicago, he had preferred Mickey Mouse and Donald Duck to Flash Gordon and Superman. "I didn't go to those Buck Rogers matinees. I don't know anything about science fiction," he explained later. Instead, he concentrated on humanizing Han Solo. "It was simply straightforward, a clear human story. I mean, I didn't have to act science fiction."

To Lucas, his most valuable contribution was the improvisational edge he brought to the script. Many of Han's scenes required him to seem befuddled by the situations in which he found himself. Two of the more insightful Solo moments—first when, lost for words, he blasts a communicator to pieces and later when he cautions a sharpshooting Luke with the words "Great, kid. Don't get cocky"—were achieved by deliberately not learning his lines. He would often turn up for a scene to announce he intended improvising in one take. "Stop me if I'm really bad," he would ask Lucas.

It was somehow appropriate that *Star Wars* was the first film that offered Harrison a commodity he had been denied until now—space. "I was being given tiny little spaces to fill, nothing where you could take the space," he divulged. "*Star Wars* was the first time in my whole career that I had a character where I could just take space . . . not just fill it anymore. I just went ahead and did it."

Yet by the time he came to leave London, there was no shortage of people convinced that *Star Wars* was a waste of space. Happy as many of them had been to take Fox's money, they were equally sure Lucas's film was an incoherent mess. The final days, in which a series of scenes had to be filmed at breakneck speed as Fox prepared to pull the plug on any more spending, seemed to sum up the shoot. "Frankly, we all thought it was a disaster," said Dave Prowse.

Harrison traveled back to America in July, as unsure as everyone else about whether Lucas could pull together the pieces of the vast jigsaw he had compiled in England. With endless hours of blue-screen footage safely in the can, Lucas went back to Los Angeles to add the special effects that would make or break the film.

Back in the kitchen at Woodrow Wilson Drive, Harrison shared a coffee with Doug Rowe. If his mood was as laconic as ever, his expectations were as low. "I was there when he got back from London, and asked him what it was he'd been doing," Rowe recalled.

"Oh, some space western," Harrison replied, his mind already half-resigned to a life once more measured in lengths of two-by-fours.

"He had all these photographs and I was looking through them. They were all unknowns," said Rowe. "In among them was this picture of Alec Guinness. I said, 'You just did a film with Alec Guinness and you call it a space western!' "

On May 1, 1977, three weeks before *Star Wars* was due to be released, a modest television audience tuned in for the NBC Sunday movie *The Possessed*, featuring Joan Hackett and James Farentino. A blatant and bullheaded attempt to plug into the public's gory taste for supernatural schlock, post William Friedkin's *Exorcist*, the film purported to be the story of how "a defrocked minister—and freelance exorcist—battles the forces of evil."

In keeping with the vile tradition established by Linda Blair, Joan Hackett as the possessed schoolgirl spent much of her time vomiting in Farentino's face. "A sicker, more witless series concept is hard to imagine," *Variety*'s television critic concluded afterward. While Harrison must have been grateful to the reviewer for overlooking his brief performance in the debacle—he had taken the job after returning from London—he must have felt as bilious as Hackett, nevertheless.

Hollywood was awash with talk of the problems George Lucas was having with the film he had turned his life upside down to make. A screening for the Fox board of directors had been a disaster. Those who had not fallen asleep had hated *Star Wars*. After several drinks, one executive had told Lucas that his film might make some money—but then he added: "Of course, I know nothing about movies."

A trailer campaign running since Christmas had to be pulled as audiences giggled at the sight of the diminutive robot, R2-D2, falling over. *Daily Variety* reflected the opinion of Hollywood when it predicted that the film would flop.

Amid all the negativity even George Lucas, who simply hoped the film would perform as well as an average Disney movie by making about $15 million, had to downgrade his hopes. He and his wife, Marcia, took the precaution of arranging to take a holiday in Hawaii the day after *Star Wars* was due to open.

Lucas's mind had been made up when he had shown an early cut to his friends Steven Spielberg, Brian De Palma, John Milius, Bill (Willard) Huyck, and Gloria Katz. At the end they had sat there in embarrassed silence. The silence was broken by condolences rather than congratulations.

Afterward a downcast Lucas simply shrugged his shoulders. "I figured, well, it's just a silly movie. It ain't going to work."

11

"Patricia, This Is a Miracle!"

The Sherry Netherland is one of Manhattan's swankier hotels, a discreet escape from the frenzy of Fifth Avenue, a monument to good taste, right down to the Italianate murals inside its elevators. It was there that Earl McGrath arranged to meet an old friend for dinner in the early summer of 1977.

As McGrath approached the hotel, he noticed a large crowd jostling for position around the green awning that extends out on to the sidewalk from the hotel lobby. No stranger to such scenes in his days as the manager of the self-styled "world's greatest rock-n-roll band," the Rolling Stones, McGrath assumed word had seeped out that some mega-celebrity was ensconced in the hotel's penthouse. The autograph hunters were stalking their prey.

As he left the hotel again moments later, McGrath was as amused as he was baffled by his dinner guest's behavior. "I have a car outside," the latter announced.

"We don't need a car," McGrath replied, puzzled.

"Yes, we do," his friend said as he grabbed his arm and ran him through the throng. The Han Solo Fan Club chased them all the way to the waiting limousine.

In the weeks after the release of *Star Wars*, Harrison Ford's friends were discovering that life would never be the same again.

A daily dose of the "trades" told Sally Kellerman that her favorite handyman would not be back to finish the work he had left behind to travel to England. She daubed the words "Harrison Ford Left These" on her garage wall, above the stepladder, paints, bag of tools, and overalls he had discarded when he landed the role of Solo. "We knew that he would get his big break one day," she smiled later. "But we never expected it to happen in the middle of a paint job to our kitchen."

Doug Rowe's first indication of what was going on came when he got a phone call from his old pal from the Laguna Playhouse. "Doug, come on over and have some peanut butter and caviar," the voice told him, laid back as ever.

There had been nothing laconic about his reaction days earlier in Patricia McQueeney's office. Harrison had sat there, just as he had seven years earlier, his head once more in his hands. He was almost as incoherent as on that first meeting. All he could keep saying was: "Patricia, this is a miracle!"

Star Wars had opened in thirty-two cinemas across America on May 25. Fox's strategy had been to open with a limited release, hoping word of mouth would talk the film toward a wider audience. The studio targeted students for the screenings, bombarding college newspapers and radio stations with advertising. No one was quite sure how it would play to grown-ups.

George Lucas had been locked in an editing suite, feverishly mixing foreign-language versions of his film on the opening night of the general release, and met his wife Marcia for a meal at a Hamburger Hamlet restaurant near the famous Mann's Chinese Theater. Since his early screening to his friends, Lucas had pushed himself to near exhaustion cutting and recutting the film in an attempt to salvage it. When the Lucases saw the size of the lines stretching along Hollywood Boulevard to see their movie, they were stunned. They spent the rest of the night simply staring at the people desperate to see *Star Wars*.

In that first week, the thirty-two cinemas alone collected $3 million dollars. By the end of August, *Star Wars* had grossed $100 million faster than any film in the eighty-year history of Hollywood.

Lucas fled mainland America during the opening days of the film's run, collapsing exhausted on a beach in Hawaii while the excitement mounted. As he lay on the edge of the Pacific, *Star Wars* grew from a hit into a phenomenon.

To *Newsday* it was "an escapist masterpiece, one of the greatest adventure movies ever made," to *Time* "a grand and glorious film, the best movie of the year," to Vincent Canby in the *New York Times* "the most elaborate, most beautiful movie serial ever made."

If the lion's share of the praise was directed at Lucas, it was Harrison who collected the acting honors. *Variety* thought he was "outstanding." There were any number of reasons why he shone more brightly than Fisher, Hamill, and even Alec Guinness. Solo offered an antidote to the decent-but-dull blandness of Luke and Leia; his character had an edge that served the film's sense of go-anywhere adventure. He was, as Harrison described him, "the rapscallion of the universe"—and Ford fitted him like a glove.

"That role was like he walked into a store and they had a tailor-made suit ready for him," said Walter Beakel. "His faux pas, his tongue-in-cheeks, his looking down at people . . . it was all there for him. That was Harry. It was perfect."

Fundamentally, however, it was his timing that was perfect. The harsh reality was that during his days at Columbia and Universal he was ill prepared for the leap into Hollywood Leading Man–hood. Not only did he lack the experience and the temperament, he did not look the part of the matinee idol. He looked what he was inside, an immature young actor. Now, a little of life behind him, he had grown up, and in return the camera began to appreciate him.

The rewards were more tangible than good reviews, however. Lucas's innovative ways extended beyond the camera lens and the cutting room. Hollywood's harder-nosed businessmen almost choked on their Havanas as he announced that he was going to reward the people who had delivered his dream personally. A total of $2 million was divided between cast and crew. His three principal players, Harrison, Hamill, and Fisher, were awarded three quarters of one percent of the net profits, to be divided among them. The precise size of the windfall is unclear. Yet it is easy to guess, given that *Star Wars* eventually made some $600 million worldwide, a figure that translates into a net profit of some $150 million.

It is safe to assume this would have made them, Harrison included, around $1 million.

As the tumult broke around him, Harrison did not totally abandon those who had relied on his handyman skills. One night, as Los Angeles was hit by a major storm, he was the first person Fred Roos thought of calling when his home in Benedict Canyon was suddenly threatened with destruction.

"There was all kinds of shit happening at my house. The roof was leaking; the hill was falling in on me," he recalled. "He came over in the middle of the night and helped do whatever needed to be done to stabilize things. He had already done *Star Wars*. But that was Harrison—he was a real good, solid friend."

Over the following months, as L.A. returned to its rainless days, Roos watched as the job offers poured down on Ford. "Once he got his break as Han Solo the roles came pretty easy to him," said Roos.

In many ways Harrison was grateful for his long wait for the lightning strike that was success. Older, and equipped with a healthily skeptical view of Hollywood, he was aware of the pitfalls that lay ahead. Fred Roos's other protégé, Jack Nicholson, had warned of the dangers of the "the big Wombassa"—the moment when success arrives. Nicholson's mantra to the newly famous was that nothing would be what it was expected to be any longer.

If Harrison had a game plan post–*Star Wars* it began with remaining loyal, hardworking and extremely wary of his new status. Luck might have struck spectacularly, but he knew that luck was not to be abused.

Before *Star Wars* was released he had honored his commitment to Fred Roos and traveled to the Philippines for nine days' work on the film that had ruptured the Lucas-Coppola friendship.

If ever a movie conformed to Norman Mailer's memorable line: "Making a film is a cross between a circus, a military campaign, a nightmare, an orgy, and a high," that film was *Apocalypse Now*. Its roots extended back to USC, where Lucas and his friend John Milius had first toyed with the idea of adapting Joseph Conrad's novel *Heart of Darkness* to the nightmare of Vietnam. During Lucas's association with Coppola's Zoetrope company, the self-proclaimed Godfather of the New Hollywood had "acquired" the film's rights. It had always been Lucas's intention to direct the film. When Coppola pressured him into handing the project over to him during the making of *Star Wars*, their often turbulent relationship was effectively over.

"All directors have egos and are insecure. But of all the people I know, Francis has the biggest ego and the biggest insecurities," Lucas let rip afterward. In return Coppola referred to his cautious colleague as "the seventy-year-old kid."

Coppola had given Fred Roos the chance to produce for the first time. Roos, familiar with the Philippines since the 1960s, offered Harrison a role as soon as he finished *Star Wars*. By the time Harrison traveled out to the Far East, however, the film was already in deep trouble. Its star, Martin Sheen, was recovering from a heart attack, the eccentric behavior of Marlon Brando, hired to play the renegade Colonel Kurtz whom Sheen's Willard is ordered to seek out and destroy, had lengthened an already epic shooting schedule, and Coppola had been forced to mortgage his home to finance the completion of filming. The movie had become Coppola's personal Vietnam.

Harrison's cameo role came in the film's "laundry list" scene in which Willard's mission is explained to him. His hair shorn back to its high school length, a pair of wire-rimmed glasses perched on his nose, Ford bore no resemblance to the flamboyant Han Solo. ("Nobody recognized me in that scene. Not even George Lucas," he happily reported afterward. "That's exactly the way I want it.") Coppola, however, easily identified the same inventive technique he had seen at work on *The Conversation*.

Harrison played his intelligence officer as nervous as a kitten. During takes he kept dropping the file of papers carrying details of Willard's orders. After the umpteenth accident one exasperated actor asked: "Look, can't you do something to help this kid?" Coppola's *sotto voce* reply carried as much contempt as it did admiration for Harrison's contribution. "He's doing it on purpose."

Harrison also helped bring some levity to Coppola's chaotic life. Once more he took it upon himself to suggest an alteration to his character's costume. Coppola could not resist agreeing and gleefully took advantage with a close-up of the name Harrison had arranged to be fixed to his breast pocket. Coppola's former assistant would not be allowed to forget his association with the film. The badge read *Col. G. Lucas.*

It was too much to expect Hollywood to rid itself of its myopia overnight. On his return from the Far East no one seemed capable of seeing the *Star Wars* discovery out of uniform.

He accepted two more roles, the first as a Vietnam veteran in *Heroes*—a film being made by the young director Jeremy Paul Kagan with Henry Winkler and Sally Field—the second as an American officer in a belated sequel to *The Guns of Navarone*—*Force Ten From Navarone.*

He had been recommended for *Heroes* by his *Graffiti* chum Ron Howard. Even though the role amounted to little more than fifteen minutes of screen time, the role of Kenny, a farmboy traumatized by his experience in Southeast Asia, offered a character with the depth he had found in *Judgment* and *The Conversation.* Keen to put as much distance as possible between himself and Han Solo, Harrison accepted.

Ironically the film's star, Henry Winkler, was looking to break a George Lucas–inspired stereotype too. *Happy Days*, the television series he was starring in with Howard, was a direct spin-off of *American Graffiti.* His performance as the oily-haired Romeo, the Fonz, had made him one of the most recognizable faces in the world.

Work began on *Heroes* before *Star Wars* was finally released. While Harrison was effusive about having worked with Alec Guinness, Peter Cushing, and company in England, he was as confused as everyone else in Hollywood about what *Star Wars* would amount to. "He had been back for a month or two. He thought it was this great experience. He knew that he had had fun, but he had no idea what the movie looked like," Winkler recalled.

The experience of working in England seemed to have unleashed a new energy in Harrison. Winkler recalls him coming round to his house for dinner. "Harrison came in with the intensity of a caged cat," he said. "He was always prowling; it was very hard for him to sit down."

The same vitality was on tap when he got down to work. "You had to be on your toes because he acted with the same passion, the same intensity that he lived with," said Winkler.

Harrison seemed ready to seize every ounce of opportunity he was now being given. When, only ten days before shooting, Kagan announced he had made Kenny a Missourian rather than a Midwesterner as planned, Harrison instantly flew down to the South to study the cadences of the local accent.

In an early scene, Winkler and Harrison played out a bus station reunion between the two friends after their return from Vietnam. The scene required Harrison to embrace Winkler. "I thought, 'This is it. This is how I am going to lose my life! This man is so strong and has completely lifted me off the ground, and I hope he hears like I hear, my ribs breaking.'" Winkler groaned.

"It wasn't so much that he was a wild card, but that he would do anything that came to his emotional mind. He did not edit himself. There were no boundaries—not that he was out of control, he was just free," added Winkler. "So you had to be on the balls of your feet at all times, or you'd be left in the dust. He would just blow you away."

In October 1977, after a spell promoting *Star Wars* around the world, Harrison traveled to Europe to make *Force Ten From Navarone*. Seventeen years after Gregory Peck, David Niven, and company had stormed the box office, Harrison teamed up with Robert Shaw, Edward Fox, and Franco Nero for another slice of Alistair MacLean hokum. Hokum, as it turned out, was exactly what director Guy Hamilton's film amounted to.

Harrison, cast as U.S. Ranger, Colonel Barnsby, admitted later the role was one of the few he had ever taken simply for the money. He regretted his decision soon after arriving in Yugoslavia. "I was lost because I didn't know what the story was about. I didn't have anything to act." A lot of his scenes, he admitted later, were "bullshit . . . I had a hard time."

His unhappiness wasn't helped by homesickness and the appalling weather that drifted in off the Adriatic coast during the winter. He was also barred from visiting the more civilized surroundings of Italy. Director Hamilton and his producers, worried by a spate of mega-lire kidnappings across the sea, insisted the cast remain in Yugoslavia. The virtually all-male cast vented their anger by drinking and organizing testosterone-charged challenges to each other. Carl Weathers, star of the *Rocky* movies and costarring in *Force 10* as Sergeant Weaver, inevitably emerged the winner.

Harrison was at least able to relieve the boredom by bringing Mary, Ben, and Willard to Europe for a brief vacation. When he spoke to journalists on the *Navarone* set back in Shepperton, he admitted that he had had problems getting the boys to join him at work during his last frenetic year away from America. "It's difficult to pull them out of school for any length of time at this stage in their lives," he shrugged. "I hope in a couple of years my family will be able to travel with me all the time."

Interviews provided a welcome escape from the tedium. Faced with a curious European press for the first time, he made a willing and witty interviewee. Most of his inquisitors were surprised to discover the braggart Solo's thoughtful, bespectacled alter ego. As he filled interviewers in on his background, tales of his "You ain't got it, kid" experience at Columbia and subsequent struggle as a carpenter quickly became staples. But there were hints of the anger he had stored up for so long.

The English filmwriter Tony Crawley, who seemed to hit it off with him in a series of interviews over the next few years, drew out the insecurities Harrison still harbored, post–*Star Wars*. Harrison admitted that he had for years avoided going to the cinema. "For a long time I didn't want to see other films and other actors working. Pure jealousy. They were getting good stuff. I wasn't," he told him.

His unease about whether he could hang on to his newfound status was obvious. Yet his determination to remain indomitably himself was as strong as it had been in the distant days of Columbia. "Acting is so intensely personal that if you're not operating totally within your own resources, there comes a moment when you'll be stuck; you won't know who to imitate," he said.

"Much better to use your own personality and keep it sharp and oiled. Otherwise you start churning out bullshit—and that lives on long after you've flushed yourself. It's still up there forty feet high and sixty feet wide screaming, 'Bullshit, bullshit, bullshit! This guy was a fraud.'"

As filming on *Force Ten* approached an end, however, there was nothing counterfeit about the transformation. "Overnight success" had arrived, he joked with Crawley. "Albeit that the night was fifteen bloody years long."

Harrison Ford may have imagined he had already paid the price required for that success. He had not. It would be higher than he could have imagined.

12

THE BLOOM OFF THE ROSE

L ate one night in January 1978, Harrison Ford sat on a wind-bat-
    tered bluff, overlooking the Atlantic on the Channel island of
    Jersey. The brutal beauty of the scene was lost on him. He felt
cold, exhausted and dreadfully homesick.

He had spent most of the previous twelve months in such isolation.
His passport now bore stamps from the Philippines, Yugoslavia and,
once more, the United Kingdom. Now he was in the Channel Islands
filming the climactic scenes on *Force Ten From Navarone*.

In most respects he was fulfilling his most cherished ambition. His
career was finally blossoming, acting had grown into what his undergraduate mind had imagined—an experience stimulated by the sights
and sounds of far-flung locations, and there were opportunities to
broaden his horizons at last. As shooting on *Force Ten* drew to a close,
however, his ambitions were humble. He was eagerly looking forward
to leaving Europe and spending time with Mary and the boys back at
Woodrow Wilson Drive.

Late that night, the earnest figure of the writer and director Peter
Hyams arrived on the set, his face flushed with the trauma of having
spent the last few days working around the clock to save his latest project. Hyams's movie, another wartime adventure, called *Hanover Street*,
was ready to start filming back in London. The sets had been built; the

script had been written. The only problem was that Hyams's original star, Kris Kristofferson, had suddenly pulled out of the lead role. The film would crumble if a new lead was not found quickly. The director had hopped on a tiny plane to the Channel Islands in the hope of persuading Harrison to fill the breach.

By the time the two men finished talking the night away, they had a deal they could shake on. In Hyams, Harrison saw something of himself. "I was impressed with his monomaniacal attitude," he said later of the high-tension New Yorker. It was a moment of awful irony, as it turned out.

Harrison's decision would have deeply contrasting repercussions in England and America. Across the Channel it would save the jobs of 120 workers and a $7 million project its backers, General Cinemas, had all but given up on. Across the moonlit Atlantic, it would also ensure that he and Mary would finally lose the fight to save their marriage.

The success of *Star Wars* had brought financial rewards seemingly reserved for the owners of the Hollywood homes Harrison Ford had set about with hammer and nails. He had toasted his first $52,000 check during filming on *Force Ten*. It was only the first of many installments on his profit share on *Star Wars*. With the money had come the opportunities he had craved through all the years of frustration on the Hollywood reject list.

Simultaneously, his new status was putting an increasing strain on his relationship with Mary. As the world became familiar with his face, so she and the boys began to regard him as a stranger. Some had detected fissures in the marriage even before success arrived. To Carrie Fisher the strains had been visible a year earlier, during filming on *Star Wars*, when they had visited Elstree. "Mary was Harrison's wife—that was what she did," she said. "She was a phenomenal cook and the mother of his kids. But when I met them, I think the bloom was sort of off the rose."

After the success of *Star Wars* it was clear to many that there had been a sudden transformation in the marriage. Hollywood had always been a transparent, tiresome place for Mary. Suddenly the wife of a hot new star, she was thrust into an unwelcome spotlight. Pictures of her on Harrison's arm in the post–*Star Wars* hysteria portrayed a woman visibly uneasy with her surroundings. "Mary was a very smart, simple, warm lady. She was a terrific mother to those boys. But she had no Hollywood social-climbing ambitions whatsoever," said Fred Roos.

For Harrison, however, the long years of frustration seemed finally over. The tensions that had made him such an awkward, irascible customer were suddenly released. It had been a triumph of his indomitable will, and he reveled in the liberation it brought with it. "He became a looser and wider person. But Mary did not change with Harry. Which is logical; Mary's background was much more downplayed," said their old friend Walter Beakel.

As Harrison spent more and more time away from home, Mary was left with the two boys. "They really were pistols," said Doug Rowe. "But it all seemed to fall apart pretty quickly after *Star Wars*."

At a time when there should have been palpable joy at Woodrow Wilson Drive, there was instead an unmistakable air of something being amiss. William Tyree recalls telephoning at the time, sensing it was time to heal the wounds of the actor's Ripon days: "I got a cold female voice—Mary, I assume, who would have known who I was from her time as an undergraduate. She just said, 'He's not available.' There was clearly something wrong."

Harrison's determination to seize the opportunities post–Han Solo was only exacerbating matters. His life had suddenly become one of constant travel. He had been able to fly Mary and the boys out to Yugoslavia for a brief vacation during filming on *Force Ten*, but in February 1978, he arrived back with just four weeks to spend at home before returning once more to London for *Hanover Street* in March.

After months of damp, depressing European winter weather, he arrived back to discover California in the grip of its own version of the Great Flood. At least now that he had been buoyed financially by the success of *Star Wars* he was able to take his family away. With Mary, Ben, and Willard he flew off to Hawaii for ten days.

The holiday failed to mend the cracks that were by now apparent in his marriage. Those wounds were only aggravated by rumors of relationships he may or may not have been forming away from home. *Star Wars* had transformed him into a newsworthy personality. The least welcome aspect of his success was the interest suddenly shown in every aspect of the private life of the buccaneering Han Solo. *Hanover Street* was to provide the press with some of its most salacious opportunities yet.

His decision to work with Hyams had a purpose beyond reconfirming his star billing. He was angry at theories circulating around Hollywood about his performance in *Star Wars*. As far as many were concerned, Lucas's film was a triumph of ironmongery over acting; Harrison, like Mark Hamill and Carrie Fisher, was an actor incapable of rising above Lucas's comic-book banality. "People started saying he was no good with women. It was something I heard a lot," said Fred Roos.

Like *Star Wars*, *Hanover Street* amounted to a ménâge à trois, this time between a beautiful English nurse, Margaret Sellinger, played by the rising English actress Lesley-Anne Down, an American airman, Lieutenant David Halloran (Harrison), and Margaret's British officer husband Paul, played by Christopher Plummer. Hyams's setting was as familiar as Lucas's had been unfamiliar—London during the blitz in World War II. Its romance was also of a kind far more familiar than that of the asexual *Star Wars* universe.

The passion of the film's central romance was the most attractive element in the film so far as Harrison was concerned. "I'd yet to kiss a girl or be involved romantically. Then along came this love story," he said.

In Lesley-Anne Down he had as alluring a leading lady as British acting had to offer in the latter half of the 1970s. Behind the classic, porcelain-perfect features burned a knowing sexuality that had been present even as a young girl. At sixteen, Down had been voted the prettiest teenager in England. Now aged twenty-four, her career launched by the transatlantic success of the TV series *Upstairs, Downstairs*, her performance in setting the elderly Olivier's pulse racing in *The Betsy* had given her a healthy notoriety. The U.S. Catholic Conference condemned the film for being "supremely trashy." She had also gone topless in *The Pink Panther Strikes Again*, where there had been rumors of a fling with Peter Sellers.

Filming got underway during more atrocious English weather. Viewing the dailies, Hyams and producer Paul Lazarus could not side with the Hollywood view of Harrison Ford. They instantly spotted sparks flying between their two leads. "One of the reasons Harrison is good for his part is that not only is he a sensitive, highly trained actor who's logged in his dues doing lots of movies, but he's also got this fierce, burning sexual energy," Lazarus told the trade magazine *Screen International* when they visited the set in April. "For me it is extremely credible that a happily married woman with a lovely child would be romantically smitten by him."

As it happened, Lesley-Anne Down was neither a mother nor happily married. Soon rumors that Harrison and she were involved were bubbling away in British newspapers. As tongues wagged, Down added credibility to the unconfirmed reports by moving out of the Wimbledon house she shared with her longtime partner, the screenwriter Bruce Robinson. Her explanation was that she had decided to "crash" with friends or stay in hotels during the *Hanover Street* shoot.

Whatever the truth, Harrison was discovering a distinct *lack* of passion for his director, Peter Hyams.

After spells as a newsman with CBS and a documentary maker in Vietnam, the sensitive, soft-spoken New Yorker was, at thirty-four, writing and directing his own movies. Back in a skeptical, post-Watergate America, *Capricorn One*, his drama about a faked space mission, with Elliott Gould and O. J. Simpson, was fast inflating his reputation; *Hanover Street* represented a step into uncharted waters. As if to add to the pressure, a few miles away at Twickenham Studios the considerably more experienced John Schlesinger was shooting *Yanks*, a similar story of wartime Anglo-American intrigue, starring Richard Gere and Vanessa Redgrave. Hyams tried to deflect his nervousness with humor in the run-up to shooting. Asked by an English reporter what the film was about, he replied: "About two hours." Soon there were those, Harrison included, who wondered whether he was really joking.

Harrison had agreed to make the film despite having major reservations about the script. He soon discovered that under Hyams, a self-confessed "plodder," the production had little scope for the kind of improvisation he had been able to suggest to George Lucas and Francis Coppola.

Hyams's dialogue made Lucas's sci-fi babble seem like Ibsen. One exchange between Harrison and Down, when the mysterious Margaret is defying David's attempts to discover who she is ran:

David: Tell me your name.
Margaret: I can't.
David: Please.
Margaret: No.
David: I'll call you Fred.

"I agreed to do it, expecting that the script, which I didn't have total faith in, would be changed as we went along," Harrison said ruefully afterward. "Well, it wasn't. And making that film was not a happy experience for me."

The personal publicity *Hanover Street* was generating only added to his unhappiness. If he had hoped to protect Mary from the links being made between him and Lesley-Anne Down, he was unsuccessful. In July, *People* magazine reported that there had been "more than a professional interest" between the two. A month later, when the same magazine asked Harrison about Down, his reaction was as indignant as it was significant. "What do you want me to do—say it's not true?"

By the time the rumors reached the Great American Public, however, events had moved on apace. The divisions in Harrison's marriage had become unbreachable. Soon after returning from England, he packed his bags and moved out of Woodrow Wilson Drive.

As it transpired, Lesley-Anne Down would not be the cause of the downfall of his marriage. The seeds of the relationship that would reinvent his life had been sown a year before. It is doubtful whether anyone involved appreciated the irony of the fact that the woman concerned was a former contributor to *People* magazine.

When Fred Roos had suggested Harrison join him and a twenty-seven-year-old screenwriter called Melissa Mathison for dinner in Toronto in 1977, matchmaking could not have been further from his mind. "I didn't introduce them as if here was going to be a romance," said the producer. That was precisely what it became, however.

Harrison had been passing through the Canadian city on the back of the *Star Wars* bandwagon. Roos and other members of the Coppola family, on location shooting *The Black Stallion*, offered a welcome relief from the silliness of the Solo circus.

Roos knew nothing of the difficulties his friend was encountering in his marriage to Mary when he suggested he join him and the film's writer-in-residence for dinner. Harrison had encountered Mathison very briefly in the Philippines. "They had met a little on the set of *Apocalypse*, but I really introduced them in Toronto," said Roos. "We had mutual friends and had worked with similar people. It was just 'let's go out for a meal.' "

Tall, willowy, and athletic, with the slightly goofy look of a Shelley Duvall, Melissa Mathison did not conform to the classic notion of beauty represented by the likes of Lesley-Anne Down or even Carrie Fisher. But over dinner her acerbic intelligence soon made an indelible mark on Harrison.

The daughter of the former *Los Angeles Times* and *Newsweek* journalist Richard Mathison and his publicist wife, Melissa's personality owed much to her upbringing. Her parents' circle of friends represented an eclectic mix of artists, writers, and moviemakers. "We weren't your mainstream 1950s family. Both my parents had wonderful, eccentric, artistic friends who treated us as friends as well," she said once.

In this fiercely intelligent environment, the young Melissa and her four brothers and sisters were judged by their ability to participate. "How your mind worked was considered important." As a result, the movie industry carried less mystique than it might have elsewhere in America. Far from being an intimidating jungle, Hollywood was the backyard in which Melissa and her brothers and sisters and school-friends roamed free. Melissa's childhood was spent in the old, unbuilt-up Hollywood Hills where jackrabbits and coyote roamed. "It used to be a great town. My mother used to let us off on Hollywood Boulevard to play! Now you'd never see your children again," she recalled.

Melissa had inherited her father's writing abilities. From UCLA she went on to Berkeley and a political science major. When, thanks to her family's friendship with Francis Coppola, for whom Melissa used to baby-sit, she was offered a job as an assistant on *The Godfather, Part II*, Melissa took leave. Even though her role was little more than that of a runner—"I just got coffee and Cokes for people"—she had been seduced by the energy of on-set life. "I had been working in a bakery. Bringing coffee to Al Pacino was exciting."

After Berkeley a family connection again helped her win work as a stringer at the San Francisco bureau of *Time* magazine and then as a reporter for *People* magazine. Spurred on by the nagging persistence of Coppola, she had eased away from journalism toward screenwriting. On the set of *The Black Stallion*, she was finally beginning to believe in her abilities.

Locked away in her Toronto hotel room, she often worked into the small hours writing script pages that would be filmed the following morning. She was as much in need of good company as Harrison. The treadmill of talk shows and press junkets, radio interviews, and public appearances alongside stormtroopers and robots, took an inevitable toll. Fisher and Hamill referred to Harrison as "Dad" on the promotional tour. But all three couldn't help behaving like adolescents to relieve the strain. "We went wild in amusement parks at night to get away," said Fisher. During their stay at the Sherry Netherland in New York the trio had a massive, frat house–style food fight. "We tried to clean up before George and Marcia Lucas came in—like Mom and Dad—but there was still a piece of spinach on the mantel," said Fisher.

In Melissa, Harrison found—as he had in Carrie Fisher—a woman who shared his slightly warped view of the world, a fellow skeptic simultaneously in love and hate with the business paying their bills. And as his horizons expanded beyond those of his Hollywood-weary wife, he found much more besides. Harrison and Melissa remained in touch when they returned to Los Angeles. Their growing friendship sustained him as he dealt with the dark and difficult early days of his separation from Mary.

In Hollywood, of course, the scenario was nothing new. Success almost required some kind of kickback. Marriage was the most common victim. There were few who would have predicted that Harrison and Mary would enact one of Hollywood's cruelest clichés, however. "When he did the typical *now I'm famous I'll get a new wife*, that was kind of disappointing. Mary had terrific character. At the time it was, 'Oh shit, Harry's gone Hollywood—too bad,'" said his old roommate Bill Haljum, who found out about the breakup through friends.

Harrison rented an apartment in West Hollywood, within an easy drive of Woodrow Wilson Drive. To the surprise of no one who knew

Mary, she ensured that the separation was amicable and that Ben and Willard were the priorities. She remained close to the boys' paternal grandparents, Christopher and Dorothy Ford, to whom divorce was becoming horribly familiar. The freewheeling Terence had just married for the second time after divorcing his first wife, a cashier at Max's Kansas City, where he had worked at the end of the 1960s. (Neither that marriage nor a subsequent one to a television executive, Terri Guitron-Ford, would last more than five years.)

Perhaps sensing his need for anchors in his now turbulent life, Mary even went so far as to encourage old friends to support Harrison during the breakup. "She urged me to try and keep in touch; I think this was while they were breaking up. I think she felt he needed his old friends," recalled Bill Russell.

Over the ensuing months, as the details of the dissolution were sorted out, Harrison and Mary adopted the attitude that they would remain "divorced to each other" for the rest of their lives. Why not, therefore, be civilized about it? The divorce was "mutual and generous," he would come to say. "As good as they get."

As news filtered its way through their circle of friends, there were those who felt more sadness than surprise. "I don't think they split up because he got famous," said Carrie Fisher. "They'd been married for fifteen years, since they were kids, and it had just gone its course."

Others shook their heads sagely, recognizing a situation as old and familiar as Hollywood itself. "I have known that to happen many, many times because there is an inward change in the person," said Walter Beakel. "It wasn't because he became a star. In all relationships there are changes and the point is both partners have to change together."

After a dozen years of being ignored by Hollywood, Mary would rather the spotlight had remained shining elsewhere. "You could never picture Mary in the Hollywood scheme of things," said Beakel. "She was very supportive, but the struggling was somehow easier to comprehend than the success."

Those who knew and loved Mary would have nothing to do with suggestions that Harrison had somehow outgrown her. "No, no. There is not a person on the face of this earth who could outgrow Mary," said Doug Rowe. "And no one knows that better than Harrison."

Certainly no one understood the cruelty of the irony more than

Harrison himself. From the Belfry to Elstree, from the heady days at Crane Hall to the grim years amid the chaos of Woodrow Wilson Drive, Mary had been his most supportive and loyal asset. Without her, he might never have risked traveling to London for *Star Wars*.

As the strain began to tell, she fought hard to save their marriage. "I had to go all over the world, and Mary and I were dragged apart more and more," Harrison explained later, time having provided him with a perspective. "Slowly but surely, our relationship began to break up. Although she tried to keep us together, traveling to see me whenever possible, the situation became unbearable. I'm not the easiest guy to be married to, but it was the outside pressures that finally drove us apart."

In the period following the breakup he was harder on himself than anyone else. Even his steel-shuttered reserve could not contain the anger he felt at what he had allowed to happen.

"Success separated us more and more—and I will never forgive it for that."

By the winter of 1978, when Harrison began work on his fourth major film since *Star Wars*, he was making no secret of his growing relationship with Melissa Mathison.

She was a familiar face on the set of *No Knife*, a western he had begun shooting in October on location in Arizona, Colorado, and northern California. Her presence helped alleviate the memory of an unpleasant experience at the hands of a figure from the Hollywood he believed he had left behind.

Michael Elias and Frank Shaw's screenplay told the picaresque story of a Polish rabbi posted from the East to a synagogue in San Francisco. During an eventful journey across America he forms an unlikely friendship with a bank robber.

Warner Brothers had given the job of directing the movie, intended as a light-touch comedy, to one of Hollywood's larger-than-life figures, Robert Aldrich. A relative of the Rockefellers and a member of a family of Rhode Island politicians, Aldrich spent his early days in Hollywood as an assistant to Jean Renoir and Charlie Chaplin. His undoubted talent extended from action movies like *Apache* and *Vera Cruz* with Gary Cooper and Burt Lancaster, to darker canvasses like *Whatever Happened to Baby Jane?* with Joan Crawford and Bette Davis and *The Killing of Sister George* with Beryl Reid, Coral Browne, and Susannah York.

A hulking, bespectacled bear of a man, Aldrich had never made a secret of his success. "The stories you hear about us [directors] being corrupt and thieves and dirty are all true. It's a swindle, and it is corrupt, but if you are tough enough you last," he once boasted. Approaching the end of a colorful, roller-coaster career, the sixty-year-old filmmaker was still standing. Indeed, as the then chairman of the Directors Guild of America, he was as powerful as he had ever been within Hollywood.

Aldrich had originally agreed to make *No Knife* with the up-and-coming Gene Wilder as the rabbi and the seventy-one-year-old John Wayne as the bank robber. The prospect of working with the greatest icon in Hollywood on what would almost certainly be his last film—Wayne died in 1979—appealed to Aldrich's ego. It would be a slice of cinematic history.

After a protracted salary row, however, Wayne dropped out shortly before filming was due to begin. Harrison once more rode to the rescue. Ironically, there were those in Hollywood who were comparing his performance as Han Solo to that of a young Wayne. "If I'm like Wayne in places, it's my subconscious supplying something that's necessary. I didn't know I was doing it," he told interviewers at the time.

From the moment he arrived on-set, however, it was apparent to everyone that the thirty-six-year-old John Wayne manqué would never be able to make up for Aldrich's disappointment at losing the real-life legend.

"It was unfortunate from Harrison's view; I think he was intimidated," recalled Mace Neufeld, the film's producer. "Every time Robert Aldrich directed a scene, in his mind he saw John Wayne. He was dealing mentally with a screen icon—it did not help Harrison as an actor, and there was enormous pressure being put on him by the director."

Neufeld, a sophisticated New Yorker who had graduated to Hollywood from photography and writing material for Rosemary Clooney and Sammy Davis Jr., spent time with his leading man and his girlfriend in an attempt to ease his anxieties.

It was already becoming apparent that the new couple were forming a mutually supportive alliance. Harrison was not shy about promoting Melissa. "You should look at some of the things she is writing," he would tell Neufeld.

"I was busy. I did not have the time," Neufeld said ruefully. (Years later, when Melissa had written her most successful film, *E.T.*, Neufeld called Harrison at home. "Tell me she was not working on *E.T.* at the time you asked me to look at her writing," he begged. "Of course she was," Harrison tortured him in reply.)

As the three-month shoot drew to an end shortly before Christmas 1978, Aldrich went out of his way to praise Wilder. "Gene is brilliant. I think it's the best job he's ever done," he told *Films & Filming* magazine when they visited the set. In the editing suite, however, Mace Neufeld was left with no illusions about what the director thought of Harrison. He was furious when he saw Aldrich's first cut, in which much of the bank robber's performance was consigned to the cutting-room floor. "I thought they were going to come to blows," recalled Pat McQueeney. Neither she nor Harrison would forget Mace Neufeld's supportiveness.

13

ENSLAVED TO THE EMPIRE

In November 1978, in his office at Twentieth Century-Fox, Alan
Ladd Jr. took delivery of the most eagerly anticipated script in years.
The attached note, written in the familiar hand of George Lucas,
read: "Here's a rough idea of the film. May The Force be with us!"

The news that Lucas was ready to begin work on the sequel to *Star
Wars*, *The Empire Strikes Back*, sent a frisson of anticipation and envy
rippling around Hollywood. As the most lucrative gravy train in cinematic history got ready to roll again, agents and publishers, food
chains and toymakers jostled for a seat, hobo class if necessary. Harrison Ford was clutching a first-class ticket. Yet he stood frozen to the
tracks wondering whether he dared climb aboard.

Lucas had always intended to use the same ensemble for the first trilogy of stories. But during the original *Star Wars* negotiations, Harrison,
recalcitrant as ever, had been the only one of the film's central triangle not to commit to all three movies. His motives had been sound—
a combination of calculation and common sense. If the film flopped,
the contract would be meaningless. If it succeeded, he could negotiate
from strength. Either way he could reserve judgment while he
attempted to build a broader career.

As it turned out, though, life away from Han Solo had been an
almost unmitigated failure. Behind his decisions to do *Heroes*, *Force Ten*

From *Navarone, Hanover Street,* and *No Knife* (now retitled *The Frisco Kid*) lay an underlying logic. "Harrison did a lot of them to consolidate his position, to get the billing," said Pat McQueeney. "You go in with high hopes, but he ran into some trouble. One thing he learned is that an actor is really at the mercy of the director."

Whatever the excuses, the net result was that he had failed to dent the convictions of those who thought he was an accident, a comic-book hero riding along on George Lucas's shirttails. *Heroes* and *Force Ten* had been released with little impact. Hopes for both *The Frisco Kid* and *Hanover Street* were low.

In the three years since *Star Wars* had lifted the profile of his former handyman, Fred Roos had heard all manner of opinion about his potential—or lack of it. "There was a whole theory in town that Harrison was a fluke. Women didn't find him attractive, he couldn't be a leading man, he had that funny little scar. Stupid theories," he said. Throughout that time, director friends would routinely ask Roos for casting advice and he would routinely suggest his old friend. "They'd say, 'No, no, no, no. Who else?' It was a really funny career in that way. Even when it got easy, it wasn't easy," he said.

At the beginning of 1979, with production due to begin in March, Lucas asked Harrison aboard, tempting him with a vastly inflated salary and, far more important, a share of the profits. The financial allure was irresistible. The scale of the *Star Wars* industry—by now ranging from books to comic strips, puzzles to pencil boxes—was overwhelming the staff at Lucasfilm. "Synergy" had become Hollywood's baby buzzword. *Star Wars* itself had already been re-released twice to satiate the phenomenal public demand.

Relations with Lucas, to whom Harrison acknowledged he owed all that had come his way in the last two years, remained solid and friendly. As a favor Harrison had agreed to make a cameo appearance in the director's ill-advised sequel to his first box-office hit, the inspiringly titled *More American Graffiti*. Denied the services of Richard Dreyfuss, now an Oscar winner for *The Goodbye Girl*, Lucas needed all the help he could get on the troubled shoot in summer 1978. Harrison did a day's work, slipping into highway patrolman gear to play "Officer Falfa," a speed cop with a passion for booking hippies. All he asked in return for the favor was that he was not credited for his contribution to the film, which some viewed as Lucas's revenge on Universal for their treatment of him six years earlier.

Now Harrison had to weigh his loyalty to Lucas plus the rewards being offered in the *Star Wars* project against the potentially crippling price of getting typecast. If he doubted the dangers, he only had to listen to the horror stories Carrie Fisher and Mark Hamill told.

In the three years since *Star Wars*, Hamill's only major roles had been in two obscure movies, *Corvette Summer* and *The Big Red One*. His fortunes had not been helped by a near-fatal car crash shortly after the release of *Star Wars* and the painful plastic surgery he had undergone as a result. As his frustration mounted, George Lucas had, half-jokingly, advised Hamill to announce his retirement. "There's no pressure to put out a product, and if you do get a part you can say: 'The role was so good it lured me out of retirement.' " While Hamill joked about his position, he found it hard to mask the resentment he felt at his fate. "Thirty years ago the studios would have built our careers."

Carrie Fisher, equally disillusioned by the offers she had received, concentrated on developing her gift for comedy and became a regular on *Saturday Night Live* with Dan Aykroyd and John Belushi. "I'm famous in this weird way because I'm this children's cartoon character," she opined. "It hasn't translated into jobs." More than Harrison and Hamill she had also suffered at the hands of obsessive fans, some of whom began to turn up at her home. "Helpless" was her one-word summation of the position she found herself in.

Unlike Fisher and Hamill, Harrison had made sure he had a choice. He knew how much hinged on his participation in the sequel, but at the same time he did not want to become even more stereotyped. To be a slave to the Empire or to fly Solo?

Exhausted by the efforts of directing *Star Wars*, Lucas brought in hired guns to guide his new film to the screen. The veteran Irvin "Kersh" Kershner had agreed to direct, and the script was being written by a former Chicago advertising copywriter called Lawrence Kasdan. The new bloods helped Harrison resolve his complex inner calculus. From what he learned of their ideas—because of Lucas's obsession with secrecy he would not see a finished script until three weeks before filming began—*Empire* would offer more opportunities for the human characters to breathe.

"You'd expect development of the characters in a second act," he said later. "I was expecting it and wasn't surprised when I saw a different version of Han Solo in the script. We get to know him better," he told the sci-fi magazine *Starlog* in August 1980.

Hopeful that the film would give him an opportunity to develop his character in a movie that was almost guaranteed to succeed, he bit the bullet. After a customary row with Lucas over his salary and profit participation, he capitulated.

A few weeks later, frozen to the seat of a snowplow as it inched its way through a violent blizzard in the remote north of Norway, he was cursing his decision. "I kept asking myself how I got into this whole mess."

As Kershner filmed the opening scenes of the *Empire*, Scandinavia was doubling for the ice planet Hoth, where Kasdan's script reintroduced Han, Leia, and Luke lying low from Darth Vader. Harrison was not originally required for the exterior scenes, shot on a glacier above the tiny outpost of Finse. A change of plan had, however, required his presence in the town (pop. around 100), one of the most inaccessible places in the region—even in good weather. With the rail service suspended, the snowplow was his only means of reaching his colleagues in time for his scenes.

"Harrison's Harrison. He can put up with things that other actors can't. That for a start. Then being out on the glaciers, where it was extremely cold. Then still being able to have a sense of humor after three or four hours out in the cold. To me he is a true professional," recalled Peter Mayhew, one of the nucleus of *Star Wars* veterans to breathe a sigh of relief when Han Solo clambered out of his makeshift transportation late the night before his early-morning call.

Mayhew saw an actor maturing both in craft and confidence. "When I first met him, he did things fairly and squarely the way he thought. But if the director thought differently, then fine," he recalled. "In *Star Wars* he played himself. He was fairly confident but then, in the *Empire*, this confidence grew."

Back at Elstree that confidence now extended to a new stridency on set as he imposed himself on Kershner, a more performance-minded director than Lucas. "The special effects take so much attention that you tend to let the action slip by. I didn't want that to happen, and

Harrison was constantly calling me on it," Kershner recalled. "If we did just two takes and I'd say, 'That's great,' he would say, 'Wait a minute, wait a minute. What's so great? Was it great for the special effects or for me?' And I'd say, 'Harrison, I wouldn't say "great" unless it was for you.' And he would give me that wonderful look of his, you know that wry look, and we would move on."

"Kersh had his own ideas, but Harrison would steam in there and say, 'This is the way it is.' He also had a lot more backing from George in what he wanted from that character," said Peter Mayhew.

If there had been a change in his approach to the on-set politics, there had been an even more significant shift in his relationship with his leading lady. These days, relations between Harrison and Carrie Fisher often made the ice-planet Hoth seem like the surface of the sun. Their former inseparability seemed to have passed, and relations often appeared strained—a development that, ironically, did little to harm the production. One of Lawrence Kasdan's greatest achievements had been to enliven the one-dimensional relationships Luke, Leia, and Han had been given in *Star Wars*. As the bond between Luke and Leia became more platonic, so the sexual chemistry between the Princess and the sardonic Solo became more obvious. Essentially it was a love-hate relationship. From what most observers could make out, the latter came easiest.

"It got a lot hotter than it should have between Harrison and Carrie," Peter Mayhew recalled.

When *Star Wars* was being made, the British press paid it no attention whatsoever. Now with the cast of the most successful movie in history once more on its shores, the gossip mill was in no mood to miss out. "You read the gossip columns of that time, there was something obviously going on. There were certain references in certain papers," recalled Mayhew.

Even the most amateur of psychologists drew the conclusion that their on-set explosions were a ritual extension of whatever had been going on elsewhere. "It was, 'Let's get rid of it through performances in front of the cameras rather than keeping it bottled up,' " said Mayhew. Tensions reached breaking point during filming of the evacuation of the ice-station on Hoth, as Han dares Leia to declare her feelings for him.

Han: Afraid I'd leave without a goodbye kiss?
Leia: I would rather kiss a Wookiee.

And later:

Han: You can't bear to let a gorgeous guy like me out of your sight.
Leia: I don't know where you get your delusions from, laser-brain.

No one was quite sure where performance began and reality ended. Either way it translated into the most human exchanges of the entire *Star Wars* era. "It would build up, build up, build up. Then one or the other of them would storm off. If you looked at Carrie's face, there were one or two lovely moments where she could cheerfully have killed Harrison," said Mayhew.

The most cataclysmic clash came in the most emotionally charged scene of the film, in which Han is turned into a giant doorstop by a carbon-freezing chamber. In Kasdan's original script, the scene ended with the couple finally acknowledging the depth of their feelings. "I love you," she tells him. "I love you," he returns as Darth Vader orders his refrigeration.

Harrison voiced his unhappiness with the exchange. It was "too much on the nose," he protested. "I wanted the moment to have another complexion," he explained later. His suggested alternative— that Han say "I know"—was the catalyst for an argument involving Kershner, who was for the subtlety of the change, and Kasdan and Lucas, who were against what they saw as its uncalled-for levity. Harrison and Fisher were heard having a screaming match in a dressing room as she protested at his arrogance. Harrison prevailed, however.

Neither Harrison nor Carrie Fisher has ever disclosed the extent of their friendship on the set. Soon Fisher would be married—disastrously—to Paul Simon. When the heat of the battle had faded, however, Ford and Fisher emerged as close and lasting friends. Whenever asked which scenes she enjoyed most in the *Star Wars* films, Fisher usually has no hesitation in answering. "I liked it whenever Harrison and I yelled at each other!"

Billy Dee Williams, the black actor hired to mend the damage done by the American media's criticism of the all-white cast of *Star Wars*, became Harrison's playmate on the *Empire* set. Williams played Lando Calrissian, a playboy pal of Solo's; he and Harrison had worked together in an episode of *Dan August* nine years earlier. They became brothers in arms.

"Billy Dee was into bodybuilding and working out," recalled David Prowse. "That seemed to stimulate an interest in Harrison too, and he would ask me for advice."

By the end of the shoot, unfortunately, *The Empire* had degenerated into the same farcical race against time that *Star Wars* had become. George Lucas had intended running the sequel from his home in Marin County, northern California, but Kershner's perfectionist's eye for detail—not to mention Harrison's increasingly voluble role on the set—had contributed to a major over-spend.

Lucas arrived at Elstree with the production $10 million over budget. At one point, according to his biographer, Dale Pollock, Lucas threw a childish tantrum, screaming: "You guys are ruining my movie." And by the time the shoot finished, the director-turned-producer was once more the most pessimistic man in the galaxy.

Two years after Han Solo had given him his first taste of triumph, Harrison came face to face with its twin impostor disaster—the only fitting description for the finished *Hanover Street*.

The film opened in America in mid-May 1979 to a deluge of derision. *New York Times* critic Vincent Canby set the tone for what was to follow by beginning his review: "Every now and then a film comes along of such painstaking, overripe foolishness that it breaks through the garbage barrier to become one of those rare movies you rush out to see for laughs." While Hyams came in for most of the criticism, Harrison did not escape. Canby thought he was "more of a comic-strip character here than he was in *Star Wars*."

By the time *Hanover Street* was laughed out of every cinema chain in America it had earned a pitiful $3 million. It fared no better around the world.

In the years that followed, Harrison denied ever having seen Hyams's finished film. "I keep saying that if fifty people tell me they like it, then I may change my mind," he said in 1981. "But so far, I'm just up to eighteen, so there's no immediate danger of that happening."

More than fifteen years later, he has still to drum up the support he needs . . .

The release of *The Frisco Kid*, a half dozen weeks later, did little to relieve the pain. There was affection for the film—and his performance. *Variety* thought Harrison "Finally lives up to the potential displayed in *Star Wars* . . . Ford provided the perfect foil for Wilder's gaffes and their scenes play wonderfully," its critic wrote. Julian Fox in *Films & Filming* also thought Harrison "an excellent and wryly funny foil" to the "Oscar-worthy" Wilder, and the film a western "head and shoulders above anything I have seen in a long time." For others, alas, Aldrich was the sledgehammer cracking the nut. "Asking Robert Aldrich to direct a sentimental Jewish comedy . . . is like putting Gen. George S. Patton Jr. in charge of a tap-dancing class for tiny tots," Vincent Canby bitched.

Damned by faint praise, *The Frisco Kid* went on to earn a mediocre $12 million at the American box office before fading from view.

The new home to which Harrison returned to lick his latest wounds was a barn-style house high up in Benedict Canyon. It had been his "second self" Han Solo, naturally, who had been largely responsible for its acquisition. The House That Han Bought was something of an alter ego in itself.

The million-dollar mock mansions of Beverly Hills and Bel Air were in neither Harrison's style nor his price range. Instead he scoured the canyons of the Hollywood Hills for a house that reflected the kind of craftsmanship he had been practicing before stardom struck.

He found precisely what he was looking for further along the same canyon as Fred Roos. The clapboard house conformed to the higher construction standards of the prewar era. It had been built in 1941, the year before he was born and ahead of the material shortages that had forced postwar builders to take sloppy shortcuts. "Everything became modularized, everything had to be built in two-foot dimensions," he explained to a vaguely bewildered interviewer shortly afterward.

With the deal done, he set about imbuing the house's interior with the atmosphere of his old childhood home in Park Ridge. He began buying up Early American furniture, hanging new doors and bringing the house's wooden floors up to a polished perfection. If the hardware and furniture shops of Los Angeles did not stock the fittings he needed, he simply retired to the garage he had once more fitted out as a work-shop and shaped them himself.

For the first time in his life, money was no object. "If somebody put $3,000 in my hand when I was a carpenter, it felt like real money," he said as the *Star Wars* money began rolling in. "Now it's just something that's happening far away and I don't see it. Except if I want something, I can have it."

His newfound fortune meant the house could receive the kind of attention Woodrow Wilson Drive had missed out on. "We just spent four months working the garden," he was soon announcing. "When I say we, I mean my workers and my money."

The picture he painted was of a boy and his new train set. Yet the reality was a little sadder than that. In the aftermath of his breakup from Mary and the boys, the metaphor was a poignant one. As the sound of hammers and saws echoed along Benedict Canyon, Harrison was not just reconstructing a property. He was also rebuilding his life.

14

THE WHIP HAND

It is one of cinema history's more intriguingly Freudian footnotes that the thirty-three-year-old George Lucas and the thirty-one-year-old Steven Spielberg were building a sand castle when, in May 1977, they conceived the idea of collaborating on the most exuberant piece of *Boy's Own* escapism of their careers.

Both were in hiding from Hollywood on the island of Hawaii, Lucas exiled from the stresses of *Star Wars*, Spielberg hoping his new UFO abduction story, *Close Encounters of the Third Kind*, could help him recover the wunderkind status confirmed by the $458 million box-office bonanza that was *Jaws* and then let slip with his $40 million budget flop *1941*.

Knee-deep in sand at the Mauna Kea Hotel, Lucas wearing rubber gloves to protect himself from the sun, they looked the oddest of couples. Yet they made a perfect, paradoxical pair: two overgrown schoolboys with a mature genius for filmmaking. As they spent an afternoon constructing the Xanadu of all sand castles, their conversation inevitably turned to fantasies of the filmic variety. After listening to Spielberg's ambitions to attain control of James Bond—he had already tried, and failed, to interest Cubby Broccoli in turning the franchise over to him—the older man outlined an idea he had been working on since before *Star Wars*.

Lucas's story belonged to the era of 1930s matinee heroes, the age of cliff-hanger classics like *Spy Smasher*, *Tailspin Tommy*, and *Tim Tyler's Luck*. It set his imagined hero—an archaeologist playboy who fought Nazis by day and wooed women by night—in a plotline suggested by another San Francisco filmmaker, Phil Kaufman. Kaufman had been inspired by *Spear of Destiny*, an account of Hitler's obsession with religious artifacts. Their adventure pitted the Germans and the dashing academic—called Indiana after Marcia Lucas's Alaskan malamute (the surname veered between Smith and Jones)—in a race to find the Lost Ark of the Covenant.

As the tide swept in toward their sand castle, Spielberg extended its life by digging a moat. After another twenty minutes, listening to Lucas's story, he turned to his friend and said: "I'd love to do that."

Lucas shocked him with his response. "Well, I've retired. I'm not directing any more, so it's yours."

By late 1979, Lucas and Spielberg had struck a deal that shook the movie industry to its very core. As surely as the Pacific had washed away their Hawaiian sand castle, their audacity was now eroding the last vestiges of Hollywood's Old Order.

Dispensing with agents and middlemen, the two had written out on the pages of a school exercise book the terms they wanted to make what had by now become *Raiders of the Lost Ark*. Their lawyer Tom Pollock offered every studio an opportunity to obtain the finished film at a cost of $20 million, including $4 million for Lucas as producer-writer and $1.5 million for Spielberg as director. The revolutionary twist was that the studio would also pay for the lion's share of the film's distribution and guarantee Lucas and Spielberg a share of the profits as soon as the first dollar of gross profit, from the cinema rentals, had been earned. In effect, they would take all the risk while Lucas and Spielberg would rake in the profits. Only if the film made in excess of $60 million would the studio start getting rich too.

Many of Hollywood's older hands, including Lew Wasserman at Universal, were outraged by what came to be known as Lucas's "killer deal." Other, less secure, executives simply could not face turning down the best script anyone had seen in years and the coming together of the two brightest talents in Hollywood. If there was a single moment when New Hollywood finally triumphed over Old Hollywood, it came when Paramount chief Michael Eisner agreed to the epoch-making terms. One senior Hollywood voice was soon calling the deal "almost as innovative and implicit with change as the advent of sound."

By late 1979, with *Empire* behind him, Lucas was ready to begin work on what was already the most talked about film in years. When he and Spielberg assembled a team to begin preproduction, it hardly required a leap of the imagination to see who should play the bull-whip-wielding hero.

Lucas had commissioned the cartoon artist Jim Steranko to produce detailed drawings of his central characters and some of his key scenes. "There were four illustrations. One was of this man fighting under the wing of a plane with a big German, another was him on a black horse chasing a truck, another was of him in a temple with a bunch of stunt snakes, and a fourth was out in the desert with a battle going on," said Howard Kazanjian, hired by his friends as coexecutive producer.

"The character had a day-old beard and he had his pouch and he had his whip and the way he was standing . . . it was Harrison Ford. It *spelled* Harrison Ford!"

It appeared to everyone that the role had been dreamed up specifically with Harrison in mind. Yet over the ensuing months Spielberg and Lucas appeared to do everything they could to avoid casting him.

Harrison was tested for the role, along with, among others, television actor John Beck, later to find worldwide fame of his own as the suave Mark Graison in the hit television series *Dallas*. To both Lucas and Spielberg, the cons of casting Han Solo heavily outweighed the pros. There was his familiarity from the *Star Wars* films—Lucas did not want a well-known face—not to mention his reluctance to commit to three outings as Han Solo up front. Lucas was worried that Harrison would simply not be up for what Paramount were insisting would be at least a trilogy of films. "I wasn't sure about what Harrison was going to say about it," he recalled. "The biggest issue was that I had three scripts basically, and it was a three-picture deal, and Harrison was one of these 'I don't know if I ever want to sign a contract for three pictures' people."

Spielberg's doubts ran deeper, mirroring the less charitable murmurings of Hollywood. Could he do it? "Steven was not enamored of the idea," Kazanjian remembered.

Instead they cast their net far and wide. With a March 1980 start date looming, Lucas and Spielberg had been impressed by a young television actor named Tom Selleck. Tall, swarthily handsome, and athletic, he fitted the mind's-eye view both men had of Indiana. Selleck had starred in a TV pilot for Universal and CBS called *Magnum P.I.* It had not excited anyone, and the option committing him to a series was within weeks of lapsing.

"The show had sat there, and nobody wanted it. And the option was about to lapse," Lucas recalled. "But we were sort of desperate to get going."

Impatient to start work with Selleck, Lucas and Spielberg tried to secure his release from the option. Universal agreed, but when CBS learned that the hottest filmmakers in town were after the star of a discarded show, they reacted predictably.

"We called CBS and asked if he could be let out of his option agreement—it literally had about ten days to go," recalled Lucas. Over the following months Lucas heard many versions of the same story. CBS found the old *Magnum* tapes, reran them, and at the eleventh hour picked up its option. "We really were about to shoot; it was right at the last minute—and we lost our star."

Spielberg still needed convincing that Harrison was the man to step into the breach. "We got three pictures for Steven to look at, at his home," Kazanjian said. "One of which was that terrible picture he made in England. Steven came back one day and said, 'He's not bad,' but he added, 'I'm not going to say okay, George.' "

Eventually the director let Lucas decide. Instead, Spielberg chose Indiana's love interest, Marion Ravenwood, opting for the New York stage actress Karen Allen rather than Lucas's preference, Debra Winger, or his own current girlfriend, Amy Irving.

The duo found Harrison quietly fuming. Up at Benedict Canyon he had been growing more and more frustrated as he monitored the situation. "They could find me if they wanted me," he told anyone who suggested he push himself forward more aggressively after his test. When *Variety* prematurely broke the news that Selleck had been cast, he was furious.

By the time Lucas phoned, feigning composure with a "Steven and

I have been kicking around the idea that you might like to do this," Ford knew the truth of the matter.

Tom Selleck's loss became Harrison Ford's gain. And he made Lucas and Spielberg pay a heavy price for the treatment they had meted out. He sensed the strength of Indiana Jones as a role. "It was clearly the most dominant single character in any of George's films," he said later. But he also knew he held the whip hand.

As usual, Harrison turned up to meet Spielberg in what Fred Roos would have called a non-office frame of mind. His no-collar, no-tie approach to doing business was the first clue the two would get on just fine. Harrison's first demand was a rewrite. Indiana Jones's snappy dialogue was too close to Han Solo. "I didn't want Jones to become some kind of Professor Solo!"

Neither Lucas nor Spielberg could have been regarded as pushovers in the negotiating stakes. Even before the "killer" deal, Hollywood had been far more dazzled by the earthly imagination of Lucas's business brain than his visions of life in some far-flung corner of the cosmos. Spielberg fed off the adrenal excitement of negotiating. His sister, the screenwriter and producer Anne Spielberg, hated haggling with him. "He's a very tough bargainer. There are times I'd be tempted to take things other places, where I know that I'd get a better deal," she opined once after a couple of collaborations with her brother.

The sheer cheek of their deal with Paramount had been the talk of the entire town for weeks. In Harrison, however, both men met a formidable foe, someone who shared their iconoclasm in business as well as in art. George Lucas had witnessed his toughness even when he was on the breadline. When he and Fred Roos offered him the part of Bob Falfa in *American Graffiti*, it had been at the going "scale" rate of $485 a week. "Harrison wouldn't do it for scale. He stood up on his high horse," said Pat McQueeney. The argument went on for days, with Harrison haranguing Roos with phone calls along the lines of "I've got a wife and two kids to feed." After fine-combing their way through their tight-as-a-kettledrum budget, Roos and Lucas finally found another $15 a week to round his salary up to $500. "Okay," said Harrison. "I think that was all about respect," said Roos.

This time Harrison had the two titans over a barrel. When it came to the details of his contract for *Indiana Jones*, he drove the hardest bargain of his career. In return for a commitment to make three films, he demanded a seven-figure salary and a 7 percent share of the film's gross profits. He knew, of course, that there would be plenty of those.

When, weeks later, signed up and preparing for the role, he finally saw the Steranko drawings, he could not suppress a sly, lopsided smile. "If you look at those alongside stills of the film, it's very striking, the similarity between the two," he mused. "It's a strange thing . . ."

On May 21, 1980, four days short of *Star Wars*'s third anniversary, The Empire struck back with a vengeance. Despite George Lucas's fears that he would not recover the $33 million of his own money which he had invested in the sequel, it never looked back after a first day's business in which 125 of the 127 cinemas that screened the film smashed their existing house records. It went on to rake in $223 million *in America alone*. Lucas once more showed his generosity, distributing more than $5 million of his profits at every level of his growing empire, from stagehands to janitors.

Kershner's attention to detail was rewarded in the reviews, which almost universally preferred the look of *Empire* to the B-movie brashness of *Star Wars*. Kasdan and Brackett's cliff-hanger–crammed story left even Pauline Kael admitting that she indulged in her fair share of yelling and cheering. "I can hardly wait for the next one."

It was Harrison Ford who once more collected most of the acting plaudits. "His Han Solo steals the show," wrote Janet Maslin in the *New York Times*. "Mr. Ford slips easily into the film's comic-book conversational style, and he also brings a real air of tragedy to Han's fate."

In the spring of 1980, Harrison Ford prepared to take on the role of the daring Doctor Jones. Up in Benedict Canyon, the whine of the bandsaw gave way to the clang of the weight machine and the crack of the bullwhip.

Physically, Harrison had survived the first thirty-seven years of his life well enough, although he had little time for exercise regimes and gymnasiums. A natural athleticism and a hyperactive metabolism had kept him trim. "I am the only person in California who doesn't jog," he joked once. "People always ask me how I keep in shape, and I say being in movies is enough exercise for me." *Raiders* presented an entirely different challenge, however; to meet it he would need to be in the best condition of his life.

He had begun to take an interest in weight-training during filming on *Empire*. Dave Prowse, the boss of his own London gym, had given him and Billy Dee Williams instruction. To continue his training, members of the Coppola clan had recommended Jake Steinfeld, one of Hollywood's first personal trainers.

While he worked with Steinfeld on his physical fitness, stunt coordinator Glenn Randall provided bullwhip coaching. The ease with which he wielded Indiana Jones's most distinctive physical prop would be fundamental to establishing his credibility. Harrison spent long hours learning how to coil and uncoil the ten-foot length of leather. "I lashed myself about the head and shoulders for at least a couple of weeks before I really figured the thing out," he said later. The pain would pale in comparison with the physical torture that lay ahead.

The extent of the punishment became obvious immediately when shooting began in June 1980. In the fertile imaginations of Spielberg and Lucas, *Raiders* would be the film equivalent of a Disneyland roller coaster ride. The opening, pre-titles scene—set inside an ancient Peruvian temple, where Indiana avoids a succession of booby traps to "reclaim" a golden statue—set the tone. The sequence climaxes with Indiana being pursued—in classic *Perils of Pauline* style—by a giant, rolling, ball-shaped rock.

On the set, at dear old Elstree, Randall's job was to get Harrison in 95 percent of the nonscreen stunts. The first five minutes of the movie was evidence of how difficult his task would be.

"A lot of people thought it was a big phoney ball, but it was made of plaster of Paris and had to weigh several hundred pounds," said Randall. "If it had hit Harrison, I'm sure he would not have known the difference between a real one and a phoney one. It would still have done great damage."

Spielberg had his doubts as to whether his star should be attempting the stunt at all, let alone at the start of the shoot. "Glenn, is it safe?" he asked. The elation that rushed through the set when Harrison safely outran the $60,000 killer ball at the first attempt was tempered by the knowledge that Spielberg would need several takes. The director made Harrison race the ball ten times. "He won ten times and beat the odds; he was lucky and I was an idiot for letting him try," he said ruefully. Harrison was not surprised at what he saw in the rushes the next day. "I looked a little scared—I'd have been crazy not to be!" That was only the beginning.

Driving Spielberg, Lucas, and Kazanjian on was the knowledge that Paramount—wary of Spielberg's newly acquired reputation for profligacy post-*1941* and *Close Encounters*—had built severe penalty clauses in if the film went over its $20 million budget.

In London there were minor crises. The scenes inside the Ark's Egyptian resting place, the Well of Souls, took ten agonizing days. In the cause of realism, Spielberg insisted on flying 4,500 extra snakes in from Denmark to add to the thousands already on hand. When they arrived it was discovered that the antivenin flown in from India was two years out of date. The tension was not eased by protests from Susan Kubrick—daughter of Stanley, directing *The Shining* at the same location—who was distressed by the cruelty being meted out to the snakes.

The problems intensified when filming shifted to the suffocating heat of Tunisia. Harrison, like everyone else, developed dysentery. (To this day Pat McQueeney knows never to mention a job that involves a return there.)

Harrison's first lucky escape came during filming of one of the four original storyboarded scenes, in which Indiana fought an oversized Nazi in the shadow of a propellor-driven airplane loosed from its moorings. Rehearsals passed off perfectly, but during the first take Harrison lost his footing and his right toe was caught under the tire of the flying-wing plane, which then proceeded to climb up his tibia. Luckily the brakes worked—"Inches before my knee was crushed," he recalled later. It then took forty crewmen to rock the giant plane off his leg. Only the blistering, 130-degree heat, which had made the tires soft and pliable, saved him from a horrendous injury. "That was our closest call," Spielberg said later.

Spielberg's reputation as a director with little patience for the peccadillos of his actors was well known in Hollywood. If there had been any doubts about the place actors occupied in the director's universe, Karen Allen provided all the evidence anyone might have needed during the *Raiders* shoot. He threw snakes at her and set her dress on fire to produce more realistic screams in The Well of Souls scene. "He looks at actors as part of the scenery," she fumed afterward.

In Harrison, however, Spielberg came across an actor no longer willing to be dominated. Their creative tension became a form of filmic alchemy as they pushed each other to new heights.

Each had landed the first blows during a ten-hour flight from Los Angeles to London. Harrison insisted on working their way through the script, line by line, scene by scene. "By the time we got to Heathrow we'd worked out the film," he said later.

As clear as his own ideas were about how the film would *look*, Spielberg was willing to bow to Harrison's ideas for adding depth and humor to Indiana. Harrison appreciated Spielberg's openness; it contrasted with the battles he had had to fight earlier in his career. "With a lot of people, you have to sorta win the whole argument," he told Tony Crawley. "You have to make the case so strong that the other person has to give up completely. That's not so with Steve. If I have a little bit of an idea, he adds to it, then I can add to it and he adds to it again and it builds into something we both think is better than we had before. Or it becomes so outrageous we collapse on the floor laughing."

Harrison had soon imposed himself on his director. Many on the set were left with the clear impression that he directed himself. "Steven would say: 'What are you going to do this time, Harrison?' " said the veteran American actor Bill Hootkins, who played Major Eaton. Spielberg would then watch the rehearsal through his camera. "If he approved he would simply say, 'Fine.' And Ford would do it," added Hootkins.

Harrison's most celebrated contribution came five weeks into his dysentery and on a morning when everyone seemed ready to drop. After a series of skirmishes in an Arabian souk, Indy was scripted to face a giant, scimitar-wielding warrior. The complexities of managing a huge crowd and the pyrotechnics of the sword fight would have taken all day.

"Why don't we just shoot the fucker?" Harrison asked Spielberg.

"Fine," said his director, suffering like everyone else in the heat. And necessity became the mother of one of the movie's most inventive moments.

Such unheroic touches also ensured that Harrison moved away from the cocksureness of Solo. As far as Harrison was concerned, the simple act of slipping into the trademark Fred C. Dobbs hat and the battered leather jacket put distance between the two characters. "Different clothes, different guy—that's the way I feel." But with Lucas and Spielberg he was ever-vigilant about slipping into Solo-esque moments. Lucas's idealism about the character helped. He did not see him simply as a playboy, bounty-hunting antiquities and landing the girl à la James Bond.

"He has to be a person we can look up to. We are doing a role model for little kids," he would say. Harrison suggested lines of dialogue to broaden the audience's understanding of Indiana. In the Himalayan barroom reunion between Indy and Marion, Allen goads him with the line: "You're not the man you used to be."

Harrison added: "It's not the years, it's the mileage." The line was funny and informative, and light-years from Han Solo—from whose lips such self-deprecatory drollness would never have passed.

He provided another, even more mordant piece of humor when Sallah, Indy's Egyptian helper, played by John Rhys-Davies, asked what the hero's plans were at the end of a sequence when the Ark has slipped out of his grasp. "Don't ask *me*," Harrison ad-libbed. "I'm making this up as I go along."

His physical characterization proved equally sure-footed. By the end of the shoot, Randall and his stunt team could only compliment their star's fitness and dedication to the physical challenges.

Harrison's argument was that if he hadn't done the stunts, "there wouldn't have been much left for me to do." "I'm the biggest coward in the world," he would routinely tell Randall as the other man explained stunts to him. Yet sequences like the one in which he clung to the front of a moving truck, inches from the ground, a leg splayed out either side of a wheel, demonstrated either bravery or a cussed kind of madness Randall had rarely come across.

"It takes only a bad turn, a bad rock or a bad bump and you are in a lot of trouble," he said. "It's a highly specialized field. There are actors who would be more than willing to try a lot of things, but they would not possess the physical attributes that it takes to do them. Harrison just happens to be capable of doing them. He will have a go at a lot of things, and he'll spend a lot of time to learn what he has to do to get the job done, instead of just going out to do it."

Randall and his team were preparing to celebrate surviving the production unscathed when their star came closest to meeting his maker. Fittingly, the *Raiders* shoot ended where the idea had been born years earlier, on Kauai in Hawaii where Spielberg filmed the climax of the opening sequence. The scene required Indiana, fleeing head-hunting natives, to swing Tarzan-style toward a waiting seaplane and clamber in as it made its takeoff. At Harrison's own insistence, as the plane eased its way into the air the door of the plane was left open so as to reveal his feet dangling in the air. Perhaps fired up by the prospect of finishing the film, none of the attendant experts saw fit to mention the potentially destabilizing effects this might have on the plane's aerodynamics . . .

The crew, and a horrified Melissa, watched helplessly as the plane reached no more than twenty feet, veered off over the treetops and dived into the overgrowth. Harrison and the pilot emerged unscathed—as, miraculously, did the plane. "But we had to do it again, of course," he joked.

During a rare trip to Los Angeles in 1981, Peter Mayhew arranged to meet his *Star Wars* sidekick Han Solo for dinner. The two men agreed to rendezvous outside Mayhew's hotel in Westwood. When a crew-cut figure in dark glasses, a battered black leather jacket and even more scruffy blue jeans pulled up at the wheel of a racy sports car, Mayhew identified the vehicle—but not its driver. "I thought, 'Who the hell's *this?*' It was a black 1956 Porsche—a beauty," he said.

As Mayhew turned away, he heard a blast on the horn, followed by a familiar bass voice. "Peter, where are ya?"

"It was Harrison. I recognized the voice, but I didn't recognize him," he said.

Harrison's chameleon-like ability to blend into the background was well practiced. Blessed with a less obvious physiognomy than Mark Hamill and Carrie Fisher, even his friends could not always pick him out. "What's so amazing about him is that on the street you will not recognize him," said Steven Spielberg.

As he shared a dinner with his *Millennium Falcon* shipmate, Mayhew detected a subtly significant change in Harrison. When he had first met him, he had been the embodiment of the buccaneering Solo, a cocky renegade, edgy and restless. Five years after the first flush of *Star Wars* success, he seemed a less tortured, calmer man.

"It was a complete change," said Mayhew. "We went out to eat somewhere in Hollywood. Harrison was a completely different character. He had mellowed; I think he was more contented, and it showed."

The prime reason for his newfound composure was sitting with him and Mayhew that night. Melissa's steadying influence had become increasingly apparent to his friends. To the occasionally broody and bad-tempered Harrison, she was a perfect foil. "She sets a good example. She's a happy person," he confessed once.

Melissa's Hollywood childhood had left her with few illusions about the city and the machinations of the industry about which a vast percentage of its citizens obsessed. "Melissa's very smart, very calm, very knowledgeable about the business, but not into it," said Fred Roos. Harrison readily admitted: "She's better at dealing with all that than I am."

One of the few occasions when she failed to retain her composure came in October 1980, when she first saw a photograph of herself splashed across a page of the tabloid *National Enquirer*.

The paper broke the news that she and Han Solo were an item under the blaring headline: HARRISON "STAR WARS" FORD AND TOP HOLLYWOOD SCRIPTWRITER TO MARRY.

Melissa had contributed to the report by confirming their romance in an interview. "You can definitely say we are together," she said as *The Black Stallion* opened. What had distressed her was the way the report built on that to dissect their relationship in lurid detail. "Harrison was a real ladykiller before he met Melissa. He would chase anything in a skirt," said a source, identified only by that ubiquitous newspaper title "a close friend." "But since the day they started dating, he hasn't even glanced at another woman." And: "Harrison fell madly in love with Melissa the first time he set eyes on her. Melissa didn't pay much attention to him, but he was persistent."

Harrison took this latest taste of tabloid infamy with a pinch of salt. "I didn't think there was anything juicy enough for people to give a shit," he shrugged afterward. "Melissa isn't very thrilled about it, though."

By now, Melissa had moved into the house up on Benedict Canyon. Unlike Mary, she was no queen in the kitchen. "We specialize in what we call 'meals in minutes,' " Harrison joked at the time.

Early in 1981 Melissa and Harrison made a little more effort in the kitchen as the English director Ridley Scott became a frequent dinner guest. Scott was in Los Angeles preparing to film *Blade Runner*, an adaptation of the futuristic novel *Do Androids Dream of Electric Sheep?* by Philip K. Dick. After initially refusing the role, Harrison had agreed to play the lead role of Deckard.

Over convivial dinners he and Scott discussed their ideas for the movie, due to start shooting on the Warners Burbank lot at the beginning of March. Soon, however, relations between the two men would be far from cordial . . . and Harrison would be only too grateful for Melissa's calming influence.

The meteoric speed with which he had risen from making commercials for the likes of British Airways to directing some of Hollywood's most ambitious movies had left the forty-one-year-old Scott shaking his head in quiet disbelief. "I think it's remarkable that people will give you $10 million to go and get your rocks off," he said as his career took off with his stylish period piece *The Duellists* in 1978.

Scott's pursuit of Harrison Ford to star in one of his films had begun in London at about the same time. While the *Empire* shoot had been underway at Elstree, Scott had offered him the role of Dallas, the ill-fated captain of the space tanker *Nostromo* in his second major feature, *Alien*. Harrison's reply had been along the lines of "Oh no, not another space pilot!" (Tom Skerritt wound up playing Dallas.)

Undeterred, Scott had then tried to cast him again, during filming of *Raiders* in London, this time suggesting he take the lead in *Blade Runner*. Scott had looked beyond Han Solo and Indiana Jones to the more sinister performances Harrison had given in *Apocalypse Now* and *The Conversation*. The "watchful, rather menacing" quality of Stett and Lucas seemed ideally suited for the part of Rick Deckard, the ambiguous anti-hero of Dick's bleak vision of the year 2020, the eponymous "Blade Runner" detailed to dispose of rogue human cyborgs or "replicants."

Harrison had turned him down a second time because he could not face another stretch on the other side of the Atlantic. As filming was switched to Burbank, however, Scott struck third-time lucky.

Harrison was soon ruing the decision. Even before shooting began on March 9, 1981, cracks had begun to appear in the relationship.

Scott had originally conceived Deckard as a "Philip Marlowe-style gumshoe"—right down to his wide-brimmed hat. He had even, briefly, considered the veteran Robert Mitchum for a reprise of his sleepy-eyed turn in *Farewell My Lovely*, six years before.

Early word on *Raiders of the Lost Ark* was strong enough for Harrison to sense that Indiana Jones would be a hit. He had no interest in playing a character whose physical props were so close. "Ridley from the beginning had wanted the character to wear a big felt hat along with the raincoat. I had just worn a big felt hat in *Raiders*; I wanted to change my physical appearance," he told Tony Crawley afterward.

When Harrison suggested he play Deckard with a close-cut haircut, Scott was equally unconvinced. "I wanted to give the impression of a character who had given up on himself, was unconscious of his appearance." Scott gave in eventually, but only on condition that he could be there to oversee the process.

"He was afraid it would make me look less gorgeous," Harrison joked. He did not find it funny at the time, however. The process took four painstaking hours—"with long pauses along the way for consideration by Ridley."

Once filming got underway, Harrison's frustrations deepened. After the exhilaration of collaborating with Spielberg and Lucas on *Raiders*, he found Scott's directorial style remote and visually obsessive. The fact that Scott's vision would eventually produce one of the most striking portrayals of the future in cinema history mattered little to Harrison. Dick's book was set forty years in the future, in a Los Angeles that had finally collapsed into anarchy. On Scott's stunning sets, designed by Laurence G. Paull, acid rain teemed down onto rat-infested streets, giant electronic billboards flashed with the faces of Coke-drinking geishas, police flew overhead in grubby jetmobiles.

If George Lucas and Irvin Kershner had occasionally irritated Harrison by their overattentiveness to machine over man, Scott represented a twenty-four-hour-a-day pain in the proverbial. As Harrison spent ages cooped up in his trailer, Scott fussed and fiddled, tweaked and tinkered with every microscopic detail. His seeming lack of interest in his actors was exacerbated by his insistence on using his own hand-held camera during many of the shots.

As the shoot progressed, Harrison became frustrated that the central relationship at the heart of the story, between Deckard and the replicant girl Rachael, played by Sean Young, seemed superfluous. "Harrison would shoot one take with Rachael, then fifty with the technology," said one friend.

"He felt that Ridley Scott did a marvelous job with the technical aspect of the project, but that the relationship between Deckard and Rachael was not explored in enough detail to give the movie the kind of heart that he thought it should have," explained Pat McQueeney, who fielded much of Ford's anger afterward.

The loss seemed even more of a pity, given the terrific on-screen chemistry Harrison and Young were displaying. In a world of repressed savagery, Deckard and Rachael's passions were almost animalistic. Brief they may have been, but Sean Young's romantic scenes with Harrison left their mark. "Every time he kissed me, the makeup people had to be all over me to repair the damage. What a beard that guy has! He completely tore my face up." Harrison's icy remoteness off-screen and his passion on it, left the impressionable Young as dizzy as Carrie Fisher. "He's one of the sexiest men I've ever met," she cooed to *People* magazine.

A schedule almost exclusively made up of night shoots did little to help Harrison's fraying nerves. As on *American Graffiti*, the sleeplessness and disorientation of his unnatural routine began to unhinge him a little. "It was very difficult to work on," said Harrison later. "Night filming . . . drives everybody a little wacko after a while."

Slowly relations between star and director cooled. One night, as Scott was puttering, for the umpteenth time, with a piece of mechanized minutiae, Harrison snapped. Only the calming, persuasive voices of others present prevented him from subjecting his director to the same treatment Richard Dreyfuss had received a decade earlier on his darkest *American Graffiti* night.

"It was a grueling movie, and Ridley demanded so many takes that it finally wore Harrison out," one colleague explained. "I know he was ready to kill Ridley. He really would have taken him on if he hadn't been talked out of it." As filming on *Blade Runner* came to a close, Burbank breathed a collective sigh of relief.

15

A FREED MAN

O n a pleasant early-autumn evening in September 1981, the
well-heeled habitués of the elegant French resort of Deauville
witnessed a charming family scene unfolding in the ornate
courtyard of the Hotel Royal.

Leaning into the camera lens, their arms outstretched like some bar-
bershop trio, two young men and their father struck a theatrical pose
for an enterprising French photographer. Each wore a tuxedo, a black
bowtie, and variations of the same square-jawed, all-American smile.
It was a memorable shot, in more ways than one.

Only one major detail distinguished the senior member of the group
from his beaming offspring. Harrison Ford's newly acquired beard helped
mask the mixture of emotions he felt. He could not have looked prouder
as he showed off his sons Willard and Ben for the first and, as it turned
out, last time in public during a visit to the American Film Festival
held in the town each autumn. "We are best friends," he volunteered
at the time. "I think—I like to think—I'm a fun dad." But behind his
playful expression lurked an enduring sense of sadness and failure.

Since separating from Mary, Harrison had spent as much time as he
could with the boys. Most weekends when he was in Los Angeles, Ben
and Willard would make the five-mile trip to spend time at Benedict
Canyon. There they would watch TV, go to the movies, or play one-

on-one basketball in the quiet street. For Harrison, however, there was never enough time. After finishing *Blade Runner* he was seeking to make amends for years of missed birthdays, Little League baseball games, and family get-togethers. He had made a commitment to spend six months off work, concentrating on his relationship with Willard, now twelve, and Ben, ten, before returning once more to London for the third and final *Star Wars* film, *Return of the Jedi*, in January 1982.

"It would take an act of Congress to get me to work before *Jedi*," he told reporters at Deauville, the final stop-off on a tour of Europe that had already taken in Venice and Paris. "I haven't had six months with the kids for a long time."

His words were not strictly true, of course. He was working at both Deauville and Venice, where he had been helping boost the openings of *Raiders of the Lost Ark*. His presence demanded public appearances and interviews. Perhaps it was his proximity to the boys—in one early-morning interview with Tony Crawley of *Cinema* magazine they were literally asleep in an adjoining room—but this latest round of publicity nudged him toward the sort of self-analysis even his friends found hard to elicit. In more than one of the many interviews he gave to publicize *Raiders* he acknowledged that during the darkest days of his marriage, it was not only the boys who were growing up.

"I'm a late bloomer. I resisted maturity because I had to learn to do my job, which takes a long time," he told the veteran British journalist David Lewin. "I still resist maturity. I like to play.

"I don't feel great about the divorce, but maybe I was hard to live with," he told George Haddad Garcia of *Photoplay*. Harrison conceded that his temperament had been a major cause. "I probably wasn't easy to be married to," he told Lewin. "I respond to a sort of barometric pressure, and this is a stressful occupation. I show it. I can be moody."

He admitted he had not, somehow, been up to the job of being a father. "I was moody at home and somewhat aggressively cynical or bitter with people I was working with," he explained on another occasion. "I was definitely not Mr. Sweetness and Light. I was as much of a pain to them as they were to me. And, frankly, I was an inadequate husband and father in my first marriage," he added on another.

As age and experience equipped him with greater hindsight, he admitted that in the midst of his battle to make Hollywood accept him on his own terms, he had lost sight of his duty to his wife and family. "In my youthful ignorance my need not to be dominated was greater than my sense of responsibility." He had already sworn never to repeat the error.

Ben and Willard could certainly not fault the five-star treatment they were getting in Europe that autumn. Their obvious enjoyment of their grand tour, along with the triumphant reception *Raiders* was receiving, went a long way toward lifting the depression their father had felt during the troubled *Blade Runner* shoot.

Raiders of the Lost Ark became an instant worldwide hit. From the moment Spielberg unfurled his first innovative image, fading the star-encrusted Paramount mountain into a mist-covered Andean peak, to his last eye-popping assault on the senses as the Ark's terrible secret was revealed, audiences everywhere were enthralled.

Vincent Canby in the *New York Times* led the plaudits, describing *Raiders* as "one of the most deliriously funny, ingenious and stylish American adventure movies ever made."

The reception was equally good in Europe. At Venice, home to one of Europe's more sniffily selective film festivals, it had won a thunderous welcome. France and Deauville reacted, if anything, even more enthusiastically.

Harrison had already watched the film three times back in America, where Paramount's Michael Eisner and Jeffrey Katzenberg had sensed their winning hand well in advance of the June 11 American opening. Advance word on the film was so strong that shares in Paramount's then parent company, Gulf and Western, rose two and a half points.

He had watched *Star Wars* with his sons countless times—"Until even I could speak the other characters' lines," he joked. *Raiders'* appeal to the same audience was the key to its box-office business. Already aware that his seven percent of the gross would earn him several million over the coming years, Harrison made no bones about the fact that it was Willard, Ben, and millions of adolescents like them who were making him an extremely wealthy man. "It's the teens, the kids who have given me this success," he admitted.

Melissa was with them as they traveled around Europe. Thanks to the civility of the divorce, the boys showed no signs of resentment toward her. A natural with children since her baby-sitting days, she reveled in their rumbustious company. "I get all the pleasure of Harrison's kids without having to discipline them or lay down the law," she said.

Melissa's closeness to the boys had indirectly helped revive her writing career. After the success of *The Black Stallion* she had worked with Coppola and writer Stephen Zito on *The Escape Artist*, an uninspiring adaptation of David Wagoner's novel about a young, Houdini-like entertainer. She had left the film disillusioned and suffering from writer's block. When she joined Harrison on the *Raiders* set her confidence was at rock bottom. Her spirits were so low in London she had told Kathleen Kennedy, one of Spielberg's trusted assistants, with whom she had forged a close friendship, that she had decided to abandon writing altogether.

An experienced hand on-set, she traveled to Tunisia instead, providing Harrison with an anchor, helping out as she could. As a former member of Coppola's coterie, she had known George Lucas well. But as filming wore on, she formed an even closer rapport with Spielberg. The latter, suffering another difficult patch in his personal life and desperately lonely as he worked punishing hours in an utterly alien environment, began to offer Melissa an intriguing insight into his mind. At one point he told her how, in the North African desert, he had invented an imaginary friend for himself as he slept in his tent. Later, over dinner, a more upbeat Spielberg told Melissa how the experience had inspired an idea for a movie. He began outlining the story of an extraterrestrial stranded on earth and befriended by a lonely young boy.

Spielberg had been impressed by Melissa's work on *The Black Stallion*. He particularly liked the way she had developed a believable relationship between a child and another creature, in this case, a horse. He had already engaged another writer, John Sayles, to develop the story, but as the dinner drew to a close, he wondered whether Melissa would like to turn the idea into a full-blown script. Her energy levels drained by a combination of her writer's block and dysentery, Melissa shook her head mournfully. "Thank you very much, but I've decided never to write again," she told him.

She instantly regretted the decision but was then too embarrassed to mention it again. When Spielberg repeated the offer days later while out with Melissa searching for scorpions in the desert, he got a differ-

ent reply. Harrison had encouraged her to accept the offer if it ever
came up again. This time even the scorpions would have been hard-
pushed to sting with such speed.

Melissa started writing on October 10, 1980, back at Benedict
Canyon. At the end of each week she would meet Spielberg in the
Marina Del Rey cutting room where he was editing *Raiders*. A first
draft for the script, called *A Boy's Life*, was finished within eight weeks.

Melissa saw the film as the story of two lonely characters from other
ends of the universe. "I was immediately sold on the story but not on
any sort of sci-fi level," she explained later. "It was the idea of an alien
creature who was benevolent, tender, emotional, and sweet that
appealed to me. And the idea of the creature striking up a relationship
with a child who came from a broken home was very affecting."

In Ben and Willard she had the perfect models for the human half
of the relationship. Melissa tuned her well-trained ear to their conversation as she wrote. "I've never had a good ear for adult dialogue,
but I've got a great ear for kids' dialogue," she said later. "I'm good at
how they talk because it's how I talk, basically. All the boys in the
movie are based on boys I know, including Harrison's."

By the time Harrison, Melissa, and the boys returned from Europe,
Spielberg had begun shooting Melissa's script, by now transformed, via
a second title, *E.T. and Me*, into *E.T. The Extra-Terrestrial*. Filming
began in Northridge, California, on September 18, 1981. Nervous of
news leaking out that he was working on another "alien" movie, Spielberg issued a low-key announcement that he was making a children's
story using the original title *A Boy's Life*. With security so important,
he kept as much of the production as possible within his tight-knit
family of friends and associates. Melissa was invited to be associate producer. The role involved her choosing and rehearsing the younger
members of the cast and overseeing some of the postproduction special effects. Melissa threw herself into the job with a vengeance, working every day with Henry Thomas, Drew Barrymore, and the film's
other young actors.

With his girlfriend so tied up, Harrison volunteered his services too.
So much for the act of Congress. Spielberg offered him a tiny cameo
as a school principal in a scene in which Elliott is disciplined after
becoming drunk in "emotional sympathy" with E.T.

Ironically, Harrison's claim to a place in another of history's biggest box-office films was denied him by his girlfriend. Melissa reluctantly agreed to play the school nurse who dragged Elliott before the principal. A combination of her crippling camera shyness and the intimidating presence of her famous boyfriend reduced the debutante actress to a nervous wreck. Her long, slim hands—the models for artist Carlo Rambaldi's model of E.T.—shook violently through every take. Afterward she begged Spielberg to leave the scene on his cutting-room floor. For the first time since *Zabriskie Point*, Harrison suffered the indignity of ending up there too . . .

On the rare occasions he subjected himself to public psychoanalysis, George Lucas frequently found himself admitting that his affection for Han Solo and Indiana Jones ran deep.

The shy, slightly built writer, withdrawn, wimpish, and unpopular with girls at his high school, projected his unfulfilled dreams and ambitions into the heroic lives of the gung-ho space pilot and the indefatigable archaeologist. They represented all he was not. "Those characters are my alter ego," he said.

At the end of 1981, Harrison Ford was not, therefore, in the least surprised when his suggestion that Lucas kill off one of his second selves was turned down flat. Filming of *Return of the Jedi* was due to begin at Elstree in January 1982. Once more the project was shrouded in a veil of secrecy even the CIA might have thought excessive.

As Harrison entered into negotiations with Lucas about playing Solo, he was adamant that the character should move forward in some way. When he read the script, once more by Lawrence Kasdan, he was even more convinced that the third installment needed something dramatic.

At least Han's carbon-freezing in *Empire*—insurance in case Harrison had walked away from the third film—had guaranteed *Jedi's* opening act would revolve around his return to the story. His rescue from the court of the intergalactic villain Jabba the Hut was the first set piece of Kasdan's screenplay, but the rest of the film seemed to offer nothing more than the answer to the riddle of Han, Luke, and Leia's love triangle—Leia, it turned out, was Luke's twin sister—Leia's unveiling as a Jedi, "the other one" obliquely referred to in *Empire*, and another showy shoot-out involving a planet-sized Death Star.

Harrison believed there should be more emotion to the story. "I was convinced that Han Solo should die," he said afterward. "I told George: 'He's got no mama, no papa, and he's got no story. Let's kill him and give some weight to this thing.' "

Lucas, however, had become deeply protective of his characters. Kasdan had suggested the same course of action earlier in the writing process and had been at the receiving end of an eccentric Lucas lecture. "You are a product of the 1980s. You don't go around killing people. It's not nice," he told him, somehow overlooking the massive body counts in both *Star Wars* and *Empire*.

Lucas was used to Harrison's feisty contributions to story conferences. "Harrison has always had opinions about things. Harrison is not someone who doesn't question what's going on. And so he's been very involved," he said.

On this occasion, despite the tigerishness of his argument, Harrison had to accept his position in the *Star Wars* chain of command. "That was the one thing I was unable to convince George of," he shrugged during filming.

His idea was a reflection of his attitude toward the series that had made him a star. Morally, he felt committed to finishing the job he had started in the becreatured cantina at Elstree in 1976, but he made no secret of the fact that he was unhappy at what he regarded as his enslavement to George Lucas's dark Empire. "Massa George says Ah kin go at the end of eighty-five—a freed man," he said, semi-joking with Lucas's biographer Dale Pollock in 1981.

At least by January 1982 he could start counting the days—all seventy-eight of them. Lucas had hired Welshman David Marquand, maker of the admired World War II drama *Eye of the Needle* to direct the movie. Marquand found Harrison as opinionated as ever: "He doesn't suffer fools gladly. If you don't know what you're going to do on the day, he gets a little confused and upset."

Harrison's boredom was obvious to those who saw him on-set. "There is no difference between doing this kind of film and playing *King Lear*. The actor's job is exactly the same: dress up and pretend," he yawned to *Time* magazine.

The pretending seemed more ludicrous than ever on *Jedi*, as the creature count surpassed anything seen on the previous movie. Part of the $8 million budget had been devoted to devising an entire language for the tiny, furry inhabitants of the moon of Endor, the Ewoks. Harrison, Carrie Fisher, and Mark Hamill were left feeling an even more minor part of the equation than they had on *Star Wars* itself. "Special-effects movies are hard on actors," Hamill said, summing up all their feelings. "You find yourself giving an impassioned speech to a big lobster in a flight suit."

The most tangible consolation during filming came when—after Elstree—location work was switched to America for the first time in the *Star Wars* cycle. The redwood forests of Crescent City in northern California and the barren Buttercup Valley in Arizona doubled for Endor and Luke's old home, the desert planet Tatooine, respectively.

The arrival of the *Star Wars* machine on American soil brought its own set of headaches. "Boring Wood" it may have been, but the beauty of Borehamwood was that it was *secure*. During the final weeks of his *Star Wars* career, Harrison was officially employed on a horror movie called *Blue Harvest*. Curious onlookers were greeted by burly men in T-shirts reading *Blue Harvest: Horror Beyond Imagination*. On the morning "call sheets,"—where Hamill was listed as "Martin"—for the first time in years, strangers referred to Han Solo as "Harry."

Lucasfilm even went so far as to announce filming on *Jedi* had actually switched to Germany. But the ruse lasted less than two weeks. After the *Los Angeles Times* reported the lengths Lucas was going to, to film secretly in his home state, crowds began to gather every day. Harrison Ford fans were the most persistent, screaming his name incessantly whenever he loped into the viewfinders of their long-lens cameras.

The end of the *Star Wars* saga was strangely muted. There was sadness, particularly among those whose lives were still inextricably linked to the films. "There was a party at the end of each shoot. It was very sad, but we did at least have a feeling that we had done something that was going to be in the history of the cinema for ever," said Peter Mayhew.

Mayhew and some of his British colleagues were anxious to know when Lucas would begin the next phase of what he had long since conceded was a nine-part series—and what part they might play in his plans. "Knowing that there were going to be another six movies, a lot us were wondering, 'Will this carry on?' " said Mayhew. "And 'Will we be in it?' "

Lucas was weary of the strain, however, and remained noncommittal. "I look upon the three *Star Wars* films as chapters in one book," he said, hinting, as he had done before, that he might now retire. "Now the book is finished and I have put it on the shelf."

For Harrison Ford, too, it marked the closing of the most eventful chapter in his life—one that had changed that life beyond all recognition. On-screen his inconsistent performances as Han Solo—from hungry cowboy through to world-weary gun for hire—reflected the emotional turbulence he himself had experienced. In many ways the trilogy mirrored the three-act mid-life drama that forged the Harrison Ford who would emerge post–*Star Wars*. In the six-year period between his arrival at Elstree Studios in 1976 and the end of principal photography on *Return of the Jedi* in 1982, he had, thanks to Lucas, won a victory over the cold and arrogant empire that was Old Hollywood. He had enjoyed the freedom and an exhilarating, life-enriching adventure. Yet his triumph had come at a huge personal price.

Life after Han Solo would be very different. "I will never forgive the film business for what it did to me," he warned at the height of his bitterness. He was to be as good as his word.

PART THREE

*"We all have big changes
in our lives that are more or less
a second chance."*

Harrison Ford

16

NEW BEGINNINGS

On the evening of Saturday, March 12, 1983, Harrison and Melissa gave the Hollywood paparazzi a rare opportunity to photograph them on the town together. Looking distinctly ill at ease in evening dress, they attended the Directors Guild of America's annual awards dinner at the Beverly Hilton Hotel. Such occasions were becoming commonplace for Melissa. The previous October she had collected a "New Generation" writer's award from the Los Angeles Film Critics Association. Four weeks before the DGA dinner, on February 17, she had been nominated for an Academy Award. Her recognition was part of the extraordinary success of Spielberg's *E.T.*

Since its premiere at Cannes the previous May, the film had seemingly masked an entire planet in tears. ("We were crying for our lost selves," the novelist Martin Amis wrote, dabbing his cold eyes in the dark.) Harrison was one of the few immune to the phenomenon. Spielberg was apparently deeply offended when he called the puckish E.T. "that ugly little fuck." He spared most of his admiration for Melissa's eye for detail. Elliott's habit of wearing thermal underwear at all times had come from Willard.

As the Hollywood award season moved toward its climax, the pre-Oscar buzz generated by the 500-plus guests at the Beverly Hilton drowned out the sound of the evening's entertainment, Bernadette

Peters and the Nelson Riddle orchestra. Nowhere was the conversation more animated than at Spielberg's table, where Harrison and Melissa joined his party.

The champagne atmosphere soon fell flat, unfortunately, as Spielberg lost the latest round in his ongoing battle with the year's other heavyweight awards contender, Sir Richard Attenborough's *Gandhi*. The effusive Sir Richard stopped at their table en route to the stage to give Spielberg a consoling hug. Behind their backslapping and smiles each man knew that only twice in history had the DGA winner failed to go on to collect the ultimate prize, an Oscar.

The mood at Spielberg's table might have lifted if the director and the other members of his extended filmmaking family had been let in on the secret Harrison and Melissa kept to themselves all night. Instead, they had to learn how the man who made Indiana Jones flesh and the woman who wrote *E.T.* planned to spend the following Monday morning like everyone else in Hollywood—in their newspapers, long after the ink had dried on the couple's marriage certificate.

By Tinseltown standards it was almost a nonevent. In comparison, Harrison's Wisconsin wedding, nineteen years earlier, had been a riot of ostentation. Days before he had quietly organized the marriage license in the chambers of a judge at the Santa Monica Courthouse. As the court started a new week's business, he and Melissa slipped the Porsche into a parking space and themselves into the chambers. At the end of a simple, fifteen-minute ceremony, they exchanged wedding bands and single white roses, thanked the courthouse staff for their discretion, jumped back into the car, and roared home along Sunset Boulevard to Benedict Canyon, where their parents joined in a small celebration.

Their timing was fiendish. In the final days before the Oscars, Hollywood was a rabbit caught in the headlight glare of its most glamorous event. Only the explosion of a small-scale thermonuclear device in Burbank would have been capable of wiping the prerace predictions off the front pages of the trades and their statuette-fixated neighbors on the L.A. newsstands.

On April 11, Melissa attended the awards where she—like Spielberg—was predictably flattened by the *Gandhi* steamroller. Attenborough's epic won eight major Oscars to *E.T.*'s three minor ones, including the screenplay award, which went to John Briley. As Spielberg memorably lamented that "popcorn had been beaten by history," Melissa, at least, was guaranteed both congratulations and commiserations.

The newlyweds managed to survive the first two weeks of their marriage without detection. When the media did catch up with them, however, it made up for lost time. From *Time* to *Cosmopolitan*—who cringingly installed them as "couple of the month"—to the *National Enquirer*, the news that Hollywood had a new golden couple was seized on with glee.

The *Enquirer* speculated that they had tied the knot in order to start a family. "They told me the only reason they got married was to have a baby," a "friend" told the tabloid. Harrison was also reported as having told friends: "I loved her from the day we met. We're going to grow old together." Melissa reportedly added: "Just having a marriage license doesn't change anything. Being at home with Harrison is always a honeymoon!"

Such quotes may have lacked the ring of even semiauthenticity, but there was no doubting the happiness the shy, sensitive screenwriter and the swashbuckling star of the Spielberg-Lucas era had found together. He may have had little interest in sharing his wedding day with the world, but in the early months and years of his marriage, Harrison made no secret of the calming influence Melissa had brought to his troubled emotional life. "When I married Melissa, I found that it was such a pleasure not to be angry and not to have that bitterness running around in my system. I no longer get moody or aggressive. I don't get crazy anymore," he said of the relationship. "Melissa and I have mutual respect for and tolerance of each other's foibles and failures."

Mary may have been a faultless mother and homemaker, but with her knowledge of the workings of her husband's industry, Melissa added another dimension to his life. Distrustful and cynical by nature, he had always relied on his own judgment. "Without minimizing the importance of anybody else, I've always made my own decisions," he said once. "I don't need a rubber stamp to continually check against." But Melissa provided a sounding board even he could have utter faith in. As he put it once: "My wife and I are very close. After we've viewed a day's filming, I'll ask her, 'Was that scene really dogshit?' and she'll say, 'Yeah, that really was dogshit.' "

Melissa in return treated her husband's fame with an even more ironic arch of an eyebrow than he did. Asked once how she dealt with being married to a "sex symbol" she said, "It never crosses my mind . . . I just joke about it—most times when he looks really rotten, like when he hasn't shaved for a while." As for being condemned to a future of flashbulbs and television cameras whenever she appeared publicly on his arm, she promised she would continue doing what she had done before she became Mrs. Harrison Ford. "I know just how far back to lean to get out of the picture."

Melissa's successes with *E.T.* had contrasted with the flat performance of *Blade Runner* at the box office.

The Ladd Company and Warner Bros. first detected problems after negative test screenings in Denver and Dallas. The dark, humorless, sometimes oppressive mood of the movie did not live up to the audiences' expectations of a Harrison Ford film.

The test cards were used as justification for major changes—including a new, less ambiguous ending and different versions of a Philip Marlowe–like narration by Harrison.

Ridley Scott's reaction to the changes was "Absolute nonsense! . . . Part and parcel of the expectation with Harrison Ford is action adventure, where it's nonstop. It's not an obvious action adventure film. It's a difficult film," he fumed.

Harrison was equally unhappy about being dragged back into a recording studio. "I was compelled by contract to record five or six different versions of the narration, each of which was found wanting on a storytelling basis," he moaned later.

In Scott's deliberately opaque original ending, the audience would be left believing it possible that Deckard, too, was a replicant, doomed to a premature death. A dream sequence featuring a unicorn set up a payoff delivered by James Edward Olmos and an origami model of the mythical creature. A new, more hopeful cut, minus the unicorn and ending with Deckard and Rachael gliding to freedom over open countryside—stock footage from Stanley Kubrick's *The Shining*—was substituted to erase any suggestion of Deckard's impending demise.

"That's the trouble with Harry." Harry Ford (left) with his schoolfriend Dennis Zetek. PHOTO © DENNIS ZETEK

"Boy least likely to succeed." Maine East graduation, 1960. PHOTO © MAINE EAST HIGH SCHOOL

The Ford family home in Park Ridge. PHOTO © GARRY JENKINS

Stagestruck. Ford (second from right) in the Tower Trotters.
Maine East High School, 1960. (*above*) PHOTO © RIPON COLLEGE

Backstage at the Red Barn, 1964. (*opposite, top*)
PHOTO © RIPON COLLEGE

Ladykiller. Harrison as Mack the Knife at Ripon's Red Barn, 1963. (*below*)
PHOTO © RIPON COLLEGE

Mary Louise Marquardt, Ripon, 1964.

Secret lovers. Harrison and Mary Lee Franke in *The Fantastics*, 1963.

Buckskin Bill. Looking bemused as one of The Not So Magnificent Seven in *Journey to Shiloh*. (*above*) PHOTO © MCA

A star at war. Ford as Barnsby in *Force Ten From Navarone*. (*left*) PHOTO COURTESY TONY CRAWLEY COLLECTION, © COLUMBIA PICTURES

The return of rent-a-hippie. Harrison lays down the law to Elliott Gould in *Getting Straight*. (*below*) PHOTO © COLUMBIA PICTURES

As Tommy in *The Frisco Kid*. (*above*) PHOTO COURTESY TONY CRAWLEY COLLECTION, © WARNER BROS.

Carpenter star. As Kenny in *Heroes*. (*right*) PHOTO COURTESY TONY CRAWLEY COLLECTION, © MCA

James Dean in a starship. Han Solo—the role that rocketed Ford to stardom. (*below*) PHOTO TONY CRAWLEY COLLECTION, © LUCASFILM LTD.

Blade Runner
PHOTO TONY
CRAWLEY COLLECTION,
© WARNER BROS.

"I'd rather kiss a Wookie." Harrison and Carrie Fisher in *The Empire Strikes Back*. (*opposite, top*) PHOTO TONY CRAWLEY COLLECTION, © LUCASFILM LTD.

On the town with Melissa Mathison in New York. (*opposite, left*)
PHOTO © REX FEATURES

"Don't tell me not to worry—I always worry." As Allie Fox in *The Mosquito Coast*. (*opposite, right*)
PHOTO © SIPA-PRESS/REX FEATURES

"And what am I—chopped liver?" With Sean Connery on the set of *The Last Crusade*. (*left*)
PHOTO © REX FEATURES

Harrison and Malcolm Ford at a New York Knicks basketball game, 1996. (*right*)

Ferreting out the truth. As Rusty Sabich in *Presumed Innocent*. (*below, right*)

The Wild One! On the set in Martha's Vineyard filming *Sabrina*. (*below*)

The tinkering was unable to salvage *Blade Runner* in the eyes of the critics when it opened in America in July and the United Kingdom in September of that year. Few were mean-spirited enough to deny the brilliance of Ridley Scott's evocation of the future. But there was no shortage of critics who found Scott's vision as lifeless as it was artful. Pauline Kael warned the director: "If anybody comes around with a test to detect humanoids, maybe Ridley Scott and his associates should hide."

Kael felt sorry for "poor Harrison Ford," particularly in the climactic scene with Rutger Hauer's Batty. "Ford is like Harold Lloyd stuck by mistake in the climax of *Duel in the Sun*." And: "Harrison Ford can't hide the strain of trying to breathe some spontaneity and wit into this off-white elephant," said Michael Sragow in *Rolling Stone*.

There was a little more warmth for Scott's film in Europe. It was well received at the Venice Film Festival. But here too the gaping holes in the film's storytelling logic failed to make up for its visual brilliance. "Maybe audiences for movies like this are not deemed to place much credence in old-fangled matters like narrative cohesion, preferring instead to lie back and think of nothing while letting the special effects have their way," wrote Tim Pulleine in the *Guardian*.

The experience left both director and star disillusioned. "I was desperately unhappy," Harrison said, and he continued to complain long after the studio's misgivings had been swept away by a viewing public's clear preference for flamboyant style over flawed content. (*Blade Runner* went on to make $27 million at the U.S. box office.) His memories of his relationship with Scott remained an itch that would never quite go away. "We engaged in a process for several weeks at my dining-room table and then very little of that seemed to make its way into the film," he said years later. "I felt more a pawn than a partner."

Scott in return once mused to a colleague who had shared the demanding experience of working with Harrison, "It's hell working with a smart actor." Even when, a decade later, the release of Scott's "director's cut" confirmed *Blade Runner*'s status as the most admired and influential sci-fi film of the 1980s, its star remained recalcitrant. "It could have been more than a cult picture."

At least *Blade Runner* contributed in a major way to Harrison's education. By now approaching a position where he could exercise an increasing level of control over the directors he worked with, he would never again allow himself to be relegated to a role on the sidelines of a production. Nobody would make him feel like a pawn again.

It was Fred Allen, the greatest star of radio's golden age, who best summed up the paradox Harrison had come to face after the successes of Han Solo and Indiana Jones. "A celebrity," America's most popular, postwar radio broadcaster used to say, "is a person who works hard all his life to become known, then wears dark glasses to avoid being recognized."

Harrison's disguise usually consisted of a pair of granny glasses, an upturned collar, and an absolute refusal to make eye contact with anyone. But even that didn't always work for the proprietor of one of the most recognizable names and faces in the world.

John Gregory Dunn and his wife Joan Didion witnessed the extent of his fame over dinner at the Ritz in Paris. A discreet and civilized meal with Harrison and Melissa was drawing to a close when a bellman appeared to announce that there was a telephone call for "Mr. Harrison Ford." Harrison, in wire-rimmed glasses, three days' stubble, and an unsuperstar-like suit, had until then spent an evening undisturbed by anything other than the dangerous good humor of his dinner guests.

Dunne described how the room suddenly erupted into activity, with hotel staff flooding out of the kitchen. "Eendeana Zhones, Eendeana Zhones," the excited crowd began to murmur, jabbing fingers in the direction of the figure sliding out of his chair and out of the unwanted limelight. The full scale of his friend's celebrity sank in that night. "Even at the Ritz," Dunne laughed afterward.

Harrison recalled his own epiphany coming far from the grandeur of Paris, in the stultifying heat and dust of Fez, in Morocco. It was there that he ventured out once to take a stroll through the Casbah. He had walked only a few hundred yards before he realized the impossibility of his situation. "There were two movie theaters in town and both were playing movies I was in," he recalled once. "I realized, this is the end, the end of privacy." By now, fortunately, he was in a position to do something about his loss.

With Ben and Willard now come of age, and his status within Hollywood sure enough for him to relocate himself, he began to make plans to move away from Los Angeles. Despite the friendships he had made there, he had never enjoyed the city, nor California—"the silly state" as he always called it. Given his Midwestern sensibility, he often felt lost when he was not working. "There's nothing for me to do in L.A. when I get up in the morning except sit by the pool and shop," he snarled once.

He had felt an affinity for the wild open spaces since he had been a Forest Ranger as a boy in Chicago. Happy memories of visits to the Marquardt family's cabin in Phelps and, more recently, Skywalker Ranch, George Lucas's Marin County hideaway, only added to the allure.

His interest in finding somewhere remote had as much to do with an almost pathological need for order, peace, and quiet as it did with his love of communing with nature. If he was not quite Garbo, neither was he Jack Nicholson, Hollywood's omnipresent party animal.

Fred Roos, who had known both Nicholson and Harrison through thick and thin, would be pushed to imagine two more dissimilar people in terms of social appetites. "Jack is a total gregarious animal; he loves people and to be out there socializing, going to parties and concerts and ball games. Harrison doesn't do any of that, hardly," he said. "They are similar in that they are smart, understand how the business works, and have a certain cynicism. But otherwise they are polar opposites."

Part of Harrison's reclusiveness was undoubtedly rooted in his belief that the less the public knew about him, the better chance he had to be accepted in new roles. "If people know too much about me, it's me they see up there instead of the character that I'm paid to represent," he told *New York Newsday* during the publicity push for *Blade Runner*.

But his fear of being trapped at a party, surrounded by sycophants or even stopped in the street, went beyond mere actorly logic. Since he was a schoolboy, Harrison had maintained an air of unknowability. Those who had befriended him over the years had, however, detected a deeper insecurity. Somewhere inside, Harrison was actually afraid of revealing too much of himself.

The novelist Susanna Moore, a close Los Angeles friend, had been familiar with his reticence since first getting to know him, pre–*Star Wars* in the early 1970s. "Unlike most actors, he is without the need to seduce or charm everyone he meets," she said. "He's not interested in getting too close, and that's not a criticism. He has a kind of reserve and coolness that I like very much."

His restraint made the naked candor of an admission he once made to Moore all the more telling. Harrison often supported his friend by turning up at her launch parties. His patronage did not, however, extend to opening the pages of her work. "He once told me he didn't like to read my work because it told him too much about me, and that scared him," she said.

If he feared the press's role in preserving his privacy, he had a peculiar way of showing it. He had no one to blame but himself for revealing more of the real Harrison Ford than he intended in London during the filming of *Jedi*.

During a photo shoot for GQ magazine with David Bailey, Harrison also agreed to give an interview to one of London's more subversive magazines, *Ritz*. For reasons best known to himself, Harrison chose to spend much of the session at Bailey's studio lost in a cloud of marijuana smoke.

The discovery that Universal television's former rent-a-hippie partook of a substance as common as cough drops in the California of the 1960s was unremarkable enough. Yet the blasé manner in which a perpetually grinning Harrison rolled joints during the Bailey photo session ranked as the least guarded and most uncharacteristic moment of his public life. The risks ran beyond damaging his clean-cut reputation, as cannabis smoking remained illegal in the United Kingdom.

At first, interviewer David Litchfield had wondered why a man as wealthy as Harrison Ford was rolling his own cigarettes. The truth dawned when his interviewee asked, "You want a toke of this all-American reefer?"

"Can you work on this stuff?" Litchfield asked Harrison.

"Nope. I can't even admit it exists," he replied.

As the joint was passed around the room, Harrison demonstrated the depth of his expertise on the subject, explaining that he was smoking a strain of dope from Humboldt County in northern California. "This is not Cannabis indicta, or Cannabis sativa, this is Cannabis rutica," he said. "A real strong dope."

"From here on the conversation took on a decidedly sixties atmosphere, which used to be translated as 'meaningful' and is now translated as 'stoned,' " Litchfield wrote.

The interview and photo session over, Litchfield and Bailey were still recovering from the experience when the doorbell rang. Harrison had left without his "herbal smoking mixture." "Some time was spent in searching before he spied the stash on the hall floor. He bent down to pick it up," Litchfield recalled in his article in *Ritz*. As he did so, David Bailey joked that the stash looked like "dogshit."

"Let's smoke it first. Then we'll make a decision," said a still-grinning Harrison. If Harrison, the husband of an ex-journalist, had trusted his interviewer to overlook his indiscretion, he had miscalculated wildly. The few platitudes he shared with Litchfied barely rated a mention as *Ritz*, understandably, concentrated on the far more revelatory behavior of America's action hero. The fact that no other publications seemed to pick up on the public relations disaster owed everything to Lady Luck and absolutely nothing to his—clearly impaired—judgment that afternoon.

The experience added further to Harrison's unease about England and journalists. It also intensified his yearning for a private place free from the risk of such pitfalls.

More than a hundred years into its history, the town of Jackson Hole, Wyoming, was still winning its war with an outside world that was determined to mold it into something it was not. In the early 1980s, genuine cowboys still walked its raised wooden sidewalks, and elkhorn-fronted, frontier-style shops still sold hardware and victuals. The town resembled nothing more than the set of a John Ford western—only for real. The original fur trappers might have left, but much of the population still earned their living off the land, in the shadow of the spectacular Grand Tetons.

It had been a homesick French trapper who gave the peaks just south of Yellowstone their mammary name. When Harrison Ford set eyes on them, he knew he could call the place home.

After rejecting Sun Valley, Idaho—already swimming with Hollywood refugees—Harrison and Melissa switched their search to central Wyoming. In Jackson he was shown a home for sale along the Snake River, a few miles outside of the town. In this case it truly was love at first sight. "I think we all get something set in our heads early on," he said years later. "And the first time I saw Jackson Hole, I said, 'This is the place that's been in my mind all the time.' "

The sheer, epic scale of the scenery overwhelmed him. "It was about water, streams, trees, animals, a grand expression of nature—the Tetons rising sharply from a flat, high mountain plateau."

The small home he was shown was set in an 800-acre stretch of land along the river. He was given the option of buying the home and a few acres or the entire tract of land. He bit the bullet and bought all the land. "It had everything I wanted," he confessed later.

His Snake River paradise would eventually cost him close to $1 million. Any doubts Harrison may have had about his ability to afford his latest investment would have been dispelled by a drive past the Egyptian Theater in Los Angeles on May 19, 1983.

A full seven days before the first screening of *Return of the Jedi*, impatient *Star Wars* fans, boys in black Luke Skywalker outfits, girls in Princess Leia braids, had formed their sleeping bags into a line already crawling around the block. From the moment their vigil ended, at 12:01 A.M. on May 26, it was apparent that Lucas, Fox, and Harrison Ford were on their way to a new set of record-breaking box-office statistics—and another phenomenal payday.

Remarkably, given that it opened on a Wednesday, *Jedi* shattered the existing record for the biggest opening day in history. Its $6,219,629 in receipts easily eclipsed anything even its sister films had achieved on a weekend. At the Egyptian Theater there was not a single vacant seat for days—despite the fact that it was the only cinema in America showing the film around the clock.

Even for the master manipulators of Lucasfilm it was a piece of perfectly organized mass hysteria. Anticipation had been whipped up through the 100,000-strong *Star Wars* fan club and a publicity blitzkrieg. Harrison had, without any effort on his part, been part of the hype, as details of whether or not Han Solo had survived his carbon freezing were withheld.

By the time audiences and critics realized the film was demonstrably the dullest of the trilogy, its success had become another sellout-fulfilling prophecy. *Return of the Jedi* was a soulless dash through a series of "Meanwhile back at . . ." sequences and creature-shop showpieces.

The resolutions of the Leia love triangle and Luke's relationship with his father Darth Vader, both handled leadenly, were lost in a sea of set pieces involving new characters like the slimy Sidney Greenstreet-like Jabba the Hut and the irritatingly cutesy Ewoks. Yet despite the fact that the magic had somehow left The Force, the film went on to outstrip *The Empire Strikes Back*, earning $263 million, $30 million more than its predecessor, at the American box office alone.

As if stung by their impotence, the critics railed not just at Richard Marquand's movie but the brash reinvention of American cinema George Lucas had inspired in the half dozen years since *Star Wars*. Pauline Kael in the *New Yorker* found the fact that the quiet-as-a-mouse Lucas and his "bam, bam, pow" films had put her vision of a more "personal" cinema "on a retrograde course," "one of the least amusing ironies of movie history." In London, Alexander Walker experienced pretty much the same sinking feeling. *Star Wars* and "juvenile pantomimes" were increasingly aiming films at "younger and more manipulated age groups."

Harrison had little time for such elitist whining. As the father of two teenage boys, he understood better than most the positive effects *Star Wars* had wrought among a new generation of moviegoers. Lucas's films were bringing people—and more important, their money—back to the cinema. Kael and the rest would just have to get used it. Indeed, even as *Jedi* was rewriting the short-lived history books, Harrison was at work on another Lucas-inspired contribution to the "bam, bam, pow" school of cinema.

When asked the most hackneyed question in the show business reporter's handbook, Harrison invariably replies that the secret of his Hollywood success is his sheer, bloody-minded stubbornness. Or as he once, rather more colorfully, put it: "They tried to kill me off with poisons, sharp sticks, and blunt objects, and I was like a fucking snake that grew a new tail."

He does not often indulge in what he sneeringly calls "farmyard psychology," but even he has conceded it is an attribute he first displayed during his daily defiance of the grade-school bullies of Des Plaines, and has never ceased displaying since. "It is a trait," he has agreed—grudgingly.

In July 1983, it took the personal intervention of George Lucas to persuade him he had finally crossed the life-threatening line that separated his hang-in-there machismo from madness.

Lucas made the 12,000-mile round trip from his San Francisco home to Elstree after receiving a series of increasingly agitated phone calls from Steven Spielberg.

Two-thirds of the way through filming *Indiana Jones and the Temple of Doom*, their follow-up to *Raiders*, Harrison was refusing to acknowledge he needed surgery on a potentially crippling back injury.

"He was on a hospital bed on the set," said Lucas, recalling the scene that greeted him at Borehamwood. "He could barely stand up. He could barely walk. Yet he was there every day so shooting would not stop. He was in incomprehensible pain, but he was still trying to make it happen."

Indiana Jones and the Temple of Doom had begun shooting in Sri Lanka in May 1983. The sequel to *Raiders*, written by *Star Wars* stalwarts Katz and Huyck, was set almost entirely in the East, where Indiana became involved in the search for an ancient stone stolen from an Indian village.

If *Raiders* had been a Disney roller coaster ride, *Temple of Doom* was to be a trip on a particularly gruesome ghost train. Along with Spielberg and Lucas, Harrison had felt the need to add a darker tone to Indy's adventures. The Nazis of *Raiders* were replaced by Chinese warlords and the brutal Thuggees of India. Scenes of torture, child brutality, and heart-ripping ritual, would by the end reduce *Raiders* to drawing-room comedy.

Harrison's stunt schedule was even more punishing than on *Raiders*. Yet Vic Armstrong, a strapping, six-foot Englishman who bore such a striking resemblance to Indiana Jones that he had been frequently mistaken for him on and off the set, spent much of the shoot fretting.

"He's a very physical actor, a natural athlete, and he wants to do it all," said Armstrong. "I say to him, 'H, we cannot afford to get you smashed up in this scene because we've got a whole crew here that needs to make a living.' And he says, 'Yes, you're right,' and does the scene anyway."

Harrison's gung-ho intentions were plain early on in the shoot at the genuine rope-bridge location scouts had discovered over a 300-foot river gorge in Sri Lanka. Spielberg, Armstrong, and his fellow stunt-men were unsure of its safety. "But I felt we had to establish a proper disdain for the rope bridge. So before anyone could do anything, I just ran across it," Harrison said later.

Cussed he may have been, but his logic was laudable. He had been stung by critics who thought Indiana another "cardboard cutout" role. The more he appeared to be in the thick of the action, the more he could use that action to deepen his characterization of Indy, a crucial part of the second movie. "Really, that is the character—and in these moments you see Indiana Jones most clearly," he explained later.

If it had not caused him such hideous pain, he might have appreci-ated the irony that his downfall came in one of the more sedentary moments of the Sri Lankan adventure—while riding an elephant.

He first began to experience twinges in his spine as he bounced along on the back of the subcontinent's most stately form of transport. "When you ride an elephant, your legs are hyper-extended in both directions to accommodate the girth of the animal," he explained later. "It's as if your legs are being pulled apart."

The twinges intensified as the shoot continued. By the time he arrived back in Elstree, where some of the most demanding stunts of all would be attempted, his discomfort was plain for all to see. The crisis came when he fell off a moving mine car.

Diagnosed as having herniated two discs, Harrison was persuaded by Lucas to fly back to be treated by specialists in sports injuries at the Centinela Hospital in Los Angeles. There he agreed to undergo a rel-atively new treatment that would avoid a full-scale laminectomy. The procedure, called "chymopapain," involved injecting an enzyme derived from papaya fruit into the damaged disc. This would then "eat" into the disc, much like acid dissolving a metal.

The risks were considerable, as they always are with back injuries. While the production was brought to a halt back in England, rumors rippled through London and Hollywood that the film was in jeopardy.

Spielberg, in damage control, tried to "shoot around" the absent Ford. Within six weeks, however, Harrison was ready to return. Ulti-mately the delay cost the production's insurers $1 million, although *Indiana Jones and the Temple of Doom* was finished a mere few days over schedule.

When he arrived back in London, Harrison began to exercise a new caution. At one stage a guard was to throw Indy into another moving mine car. "Since I had just come back from surgery, I had second thoughts about being the throwee," he said. He let Vic Armstrong do the shot.

By September he was cautiously picking his way through the final days of shooting. It is debatable whether an elaborate surprise Paramount executives arranged for Harrison during the final scenes was a token of their affection or of their profound relief at the completion of their most expensive film of the year.

Chained to a rock where he was about to be beaten by a turbanned torturer, played by Pat Roach, Harrison was suddenly greeted by the sight of Barbra Streisand, dressed in kinky black leather, brandishing a bullwhip. The diva-turned-dominatrix proceeded to rain lashes on his exposed back. "That's for *Hanover Street*," she said as the first stroke landed. "That's for making so much money out of *Star Wars*," she added as another one hit home.

Before Streisand could punish him for some of his earlier television cameos, or perhaps for his decision to pass on working with her the previously year, the diminutive figure of Carrie Fisher arrived on the set. Screaming "No, no, no!" with more passion than Princess Leia had ever shown, she draped herself across Harrison's back to protect him from his assailant. The tableau was completed when the tall, patrician figure of Irvin Kershner appeared at Steven Spielberg's side and deadpanned: "Is this the way you run your movies?"

17

BOOKWORK

Pat McQueeney acquired her air of ice-chip unflappability hosting NBC television's flagship *Today* show. It was a quality which stood her in good stead when she left New York for Los Angeles and the card-sharping politics of Hollywood.

She was lacking her normal composure when, one Monday morning in 1984, she left her office on Century Woods Drive and drove "up the hill" toward Benedict Canyon.

She had spent the previous day doing what she routinely did on Sundays, ploughing through the minimountain of scripts that had piled up in her office the previous week. It had been the normal, uninspiring material: formulaic, predictable pap. Until, that is, she settled into the fifth and final script she had set herself the task of reading.

"Harrison, I think I've found it!" she told her most successful client the next morning, sliding the script onto his kitchen table, her excitement visible. "See what you think."

As she remembers it, the phone rang at around 1 P.M. "Patricia—Harrison. I think you have!"

Called Home, the story of a big-city homicide cop drawn into the mysterious world of the Pennsylvania Amish community during an investigation, the script had been bouncing around town like a bad check. When McQueeney called Harrison's then agent, Phil Gersh,

197

about the script, he had advised her, "Don't embarrass yourself by giving it to Harrison. Everyone in town has passed on it."

McQueeney was unfazed, however. Frustrated by his failure to break through into the "serious" roles that would take him beyond Indiana Jones and Han Solo, Harrison was looking for something just like this. "I had begun to really beat the bushes for a script that would bail him out of that mold. I fell in love with it—I thought it was exactly what he was looking for," she said.

Soon Gersh—and everyone else in town—was trying to discover her "secret" in spotting scripts. "They would ask me, 'How did you recognize it?' " Normally her reply was, "I read it." This script, which eventually became the movie *Witness*, was to represent a turning point in both McQueeney's and Harrison Ford's careers.

Created by TV writers Earl W. Wallace and William Kelley, and undoubtedly inspired by the 1947 John Wayne western *The Angel and the Badman*, the story of *Witness* revolves around a young Amish boy pursued by corrupt policemen after witnessing one of them committing a murder. A high-principled detective assigned to investigate the killing immerses himself in the strange world of the religious sect as he protects the boy and his beautiful mother.

Harrison saw that the script was not without its flaws. For instance, there was violence, too much of it—but at its heart was the highly moral struggle of a just man in an unjust world. Even the name of its honest-cop hero, John Book, resonated with decency. And the cultural clash between the outside world and the pacifist Amish, one of America's most closed communities, gave it unique possibilities. "Without the Amish serving as a kind of parameter to the violence, this would have been the usual indulgence," he said later.

Harrison had a clear idea of how it could be made to work on screen. Equally he now had enough experience to know how it could be made to fail dismally. Time to flex a little muscle. *Witness* became the first film over which Harrison Ford exercised the kind of tasteful control he had until then reserved for constructing cabinets and sundecks.

The script was by no means perfect. "About ninety percent there," he told producer Ed Feldman and Paramount's Jeffrey Katzenberg, who agreed to a $12 million budget on the back of his Indy popularity. Harrison insisted on script and director approval. "If we didn't have a really good director, we wouldn't have anything—in fact, it would most likely lose something in the translation," he said later.

Convinced that the film should be shot through an outsider's eye, Harrison's first choice was the Australian director Peter Weir, maker of three moodily atmospheric films, *Picnic at Hanging Rock*, *Gallipoli*, and *The Year of Living Dangerously*, the latter two with the emerging Mel Gibson. The drawback was that Weir was ready to start shooting an adaptation of Paul Theroux's acclaimed novel *The Mosquito Coast*.

Harrison would have been happy to wait. However, Paramount, keen to make the film as soon as possible now that its most saleable star was on board, suggested other directors. When Harrison refused to budge on Weir, Jeffrey Katzenberg began playing a faintly ludicrous game of Hollywood hardball with McQueeney. "Jeffrey started calling me up and threatening me and saying: 'Pat, if he doesn't agree to one of these guys, we're going to have to go on. We'll really have to get another actor.' And I'd say: 'Well, Jeffrey, you can't do that. I brought the project to you. That's not fair.'"

The deal was close to collapse when word arrived that Weir and producer Jerome Hellman's plans to make *The Mosquito Coast* had turned to dust. Deeply frustrated and now facing a year without work, the forty-year-old Weir decided to dispense with the usual agonizing over choosing films and "just take something, just fly it. . . . I decided it was a good idea not just to make films that obsessed me. I wanted to be like those directors in the 1940s who took assignments from their studios and got on with them," he said.

Quickly shown three scripts that were financed and green-lighted, Weir chose the only one that he regarded as "halfway good"—*Witness*. After meeting with Paramount and Feldman in Los Angeles, he flew out to Jackson Hole simultaneously suspicious and attracted by the prospect of working for the first time with a five-star Hollywood phenomenon. "It being my first American film, and my first time with such a big star, I was a little bit uneasy. It was conditional on the way we got on when we met," he recalled.

It took Weir only a few moments to realize he was dealing with a different kind of star. He found Harrison standing in the arrivals lounge, looking more like the Marlboro Man than the world's biggest box-office draw. En route to the new ranch they stopped off at a local supermarket. "We went to pick up some groceries and there was a picture of Han Solo on a cereal package. He gave me a laconic rise of his eyebrows—'Is there no end to this?' I could tell right away he was different; he had his head screwed on right."

As the two men talked, Weir got his first glimpse of the master carpenter-actor at work. "The thing that struck me about that discussion was that it was more like talking with a filmmaker than with an actor," he mused. "His interest is in the whole, so he will be quite happy and suggest a scene be removed in which he plays some prominent part because he doesn't feel that it sits well with the whole. And that's rather unusual."

The two men spent several hours talking. Farcically, it was only afterward that each realized he was effectively interviewing the other. Weir asked whether he could use the phone and rang his agent in Los Angeles. Over dinner that night, Harrison confessed he had done the same thing immediately afterward. "I had no idea I was having a big audition with Harrison," laughed Weir.

Both director and star agreed that the key casting decision was Rachel, the Amish mother with whom Book would become romantically involved in the film's second and third acts as he fled Philadelphia with her and her son. Weir had admired the performance of a young actress called Kelly McGillis in Robert Ellis Miller's *Reuben, Reuben*. He sent her the script and, with Harrison, flew to Jimmy Day's, a Greenwich Village coffeehouse where she was working to offer her the part. "Harrison and Peter came to pick me up at my job, and I never went back," she said later.

As he prepared for his American debut, Weir discovered a common ground with his star. "I had a certain devil-may-care feeling, a certain recklessness," he admitted. "And I think he had the same quality at that time. Like, 'Let's be loose about it. Let's see what happens, not be uptight about it.'"

This faintly kamikaze streak had become apparent during the period the two men spent researching the film. While Weir and McGillis hung out in Lancaster County, quietly observing the Amish, Harrison spent time with the Philadelphia police. His search for authenticity could easily have gotten him killed.

Harrison teamed up with Captain Eugene Dooley of the Philadelphia police department. During an intensive fortnight as Dooley's "partner," he spent days and nights on the streets, where he was served up some unsettling sights. "The first corpse was shocking and the fifth was just as shocking." He even accompanied Dooley and colleagues on raids to serve warrants on murder suspects. Asked later whether his celebrity had inhibited the operations, he joked: "Listen, when you are a citizen in distress or you're standing there with a cop's pistol pressed against your head, you are not looking to see if there are any movie stars present!"

Fortunately, that principle applied one night when he and Dooley moved in on a bar popular with Philadelphia's underworld, in search of an informant. Harrison told the story to a horrified Peter Weir the next day. "Gene said to Harrison: 'If you really want to go the next stage, this is what partners do. You go in through the front door, I'll go in through the back door. Don't look to the left or right, just move in cool, they'll know you're a cop. Go to the center of the bar and I will join you,' " Weir related.

As Harrison duly did what he was told, Dooley went to the rear door, only to discover it was locked. "Harrison went into this bar, with a bunch of fairly tough characters and suddenly there is this white guy and he's not in there for a beer. So there is a critical moment where you had better do something coplike," added the director. "He carried it off with no backup partner through an agonizing several minutes until Gene made his way back in through the front door. Thank God he was not armed. Harrison told me this story the next morning and I said: 'Look, Harrison, this is just a movie! What am I going to say if you get killed or something?' "

Filming went ahead through the sweltering heat of May and June 1984, in Philadelphia and Lancaster County, home of the Amish. The descendants of German Mennonites, the Amish had maintained a lifestyle their ancestors had established more than a century before. There were no cars, no televisions, no cameras in their world. Wary of the outsiders, all but a few of the Amish community kept a safe distance from Weir's film set.

One mother confided that while her child had a poster of Han Solo on her bedroom wall, she had no real idea who the heroic figure was, as her religion forbade her from seeing *Star Wars*.

For Harrison, no role—not even Han Solo—could have been as perfectly dovetailed as John Book. As shooting got underway, he was even able to bring his carpentry skills to bear.

A crucial scene within the Amish community had Book helping erect a barn. Weir wanted to make the scene as visual as possible, to allow action rather than dialogue to define its communal mood. Weir and his star were not about to ignore the opportunities Harrison's alternative master-craftsmanship provided. To gently heighten the tension between him and an Amish admirer of Rachel's, played by Alexander Godunov, Book was seen demonstrating a flair with hammer and nails his rival lacked. "We took advantage of my past experience," Harrison said wryly afterward.

He has admitted many times that there are similarities between the two crafts at which he excels. "There's a real simpleminded analogy: you have to have a logical plan. You have to perceive it from the ground up. You have to lay a firm foundation. Then every step becomes part of a logical process," he explained once.

On *Witness* Weir saw much more than Harrison combining his first- and second-string careers on film. He also watched a master class in the construction of a screen character. John Book may well be the most perfectly assembled performance of Harrison's career so far.

"He's got guts. He has two sides to his nature; he has the very careful eye of the craftsman, and he has a kind of wild side. And he can be very funny in that reckless area, both on and off the screen. I can remember him being very funny with my kids," recalled Weir.

Weir also sensed Harrison's determination to break away from the shackles of Solo and Jones. "Often major film stars can become extremely inhibited as their success mounts, and it can make working a painful process. But when you do strike somebody on the point of change, where they feel they're really going to burn their bridges, it's very exciting."

The relationship between Book and Rachel provided the subtlest glimpses of Harrison's skill. His touches ensured that no one would ever question his ability to share romantic scenes again.

Harrison suggested music should play while he and Rachel were alone in a barn together. Sam Cooke's *What a Wonderful World* was one of his choices. The gentle intimacy of the moment fitted perfectly. Years later, Harrison summed up the satisfaction of one of *Witness*'s finest moments with considerably less finesse. "It's much more fun to watch the tension and anticipation than it is to watch people *shtup!*"

In another scene, Book recovers the bullets Rachel has hidden in a flour tin. "And she sort of tips them into his hand and flour trails into his hand and he, with his own gesture, just blew the dust off the bullets, and looked at her with that kind of Harrison look," said Weir. "It's a type of cool, but it's at its best when there's that trace of bittersweet humor, that squeeze of lemon in Harrison's smile. It's what you love about a screen hero of Harrison's American type—there have only been a handful of them in this century of film."

For all the repressed passion she generated with her star on-set, Kelly McGillis found Harrison a cold fish. Sean Young had found him equally distant at times. "He doesn't open up easily to people."

Steven Spielberg had observed a similar phenomenon. "I've seen him during a shooting day, drift off—he already knows how to play the scene and I think he is just drifting away from the fakery," he said. "He's planting a crop or building a bookshelf in Wyoming."

Harrison does not deny his insularity. His defense is that it is part of his craft. "Actors have to wait a long time between takes. I sit and stare at the walls or I walk around and bump into the front and the back of my trailer," he told the American writer Joan Goodman. "Either I'm thinking about the next scene or I'm in a state of mental suspension. I can't read or concentrate on anything. For me it is the worst part of being an actor."

The week-long break he took from filming *Witness* in mid-May might have offered some welcome relief, but the publicity push for *Temple of Doom* turned out to be about as far removed from a holiday as he could imagine. He walked from the tranquil world of the Amish straight into the middle of a media war.

Clouds of controversy had been gathering for weeks. Since handing in their final cut, Paramount, Spielberg, and Lucas had been embroiled in a running dispute with the U.S. censors, the Motion Picture Association of America's Classification and Rating Administration, over *Temple of Doom*'s violent content. Spielberg's gruesome Thuggee sacrifice scenes—complete with the removal of one victim's heart and the immersion of another in a pit of boiling lava—along with the film's images of child brutality, and the banquet in which Indy's hosts ate monkey brains and live eels, turned more than one stomach on the seven-member board. At the same time, the British Board of Film Censors were warning Paramount that twenty-five major cuts would be needed for the film to get its 15 rating—fifteen-years-old and over only—let alone an equivalent *PG*.

Eventually a penitent Paramount helped sway the American censors' decision to award a *PG* rather than an *R* rating, thus allowing under-seventeens in without an accompanying parent, by agreeing to issue a warning that the film "may be too intense for younger children." In Britain the requisite cuts were made before the film was given its *PG* there.

On the eve of the film's release, an embattled Spielberg conceded on television that there was a twenty-minute section in the middle of the movie that he would not allow a ten-year-old child to see, even if he had to hold his hand over the child's eyes. And in the face of growing flak from critics who had seen early screenings, he and Lucas issued a joint statement admitting that their film was more "intense than *Raiders* . . . A story with children in jeopardy is going to get a more emotional reaction than a story with Indiana Jones battling Nazis."

None of this was sufficient to appease critics and parents on both sides of the Atlantic. Gary Franklin, reviewer for Los Angeles' KCBS-TV, became the fulminating flag bearer in America, noisily refusing to attend a Paramount lunch after the screening, awarding the film 0 out of 10, and then publicly berating Spielberg and Lucas as they were immortalized in cement on Hollywood Boulevard. ("Who do you think shouldn't see this film?" the critic asked Spielberg. "I think everybody can see this film except Gary Franklin," the director replied.)

"Someone has misread the voltage on state-of-the-art effects, and they're going to have to scrape youngsters out from under the seats like old chewing gum with this one," wrote Sheila Benson in the *Los Angeles Times*. "I don't understand how Spielberg could have lost his way so badly," wrote Alix Palmer, launching a negative campaign in the *Daily Star*. By the time the film arrived in London in early June, a chastened Spielberg suggested the pregnant Princess of Wales cover her eyes as she sat next to him during its gala premiere!

As if all this was not enough, back in America, Indian immigrant groups further fanned the flames by demonstrating outside a cinema in Seattle, waving placards branding Spielberg and Lucas "Raiders of the Third World."

"Imagine a child of Indian background confronted with questions from his classmates," said Aslam Khan, a science teacher who organized the protest. "Do you eat snakes? Do you have voodoo dolls at home? Why is your religion so stupid?"

Cast into the eye of this storm in mid-May, Harrison publicly defended the film as best he could. "This is a completely moral tale," he told the *New York Times*. "And in order to have moral resolve, evil must be seen to inflict pain. The end of the movie is a proof of the viability of goodness . . . I do not seek out movies that are bathed in blood," he added testily when it was suggested *Temple of Doom* picked up where the sadistic finale of *Blade Runner* left off. "Quite the contrary."

Privately, however, he was angry at the excesses Spielberg and Lucas had included in the film, some of which had come as a surprise to him. It had been after he left the set, for instance, that Lucas had insisted on adding additional horrors to the dinner scene, including giant bugs, soup with bobbing eyeballs, and a python filled with wriggling eels. No one had been keener on adding a darker edge to Indy's character than Harrison, but he felt much of the movie overstepped the mark. Philosophically, he licked his wounds and wondered whether he should have been more vociferous in objecting to Spielberg and Lucas's taste for the macabre. "Occasionally I rose to protest, but moviemaking is a collaborative effort, and while my attitude was noted, it did not prevail," he explained later. He returned to the set of *Witness* determined not to make the same mistake when Indy returned for a third time.

Temple of Doom was released at the same time as another gory piece of Spielbergian fantasy—*Gremlins*, directed by his protégé Joe Dante. Together, these movies came to represent a twin milestone in the history of mainstream cinema. The furor became the catalyst for a broader debate about what was and was not suitable entertainment for children, and the establishment of a new rating in America—*PG-13*. More predictably, public awareness buoyed to a remarkable 80 percent before Paramount had paid a cent on advertising. It ensured *Temple of Doom* erased *Return of the Jedi* from the record books when it opened over America's Memorial Day weekend. Indiana Jones's return earned a truly terrifying $42,267,345 in its first six days. It went on to earn $179 million at the U.S. box office and almost as much again overseas.

Peter Weir got his first clue that the reception to *Witness* might prove tricky when he went to a preview screening in Los Angeles. Mindful of the experience Ridley Scott suffered on *Blade Runner*, Weir had tried to ensure that the audience knew this was *not* a sneak preview of *Indiana Jones Rides Again*.

When he arrived for the 7:30 P.M. screening early, so as to make a few last-minute changes: "There, to my horror, stretched a line of people several hundred yards long, all of them chattering and laughing." It was instantly clear what they were expecting. "The anticipation for *Raiders Mark III* was terrifying," he said.

As the audience watched *Witness*, they were restless and confused at first. "They were puzzled because they expected more action, but by the middle of the film they were loving the humor," Weir said. At the end people filed out, smiling positively, and Weir felt the film had a good chance. "I thought it was a good little movie that would find its own audience and make a dollar or two," he concluded.

Within weeks it was earning a little more than that. In its opening weekend at the beginning of February 1985, *Witness* grossed $4,540,000—an exceptionally good figure for a picture of its kind. To most critics, the sight of Harrison demonstrating abilities undreamed of in the world of Lucas and Spielberg, was the most pleasant surprise in years.

"In *Witness* Harrison Ford has become a real movie star in the old-fashioned sense—he's interesting no matter what he's doing," wrote David Denby in *New York* magazine.

Encouraged by its opening, *Witness* was taken to Cannes. Harrison once more submitted himself to the peculiar madness of the Croisette in May as *Witness* opened the festival. The sniffiness of some of the reviews may have been colored by Paramount's refusal to allow the film to slug it out in competition. "A flop d'estime," the *Guardian's* Richard Roud called it. Most, however, simply chided Paramount for their cowardice. "They were wrong, for this is a triple-tiered story that works extraordinarily well."

Harrison's acting range, so far only hinted at in *Empire* and *Blade Runner*, *Heroes*, and *The Conversation*, was finally recognized and allowed to flourish. "His performance is gripping," said Iain Johnstone, the urbane critic of the *Sunday Times* (London).

Harrison, as ever, could not accept the praise without an acidic aside. "The reviews were among the first I'd had as an *actor*," he told the respected British writer Victor Davis. "Although that's what I'd always been doing." But even he could not deny the sea change in his fortunes.

"*Witness* changed everything for Harrison," said Fred Roos. "People started saying, 'He's really good!' But he was always that good—they just couldn't see it," he sighed, with "I told you so" written all over his face.

The Weir-Ford team was soon on the road again. As *Witness* opened new doors for Harrison, so too it presented new opportunities for the Australian. With Oscar talk already bubbling away, Weir seized his chance to finally make *The Mosquito Coast*.

At the dark heart of Theroux's nightmarish Conradian novel was Allie Fox, an American original, an inventor, philosopher, and perpetual nitpicker. Driven by his hatred of the cops, crooks, scavengers and "funny bunnies" of the late twentieth century—not to mention his loathing of all things junky and Japanese—Fox transports his confused young family from their life on a Massachusetts farm to the jungles of Central America, where he dreams of establishing an independent civilization. However, his vision of a new Eden—built around his greatest invention, Fat Boy, a vast ice-making machine—dissolves into disappointment, disillusionment, and ultimately, tragedy.

The battle to bring Theroux's disturbingly eloquent commentary on the madness of the modern world to the screen had already proved something of an epic. Producer Jerome Hellman had spent the early part of the 1980s hawking the screenplay around the world. Only Jack Nicholson's brief interest in playing Allie had brought Hollywood to life, although it had concerns about the darkness of the film's subject and its $16 million budget. The studios' appetite waned completely when Hellman refused to film anywhere other than the real Mosquito Coast—the jagged coastline that skirts the jungles of Central America from Belize to Nicaragua.

By 1985, however, the landscape had changed out of all recognition. *Witness* had transformed Weir, who had been keen to direct the movie since being given the book by Sigourney Weaver on the set of *The Year of Living Dangerously*. And when the producer Saul Zaentz, buoyed by his Oscar success with *Amadeus*, offered financing, Hellman was finally in business.

When Robert De Niro's brief interest also faded, Weir suggested Harrison step into the breach. He had seen enough of the actor by now to recognize the resonances Allie Fox had within his own life. On *Witness* he also sensed that Ford was entering a new maturity in his acting. In Albert Camus's phrase—experience had not been created, it had been undergone. "He was socking away, storing up important observations of life that become impossible once you reach the kind of private-jet status he has now, sort of cut off from life," Weir commented.

Not everyone shared Weir's enthusiasm. Patricia McQueeney, for one, feared only the worst. As sure as she had been that *Witness* would reinvent his career, she was even more certain *The Mosquito Coast* could deal it a mortal blow. "We had friendly fights, friendly arguments, but on that one we really had a knock-down-and-drag-out," she said. "Harrison is very much into the environment and antipollution and all of those good things that Allie Fox was also into. But what I *didn't* like was the torture that he put his wife and kids through."

John Book presented a more human, vulnerable side of Harrison Ford—a character his audience wanted to root for, a flawed man made whole by the end of the movie. Allie Fox, arrogant, self-absorbed, and ultimately self-destructive, would confuse his fans, McQueeney argued. Here was a man whose life was heading downhill all the way. "I said, 'The audience thinks you're a hero. They aren't going to want you to be this mean guy who drags people through the jungle.' " But Harrison had rarely felt so passionately about a character. For him it was a story with strong personal meaning, the role of his career. And with John Book and *Witness* by now on its way to nominations in all the major awards, from the Golden Globes to the Oscars, Hollywood finally seemed ready to take him seriously.

"He has something to say," he repeated vehemently to McQueeney during their disagreements. "Allie says more in one scene than other characters I've played said in the whole film!"

Eventually agent and actor had to agree to differ. "It's his face and body up there on a fifty-foot screen" was McQueeney's final word on the subject.

18

A Lion in a Cage

In 1986, five years after independence ended its status as Britain's last colony on continental America, the fledgling nation of Belize still clung to the very lowest rung of the world economic ladder. Its population, a mix of mestizos, Creoles, and Mayan Indians, scrabbled a living on either side of the law, farming the area's staple crops, sugar and marijuana. They earned, on average, ten dollars or so a week.

For almost five months during that spring and summer, few who walked the coast on the edge of the country's most populous settlement, Belize City, could help but cast an envious eye out at the bobbing silhouette of the 126-foot yacht *Mariner II*, moored a few hundred yards out to sea. The vessel, a palace of polished mahogany and brass, replete with awnings and lead crystal windows, a staff of five, and a look of presidential impregnability, somehow symbolized the gulf that separated Belize from America and the developed world. At night, its lights winking in the distance, it appeared a sanctuary from the street crime and the squalor—a monument to the peace that money can provide.

A brief conversation with the novelist and travel writer Paul Theroux would have quickly disabused them. Theroux's globe-trotting had shown him a thousand shades of human nature, but he had never encountered anyone quite as insecure as the man who had chartered the *Mariner II*.

"Don't tell me not to worry. I worry all the time," Theroux recalled Harrison Ford snapping at one point.

As news that he was to play Allie Fox had drifted through Hollywood, friends familiar with the book offered the film an alternative title: *The Harrison Ford Story.*

Brilliant but crotchety, driven by often nonexistent demons, at war with a world filled with junk food and junk philosophy, Fox was to them merely a more militant version of the man they knew and, for all his faults, loved.

"He was always cranky," said Fred Roos, who had felt the rasping edge of his tongue whether employing him as a carpenter or an actor. "He was crotchety, but charming crotchety. He would bark at people, but he was never mean . . . He was a beautiful carpenter. Each piece was a work of art, and he would not compromise. If I ever quibbled about the cost, he would just browbeat me. He'd say: 'Do you want a piece of shit, or do you want something your grandchildren will still have!' "

Over the years, some of Harrison's public pronouncements had added support to the thesis. His voice and that of Allie Fox had often been indistinguishable. Once, for instance, midway through an interview he set off on a tirade against the declining standards of hardware stores. "There was a wonderful place near downtown Los Angeles, Andrew's Hardware. It had five floors of hardware. It was heaven. You'd walk in and smell that red or green sweeping compound on the well-worn wood floor. Gave it that woody smell. Now it's been replaced by a neighborhood Ace store with those plastic packages of ten little screws." He added: "We're living in a disposable, replaceable, jerry-built world." The speech could have been lifted straight from the opening pages of Theroux's book, in which Allie launches an almost identical rant—also in a hardware store.

On other occasions his scabrous turns of phrase might have been scripted by Paul Theroux. There was, for instance, Harrison's rationale for not going to the movies: "Maybe it's the same as not eating hot dogs after you've worked in a slaughterhouse. You know it's all made from ears and ass parts." And his objection to the cult of celebrity and magazines like Melissa's former employers, *"Peephole"* magazine. "It absorbs, digests, and shits out personalities just like yesterday's prunes."

Anyone who doubted how dangerously close Allie Fox was to the real Harrison only needed to listen to the testimony of Paul Theroux himself. At times the author could not disguise his amazement at the similarities between the actor and the character he had only imagined.

Theroux traveled to the set midway through filming and spent time with Harrison and Melissa on board the *Mariner II*. He sensed he had met his fictional hero's doppelgänger the moment Harrison began trying to justify his decision to charter the floating palace.

Harrison had traveled down on a scouting mission months earlier. With Weir and a group of locals, he had utilized Indiana Jones's machete-wielding skills to help clear an area of jungle near the shantytown of Gracey Rock, on the edge of the Sibun River. The prospect of spending three months in the production's makeshift headquarters at the Villa Hotel—or anywhere else in Belize for that matter—had filled him with horror. His original plan, he told Theroux, was to airlift a ready-to-assemble home into the jungle. "I said, 'Get a cargo plane. One of these C-130s—a big mother. Fill it up with a prefab house in lots of sections, all the plumbing, all the wires, maybe a helicopter too. Drop the whole thing into Belize in one package and bolt it together.' "

Theroux listened in barely concealed awe. "Without any apparent effort he had turned into Allie Fox—the beaky cap, the flapping shirt, the pushed-back hair, the I-know-best eyes, and the gently maniacal voice explaining his brilliant plan," he said.

One evening aboard the *Mariner*, Harrison had been obsessively chinning himself up and down over the taffrail. When he admitted he was worried that his portrayal of Allie might not be authentic, Theroux had smiled and reassured him. "You *are* Allie Fox. That's straight from the horse's mouth."

"Does Allie Fox worry?" Harrison had shot back, almost forcing the author to nod in agreement. "Right. That's why I worry."

"Pure Allie," Theroux would say to himself time and time again.

Peter Weir got his first glimpse of the vaguely unsettling transformation earlier. The gifted English actress Helen Mirren had been cast as Allie's wife, while the fifteen-year-old River Phoenix, star of Joe Dante's offbeat space adventure *The Explorers* and soon to shine in Rob Reiner's *Stand by Me*, was chosen as the narrator of the story, Allie's son Charlie. Two porcelain-pretty eight-year-olds, the Gordon twins, had been chosen to play the youngest members of the clan.

Before filming was due to begin, Weir organized a picnic for the Fox family and other key members of the production. The director crammed into a van being driven by Harrison and sat in the back while Mirren, Phoenix and the ash-blond Gordon twins rode up front. "It was the first time they were together," he said. "I didn't say anything, I just listened and watched them. Then I noticed Helen and Harrison starting to use dialogue and ideas from the movie."

If the twins began playing around, Mirren would say: "Don't distract Harrison, he's concentrating." On one occasion she turned to him and asked: "Are you lost?" "I'm never lost," he shot back. "It was almost Mother and Allie," said Weir.

Yet Harrison also displayed the other side of his character. If he shared Allie's frantic manner, he also shared his protective, fatherly instincts.

Mirren admitted her role as the servile, intimidated, yet adoring wife was helped by the fact that she was hopelessly star-struck by her screen husband. Despite having shared a Shakespearean stage with Gielgud and Olivier, she later confessed: "It's stupid, but I'm scared of people who are famous. I went absolutely to pieces when I met Harrison Ford."

Harrison's ability to work well with children—a rarity in leading men—shone throughout. Between takes he would play with the Gordon twins, whom he called "the Munchkins." His manner was that of a natural father. "I want a finger. I collect fingers from all the kids I work with," he teased one of them, as she held his hand one day. "How about this one?" "They play with Ford as cubs would play with a grizzly," joked one observer.

To Phoenix he was the voice of common sense. His advice to the young actor—sadly ignored as it turned out—was: "Keep your head on your shoulders. It's just a job." "He's sturdy, a real father figure. In control, very centered," the young star said later.

His relationship with Peter Weir was less straightforward. Having spent two years shooting the film in his head—rather than the eight weeks he had had on *Witness*—Weir's vision was clear. He was horri-

fied by some of Harrison's ideas for the role. Early on he had to talk
him out of playing Allie as a slimmed-down version of Brando's Kurtz
in *Apocalypse Now*.

Once filming was underway, Harrison was as willing to use his Allie-
like gift for invention as he had been on *Witness*. He went so far as
improvising a design for the pedal-driven washing machine that was
used in the film. His carpenter's eye for detail was as well honed as
ever, too. At one point he indicated a "flaw" no one else would possibly have worried about. "This is the wrong kind of lathe: Allie would
have a metal lathe, not just a wood lathe," he announced to the befud-
dlement of most. Nevertheless a metal lathe was brought into the
jungle as a result.

Having been a more vocal, collaborative voice on *Witness*, Harrison
concentrated his efforts far more on his performance this time around.
"In some ways it's easier to play a character that has so much complexity," he said later. "It's like trying to fill a big room with an accordion band or a large orchestra where you can bring up the violins and
tinkle the bass."

He left it to Weir to conduct his performance.

"I wanted *not* to have control of the situation," he explained. "I
wanted to be able to give in to the excesses of the character, to be
pulled back from the brink by Peter when he thought it was necessary,
or encouraged to go close to the edge when he thought I should."

Weir in return watched out for the moments when Harrison's looseness produced its best results. "I'm a tremendous believer in craft, but
there are times when all you can do is prepare yourself to take advantage of the happy accidents," he said during the shoot.

For all the empathy Harrison felt for his character, the shoot took
a punishing toll. Back on the *Mariner* at night, he would collapse,
exhausted. His sanity was only preserved by the stabilizing influence
of Melissa. She traveled with him, staying on board the yacht, working on a television adaptation of Evan Connell's bestseller on Custer
and the Battle of the Little Big Horn—*Son of the Morning Star*—while
her husband was ferried out into the jungle each day. Harrison and she
had agreed to avoid separations, whatever the cost. "She works anywhere she can, in the back of the car if she has to," he said.

Melissa's protectiveness by now extended to buffering journalists from Harrison's occasional hostility. The *Star Wars* and *Indiana Jones* movies had given Harrison a relatively easy ride with the press. In *Witness* and now again on *The Mosquito Coast*, he had become the sole focus of the media's interest. Since his run-in with *Ritz* magazine, he had harbored a healthy distrust of journalists. With his Allie Fox hat on, he became almost paranoid. His greatest fear was that writers would reveal the location of his new home in Wyoming. "It's not marked or anything, but we already have people standing outside the gate. And I've started getting mail addressed to Harrison Ford, care of His Ranch, with just the name of the state," he said incredulously in Belize, interviewed by the *Esquire* magazine writer Guy Martin.

Martin described the process of trailing Harrison around the jungle for a few days as "good fun, of course, but it's like good fun with a lion in a cage." When the subject of his profile spotted Martin having a drink with Melissa at the end of one day spent in his intense company, the lion snarled: "You know you are a spy. You are all spies."

Melissa defused the situation with a rub of her husband's back and an arch of her eyebrow to Martin. "Oh, he's just being an *actor*," she smiled.

The next day, Martin once more watched Harrison prowling around the set as he prepared to go home. After three months in the bug-infested jungle and the saunalike heat, Harrison was desperate to leave. He rifled through the cupboards of his trailer at the Gracey Rock location, discarding magazines, papers, and cassettes like some demented burglar. "I'm never coming back here," he muttered. "*Never!*"

As he left Martin in the jungle, he was still blurring the lines between himself and Allie Fox. Spotting the mosquito bites on the writer's ankles, he tipped his cap and barked: "You should always wear repellent!"

Fetid and flea-infested it may have been, but on March 24, 1986, Belize briefly appeared bearable—as jungles went. With fellow nominees Peter Weir and Thom Mount, Harrison watched the 58th Academy Awards on satellite television. The show began with host Robin Williams arriving on stage weighed down by a sealed briefcase of winners' envelopes.

As he joked: "What say we open the suckers right now?" Harrison—for one—was almost certainly in favor. Anything to avoid three and a half hours of excruciating schmaltz and sentimentality.

For some the ceremony was the emotional high point of their careers. Don Ameche, a talent so modest Hollywood had overlooked it for fifty years, was given the night's biggest standing ovation for his Best Supporting Actor award for *Cocoon*. Geraldine Page, another stalwart rather than a major star, collected the Best Actress prize for *The Trip to Bountiful*. For Harrison and *Witness*, it proved a muted occasion. There was cause for some celebration: Thom Noble won the Oscar for Best Film Editing, and William Kelley and Earl and Pamela Wallace, collected a statuette for the Best Original Screenplay. But in the major categories Peter Weir was already being eclipsed by Sydney Pollack and his *Out of Africa*, the film that would go on to dominate the night with seven wins.

By the time Sally Field, presenting the Best Actor Oscar, attempted to undo the damage she had inflicted on her image with her infamous "you really like me" acceptance speech a year earlier, Harrison prepared himself for the worst. "Let's see who you really liked," his *Heroes* colleague giggled before adding: ". . . and the Oscar goes to William Hurt for *Kiss of the Spider Woman*."

It was what Harrison and almost everyone else had expected. Hurt's outrageous turn as a gay window dresser, imprisoned in a South American jail cell, had been sucking up awards since the previous year's Cannes Film Festival.

Some, like David Puttnam, saw Hurt's award as a "watershed"—the dawning of a new maturity in the acting awards. Others wondered whether Harrison had suffered a smaller-scale version of the biggest snub in the history of the Oscars; it became the dominant talking point that night and for months afterward.

Steven Spielberg's *The Color Purple* had matched *Out of Africa* with eleven nominations. Harrison and Peter Weir shared in the audience's growing disbelief as the director's first "mature" movie lost out in every single category. "Anyone who says that envy didn't affect Spielberg's chances would be crazy," Peter Bogdanovich told the Oscar historian Anthony Holden afterward.

As the most visible star of the so-called Lucas-Berg phenomenon, there were many who felt Harrison suffered vicariously. If the Academy had not yet forgiven Spielberg for making so much money, it was certainly not ready to recognize the comic-book hero he had made a fellow millionaire.

Later, Harrison diplomatically acknowledged his gratitude for the nomination. "I was very flattered by the company," he said. But he went on to express his distaste for the whole event. "I don't believe in the competition. You can't compare two different efforts in two different movies and say one is better than the other. Nonsense as far as I'm concerned." His relationship with the Oscar show would remain a long-distance one for years to come.

Harrison's image as a "cartoon hero" was not the only casualty of *Witness* and its ground-shifting success. In June, as he returned from Belize, he cut loose from his representatives, the Gersh Agency. The trade announcements said the split ended "many, many years of togetherness," but few in Hollywood would have been fooled by the cozy tone of the reports.

His relationships with agents had been mercurial since the breakthroughs of the mid-1970s. Gersh, twice, Joan Scott at Writers and Artists, and the giant William Morris Agency had counted him as a client—but no agent was ever made to feel indispensable.

Harrison's contempt for the leviathan agencies, so powerful in Hollywood's New Order, was based on his own brief experience. "I was with a monster agency once. I rode up on the elevator with three guys who were supposed to be my agents," he recalled once. "By the time we got to the top floor of the building they still hadn't figured out who I was. So I never got out of the elevator. I just went right back down."

His mentor George Lucas had added to his distaste with tales of his battle with Jeff Berg of ICM. Berg had helped broker the deal with Fox over *Star Wars*. ICM's ten percent had earned the agency $4.5 million. But by the time of *The Empire Strikes Back*, Lucas felt powerful enough to conduct his own affairs, and experienced few qualms in telling Berg to "buzz off" before negotiating the sequel rights with Alan Ladd at Fox himself. From there he had gone on to clinch his "killer" *Raiders* deal using only the services of a sharp lawyer, Tom Pollock.

In the wake of *Witness*, Harrison finally felt confident enough to set himself free. In a different time the agents had not wanted anything to do with him. Now his ten percent alone would have been enough to keep a medium-sized agency in antique Chippendale furniture. It was too late. Now he didn't want anything to do with them.

Asked once what he likes least about his personality, Harrison answered: "Not letting go . . . I do keep score and I shouldn't." There was a tangible taste of retribution in the air afterward.

Typically, he decided to fly in the face of Hollywood convention. By now Pat McQueeney had been handling his affairs as a manager for more than a decade. As *Witness* had proven, she possessed as much—if not more—instinct for spotting scripts than most of the agents he had come across. Her loyalty had been taken for granted years ago. After the Oscars he proposed she became his agent as well as his manager.

When McQueeney pointed out the complexities of the situation—Californian law made it difficult for anyone to perform both roles—he simply offered a smile and a shrug. "I'm sure you'll work it out, Pat."

She did.

19

MILDLY DISTURBED

When, in 1982, *E.T.* transformed the former *People* magazine writer Melissa Mathison into a celebrity in her own right, journalists were often surprised to discover the slightly menacing presence of Harrison Ford watching over her during interviews. He would sit in the background, wearing what Philip Wuntch of the *New York Times* described as a "don't even try to interview me" scowl on his face.

The few who were given the opportunity to profile her found Melissa deeply uncomfortable in her new, poacher-turned-gamekeeper role. She would shift nervously in her chair, her hands would sometimes shake visibly, and she would almost invariably refuse to be photographed for the article. "My whole life I've been horrified to have my picture taken. I really, like, get so nervous it's not worth the experience," she told one writer. Her shyness made her taciturn boyfriend seem like Oscar Wilde in comparison.

Melissa's interrogators usually left wondering quite what role the hero of *Star Wars* and *Indiana Jones* performed in her life. Was he Svengali or spin doctor, a minder or a Machiavelli overseeing the launch of another career and the protection of his own at the same time? There may have been elements of all this, but, as so often with Harrison Ford, the complexities boil down to a simpler, rather more neurotic truth. "I'm always worried about her," he would come to explain. "That pretty much defines my reality."

In June 1986, with the grueling experience of Belize and *The Mosquito Coast* behind him, Melissa gently broke the news that he had something new to worry over. Back home in Jackson, she told him she was expecting their first child. By now Melissa had finished writing *Son of the Morning Star* and had begun working on an adaptation of the classic cartoon series *Tin Tin* for Roman Polanski. Just before Christmas 1986, six months into her pregnancy, Polanski asked her over to Paris for a script conference.

Harrison would have done all he could to travel with her anyway. But after a recent spate of terrorist bombings he was insistent that he be at her side in France. He had been the beneficiary of more than his fair share of luck over the years. Now it was Polanski's turn to enjoy a slice of good fortune.

In the eight years since Polanski's worldwide notoriety had been cemented by his decision to flee America while facing sex-offense charges, including the alleged rape of a thirteen-year-old girl, his filmic output had been patchy. *Tess*, starring his former lover Nastassja Kinski, had been as exquisite as *Pirates*, with Walter Matthau, had been excruciating.

Polanski had been friendly with Jack Nicholson's circle in Hollywood, but when Harrison met him in Paris it was for the first time. Harrison was entertained by the Polish-born auteur's demonic intelligence, and within days Polanski had asked whether he might be interested in his latest project. Unable to read the French script, Harrison asked for a broad outline.

Over the next two hours, Polanski provided a typically extravagant enactment of his idea, the story of an American doctor searching for his kidnapped wife in Paris. "It was terrific—a compelling story about a man who loved his wife," recalled Harrison. For Polanski, who endured the murder of his wife Sharon Tate by Charles Manson in 1969, the resonances were clear. For Harrison, isolated in Paris, a city he confessed to being able to take or leave, while he watched over his own pregnant wife, it struck a powerful chord nearer home. "I was very receptive," Harrison said later.

It was a measure of how strongly Polanski's story affected him that Harrison immediately registered his interest in traveling to Paris to make the movie. The by now painful process of evaluating a project in all its details was short-circuited by the intensity of Polanski's bravura pitch. "It was clear that this was deeply emotional for Roman," he explained later. "I said, 'If that is what it's going to be like when it's written down, I'll do it.' "

He had other reasons for wanting to leave America. *The Mosquito Coast* opened to reviews—and box-office business—that left Harrison feeling deeply wounded. The film was hardly comfortable viewing. With his hair oiled back, a scowl stapled to his ravaged-looking face, and his eyes dancing like some malevolent mad professor, he looked and sounded the antithesis of the dashing Jones and Solo. Flawless it was not, yet it was easily the most interesting and edgy role of his career. Both Harrison and Weir were widely derided. Whatever hopes they might have had of a second consecutive Oscar nomination together faded almost instantly.

America's heavyweight critics were almost united in their hostility. "One escapes from *The Mosquito Coast* as one might from a plague of the title insects, itching and irritable," wrote Richard Schickel in *Time*.

"This ambitious movie is a complete disaster—monomaniacal, tiresome, pointless, and for all its devotion to the great outdoors, surprisingly claustrophobic," said David Denby in *New York* magazine. Denby went on to accuse Harrison of self-indulgence. "Ford never develops the slightest complicity with the audience. He's out there by himself, fulfilling his actor's dream of intransigence. He doesn't bring us into his way of looking at things and we don't care what happens to him."

Vincent Canby in the *New York Times* simply thought the film "flat." Harrison "looks and sounds right," he said, "yet the audience can never understand the hold he has over his loyal wife."

"At first glance *The Mosquito Coast* must have appeared to have everything: adventure, social criticism, a family story, an exotic locale," wrote Canby's colleague Janet Maslin. But she went on: "If the characters in a film wind up alienating the audience as thoroughly as Allie Fox does (despite the canny, snappish performance of Harrison Ford in the role), then the specifics of what happens to them hardly matter at all."

As the film crept its way to a $14 million return at the box office and began disappearing from view, Harrison gamely took to the publicity trail. He invariably found himself defending his decision to tackle the role in the first place. "I have always tried to do different things. It seems to me the logical ambition of an actor," he told the Associated Press's respected film writer Bob Thomas during a blitzkrieg day of interviews at the Century Plaza Hotel in Los Angeles. "What sense is it to be an actor if you play the same thing over and over again? You need to challenge and broaden yourself."

He also, perhaps misguidedly, given that the film needed any help it could get at the box office, swatted the "Ford is Fox" theory away as if it were another insect back in Belize.

"The role of an actor is to serve as a mirror," he told the American critic Gene Siskel, impatience etched deep in his voice. "My job is *not* to show you that the character and I have something in common. My job is to show you that *you* and the character—even one who may seem a little crazy—have something in common."

While Theroux joined in the defense, writing passionate appreciations of the film of his book to *Time* and *Newsweek*, who had both been critical, Harrison slipped easily into the role of the avenger of injustice, even writing to a number of American newspapers who had run negative reviews. "I have never seen a serious film treated so badly by the critics," he protested in the *Philadelphia Inquirer*. "And I think they're wrong. The picture is well worth seeing. I would like to do whatever I can to help that happen."

His performance was not without its admirers. For the second year running he picked up a Golden Globe nomination from the Hollywood Foreign Press Association. But the real consolation for the public's coolness toward *The Mosquito Coast* lay in the warm reaction of people close to him, Willard and Ben in particular. They greeted his latest character with an ironically arched eyebrow, he admitted. "Even though I haven't been nearly as tough on them as Allie is on Charlie, I know that I have been close to the loss of control that Allie exhibits," he told the *Chicago Tribune*. "I know what they're thinking," he added with a smile.

"One thing that did amaze them, I think, is just how personal the process of being an actor is. I think they were surprised to see me use so much of myself on the screen." Father and sons would carry on talking about the film, "for the rest of our lives," he said.

Afterward he traveled to London to continue beating the drum. It was a measure of his belief in the film that he even agreed to a rare television interview in Britain, appearing, albeit uneasily, on the *Michael Aspel Show*. Britain's critics warmed to his performance in a way their transatlantic cousins had not been able to. "Ford imbues the fast-talking, hyperactive, infuriating, know-all Allie with a kind of tragic grandeur," wrote the *Observer*'s Philip French. The *Financial Times*'s Nigel Andrews thought the book was "wonderfully brought to life" and praised the plausibility of Harrison's Allie. "He is such an overgrown baby and appealing loudmouth . . . a hybrid of matinee idol and Midwest tourist with a dash of mad scientist thrown in." Once more, however, there were those who mourned the fact that Nicholson had not taken on the role. He was the one actor with "the charisma to carry the audience with him" in such an unsympathetic role, thought Iain Johnstone in the *Sunday Times*.

Despite all efforts, however, *The Mosquito Coast* fared little better in Europe. In the end the film's fate was decided by its lack of audience appeal. The critics had their own set of intellectual misgivings; for Harrison's fans it boiled down to a plainer truth. It seems they were simply not interested in seeing the most heroic screen actor of his generation playing a complex and ultimately antiheroic character like Allie Fox.

Patricia McQueeney took no pleasure in seeing her doubts vindicated, but she knew the commercial failure of *Mosquito Coast* would not shake Harrison from a principle he now intended sticking to. "He loved *Mosquito Coast*. He loved what Allie Fox had to say, and he loved playing that character," said McQueeney. "No one has had as many blockbusters as he has had. But he says: 'I'll do these others, but once in a while I gotta do one for me.'"

His disappointment was overshadowed by the birth of his first child with Melissa. The arrival of his first two sons had hardly set the Los Angeles media on red alert. Two decades on, Harrison's second taste of fatherhood constituted a news event of such significance that questions cropped up for years afterward. The softening of his temperament begun by Melissa seemed, if anything, to be accelerated by the arrival of tiny Malcolm Ford in March 1987.

At one time, he would have chewed reporters' heads off for asking about something as intimate as his new baby. It could still happen, depending on his mood. But more often than not he was willing to open a window on the emotions released as he once more became a father.

In London to promote *The Mosquito Coast* toward the end of the pregnancy, he confessed to harboring his usual share of insecurities. "I'll be there at the birth, which I'm really excited about. At forty-four I can only hope that the old adage that having children keeps you young is true. I know I'm going to need a lot of energy."

And he once more admitted to his failings as a father. "There's a chance that this time round I'll do a better job than last time," he said. "I've learned about patience and I have more experience about being a father. The thing about having a child when you're young, as I was then, is the loss of freedom. You sometimes resent that," he told the *Daily Mail*.

Back in America after the birth, the new arrival inspired more uncharacteristic intimacies. "I'm a lot more settled and content in my own life, and it's much easier to deal with all the frustrations and anxieties of parenting," he told *Playboy*'s Bill Zehme in an interview in which he even went on to discuss the merits of disposable diapers. "I'm all for 'em," he said with a grin.

Elsewhere he gave the first indications that Malcolm might be a chip off the old block. "He's remarkably self-possessed," he told writer Jeanne Wolf in an interview with the American magazine *Redbook*. "And I mean from the time he was born. After the birth he just rested on Melissa's chest for about seven hours, while she and I talked to him. He kept looking back and forth at us. It was strange—not how you expect a newborn to act."

The most serious threat to Harrison's newfound equilibrium came not from the media, but from working with Polanski in Paris. The experience was to be the most psychologically demanding of his career so far.

He traveled to Paris with Melissa and baby Malcolm to begin filming in May 1987. The screenplay for *Frantic*, as the film was now called, had been written by Polanski and long-time associate Gérard Brach. Their story described how an eminent American cardiologist, Dr.

Richard Walker, descends into a personal nightmare after his wife goes missing in Paris. Discovering she has been kidnapped, he is drawn into the Parisian demimonde by a mysterious young girl, to be played by Polanski's beautiful girlfriend, Emmanuelle Seigner. Walker's perfectly controlled demeanor slowly unravels itself as he is literally driven frantic by his search.

Harrison had researched the part by spending time with two heart surgeons and talking to other surgeons about the specialists who regard themselves as the crême de la crême of their profession. "Heart surgeons, I discovered, are among the élite of the doctor world. I also found a certain elegance or vanity of gesture that was common to these guys," he explained later. "Lots of hand movements. I already gesture enough with my hands, so that wasn't a challenge."

It was the mechanics of his character's mind rather than his body that he found taxing, however. Polanski was open to improvisation, and with Harrison introduced new and helpful elements to the story. "Roman is actually pretty free in the shooting process," he said later. But he was also one of the most skilled performance directors he had encountered. Perhaps more than any other director in his career, Polanski tapped into his star's duality, his ability to be uptight one moment and unrestrained the next, a coiled spring forever in danger of unleashing itself. On the set, Walker's air of calm authority slowly gave way to the frenzy of a man losing control of his life. And it began to take its toll after-hours, too.

Harrison immersed himself in the role of Walker in his customary way. He had found himself overly absorbed in his characters before: "When it's over, I need to patch up everything and get my life back on its feet again," he said once. At first he was unaware of how Walker was affecting him until, heading back to his hotel to see Melissa and Malcolm each night, he became aware that the role was getting to him like no other role before. And it was Melissa who suffered.

"To imagine how terrible someone would feel if his wife were kidnapped wasn't hard," he explained later. "The frustration and anxiety I had to create had a serious residual effect on me. I took it home with me every night in a way I never had before. I usually get that out of my system, but this one was unremitting, relentless . . . My wife often found me in the same frustrated mood as my character, a mood I thought I'd been able to drop. It was more of a strain than I'd anticipated."

His coolness toward Paris did little to help. He admitted he did not enjoy the louche lifestyle of the average Parisian. "I find the whole routine completely unattractive: eating late, staying up, smoky bistros and all of that. It doesn't have the charm for me that it might once have had."

Perhaps sensing his mood, Polanski and Melissa organized a party to celebrate his forty-fifth birthday. The decadent atmosphere of Ibiza's Ku Club, a favorite hangout for rock stars and royalty, from George Michael to Princess Diana, lifted the gloom.

Harrison also had the distraction of composing a tribute to George Lucas, celebrating the tenth anniversary of *Star Wars* back in America. No writer (his claim that he never writes letters or even sends postcards is challenged by his old Park Ridge friend Bill Russell, who would receive cards from the edge of America in the 1960s simply signed, "I'm rich and famous, you bastard. Harry."), his message was short and sweet:

George Lucas.
Maker of myths.
Champion of the innocent.
Defender of the faith—or Force, if you will.
My colleague.
My friend.
Let's face it—my mentor.
Best wishes on the 10th anniversary of *Star Wars*.
Love, Harrison.

On the *Indiana Jones* movies, stuntwork had been the most demanding element. On *Frantic* in many ways it became a welcome escape from the pressures of playing the disintegrating Dr. Walker—although Harrison's willingness to take risks horrified some of the crew.

The most testing sequence took place on a steep Parisian rooftop. At one point Harrison had to dangle thirty-five feet above a courtyard. In his enthusiasm to make the most of his star's courage, Polanski spent hours on the rooftop with him. "Polanski and Harrison were up on that steep roof, climbing around like a couple of ten-year-olds, trying to work out the shots," said the film's editor Sam O'Steen. "Had either of them slipped, they would have been killed. I watched three takes and had to leave the set, it was so scary."

Both men survived the scene—and indeed the shoot, which came to a close in August, as France collectively closed down for its annual summer holiday. Harrison and Melissa's troubles did not end when their plane left French soil. The private jet they were sharing with Clint Eastwood and his girlfriend Sondra Locke, who had been in Paris researching *Bird*, Eastwood's jazz movie based on Charlie Parker, experienced landing-gear failure as they were due to make a refueling stop in the eastern United States. After a period of mild panic amongst the high-profile passengers, the backup system allowed them to make an emergency landing at the small airstrip in Bangor, Maine. While a crew of mechanics was flown out from California, two of Hollywood's strong-but-silent heroes holed up at a local hotel. Harrison Ford remained frantic about the safety of his wife and new baby all the way back to Wyoming.

By the time he returned to Jackson Hole, what had begun as a series of drawings on the back of Parisian paper napkins had been transformed into a new house on the edge of the Snake River.

Harrison relieved the stress of filming *Frantic* most effectively by scratching out detailed plans for the dwelling—a classical, white clapboarded building in the tradition of the Massachusetts mansions. Each morning, as the workmen rose in Jackson, a new set of instructions was waiting at the foot of the fax machine in their employer's workshop.

If Harrison had been exacting as a contractor, he was even more so as a client. "I'd hate to work for him," said the writer Jim Harrison. "He'd be incredibly demanding."

The large house had been intended as a home for the caretaker employed to watch over the land when they were away. It was a measure of how happy Harrison was with the work that had been done in executing his designs that he and Melissa quickly changed their minds and made it their own.

The house was a wonder of inch-perfect joinery, a burnished miracle with gleaming wooden floors the size of basketball courts and flaw-lessly proportioned cabinetwork everywhere. Its angles were so carefully coordinated with its environment that the view through every window was an Ansell Adams landscape. It was, as one visitor put it, "the kind of place that John Book might have built had he stayed around to marry Rachel in *Witness*." Jim Harrison, who visited them there, called it a "marvel. . . . In terms of details, people don't build houses like that."

As he watched autumn breaking under the shadow of the watchful Tetons, Harrison helped his contractors build new guest quarters and a large red barn. The barn became his workshop, the inner sanctum where he continued to enjoy the pleasures of carpentry. Slowly, like Skywalker Ranch, the personal paradise George Lucas built from the profits of *Star Wars*, the Jackson homestead evolved into an extension of its owner's unique personality. Lucas furnished himself with the science to take cinema into the twenty-first century. Harrison harked back to the simplicity of a life lived a hundred years earlier.

His 800 acres was home to some of the area's most precious wildlife. A year earlier, in June 1986, he and Melissa had granted an easement to the Jackson Hole Land Trust. The move ensured that 132 acres of their land, home to two bald eagles, red-tailed hawks, moose, elk, deer, and trumpeter swans, could no longer be built upon.

The town, still getting to know its famous new residents, were grateful. "It's hard to imagine such a place covered with buildings, but that certainly could have happened some day. The Fords have done a splendid thing by making sure that it never will," Jean Hocker, the trust's executive director said.

Miles from the gates marked PRIVATE PROPERTY: PLEASE NO TRESPASSING, Harrison Ford had finally found a refuge where he could merge with nature, become a detail in the landscape.

By the late 1980s, few men in Hollywood remained immune to the elegantly persuasive powers of Patricia McQueeney. Even she was amazed when one of this rare breed performed the volte-face that led to the role of Jack Trainer in *Working Girl*, one of the most enjoyable and successful experiences of Harrison Ford's career.

McQueeney had loved the script by Kevin Wade and first suggested it to Harrison early in 1986. "I wanted him to do romantic comedy but they are very hard to find," she said. His rejection of Wade's feminist fairy tale, in which an ambitious secretary from Staten Island bluffs her way to the negotiating table in a Wall Street takeover deal, out-smarting her arrogant female boss and landing her WASPish, invest-ment broker boyfriend in the process, boiled down to four little words. "It's the girls' movie," he told McQueeney.

Even the prospect of working with Mike Nichols, rehabilitated in the eyes of Hollywood after a disastrous decade in the 1970s and fresh from the Oscar-nominated success of *Silkwood* with Meryl Streep, exerted less pulling power than it might.

Her client was not the only stubborn son-of-a-bitch in Hollywood, however. By the time McQueeney once more raised the subject of the movie over dinner with Harrison and Melissa one evening, it was the sixth time she had done so.

Harrison, Melissa, and Malcolm were preparing to head to Wyoming for the winter. "I said: 'Why spend January and February with snow on the roof when you could be in New York having fun with Mike Nichols?' " she recalled. Sensing a change in his mood she added: "Maybe somebody will get an idea from this and sit down and write something for you. What can you lose?"

The phrase, "Okay," had barely passed her client's lips before McQueeney was racing down Sunset Boulevard plying her charms on producer Larry Mark. "He said, 'It's interesting you should call; we are going to make Alec Baldwin an offer tomorrow morning.' I said, 'See if you can change their minds.' . . . They didn't call back for five days—I almost had a heart attack."

Such was Harrison's drawing power now that Larry Mark could not resist adding him to a cast list that already included the rising Melanie Griffith and Sigourney Weaver. As recompense, Alec Baldwin was offered the role of Griffith's habitually unfaithful, blue-collar boyfriend. A magnanimous Baldwin later summed up the simplicity of the expe-rience—and the appreciation his peers now had for Harrison's ubiqui-tous ability. "The minute Harrison Ford shows up, you drop everything and you sign up Harrison Ford."

Harrison's reasons for accepting ran much deeper than mere meteo-rology. He was keen to put the nightmarish experience of *Frantic* behind him. Such suffering might have been meat and drink to Method

masochists like Pacino and De Niro, Hoffman and the young Daniel
Day-Lewis, but it wasn't Harrison's idea of fun. "Taking that amount of
anxiety and pent-up frustration around with you all the time is difficult.
It affected me internally," he told the *New York Post*. "I was happy to
do a comedy because you go home at the end of the day feeling great.
What you're working on is not so serious that it obsesses you."

The tepid reception *Frantic* received when it was released in February did little to justify the anguish he had been through, although there
was widespread praise for both his performance and Polanski's direction. *Newsweek* thought it a revelatory performance: "Ford makes you
realize what a movie star really is—someone whose every on-screen
move is totally enjoyable, an indefinable synthesis of his own personality and the role he's playing." *USA Today* called *Frantic* "the most
underrated '88 film to date." Janet Maslin in the *New York Times*
described Harrison as "a compelling if rather uncomplicated hero" but
thought Polanski "succeeded in picking up the clever, unnerving thread
of his earlier career."

Frantic failed to ignite much interest at the box office, unfortunately.
Its $17 million at the U.S. box office made it only marginally more suc-
cessful than *The Mosquito Coast*. After a flawless run of success between
Empire and *Witness*, Harrison had misfired twice in succession.

While Polanski undoubtedly proved the legend that had preceded
him in terms of pushing his actors to the limit, his treatment of Harrison was entirely different from that of, say, Ridley Scott's on *Blade
Runner*. Harrison knew Polanski was simply seeking the best possible
performance. In combining Harrison's simultaneous looseness and
tightness, he almost, but not quite, achieved that.

The two men have remained friends despite *Frantic*'s failure at the
box office—and Harrison's occasionally acidic remarks about the
movie. "I always knew calling it *Frantic* was a mistake. I told Polanski
we should call it *Moderately Disturbed*," he joked once. Later, looking
back at the film, he called it a "fish out of water" story. The familiar,
sideways snarl of a smile slid into place as he added: "Fish out of water
sometimes die from a lack of something to breathe."

The roots of Harrison's friendship with Mike Nichols stretched back
to his days as a studio-fodder freshman at Columbia. At different times

Walter Beakel had been each man's mentor, tutoring Nichols at Chicago's Compass Theater with Elaine May, and Harrison when he was the most recalcitrant member of his New Talent Program on Gower Street.

The Harrison Ford who turned up for rehearsals now bore no resemblance to the raw, undisciplined newcomer Nichols had rejected in favor of Dustin Hoffman for *The Graduate* more than two decades earlier. Callowness had given way to consummate control.

Nichols shared Harrison's belief that God lies in the details. He later attributed *Working Girl*'s success to the simple fact that "the makeup was right . . . When the girls got off the Staten Island ferry right at the beginning, you thought—I get it, this is about real Staten Island girls."

Harrison contributed much to his character Jack Trainer's comic personality in the same way. He even worked in a joke about his famous facial scar. While rehearsing a postcoital moment between Trainer and Tess, Harrison, Nichols, and Melanie Griffith came up with the idea of her stroking his distinctive cicatrix and wondering how he had got it. As they played around with the idea, Harrison suggested that Trainer initially brags it is a battle scar, won in a knife fight. When Tess seems alarmed by this he tells her the truth, that he fainted while having his ear pierced as a teenager and had knocked his chin on the toilet seat.

"Many of the changes that came about in *Working Girl* came about through Harrison," said Nichols. "The fact that his character was in trouble, the fact that Jack risked his position by refusing to go on without Tess—those were Harrison's contributions. He's as intelligent an actor as I have ever met."

The chemistry between him and the effervescent Griffith proved to be one of the film's great assets. "He was so easy to act with, because you look in his eyes and there's a real person there. He listens, he reacts, he gives a lot," she said later. "He helped me enormously."

The relief of working on a production which did not leave him as mentally burdened as *Frantic* and *The Mosquito Coast* was frequently in evidence, although producer Douglas Wick recalls a moment when Harrison's patience snapped. During a seemingly interminable night shoot, he had been left sitting with Griffith in the back of a taxi for more than two hours. He summoned Wick and, raising his voice slightly, demanded to know, "What the hell is going on here?" By the high-strung standards of other leading men he had worked with, the eruption hardly registered on the Richter scale. Yet Harrison later sought Wick out to apologize.

"When so many people want something of you, and are trying to ingratiate themselves, they're very complicitous in allowing you to be an asshole," said the Hollywood-weathered producer. "Harrison has a very strong sense of how it's right for a person to act."

Nichols saw the same principles at work when a shy young autograph hunter wandered on to the set, eager to meet the man who plays Indiana Jones. Looking nervously around, the boy failed to recognize the film's male star and approached him.

"Excuse me, sir, could you tell me where I can find Harrison Ford?"

"Harrison said: 'Oh, he's around here somewhere. He's wearing tan pants and a jacket,' and he went on to describe what he was wearing," Nichols recalled.

Soon the words connected. The little boy smiled. "It's you."

"That was typical Harrison. He found the kindest possible way of letting the kid know without hurting him."

20

NEVER SAY NEVER

F or a definitive portrait of the determination with which Harrison Ford was driving his career by the end of the 1980s we need look no further than a set of statistics provided by his personal trainer at the time.

At 6 or 6:30 A.M. each morning, Fran Horneff would oversee a workout consisting of :

100 bench-presses with 115-pound weights
100 leg extensions with 70-pound weights
100 leg curls with 50-pound weights
100 squats with 100-pound weights
200 assorted arm, upper body and back exercises with 15- to 25-pound weights
100 gridiron-style "squat thrusts"
up to 400 sit-ups

At the end of each session Horneff's pupil would go off to makeup and prepare for another dawn-till-dusk day at the office of Professor Indiana Jones. The traumas of filming *The Temple of Doom* in Sri Lanka had left him in no doubt about the physical demands that came with his most popular role. For years afterward Harrison complained of feeling like "a creaky old bag of bones." Late in 1987, long before Paramount set a shooting date for the third adventure in the series, Harrison had begun to prepare for the challenge.

A lasting legacy of his second outing as Indy was a nagging back-ache. Some gym equipment had been installed at Jackson Hole, and skiing and tennis were added to the fitness routine that had, at the age of forty-five, become a tedious necessity of his job. His approach to his tennis was as rigorously practical as ever. Having discovered a knack for it, Harrison made it part of his routine wherever he went. "I like to get out there and work on skills and run around and sweat," he explained once. In his search for a new perfectionism there was no room for friendly family knockabouts. "I never play socially because it seems like a waste of time!"

The daily routine he went through with Fran Horneff had been designed with Jake Steinfeld for the specific purpose of helping Harri-son's fragile back survive a four-month shoot that would take in Spain, Jordan, and Venice as well as Elstree. "He is very strong; he has a lot of determination and doesn't quit," Steinfeld said admiringly later. By May 1988, their preparation was ready for its ultimate test.

The third Indy film, *Indiana Jones and the Last Crusade*, had been more than three years in coming. The trinity of Harrison, Spielberg, and Lucas had demanded a series of rewrites. Each knew the latest revival would require a more finely judged development of the character than in the flawed *Temple of Doom*.

Harrison had quietly voiced his dissatisfaction with the film's vio-lence in the intervening years. "It was unnecessarily graphic," he con-ceded. Lucas in particular felt the next adventure should return to the *Raiders* theme of Hitler and his quest for religious artifacts. Five drafts of a script had been presented and rejected before all three agreed on an acceptable story.

Writer Jeffrey Boam's adventure introduced Indiana's archaeologist father, Henry Jones, who became involved with his son in a race against the Nazis to find the ultimate prize, the Holy Grail. Part of the story's appeal was that it also featured a lengthy opening sequence, priming the audience for the main event, with an introduction to the young Indiana and his father set in Utah in 1912.

Spielberg was credited with the inspirational idea of casting Sean Connery as Henry Jones. As the spiritual father of the *Indiana Jones* adventures, who better than James Bond himself to play Jones senior? River Phoenix's performance in *The Mosquito Coast*—not to mention his striking physical resemblance to Harrison—landed him the role of the young Indiana.

Harrison was, on the face of it, delighted by the casting of Phoenix. He insisted on working with him on the physicality of his part. "I wanted to make sure he got the moves right," he said later. Some, however, interpreted his interest in Phoenix's performance as mild paranoia brought on by fears that he might be about to be permanently usurped by Young Indy. "The young actor [Phoenix] was warned never to imitate Ford's mannerisms on-screen, nor to suggest he had any interest in taking over the Indy role," wrote Spielberg biographer John Baxter. Certainly the success of Phoenix's performance was strong enough to inspire a Lucasfilm television series, *The Young Indiana Jones Chronicles*. Fate, however, would not allow a definitive answer to the rumors that circulated in Hollywood. Within six years, Phoenix would be dead.

If Harrison had been perturbed by Phoenix's role, he was initially confused by the casting of Connery. At fifty-eight, the Scot was still in prime physical condition. To judge by the "World's Sexiest Man" polls he kept topping, his looks were if anything growing more appealing.

"My first reaction was he's not old enough. Then I forgot—*I'm* too old," Harrison said. According to the script, Indiana was thirty-five. In reality, Harrison would soon be forty-six. His youthfulness had not deserted him, however. The chemistry between the two men would prove the film's greatest asset.

Filming began in Almeria, Spain, on May 16, 1988. The complex opening sequence provided biographical background ranging from Indy's problematic relationship with his father and the acquisition of his bullwhip and fedora, to his phobia for snakes and the latest explanation of the most famous facial scar in cinema—a misguided crack of his whip.

While the young Indiana was revealing new and surprising psychological insights, his alter ego served up more familiar fare. In the most highly tuned physical condition of his career, Harrison seemed intent on proving his fitness.

"If he hits you, he really hits you," confided actor Kevork Malikyan, with whom Harrison staged an elaborate fight on board a speedboat in Venice. "I found him very rough in that way. No nonsense—and no apologies, either." Malikyan went so far as to suggest Harrison was "not all that concerned about the other people in the scene with him . . . who didn't have any dialogue." During their fight scene, at which Alison Doody was also present, he said: "Sometimes one foot would be up in the air, hitting Alison [Doody] in the face."

Vic Armstrong was once more a frequently bored onlooker. ("Using a stunt person is like going off on vacation and asking somebody else to make love to your wife while you're gone," Harrison philosophized once. "If you can do it yourself, you certainly should.")

The most expensive part of the film was an extended sequence featuring a giant German tank. The action, reminiscent of the convoy chase in *Raiders*, was the first major test of Harrison's fitness.

The most difficult stunt involved hanging on to the turret of the tank as it ploughed through the crumbling rocks of a gorge. Harrison called that "one of the hairiest stunts I've ever been involved in." The one scene he accepted as being too difficult was a fourteen-foot leap from a galloping horse on to the rumbling German behemoth. That was "deemed too dangerous for me to do," he said later.

The film's locations also took in Jordan and Venice. Melissa and Spielberg's girlfriend, Kate Capshaw, traveled with them to the Italian city but found the stench from its polluted canals so overwhelming that they relocated to London, where filming would be completed.

For the seventh time in his career to date, Harrison found himself back at Elstree. London had long since lost its allure. And when, in July, a burglar broke into the Hampstead mansion he and Melissa were renting and removed some of her jewelry worth $33,000, the sparkle faded even more. Harrison had seen a figure trying to break into a neighboring house. It was only an hour later that he realized the burglar had beaten his home's elaborate security system to snatch gems from the master bedroom.

While details of the burglary made newspapers on both sides of the Atlantic, it was a series of other reports that angered him most. In the wake of his back problems on *Temple of Doom*, there were rumors of dire warnings over his stuntwork. In New York, the *Globe* had run a story claiming doctors had warned him that continuing to play Indiana Jones "could kill him." This was followed up by stories suggesting he did not actually do his stuntwork and was regarded with disdain by the stuntman. The final straw came when the *News of the World*'s Sunday magazine ran an article alleging cowardice on the set and some equally lily-livered behavior back home in Wyoming.

As the production settled into routine, Harrison found his greatest exhilaration in the opportunities he had to play off Connery. Spielberg claimed later that he had hired Connery to "give Harrison a run for his money." If that is true, it was inspired casting. In *Last Crusade* Harrison gave by far his most engaging performance as Indiana.

The two men formed a respectful relationship, Connery warming to his costar's wit—"his humor is sly and sneaks up on you"—Harrison responding to his partner's love of improvisation. "We like to work fast and loose, and we like to have fun," he said.

As Jones senior and junior fled Germany on a Zeppelin, Indiana was called on to deal with a Nazi on the verge of capturing them. Rather than disposing of him with a conventional punch—or a variation on the series' long-running gun gag—Harrison suggested Indiana pose as a flight attendant and hurl him out of the window. He could then announce that the man had no ticket. "Well, we all agreed it was stupid, but we all agreed it would work, and it does," he explained afterward. "That's because it's dumb while being inspired and gleeful."

Even funnier was an exchange cooked up between Harrison and Connery involving the film's blond villainess Elsa, played by the stunning English actress Alison Doody. ("I can't play opposite someone called Doody," he had japed with English actor Julian Glover. "You know what that means?") Indiana inevitably ends up in bed with the spy who has been posing as an archaeologist, but then discovers his father has had carnal knowledge before his arrival in Germany. "I'm as human as the next man," Jones senior protests. "I *was* the next man!" replies Indy in one of the film's most memorable jokes.

"I was bound to have fun playing a gruff, Victorian Scottish father," said Connery, who had fought a typically tenacious battle to give his character more depth and had succeeded in getting the playwright Tom Stoppard to beef up his lines.

The fifty-eight-year-old legend even found time to provide the most successful box-office star in the world with an unnecessary but rather hilarious refresher in humility. One morning he and Harrison were sitting beside a road during a break in filming in California. Spotting the scene, a passing car slowed down. Soon shrill female voices were to be heard shouting, "Oh my God, it's Sean Connery!" "And what am I, chopped liver?" enquired James Bond's sardonic sidekick.

"The pleasure of my life," Harrison admitted during filming on *The Last Crusade*, "is that, however long it takes to make a movie, when it's over, I'm back to reality. Back to the banal tasks where I belong."

As he watched autumn pass into winter back at Jackson Hole, he devoted himself to six months of blissful banality. Determined not to look at another script for the duration, Harrison filled his time with the minutiae of running a working ranch of Ponderosa proportions. "I'll fix a fence, repair a piece of equipment, or plough the driveway if there's snow. There's always plenty of work to do," he explained at the time.

As the father of an eighteen-month-old child, his days were no shorter than those he put in as Indiana. He and Melissa would rise at 5:30 A.M. or so, attend to the baby, and get on with the business of the day. Once their small staff of farmhands and a secretary had headed home, they would, weather allowing, pop Malcolm into his papoose carrier and end their day with a walk along the riverbank or through the glades of blue spruce and cottonwood, soaking up the Thoreau-like simplicity of their life there.

At work he had once more existed within the surreal bubble of superstardom: the five-star suites, the infinite indulgence of hotel and film-set assistants, an environment where every whim would be catered for. On his ranch he was able once more to restore his equilibrium. "I need balance," he said. "I need to be in a situation where my every whim is *not* attended to, where I have to fetch my own nails, do my own shopping and wash my own dishes. . . . Being normal," he would often say, "is a kind of victory."

He only emerged from his exile to help Mike Nichols promote *Working Girl*. In New York in December he once more dutifully presented himself for a round of television and print interviews.

His relationship with the press had hardened into a kind of stand-off. He had all but given up on his efforts to preserve the privacy of

the ranch. (Soon he would be admitting he had "lost the war" by inviting the celebrity photographer Annie Leibovitz to capture the beauty
of his hideaway.) But the experiences of the past, particularly with *Ritz*
in London years earlier, had made him one of the wariest interviewees
on the Hollywood circuit.

His reticence often gave journalists only half their story. Writers
would talk of his habit of handling words like hand grenades, listen to
him leave sentences hanging in the air, tie himself up in narrative
knots as he attempted to talk and edit himself as he went along.

His precision also reduced the risk of his losing his temper. The last
time he had blown a fuse had been in London during filming of *The
Last Crusade* at Shepperton, as *Frantic* had been released in the United
Kingdom. Ironically, drug-taking was the subject which snapped his
patience during the interview with Tim Willis of *You* magazine. Willis
had asked Harrison to explain why he had insisted on showing Walker
in *Frantic* washing his nose clean after a scene in which he snorted
cocaine with the mysterious Seigner.

"I guess on account of how I was raised, I feel obliged by a certain
responsibility toward myself, my children, and my audience to work
that is positive rather than negative," he tried to explain. "My intention was to show the audience that the doctor had not done that on
purpose."

When Willis wondered whether this reflected his own attitude to
drug-taking, Harrison, "slammed one hand on the table, jutted his head
forward and spat: 'That's none of your ****ing business!' . . . I thought
he was going to nut me," Willis wrote in his piece.

In New York, however, his composure remained intact—helped in
no small measure by the almost universal praise his comic turn as Jack
Trainer in *Working Girl* was winning. For once it was Pat McQueeney
for whom persistence had paid off.

"He displays a comic talent never before explored," said the *Hollywood Reporter*. *USA Today* echoed the reaction of many who did a
double take at his wonderfully deadpan turn. "Ford's comic abilities
are a total surprise; he's been so good recently that a critical reevalu-
ation is due."

Thoroughly in tune with the aspirational 1980s, *Working Girl* went
on to reap six Oscar nominations, including one for Melanie Griffith

as Best Actress. Predictably, alas, Harrison was *not* among the hallowed half dozen.

While *Star Wars* had gone out with a critical whimper, *Indiana Jones* bowed out with a resounding crack of a bullwhip. On both sides of the Atlantic, it was difficult to find a critic willing to dislike the wittiest, most gleefully absurd, and hopelessly theatrical of the trilogy. Nor were there many foolish enough to fault Connery's jewel of a performance as Henry Jones. *People* magazine summed up the popular view: "In this imperfect world you're not likely to see many man-made objects this close to perfection."

As the cycle of films came to an end, it was left to more cerebral minds to place the trilogy and its makers in a proper historical context, bestowing comparisons with the Frenchmen who made such fantasy filmmaking possible in the first place. Derek Malcolm in the *Guardian* bracketed Spielberg and Lucas with Méliès and Feuillade. "If they were among the real pioneers, this lot at least are keeping the popular cinema alive and kicking," his benediction ended.

In reality the reviews mattered not at all. Once more Harrison Ford found himself the star of the most successful film in history. As it opened over the weekend of May 24, 1989, *The Last Crusade* raked in a staggering $46.9 million from 2,327 American cinemas. Thanks in no small measure to the additional fifty cents exhibitors had charged for the hottest seats of the summer, Paramount were able to boast the biggest box-office opening weekend of any film to date. Worldwide it went on to outgun even the other success of the summer, Warner's *Batman*, Jack Nicholson's Joker and all. Its global box office pushed the $450 million mark.

Lucas yielded to the instant pressure for more Indy adventures by developing the River Phoenix character into a small screen spin-off. When, four years later, ABC's *Young Indiana Jones Chronicles* was struggling in the ratings, Harrison once more rode to the rescue, appearing in a two-hour special, "The Mystery of the Blues." From a snowbound Wyoming, a bearded Indiana cast his mind back to his youth in Chicago and his adventures with his college roommate Eliot Ness!

As far as a fourth film was concerned, Lucas, Spielberg, and Harrison presented a united front. There were no plans for any more. Harrison's flourish of finality was to donate his fedora to the Smithsonian Institution. (He kept another at home in Wyoming.)

For the devoted, however, there was enough ambivalence to leave a semblance of hope. Given the length of time it had taken to find a satisfactory script for the third film, Harrison told interviewers that he did not foresee himself being able to play Indiana again until he was in his early fifties. "It might appear unseemly," he said.

It was, perhaps inevitably, Connery who provided him with the perfect cliff-hanging ending to the Indiana Jones era. Asked what he had learned most from working alongside the man who made James Bond flesh, the line was irresistible. "Never say never again . . ."

The Last Crusade marked the end of Harrison's commitment to Lucas and Spielberg. As Indy and his father rode off into the sunset, the most significant collaborations of his life so far were complete. Appropriately, the severing of the cord came at the end of the decade during which the trio had exerted an enormous influence within their industry—an era in which the ethos of the New Hollywood had taken triumphant hold.

No films characterized Hollywood in the 1980s as simply and profoundly as the Indiana Jones adventures. Old Hollywood had had its run at catering for the postwar baby boomers; Indiana Jones was the champion of a New Hollywood that was making undreamed-of profits by aiming its guns at a new market. Indy appealed to older audiences too. But it was the teens and preteens, the Nike-and-baseball-cap generation, with their love of comics and computer games, McDonald's hamburgers and nights out at the multiplex, who made him a phenomenon. Harrison, much as he tried to deny it with roles like Allie Fox and John Book, personified the new age. If Spielberg and Lucas were the dashing duo in the vanguard of this new movement Michael Pye and Linda Myles christened the Movie Brats, then he was their whip-wielding champion.

Luck, of course, had played a part in his triumph. But fortune had also smiled on the likes of Richard Dreyfuss and Mark Hamill. Harrison, more than any other of the Lucas-Berg protégés, had remembered—as Yeats put it—"Not a man alive / Has so much luck he can play with it."

In truth, the foundations of his triumph were laid long before *Star Wars* and *Indiana Jones*, *Jaws* and *E.T.* His lean years in Hollywood underpinned his will to win. And the means with which he won his victory had been learned long before that. "Right from the beginning, I believed that staying on course was what counted. The sheer process of attrition would wear others down," he said at the peak of his powers in the early 1980s. "Them that stuck it out was them that won. That was my belief then. It still is."

If his mulish stubbornness had been an asset within his career, it could still offend those who had befriended him away from Hollywood. Seven dollars or so of *The Last Crusade*'s mega-million takings came from the pocket of Professor William Tyree. He was persuaded to see the film by a friend at Ripon College who had watched it the previous weekend. Harrison's former friend and philosophy master was touched by a line early in the film: "Archaeology is the search for fact not truth," Indiana told a class of star-struck students. "If it's the truth you're interested in, Dr. Tyree's philosophy class is right down the hall."

Since leaving under a cloud, Harrison's contact with Ripon had been limited to his phone conversation with Tyree during the draft-board troubles of the 1960s. The college authorities had watched with pride as the career born at the Red Barn went on to confound almost everyone's expectations. Tyree, by now retired, was aware that Harrison had been approached by Ripon with a view to being given an honorary degree. The offer had been made through Pat McQueeney's office, but no reply had been received. He sensed a chance to rebuild bridges, but was disappointed by his treatment. "I thought here is another opportunity to say something conciliatory," he explained.

Tyree, a proud man, tried to contact Harrison directly through Pat McQueeney's office but was told to write care of her address in Los Angeles. "Underneath I was resentful about having to go through an agent. We had been friends. I was not writing a fan letter. That offended me deeply, but I swallowed that," he said.

He penned a long letter thanking Harrison first for remembering him in *The Last Crusade*. "I congratulated him on his career, said that I had followed it closely and was gratified that he had done so well. Second, I said that I had been made aware that he had been offered an honorary degree. I then expressed the hope that if the offer were to be renewed, he would reconsider. I also made a vague but intelligible reference to the effect that I too have been unhappy about the time since he left and that I had perhaps not done as much as I could have," he added. "It was as nice a letter as one could hope to write."

To his disappointment, Tyree—like Ripon itself—never received a reply; "I was saddened by that. But with the college it is still a stronger point. Here is an institution extending itself to him. It didn't have the respect of a courteous personal reply," he said.

In the years that followed, Ripon made another attempt to offer Harrison an honorary degree. Rather than softening, his attitude hardened to the point of hostility.

"Why don't they all do that?" he snapped once. "Invite those flunkies who've become notably successful—and most likely well off—to return, with the very firm belief that such an honor would loosen the purse strings? Is that not the reality of the situation?"

If the college was as offended as Harrison's old mentor, it is unlikely Ripon will extend the hand of friendship again.

21

LEGAL TENDER

Locked away in an editing suite at the beginning of March 1989, Steven Spielberg could probably have done without the sight of Harrison Ford, sardonically smiling at him in virtually every frame of the yet-to-be-completed *Indiana Jones and the Last Crusade*.

Elsewhere in Hollywood, amid much rancor, the man who had called the director's most cherished screen character "that ugly little fuck" was about to become the indirect beneficiary of a sizable chunk of *E.T.*'s mega-millions. Melissa had been locked in a protracted legal row with MCA/Universal over who exactly had created the most familiar alien face this side of Alpha Centauri. She claimed she was due a slice of the enormous merchandising business that had spun off from the film's success.

On March 1, the Writers Guild of America, arbitrating the dispute, ruled that *E.T.* was Melissa's "unique and original" creation. As a result she was due between four and five percent of any merchandising of E.T.'s likeness. Given that at the peak of E.T.'s popularity, MCA had licensing agreements with forty-three companies to produce more than five hundred E.T. items, from dolls to lunch boxes, the word *substantial* substantially understated the scale of the back-dated royalties now due. As a newspaper in her husband's hometown put it: "If they ever get divorced, this could mean he gets a bigger alimony check than she does!"

The decision left Spielberg fuming. Days after it had splashed the story across its news pages, his attorney Bruce M. Ramer protested at the Hollywood trade paper *Variety*'s "implied denigration" that "Mr. Spielberg had nothing to do with the birth and shaping of the character and concept central to the most successful motion picture in history. . . . Without [Spielberg] there would have been no *E.T.*," he berated. "As Ms. Mathison would unquestionably confirm to you, Mr. Spielberg conveyed his views and concepts to her respecting *E.T.* in the most minute detail, both before and during the writing process."

Spielberg's "views and concepts" were not what Melissa had been arguing over, however. At the heart of the matter was the question of who had been responsible for first describing in writing the distinctive features of the creature an entire planet had fallen in love with six years earlier.

MCA/Universal argued that E.T. had been described in written material by Spielberg and John Sayles *before* Melissa was hired. The studio had additionally argued that artist Carlo Rambaldi, who had designed the model used in the film, was also responsible for its unique features. Arbitrator Sol Rosenthal saw things differently, however. Melissa was the only credited screenwriter, and her brief from Spielberg had been simply to "write a children's story about a man from outer space." She had never read Sayles's script, in which the alien had a beaklike mouth and eyes like a grasshopper's, and had described her version of the character in intricate detail in her two draft scripts.

Rosenthal had no doubt that E.T. was her creature: "Mathison did not stop at writing only that E.T.'s finger glowed. She described his unique hands and fingers," he said. "Mathison did not only write that E.T. was three and a half feet tall; she created short, squashed legs, a telescopic neck, a protruding belly, long thin arms and a glowing heart. She did not simply write that E.T.'s face was round, but detailed his wide head, the softness in his face, his large, round eyes, the leathery creases and furrows in his brow."

Whatever damage the case inflicted on relations between Harrison and Spielberg, the two men presented a friendly front weeks later as *The Last Crusade* was released. Spielberg, far from the most adept interviewee, rambled on about Connery and Harrison's status as Hollywood "royalty. . . . Not the royalty you fear because they can tax you, but the

royalty you love because they will make your lives better." Harrison
dutifully returned the compliment, but in his customary careful tones.
"He and I have a process that doesn't involve arguing. It's as if our
brains are built to run very well as a team," he said.

In the months that followed, Melissa, Harrison, and Spielberg maintained a dignified silence over their feelings about the E.T. ruling. By the
time, two years later, Spielberg married his second wife, *Temple of Doom*
leading lady Kate Capshaw, on Long Island, Harrison was invited not just
to the wedding but the raucous stag night beforehand. However, the
case publicly confirmed what those who knew Harrison Ford had privately known for years. No one took him—or his wife—for a ride.

The case had been difficult and potentially ruinous for Melissa. Her
public argument, though not directly with Spielberg, risked wounding
her relationship with one of the most powerful figures in Hollywood.
Yet her decision to pursue it was thoroughly in keeping with the principles Harrison had displayed ever since he had arrived in Hollywood.
On-screen he was the public embodiment of the all-American hero, an
heir to the family-loving frontiersman who quietly got on with his business until injustice forced him to pick up his shotgun and defend himself. Offscreen he was no different. And bitter experience had taught
him how to look after himself.

Even as Melissa had been involved in her case, he had been instruct-
ing lawyers to act on the sensationalist stories that had run on him in
Britain. Harrison had never before complained about his treatment by
the press, even if he found the experience of giving interviews as appealing as root canal work. "I'd just as soon people knew as little about me
as possible, for a variety of reasons. One is I don't think it helps with
your work. Two, I think people get bored with you. And three, I think
that there's just too much emphasis on celebrity and success in this
country," he told an American interviewer once. Despite the fact that
he had given interviews to the first two, and his wife was a former writer
at the third, he referred to America's three leading celebrity magazines
as "Vanity is Fair," "US, as opposed to them," and "Peephole."

He understood his function within the complex calculus of advertising and media manipulation, recognized the correlation between magazine covers and opening weekends. As "the money," he dutifully
submitted himself to the process—but only when he had a movie to sell.

For the first time, however, he felt journalists had overstepped the mark. To his mind, the two stories printed while he had been in London making *Last Crusade* had bordered on character assassination. By the autumn of 1990, the *News of the World* had admitted libel and apologized "wholeheartedly" for the wild allegations that he was a coward obsessed with his tough-guy image and that he had covered up a serious accident he had caused in Jackson Hole.

In his case the substantial damages he received ran into six rather than the eight or more figures Melissa's win had brought. His English solicitor Michael Skrein made it clear that Harrison had not sued for financial reasons but to vindicate his reputation. Skrein told the court his client would give the award to charity.

The director Alan J. Pakula was probably unaware of the flurry of legal activity in the Ford household when, at the beginning of the year, he offered Harrison the role every leading man in Hollywood was desperate to play. His Everyman qualities were what seemed to make him perfect to play Rusty Sabich, the central character in the runaway bestseller *Presumed Innocent*.

If Pakula had known how much time Harrison and Melissa had been spending with members of the legal profession, he might have asked him to start his research a little earlier. Rusty Sabich happened to be a lawyer too.

The author Scott Turow had begun writing *Presumed Innocent* in 1981 as he commuted in and out of his Chicago legal practice. Six painstaking years later, his finished book had become the publishing sensation of 1987. A triumph of powerfully plausible setting and fiendishly clever plotting, in which Sabich is accused of murdering a beautiful colleague with whom he has been conducting an affair, it took immovable root at the head of the bestsellers list.

Presumed Innocent sparked the most ferocious bidding war Hollywood had seen in a decade. When the producer and director Sydney Pollack emerged as the owner of the book rights, it had been assumed that his longtime leading man, Robert Redford, would play Sabich. Instead, Pollack had passed the book on to Alan J. Pakula, successful translator of the seemingly unfilmable *All the President's Men* and *Sophie's Choice*. Pakula was convinced Redford was too old. The only

other actor he could picture in the role at first was a dead one. "Someone asked me who I wanted for Rusty, and I had no idea. Maybe Henry
Fonda as he was forty years ago, because he had that decency, and he
looked like the average American, and yet you felt there was something
dark and repressed," he said. Soon, however, Pakula was pursuing the
only modern leading man who could present the same qualities.

Harrison took his time weighing the role. By now, the balance was
a familiar one. On the one hand, Sabich—a dour but devoted family
man whose life is flipped upside down by his sexual obsession with his
colleague, Carolyn Polhemus—represented another ambiguous hero, a
risk so soon after the experience of *The Mosquito Coast*. On the other,
the bidding war Hollywood had fought over Turow's book had made it
the most talked-about project of the year. After laying Indy to rest,
what better way to reestablish the momentum he had been given by
Witness? Harrison needed time to think. "He is very quick to make
negative decisions. A positive one takes a lot longer," said his friend
Earl McGrath.

By the summer of 1989, Harrison had made up his mind: he agreed
to the role and began his preparation.

His first call was on a city prosecutor's office in Wayne County,
Detroit, where he spent a month immersing himself in the day-to-day
details of legal life. "I wasn't so much interested in the courtroom
behavior, but I wanted to observe the more banal aspects—the little
details such as the handling of files, or how attorneys interact with
each other at the coffee machine," he explained later.

Eventually, he found the keys to his character in the minutiae of a
pair of shoes and a battered briefcase. He always wore the same working shoes regardless of whether he was in close-up or long-shot; and his
briefcase was always loaded with paperwork. "It affected how the character walks," he explained when the film was released. "And if you are
playing a lawyer who wears wingtip Oxfords, you don't go to work in
tennis shoes because they're shooting that day only from the waist up,
because suddenly you're not walking the same."

Harrison's most pressing need was to find a way of conveying that
Rusty was a man utterly lacking in vanity—"someone looking for love
in all the wrong places."

When he telephoned Pakula to let him know he was thinking of having the kind of short, military-style buzz cut he had worn back in high school, he might as well have announced he was going to play Rusty as a hunchback. "God, you're going to look like a marine," the director said down the phone, diluting the apoplexy the studio had displayed when they heard the news. "I hired a movie star and I'm getting a character actor." After two months Pakula relented, for one reason: "It worked for him."

News that shooting was underway leaked out in the neighborhoods of Detroit, Newark, and New York throughout the summer. Occasionally thickets of curious locals would gather in the hope of catching a glimpse of the action. "Isn't this the movie where Indiana Jones kills his wife?" one excitable youngster asked one day.

If the Indy adventures represented the ultimate adolescent male fantasy, *Presumed Innocent* showed a different, more disturbing aspect of masculinity. Harrison's aura of repressed rage had been a crucial part of his attraction to Pakula. Throughout the shoot, his bottled-up emotions were the focus of the production.

"The complicated thing in playing Rusty Sabich is that this is a character who feels very deeply and shows very little to the world because he's so repressed," he explained on the set.

As Harrison returned to the tautly strung frame of mind he had portrayed in *Frantic*, the experience of working with Polanski reemerged, to improve his ability to combine control and recklessness. Pakula, as precise and measured a director as Hollywood had within its upper ranks, found himself embarrassed by the quality of his star's performance. "Halfway through the film I said to him: 'At the risk of sounding patronizing, Harrison, when we started the film I thought you were a very good movie-star actor, which I respect a lot,' " he recalled later. " 'But you're more than that. You know what surprised me a lot of times? When I didn't know what you were going to do next.' "

That element of the unexpected was evident in Harrison's "choreographing" of the office-bound love scene between himself and Carolyn Polhemus (Greta Scacchi). As Scacchi led him into the dingily lit office, purring, "This is going to be so-o-o good," Harrison played

Sabich all fingers and thumbs, an uncoiled spring suddenly unable to keep pace physically with the emotions racing through his mind.

"I give him the credit for that scene. He really staged it himself," Pakula said afterward. The scene's subtlety was an overture to the most unexpected improvisation of the shoot.

The script required Rusty, in the depths of his despair, to tell his wife they face financial ruin because of his fight to clear his name. In what was to be one of the most intimate scenes of the film, Pakula prepared to focus on Bonnie Bedelia, who would deliver a highly charged speech as the supportive wife. As the cameras rolled, however, the emotional energy of the scene was coming from Harrison. Unexpected tears had begun to roll down his cheeks.

Pakula hadn't expected to see such raw emotion in his leading man. "It's not manly to cry, and I didn't ask him to cry," he said later. Take after take, however, Harrison provided the same powerful reaction. The tears flowed each time.

Afterward, Harrison ascribed the moment to "magic." But there were those, his director included, who saw nothing fake in his performance. For the one—and perhaps only—time in his public life, the emotions of a character had merged seamlessly with his own. To allow Rusty to show his repressed feelings, Harrison had seemingly tapped openly into his own. Somewhere he appeared to be drawing on the anguish of his own marital failure.

"Here's a responsible man who prided himself on taking care of his family and is now realizing that his behavior is destroying them," Pakula noted sombrely. "The pain in him was just so real. What happened in that take is what happened to Harrison."

The scene represented a milestone in his development as an actor. By providing Rusty Sabich with a brief but profound moment of vulnerability, he brilliantly humanized a man who could easily have remained a cold and forbidding character.

By the turn of 1990, Harrison had completed his cinematic quarter century. *Presumed Innocent* was his twenty-fifth feature film. Since his bellboy walked on-screen in *Dead Heat on a Merry-Go-Round* in 1966, he had averaged around one film a year.

Like every other actor alive, his actual film output represented only a fraction of rejected scripts. Such was his popularity in the 1980s, it was inevitable that he had passed up a succession of high-profile opportunities. How different would his career had been if he, rather than Kevin Costner, had accepted the role of Elliott Ness in Brian De Palma's version of *The Untouchables*? How might he have looked if he had swapped Indy's fedora for a panama hat, and the breathless charms of Madonna in *Dick Tracy*—a role eventually taken up by Warren Beatty? And what carnage might have been caused if he, rather than Al Pacino, had taken the lead in the disastrous American Revolution movie *Revolution* in 1986?

Harrison claims never to consider such questions himself. Given the number of scripts he receives it is a philosophy designed to preserve his sanity. "I don't regret those choices that I didn't make that went on to be big successes for someone else," he said once. "The reason that I didn't take the job was that I didn't know how to do it, or it was too close to something I'd already done, or I didn't like the idea. If you can't do it, you can't do it. There's no sense regretting it."

If there was one project that had left Harrison wondering "what if?" it was *Big*, the Penny Marshall–directed comedy about a thirteen-year-old boy who has his wish to grow up granted by a fairground fortune teller. Harrison and Robert De Niro had passed on the script by Gary Ross and Anne Spielberg. The semiseriousness of the issues it tackled—aren't we all children in grown-up bodies?—was overwhelmed by the slapstick comedy as far as both actors were concerned. Their decision opened the door for a rising young Tom Hanks to construct a brilliantly funny and touching new role.

Big had become Huge at the box office, touching a nerve that role-reversal movies had found as far back as *Turnabout*, Hal Roach's 1940 hit about a quarrelsome couple who swap bodies, and inspiring a slew of inferior copies. Harrison recognized a similar theme when, one night in 1990, he read a script by a twenty-two-year-old student from New York's Sarah Lawrence College, Jeffrey Abrams. The fact that he read a script end-to-end in one evening was in itself remarkable; the fact that it was by an unknown, first-time writer even more so. "Most scripts I read, I don't get past page twenty, because they don't have any ambition or any focus or any skill," he explained once.

Abrams's script, called *Regarding Henry*, told the story of a cold, ruthlessly brilliant New York lawyer, Henry Turner, who is reduced to a childlike mental state when he is shot in the head during a petty drugstore holdup. Overbearing, obsessive and distant from his wife and daughter before the shooting, Henry starts life afresh—and learns the ugly reality of his old life along the way.

Even the hyperactive young Abrams, who had written the script in just seven days, was dumbstruck by the speed with which events unfolded after producer Scott Rudin became involved. Having persuaded Paramount to pay $450,000 for the script, Rudin sent it straight to Harrison, who quickly established contact with Mike Nichols. Nichols, while spotting the flaws, was equally impressed by the emotional maturity that the young college graduate had given his script. Abrams was, of course, told that their decision was based on the originality and appeal of his idea. But Nichols, in particular, left him with the clear impression that *Big* was the reason Harrison Ford and he were moving so uncharacteristically quickly.

"He and Harrison wished that they had made that film," said Abrams. "Well, here was another film about a man's body that was essentially filled with a child."

Since *Working Girl*, Nichols and Harrison had become close personal friends. They had much in common. Nichols, like Harrison the descendant of Russian Jews, salted his conversation with the same brand of civilized cynicism. He too had drifted into acting after spending much of his college life sleeping, "seventeen to eighteen hours a day" in his case. "I was very bad for a while and then I was pretty good. And then, like everybody, if you figure it out long enough, you figure how to do it," he said. Regular dinner companions at the Russian Tea Room, they even shared similar friends, like Jim Harrison the writer.

As far as their mentor Walter Beakel was concerned, his former pupils were two sides of the same coin. "I can't think of anyone I have ever worked with who was like Harrison except maybe Mike," said Beakel. "If you said anything wrong to Mike, you would truly hurt him. He would break down. Mike Nichols would ring me at two in the morning. Young Harrison was very fragile too. But he didn't wear it on his sleeve because he would not want you to think that—it would be demeaning. In different ways they were very much alike."

It was Harrison's similarities to Henry Turner that would be the focus of the film. His latest character offered him a rare chance to roll a villain and a hero into one. Before the accident transforms his life, Henry Turner is an elitist, arrogant, self-centered son of a bitch with little time for anything other than his career. A bullet transforms him into a gentler, more thoughtful human being. Nichols recognized both sides of Henry within his friend. "I've seen him make a fuss about a suite at the Savoy, and then I've seen him be wonderful with his kids and with mine," said Nichols.

Harrison didn't deny it. "Both Henrys are in me, and all of us."

Shooting began on September 14 and went on through the autumn, in and around Manhattan. Aware of his responsibility to neither sentimentalize nor send up the real-life victims of brain damage, Harrison researched the role more thoroughly than any other in his career.

He spent two months poring over every book he could find on brain injuries and visited a rehabilitation clinic where he interviewed neurologists and brain surgeons and discreetly observed patients.

By the time he arrived on-set, he was equipped with a complex series of index cards on which he had mapped out the slow recovery process he—and Henry—would have to go through. Every card was divided up into the three main criteria—physical, mental, and speaking skills—with gradings between one and ten on each. On a film in which, as ever, scenes would be shot out of sequence, his aide-mémoire would ensure he always knew at which stage in his recovery Henry was at any one time.

His most precious pieces of advice came from Tom Frost, a Princeton-educated lawyer who had suffered similar injuries to the fictional Henry in real life. Harrison spent hours with Frost, basing many of his nuances and mannerisms on him. The slightly disabled walk he used in his performance was based on Frost and achieved by slipping a stone into his sneaker.

"We all felt a great sense of responsibility to get it right. Not to offend reality," Harrison said later.

The job of portraying Henry Turner's transformation from tough to tender was made easier by events in Harrison's own life that summer. On June 30, 1990, Melissa gave birth to a baby girl, later named Georgia. After three sons, her husband was caught off guard by the emotions released by the arrival of his first daughter. "Girls are different from boys from the git-go—to my surprise," he said afterward. "Helpless creatures of whatever sex engender certain feelings, but there's something, um, that I can't define which is female about Georgia."

His second family had laid down the flagstones of a second stab at happiness. If he had needed a reminder of just how precious an opportunity he had with Melissa, Malcolm, and Georgia, *Regarding Henry*, with its profound echoes of his own myopic past, provided it. "We all have big changes in our life that are more or less a second chance," he said, discussing the film later. He had no intention of messing his own life up twice.

It had been a dozen years since his marriage to Mary had crumbled. Second time around he had eliminated the mistakes that had contributed to the failure. It had, for some time, been a condition of any job he took that Melissa and the children accompany him. Patricia McQueeney would pass on the message. "If I can't take them along with me, there's no deal."

Their presence did not, of course, guarantee that he remained Mr. Sweetness and Light. "When I work on a picture, I don't want to go out to dinner, I have no energy left for weekends, I neglect my children, I neglect everything," he confided at the time.

But it did at least allow him to avoid the pressures—and the temptations—of life away from home. "When my eldest kids were growing up, I wasn't being paid enough money even to be able to take them along on location. I didn't miss years on end, but I did miss some very important times in their lives. These days I make sure my family is properly provided for," he told one interviewer at the time.

"I've learned a lot since then—not just about being a father, but about being a human being," he told another.

His on-screen family in *Regarding Henry* consisted of Annette Bening and Mikki Allen, the thirteen-year-old actress who played Henry's daughter. Allen, for one, was in no doubt about which of the two Henrys her screen father most resembled after hours. "He was really good to me, teasing me, keeping me happy. But he kept himself to himself very much," she said. "As soon as work finished, he'd just rush home to be with his own boy and girl. People on-set learned to understand; as soon as his hours were over, he was home."

As the realities of new fatherhood once more entered his life, moments in Abrams's script hit poignantly home. Before being shot, the stern, unfeeling Henry is coerced by his wife into apologizing to his daughter for having rebuked her too sternly. Instead, he ends up delivering an even harsher lecture.

"I know that moment when you go in to apologize to your kid and you end up hectoring him. I've known that as a father and I've known that as a son," he told interviewers as he discussed the film later. "I found myself having a real strong reaction to that."

On-set, at least, the Fords presented a picture of the perfect, nuclear, nineties family. Melissa, content with the two children she wanted, radiated an earth-mother warmth that left some sorely star-struck. "You love Harrison, and then when you meet Melissa you love him more," Abrams recalled. "She is so great and brilliant and funny, she charms you like a great mom."

Such sentimentality seemed to have no place in the world of young Malcolm Ford—now two going on thirty-two. During filming on a Manhattan street, Malcolm was sitting in his father's chair, when Harrison introduced him to Abrams.

"This is Jeffrey. He wrote this movie," he told his son.

Malcolm looked up and nodded. "I like your work," he said.

Harrison enjoyed dismissing his superstar status with claims that he was "nothing more than a worker in a service occupation . . . It's like being a waiter or a gas station attendant, but I'm waiting on six million people a week if I'm lucky." He was entitled to his sanity-preserving perspective, although even he would have to concede there were few hamburger chefs whose homes had become the mecca for transcontinental pilgrimages.

Often he would find people camped on the roads outside Jackson, out-of-state license plates on their cars, zoom lenses fixed on the distant dot on the horizon that was his well-secured home. "I am just not on their wavelength," he would say, baffled. As *Presumed Innocent* was released in August 1990, his detachment from the real world seemed greater than ever.

Harrison may have imagined that there was little left to shock him, but nothing had prepared him for the acres of newsprint devoted to his choice of Rusty Sabich's haircut. Even Georgia Brown, film critic of New York's supposedly highbrow *Village Voice*, could not resist cracking: "That crew cut makes Ford look like a ferret."

Most eventually moved on to praise the most fully self-contained performance of his career. "Ford . . . is astonishingly fine in a performance of controlled intensity," wrote *Rolling Stone*'s Pete Travers. "Harrison Ford proves once again that he is steadily developing into one of the most powerful and versatile actors in American films," wrote the critic at the *Seattle Post-Intelligencer*. And in competition with the husband-and-wife-to-be combination of Bruce Willis in *Die Hard II* and Demi Moore in *Ghost*, *Presumed Innocent* punched its weight at the box office, pulling in a highly respectable $43 million in America.

Yet pleased as he was by both his and the film's performance, the moment represented another watershed. The iconoclast had to finally accept that he had become an icon.

"Nearly every article and review had some reference to my haircut. That was the one time I was absolutely befuddled," he said later. "I guess I finally began to understand that people felt they owned me in a way."

22

WHO WANTS TO BE
A HUNDREDAIRE?

I n the spring of 1990, with Melissa pregnant with baby Georgia and *Regarding Henry*, his third consecutive film in New York looming, Harrison had been growing frustrated in his attempts to find his family a new home.

His dislike of big-city life had faded over the years, and with Malcolm now fast approaching school age and Melissa keen to have their second child in a New York hospital, a base in Manhattan as well as his main home in Wyoming and another in Los Angeles had become a necessity.

The previous autumn he had lost out on a spectacular, twelve-room apartment on Central Park West. His offer had seemingly been accepted when, to his disgust, the seller agreed to an improved bid from a Wall Street tycoon.

When he heard Debra Winger was considering selling an equally sumptuous apartment directly overlooking Central Park, he was determined not to miss out again. He reached Winger by phone in Nairobi, where she was filming Bernardo Bertolucci's *Sheltering Sky*, and by the time their long-distance conversation was over, Harrison had made her an offer that she found simply too good to refuse. Weeks later he took over ownership of the apartment for the princely sum of $2 million.

The days when he had holes in his living-room floor and struggled to scrabble together $70 for a family holiday were a distant memory. And since the first *Star Wars* windfall, he had managed his financial affairs with the same care he employed when constructing a cabinet or working on a new set of storm windows in Wyoming. A bonus from *Blade Runner* had been used to buy five drawings by Vuillard. The masterpieces formed the foundation stones of his greatest indulgence—a collection of works by important nineteenth- and early twentieth-century artists like the American Robert Henri. New pieces were acquired with the help of friends like Earl McGrath and Arnold Glimcher, the producer and owner of New York's Pace Gallery.

There had been no rush-of-blood investments, no risky ventures into producing his own movies. There had certainly been none of the wild living that had parted so many of his peers from their hard-earned cash. His attitude was grounded in his Midwestern past. "If you don't have it, don't spend it," had been the dictum drilled into him by his parents.

"I am never far from saying, 'Oh, wow—how did this come to pass?' " he confided once, offering a rare insight into his attitude to his wealth as he talked about his latest acquisition. "But because I did it myself and I waited to buy it until I could afford it, I can walk away from it. That is part of the way I was brought up." In the past a shopping mall in Malibu and a home in the West Indies had been among the investments he had made and moved on from without fuss or financial pain.

Generally, he had been as guarded about the precise details of his fortune as he had about the rest of his offscreen life. Journalists brave enough to put out feelers could usually expect both barrels. "It's none of their goddamn business!" On less cloudy days, however, he was capable of turning the subject into a joke.

In the run up to *Regarding Henry*'s release in the summer of 1991, Jeffrey Abrams, turned interviewer for the day, asked how much money he had made.

"Hundreds and hundreds of dollars."

"So you're saying you're a hundredaire?"

"Yes, that's correct."

"Money is only important when you don't have any," Harrison was fond of saying. In that case, by 1991 he could no longer hide the fact that it had become truly unimportant. For the first time, that year he joined more ostentatious Hollywood earners like Sylvester Stallone, Arnold Schwarzenegger, Jack Nicholson, and Eddie Murphy on the elite *Forbes* Top 40 list.

According to *Forbes*'s meticulous researchers, Harrison's total earnings in 1989 and 1990 were $22 million, slightly less than composer Andrew Lloyd Webber and writer Stephen King, but many millions more than musicians like George Michael and Guns 'n' Roses in the same period.

Weeks after the poll was published, on the morning of September 12, the magazine's statisticians began planning Harrison's promotion to an even more Olympian position on their list. The Hollywood trades broke the news that he was about to come into several hundred dollars more.

Rumors that he was to take on the lead in an adaptation of Tom Clancy's bestselling novel *Patriot Games* had been circulating for weeks. But to the surprise of many in Hollywood, Paramount president David Kirkpatrick announced the studio had signed him for not one, but three films in the role of Clancy's hero, the CIA analyst Jack Ryan. Accounts varied, but his fee for *Patriot Games* was by common consensus $9 million, with a further $20 million to follow for the two sequels. Harrison's percentage of the gross would be of the order of ten percent. At near enough $30 million plus the promise of as much again in profit-point bonuses, the package eclipsed anything Harrison—or Hollywood—had seen before.

To the outside world the figures seemed insane. Yet within the warped logic of Hollywood it made a kind of perfect sense. Kirkpatrick and Paramount's generosity was based on the $120 million the studio had made from its screen adaptation of *The Hunt for Red October*, the first book by the million-selling Clancy to be adapted to the screen. It also reflected the more than $600 million the studio had made from Harrison's three outings as Indiana Jones. "With *Patriot Games* Harrison Ford can propel successive films as he has done in the past," Kirkpatrick said in his corporate sound bite to the *Hollywood Reporter*.

While the press pedaled out features on Ryan's arrival as a "James Bond for the '90s," the size of the fee set Hollywood's talent agents into a spin. Every major negotiation in town was reconsidered in its wake. Stallone, Schwarzenegger, and Bruce Willis enjoyed what many came to regard as the obscene fruits of the spiral that ensued as salaries passed $10 million a movie for the first time in Hollywood history.

A dozen years spent scraping a living below the Hollywood poverty level had removed any sense of guilt or embarrassment Harrison might have had about his earning power. "I'm well adjusted to the situation. I was lucky to serve a long apprenticeship," he said later, as his salary began to dominate journalists' agendas. And as long as money and respect remained inextricably entangled in the Hollywood psyche, he, for one, had no intention of weakening—even if he agreed the salaries were now "outrageous. . . . No one is worth these amounts—except to someone else who has the potential to make even more from engaging us," he explained.

"I don't *need* to make the money. You don't *have* to keep your price up. But no one in this business would be impressed if I reduced it."

If Harrison had to thank anyone for the biggest payday of his life so far, it was Alec Baldwin rather than the Paramount powers-that-be. Baldwin turned out to be less gracious than he had been after losing *Working Girl*, however.

When Mace Neufeld and his business partner Bob Rehme had picked up the rights to the yet-to-be-published *Hunt for Red October* in 1984, they had done so with Harrison Ford in mind for the role of Jack Ryan.

Clancy's cold war potboiler centered on a disenchanted Soviet submarine commander, Marko Ramius, and his attempts to steer his fleet's ultimate underwater weapon into the hands of the West. Ryan, an intelligence expert familiar with the renegade captain, was dispatched to deliver him into American waters. The gifted Klaus Maria Brandauer had originally been lined up for the role of Ramius, but when Sean Connery had made his considerable star power available, Brandauer had accepted a handsome fee to stand down. For a moment it appeared that the film might recreate the memorable chemistry of *The Last Crusade*.

The most difficult element in Neufeld's equation was not his cast but Clancy. The brilliant but brittle-tempered novelist bombarded him with notes and suggestions as he put the production together. To Neufeld's relief Clancy was delighted when he heard Harrison had been offered the part of his hero, Ryan. "Absolutely right," he wrote in one of his many missives. "Harrison Ford *is* Jack Ryan." When Harrison was shown the script by Donald Stewart and Larry Ferguson, however, his doubts were considerable.

The main problem was that the role of Ryan, while substantial, seemed secondary to that of Ramius. Enjoyable as it might have been to be reunited with Connery, he made an alternative suggestion. "He said, 'I'll do it if I can be Ramius.' He ain't no fool," said screenwriter Stewart, who with Ferguson had concentrated the film's most powerful moments inside the state-of-the-art submarine. "It was pretty much Sean's picture—if it wasn't Sean's, it was the boat's."

Neufeld, however, was committed to Connery.

In a reversal of his fortunes on *Working Girl*, Alec Baldwin stepped into the breach, turning in a polished performance as Ryan in a film that was, predictably, dominated by a bouffant-haired Connery. Released in the summer of 1990, *Red October* pulled off the double whammy of major box-office success and a grudging seal of approval from the hypercritical Clancy. "They didn't screw it up too much," he said afterward. In Clancy-speak that amounted to an Academy Award, and in recognition he signed the rights to two more of his Ryan books, *Patriot Games* and *Clear and Present Danger*, to Neufeld and Rehme.

As the first of the sequels rolled on to the Paramount production schedules Baldwin was given first option to reprise his role. To his horror, shooting had been moved forward two months and now clashed with his long-cherished plans to star in *A Streetcar Named Desire* on the New York stage. Amid "did he jump or was he pushed?" inquests and rumors that the debonair star had been asking for too many perks on top of his $4 million salary, Baldwin dropped out, and Neufeld and Paramount began the pursuit of their original Ryan.

This time, Harrison found Clancy's hero at the very heart of the script by Stewart and W. Peter Iliff. Ryan, retired from the CIA, foils an IRA attempt to assassinate a minor British Royal. He is then drawn back into the secret world of "the Company" as the bloodthirsty brother of a terrorist killed in the incident seeks revenge on his own family. Harrison quickly signaled his interest.

The machinations left a bitter taste in Baldwin's mouth. "Harrison's not sexy and audiences will not turn out to see him," he bitched later.

Whatever the background to Baldwin's departure, Fate could not have played its hand more sweetly as far as Mace Neufeld was concerned. The friendship he had formed with Harrison had been one of the few positive elements of his run-in with Robert Aldrich on *The Frisco Kid*. Harrison agreed to the role and the multipicture deal—subject, of course, to his standard script and director approval.

He was soon to regard his record-breaking price tag as cheap at twice the price.

When his nursery-school teacher asked Malcolm Ford and his classmates to describe what their fathers did for a living, Harrison's youngest son replied: "My daddy is a movie actor, and sometimes he plays the good guy, and sometimes he plays the lawyer."

Even Malcolm, it seemed, sensed Harrison needed to break away from what he called "coat and tie jobs" after *Presumed Innocent* and *Regarding Henry*. Somewhere in his rapidly forming young mind he probably understood what his father meant when he said: "I reckoned I needed to hit somebody in my next movie."

Regarding Henry's lukewarm reception on both sides of the Atlantic had only added weight to the argument. The critics left Nichols's film feeling either cold or conned. Some called it "a gimmick" and chided the director of *The Graduate* for a classy-looking but ultimately soft-centered film. "*Regarding Henry* is facile and commits the cardinal sin in my book of making brain damage look cute," wrote Christopher Tookey in the *Sunday Telegraph*. "It's another bland postcard from the edge by director Mike Nichols to make you glad you are not there," sniped Tom Hutchinson in the *Mail on Sunday*.

In New York, Vincent Canby detected traces of Tom Hanks's *Big* performance in Harrison's Henry, with a slice of Peter Sellers in *Being There* thrown in for good measure. "It's a ponderous, toned-down, golly-gee-whizz performance," the critic wrote. At $43 million, *Regarding Henry*'s American box office was exactly half that of *Presumed Innocent*. At that rate of depreciation, a third successive sighting of Harrison in a "coat and tie" would interest no one.

As he took stock, his concerns over his shift away from man-of-action movies was a primary influence in his decision *not* to accept the role of Jim Garrison, the crusading New Orleans attorney in Oliver Stone's *JFK*. He had liked both the script and the idea of working with Stone, but had reservations that the film revolved around events that were too fresh in the memories of Americans.

More appealing was *Night Ride Down*, set against the backdrop of a more distant, and considerably more obscure, incident in his country's history—the Pullman porter strike of 1936. Willard Huyck and Gloria Katz's script revolved around the story of a Pullman Company executive whose daughter is kidnapped. Harrison was close to signing when, following the arrival of the newly installed Paramount chairman, Brandon Tartikoff, the plug was pulled because of a ballooning budget.

Another film doomed to disintegration was *Hickok and Cody*, a fictional account of two great icons of the West, as they made their way to New York with Buffalo Bill's Wild West Show in 1873. Bruce Willis had been tentatively lined up to play Cody to Harrison's Hickok.

Shooting on *Patriot Games* began in London with Phillip Noyce, the Australian director of the taut thriller *Dead Calm* at the helm, Anne Archer in the role of Ryan's wife, and the rising Sean Bean as the vengeful IRA hitman Sean Miller.

Mace Neufeld had been warned about Harrison's perfectionism. "I have friends in the construction business who have done work for him. He is the most difficult client they know. Nothing can be almost right," he said.

The same rules applied on-set. "You know that the script that he has approved is not the script we're going to end up shooting, because we're going to work on it every day up to and while we're shooting," he said. "Every scene in a film and ergo every line that makes up the scene has got to advance the story and be consistent with the character. He's always looking to eliminate false notes, writer's directions that look good on paper but just don't work."

Shooting was spread out between Greenwich in London, the U.S. Naval Academy at Annapolis, Maryland, Brawley in the California desert, and Sea World near San Diego, where Ryan's home was built on a bluff overlooking beautiful Mission Bay.

As he prepared for the role, Harrison had been granted access to the CIA's headquarters in Langley, Virginia. He had signed a secrecy order prohibiting him from talking about what he saw of the agency's global war against drug trafficking and terrorism, but not even that could prevent him from revealing his horror at their activities with his face.

When filming got underway, his most telling contribution came in a scene in which Ryan reluctantly oversees a search-and-destroy SAS (Special Army Squadron) attack on the terrorist camp he suspects is harboring Sean Bean's character Miller. In Iliff and Stewart's script, a room full of staff watched the operation via a powerful spy satellite. Harrison came up with the idea of conveying Ryan's unease at the ruthlessness of the operation by concentrating solely on his facial emotions.

Noyce, Neufeld, and Rehme had no arguments when they saw him run through what he had in mind. "It was originally a dialogue-heavy scene. Harrison suggested no dialogue except one line at the end of the scene implying 'a kill.' Everything else was played out on Harrison's face," said Neufeld.

Elsewhere this might have been an exercise in rank-pulling, but Noyce saw it as an example of his star's understanding of the nature of his appeal. "He has an innate relationship with the audience, and that relationship is probably the key to his continuing success," said the director. "He never mentions the audience, but you know that he can feel them. They're behind that camera, they're there, and you know that he's reaching out to them."

Noyce was impressed by his star's sheer knowledge. "He is a walking encyclopedia. He's worked with so many great directors, and seen the shots that work and the shots that don't."

The director did not always bow to his star's judgment. "He understands the collaborative process, and that is that you have a deadline, which is the amount of money or the number of days you have to shoot the film, and the winner is the movie that can come up with the most good ideas before the bell sounds," shrugged Noyce.

Even screenwriter Stewart, a hardy, Oscar-winning veteran with a reputation for defending his material to the hilt, assented to the sharpest acting mind he had come across. "After twenty odd years in this business, I have learned to kind of tune out to a lot of these story meetings. But you don't with him, because you know he's going to say something that you want to remember," he stated. "He's the only actor that I really take notes on."

While the nuances of his performance as Ryan were being polished with customary precision, the same could hardly be said of the film's climactic moments. Sledgehammers were being wielded to crack nuts.

In Iliff and Stewart's screenplay, Miller and Ryan fought it out hand-to-hand in a lengthy underwater scene. Shot over three nights on the Paramount lot in the same half-acre, million-gallon water tank in which DeMille had parted the Red Sea, the portents were ominous from the beginning.

"The water was very cold, you can't heat that water, and it was dirty because you couldn't filter it either," said Bob Rehme, who spent each night working with Harrison. "He was in the water all the time and wore a wet suit under his business suit to keep warm. We had been doing this for three nights and on the third night he said: 'Gee, I hope we get this done tonight.'"

Rehme assumed his star was simply tired but, as he unzipped his suit, realized it was more serious. "He was beginning to get infected by the dirty water. He had broken out in a rash. I'm sure it was very painful and very uncomfortable, but he had silently carried on doing his scenes," said Rehme.

Then Harrison, an experienced diver, hit his head while grappling underwater with Bean. The on-hand divers had to rush to his aid as he struggled for air. The incident was serious enough to be picked up by the press days later. By then an accident which had left Harrison with a small cut to his forehead had become a near-death experience.

The sequence's complex, *Man From Atlantis*-style balletics simply did not work. A month before the film was due to be released, he and Bean returned to the Paramount set and shot a more straightforward fistfight on board an out-of-control speedboat. "We made a mistake," Harrison concluded later.

At 2:30 P.M. on June 3, 1992, a hundred or so film fans, foreign tourists and members of the flotsam and jetsam of Los Angeles street life jammed together at the seediest end of Hollywood Boulevard to witness one of Tinseltown's tackier rituals.

Crouched on all fours, his work-hardened hands spread out in a patch of wet concrete, Harrison managed to force the falsest of smiles for the cameras. If it appeared that he was not exactly relishing the experience of having his hand and footprints installed alongside Chaplin, Gable, Monroe, and the rest outside the gaudy Mann's Chinese Theater, that was absolutely fine by him. To clarify matters, he even told reporters so afterward. "I'll tell you very frankly I didn't consider it an honor," he said, the sourpuss smile still locked in place. "It was just in order to sell *Patriot Games.*" Later he boasted that he had kept the motor of his car running and completed the entire process "in and out in seven minutes," after which he roared off to celebrate a far more worthy event—Melissa's birthday.

For years he had resisted having to endure the ceremony on the so-called Boulevard of Stars. Hollywood had failed to bring him to his knees back in the bad old days, why should it succeed in doing so now? Anyhow, "Harrison Ford" was already installed among the immortals, he argued. So what if it was the *other* Harrison Ford—the old actor who had died in the Motion Picture County Hospital outside Los Angeles in 1957?

Coincidentally, the silent star had also had little time for Hollywood and all its absurdities. According to a 1926 profile in *Photoplay,* he was "remote" and "aloof," "not only the hermit of Hollywood, but of the entire motion-picture industry." Harrison Ford I would probably have appreciated his namesake's cussedness!

Harrison's Seven Minutes From Hell added psychological scars to the physical bumps and bruises he had picked up on *Patriot Games.* In general, he wore his battle wounds with pride. There were, however, moments when Harrison must have questioned whether even his record fee was worth the cost of Tom Clancy's constant carping.

Soon after he signed for the role of Jack Ryan he had traveled to the writer's Maryland home with Mace Neufeld. "He insisted that we come to Maryland. We had lunch and Harrison signed all kinds of stuff for him," said Neufeld.

Days before the opening, the mercurial master novelist showed his gratitude by moaning that the film had bastardized his script. What was worse, Clancy told reporters that Harrison, weeks away from his fiftieth birthday, was "too old" to play the thirty-one-year-old Ryan.

Along with Neufeld and Noyce, Harrison played down the author's hostility during the publicity interviews. Asked how he felt about the criticism, Harrison bit his tongue and joshed: "I don't think I can afford to be very honest about that."

Precisely how damaging Clancy's remarks had been, particularly to his multitude of fans, was impossible to gauge—although Paramount was sufficiently rattled to use its checkbook and the promise of future deals to buy his silence. Neither was there any way of measuring the effects of a public row between *Variety* magazine and Paramount over a negative review from a misty-eyed Irish-American in which the film's supposedly anti-Irish prejudice was the central issue. Joseph McBride's description of the film as "mindless and morally repugnant" erupted into a media tempest-in-a-teapot with the studio pulling its lucrative advertising business, the editor chastising the hapless critic and then facing a full-blown revolt from his journalistic staff.

But according to Hollywood's tried-and-trusted barometer—the box office—*Patriot Games* was marked down as a satisfactory if not spectacular opening mission for the new Jack Ryan. Its gross of $83 million in America was one of the season's highs, but still a third down on *Red October.* Critically, the world agreed that Harrison made a more plausible, wholesome hero than Baldwin's Jack Ryan, but that for a thriller from the Clancy canon of high-technodrama it was a strangely cool and clinical film.

"Even third-rate Hitchcock exposes the dramatic and psychological feebleness," wrote Philip French in the *Observer*; he thought Harrison "dull" in the Ryan role.

Harrison's headline-hogging salary was also fair game for many. *Time Out* thought the film was "so duff you wonder why they didn't ask Roger Moore to star."

Others appreciated Harrison's minimalism, particularly in the satellite raid scene. The *European* thought him worth $9 million for that alone. "At that moment Harrison Ford amply earns his fee. Even in the silliest films he always shows genuine intelligence and a go-with-it, go-for-it commitment that puts flesh and blood on cardboard roles . . . He is the linchpin of the entertainment. He has been here before; he knows that insuperable odds are just what a hero needs to bring out the beast in him."

Tom Clancy would soon bring the beast in him out again.

23

RUNNING HOME

In December 1992, Dr. Jim McKinsey would begin his morning calls at the University of Chicago Medical Center by introducing his patients to the studious six-foot figure accompanying him on his rounds.

Some responded to the bespectacled, lightly bearded attendant with a surprised smile, others simply with a look of mild bewilderment. "Some of our elderly patients didn't recognize him," said Dr. McKinsey. "Later they'd tell their kids, 'I had a visit today from some actor named Harrison Ford. Ever hear of him?'"

Harrison had learned the knack of settling into the landscape over the years. In hospitals and courtrooms, he had become part of the furniture, could transform himself into the observer rather than the observed.

As he returned to Chicago a month later, however, such opportunities were suddenly nonexistent. As news spilled out that he was to make the first film in his city of birth, the rest of the Windy City celebrated the return of a favorite son.

The fuss had begun almost as soon as it was announced that a new Warner Bros. production of the classic 1960s television series *The Fugitive*, was to be made in Chicago, produced by Arnold Kopelson and directed by Andrew Davis. Mayor Richard Daley—son of the late

"Big Boss" Daley who had molded the metropolis of Harrison's teens—was among the first to muscle in on the act, organizing a photo call as the boy from Maine East High School arrived to film at city hall.

Throughout the four-month shoot, crowds had to be cordoned off as the production moved from the civic headquarters to the Gothic quadrangles of the university and the gleaming glass and steel of the business sections of the Loop. Harrison's visits to Chicago had become infrequent. His mother and father had long since retired to the Laguna Hills, south of Los Angeles. The few school friends he remained in contact with had moved elsewhere, Bill Russell to Virginia, Stu Shakman to Los Angeles. His closest acquaintances now were couples like Scott and Annette Turow, to whom he and Melissa had become close during the making of *Presumed Innocent*.

His affinity with his hometown had not diminished, though—quite the opposite. His belief in the Midwestern way—the local work ethic—had grown stronger over the years. "I think there *is* such a thing. Maybe because there isn't the opportunity for easy success there, work becomes an end in itself, and people look to gain satisfaction from their work," he explained once. "Maybe they don't have such high aspirations, such vain hopes as you sometimes find in those who live on the edge of the country."

Yet Chicago was no longer the city of his youth. When he went for a drive to find his old home in Morton Grove, he struggled to locate Davis Street. The old water tower was there to welcome visitors, but the open fields of the new suburb he had known in the 1950s were now a seamless extension of the modern metropolis. "I didn't know the streets anymore. I was really lost," he confessed later. "I just kept driving around the suburbs until I found my house almost instinctively."

When he finally pinpointed the old bi-level, his excitement gave way to sadness. "It looked so different. The house was tiny. I remember it from my scale at the time; it seemed bigger," he said.

Arnold Kopelson was a former New York banking lawyer who had carved himself a position as a major Hollywood player through a formidable combination of Wall Street savvy and never-say-die determination. His persistence had paid off spectacularly in 1986 when he collected the Best Picture Oscar for *Platoon*, Oliver Stone's highly personal Vietnam memoir, a film that took ten tenacious years to progress from script to screen.

Kopelson had been nurturing the idea of reviving *The Fugitive* even longer. He had narrowly failed to buy the rights from Quinn Martin, the executive producer of the phenomenally successful television series and a client, during his legal days in the early 1970s. By 1987, however, Kopelson had done a deal to make a movie with Keith Barish, who had beaten him to the rights years earlier. Five years later, unfortunately, *The Fugitive*, by now switched by Kopelson from Orion to Warner Bros., still seemed no nearer the screen. Director Walter Hill and Alec Baldwin had been attached and then unattached to the project. Six scripts had been rejected as too weak and too similar to the original television show.

As sharp and shrewd an operator as he was, even Kopelson was impressed by the star power displayed in the days that followed his first phone call to Patricia McQueeney in 1992.

His first surprise came when he offered Harrison's agent the seventh—and by far the best—*Fugitive* script, written by Jeb Stuart and David Twohy.

"I called Pat McQueeney and I said: 'I have this terrific draft of *The Fugitive*,'" said Kopelson. "And she said: 'Well, you know, Arnold, we've seen every other draft before this and Harrison likes this role a lot.' I never knew this. Apparently somebody was feeding it to him."

His second shock came when McQueeney called him a week later to say that Harrison wanted to make the film. Within days Warner Bros. had confirmed a budget and a start date for principal photography. Usually a decision on a precise release date would be decided once production was underway or completed, but with Harrison Ford attached to his project, Kopelson was given that too.

Over 120 grittily *noir* episodes, climaxing in the most watched single show of its time on August 29, 1967, *The Fugitive* dominated the television ratings of the mid-1960s and turned its brooding star, David Janssen, into an international icon. At a bullfight in Madrid at the height of his fame, the entire crowd ignored the bloodthirsty spectacle and stood and cheered "El Fugitive" when he was spotted there on holiday.

Based on the simplest of stories, by prolific writer Roy Huggins, the series told the story of Dr. Richard Kimble, a Midwestern surgeon convicted of killing his wife but freed by a freak rail accident to spend a life on the run. As Kimble drifted from one nondescript town to another, he was relentlessly pursued by Detective Sam Gerard, an obsessive police officer intent on recapturing him, played by British actor Barry Morse. Each week, as Gerard hunted for Kimble, so too did Kimble draw closer to finding the "one-armed man" whom he claimed was his wife's real killer.

The seven-day-a-week shooting schedule took its toll on Janssen, who by the end of his time as Kimble had developed a stomach ulcer and a limp. A hardened drinker as well, he died aged just fifty.

Planned to last only fifteen weeks, the shooting schedule that began on February 3, 1993, would not amount to the epic trial Janssen's role became. But with a succession of spectacular set pieces that would have given even Indiana Jones palpitations, it would claim its own high physical price, nevertheless.

Harrison's research had been sedentary enough. At the University of Chicago he had immersed himself in the techniques of vascular surgeons, going so far as to assist in a complicated bypass operation on an elderly diabetic. "I wanted to know the minutiae. I wanted to know how a surgeon would turn toward a nurse to put on his gown, not as if he'd done it once but after he'd done it a thousand times. That's the truth of a part," he explained later.

In Stuart and Twohy's script, Kimble was portrayed as a maverick figure within the medical world. Harrison decided Kimble should begin the film, when he is seen under arrest, wearing a shaggy beard. One of his first acts after escaping would be to shave it off—a perfect symbolic moment of his newfound freedom. Warner Bros. were unconvinced, to say the least, and his hairstyle once more became an issue.

"The studio was petrified by that," said director Andrew Davis. "I totally agreed with him that that was a great way to go, because you were going to be able to see his bohemian, irreverent side, and then his having to be a chameleon and change."

The physical discomfort began in North Carolina where, in one of the film's most stunning set pieces, Kimble was seen evading arrest by jumping off a dam and swimming for his life through frozen waters. At the scenic Cheoah Dam, Harrison's first problem was overcoming his slight vertigo. "It takes me a minute or two to steel myself for heights," he confessed later. He survived hours hovering over the edge of the 200-foot dam only to suffer an injury to his back on terra firma. Three weeks into filming, Harrison damaged his right knee. (It had been the left leg he had damaged during filming on *Raiders*.) The anterior cruciate ligament was torn as he took a sharp turn while running through the Carolina countryside, leaving his knee severely swollen.

Still in excruciating pain, Harrison then had to spend long hours waist-deep in freezing water. Tubs of steaming hot water were kept off-camera, allowing him to avoid hypothermia from the cold. "He took a lot of abuse," Davis admitted. "It was a rough experience because we were working in the middle of winter. He was in pain, and he was cold, freezing. He's a real trouper."

When shooting moved to Chicago, however, he aggravated the injury even more. Another sharp turn, this time as he ran down a staircase in city hall, was once again responsible. "That was the angriest I've seen him. The first time was bad, but that time it did more serious damage," said Peter Robb-King, his longtime makeup assistant.

Much as it may have added to the audience's sympathy for the beleaguered Kimble, Harrison would have preferred the limp with which he dragged himself through the rest of the movie to have been a little less naturalistic!

The constant pain did little to stem his stubborn insistence on contributing changes to the complex sequence. "He brings a lot to the party in terms of point of view and ideas, which is much better than having somebody with an empty head who says, 'Tell me how to hold the apple!'" approved Davis.

At one stage Kimble was being pursued by Gerard through the congested corridors of a hospital. Harrison suggested Kimble slow the policeman down by shouting, "There's a man with a gun chasing a woman!" The ensuing chaos added to the visceral thrill of the chase and provided the film with another moment in which to root for the hero.

Davis was surprised at the amount of improvisation Harrison introduced. In an early scene he was to be interrogated over the death of his wife. "That scene was highly scripted. Harrison didn't want to know the questions the cops were going to ask him," said Davis. Throughout the lengthy shooting process that day, his off-the-cuff responses added to the sense of Kimble's confusion.

Davis discovered that his star's perfectionism did not end when his scenes had been completed. One day, the director decided to shoot extra footage of actor Ron Dean conducting the interrogation. "Harrison had worked all day, so I let him go home." As he was climbing into his car, however, Harrison got wind of what was going on. "What are we shooting? I thought we were done," he queried. When Davis explained, Harrison stayed on, sitting off-camera in Dean's sightline so that the angles would look absolutely accurate on film.

Even on the occasions when Davis did overrule him, Harrison had his own methods of prevailing. In one shot Harrison argued that the camera was not framing his head properly. Davis insisted it was fine, yet as soon as the cameras rolled, Harrison crouched the extra half inch he needed to lower his head into the right position. Melissa, watching, smiled quietly. "That's our Harrison," she whispered.

Harrison, Davis and company had precisely six months—between February 3 and August 3—to shoot and edit one of the biggest movies of the year. Predictably, the pressures boiled over. Writer Jeb Stuart with Harrison, Davis, Jones, and Arnold Kopelson, worked continuously at rewriting and improving the script. Harrison once more made no apologies for his interventions. "It's my face the people remember, and I don't like to disappoint my customers," he said matter-of-factly. Harrison's antenna was tuned to pick up anything that veered toward the *Raiders* school of heroism. Writer Jeb Stuart would regularly have action scenes rejected. "There would be constant arguments. Harrison would say: 'This is a great scene. It would just steal the movie, it would be fabulous, but it goes into the zone of *Indiana Jones*, so you can't do it,' " Stuart recalls.

Harrison was also ever-vigilant about Kimble's motivation. "He would be constantly saying: 'Why would I go into a diner filled with people?' or 'Why would I color my hair?' He would not relinquish any aspect of the storytelling to anybody," said Stuart.

Tommy Lee Jones, a talent hopelessly underappreciated by Hollywood over the years, was as potent an improvisational force in the role of the Rottweiler-like Gerard. In the opening act, when Kimble, protesting his innocence, warns that he will jump off the edge of the dam, Jones suggested that Gerard counter "I don't care." In a scene that could have been overwhelmed by the raw power of its visuals, the line established—to Kimble and the audience—an obsessiveness that would never allow Gerard to quit hunting the fugitive.

There were inevitable clashes. Harrison and Kopelson disagreed violently about whether Kimble should be sentenced to death at the beginning of the story. To support his theory, Harrison recruited his friend Scott Turow. "They had dinner while the writing was going on," Kopelson recounted. "He came in and said: 'Scott says that Kimble would never have received the death penalty; instead he should get life imprisonment without the possibility of parole. A rich doctor would be able to beat this.'"

In Kopelson, however, Harrison had met his match. On the night the opening sentencing scene was shot in a Chicago courthouse, Kopelson visited the chambers of one of the city's leading criminal judges. His view was that Kimble *could* have been given the death sentence—if there was tremendous malice in the murder.

Triumphant, Kopelson returned to the set. "Do me a favor, let's shoot it two ways," he suggested to Harrison. The latter agreed, and the death sentence was left in the final movie. "There are actors who will challenge you when they're trying to make their role better, to give themselves more lines—or just being a pain in the ass. He is challenging, but it was never about his role; it was about what's best for the movie," said Kopelson.

The producer left Chicago under no illusion about the forces that made his Richard Kimble run. Underpinning Harrison's drive for shot-by-shot perfection was an even more profound determination not to trip up. Harrison's climb had been a long and punishing one: it was now too far to fall. "I suspect he has a fear of failure because he is on top, and it takes a great deal to stay there," Kopelson decided. "I don't think he wants to fuck up."

Suddenly there seemed no escaping the wards and the waiting rooms. Within days of completing shooting, in mid-June Harrison was admitted to a hospital in Jackson Hole. Once more, by ignoring pain in order to finish filming, he had exacerbated what might have been a less serious problem. Ten years after his back operation, doctors performed reconstructive surgery to connect the torn cartilage to the joints in his knee. (He would need a second operation the following year.) He spent six weeks of the summer hobbling around the ranch on crutches. Shooting on his next picture, his second outing as Jack Ryan, in *Clear and Present Danger*, was put back to October while he recovered.

Unfortunately almost as soon as he was throwing the crutches away, he was back in hospital. His father suffered a brain aneurism at the beginning of July and was admitted to Los Angeles' UCLA Medical Center. Harrison remained at his bedside as Christopher, now eighty-seven, made a recovery. "He didn't even go home to sleep," one hospital worker was quoted as saying.

Family remained the bedrock of his life, the anchor of his soul. Months later he would be back at a relative's bedside in happier circumstances. His first grandchild, a boy called Eliel, was born to Willard and his wife in Oakland, northern California.

Neither Ben, now twenty-six, nor Willard, twenty-four, had shown any interest in following their father into acting. Ben had qualified as a chef at the California Culinary Academy and now worked at the chic Campanile Restaurant in Los Angeles. Willard had graduated in American history from the University of California, Santa Cruz and—much to his father's pride—worked as a substitute teacher specializing in Chicano, Hispanic, and African-American history in one of the poorer sections of Oakland.

Harrison had been neither dismayed nor surprised at their choices. Like his father before him, he had deglamorized his profession at every possible turn. In his case it had been a relatively easy job. Nothing could have been less dazzling than the life he had led during their most impressionable years when he had been driven to distraction by his struggles to meet the mortgage and finish work on the family home. They recognized the pain that lay behind the millions. "They knew me when I was just a poor carpenter and a bad actor," he said.

As his family extended its roots further, Harrison had come to regard the ranch more and more as his greatest legacy to his children and grandchildren. "I have more a sense of stewardship about it than ownership. I really want to preserve it for my kids—to let them know this is what's dear to me rather than a pile of money in the middle of the floor. . . . I realize that what's most sustaining is having kids," he said that summer.

Elsewhere in an America in love with its New Age self, such pronouncements were becoming as transparent as they were tiresome. Parenthood, no longer an unfashionable, stolid interview subject, had replaced sex and substance abuse on the celebrity confessional couch. Even Warren Beatty and Jack Nicholson were babbling on about it!

Yet, despite the failures he had admitted to with his first children, it would have taken the toughest of cynics to question the sincerity of Harrison's fatherly feelings. And his family extended well beyond blood ties.

"It's no accident that he plays a lot of heroes," said Carrie Fisher, who benefited from his paternal hand in her long fight to rid herself of drug addiction. (Harrison and Melissa receive a dedication in her novel *Postcards From the Edge*.) "He plays somebody you can rely on, who will take care of whatever it is, from a kid's hurt finger to a murder, or to saving the galaxy. He has that quality."

Ever since his arrival in Hollywood, members of his immediate and extended family had seen different shades of his generosity. He had, according to one report that he did his best to suppress, paid for the exorbitant, six-figure hospital bills of a dying friend.

His generosity could not be dismissed as a matter of money talking. Back in the depression days of the early 1970s, Cindy Williams had been surprised by his thoughtfulness during filming on *The Conversation* in San Francisco. Hospitalized with Russian flu, her flagging spirits were raised as she woke one morning to find a violinist playing at the foot of her bed. The musician had been sent not by Francis Coppola or Fred Roos, but by one of the poorest members of the team— "the guy in the green silk suit."

In the summer of 1994, it was his brother Terence who received the rude awakening.

Terence's troubled life since the 1960s had hardly been made any easier by his decision to take up full-time acting in the mid-1980s. Blessed with, if anything, even more appealing looks than his brother, he had at first found it relatively easy to charm casting agents. Tall, gipsyish in appearance and manner and, as three broken marriages seemed to indicate, "a terrible flirt," he fitted photogenically into shows like *Dynasty* and *Falcon Crest*.

The shadow of his famous brother was ever-present, unfortunately. Through the decade of *Star Wars* and the Indy adventures, *Blade Runner*, and *Witness*, the burden of expectation became unbearable.

On the rare occasions he admitted his lineage—"I'm a lot happier it's not Terence Costner or Terence Belushi," he confessed once—casting agents were inevitably disappointed by the lack of an obvious resemblance to Harrison. "When producers hear that I am Harrison Ford's brother, they think they are going to get Indiana Jones on the cheap. And they hate it when they find out they are not."

Europe had briefly offered him a warmer welcome. In 1992 he played an American photographer in Paris, in the pan-European soap *Riviera*. Yet by now he had drifted out of acting again to settle in Humboldt County, northern California, where he had set up a small landscape gardening business.

Without his brother's support, Terence's patience would have failed him much sooner when things got tough. "Harrison was the one who forced me to keep going," he acknowledged. "He begged me to hang in there. And he told me that he was one of the greatest examples of someone who could be a success story eventually."

As *The Fugitive* opened that August, Terence was once more experiencing difficulties. The Dodge pickup truck he used to run his business had given up after months of misbehavior. News of his problem somehow drifted back to Wyoming.

At dawn one morning, Terence woke to find a brand-new pickup, identical to the previous one, parked outside his house wrapped in a red ribbon. The attached note joked: "If this truck is found, please return to Dr. Richard Kimble."

As it happened, Harrison had every reason to be generous after *The Fugitive*. It swiftly delivered his biggest critical and commercial success away from the world of Lucas-Berg. Despite his intimidating deadline, Andrew Davis erased even the fondest memories of the original television series. Powered by two exemplary performances by Harrison and Tommy Lee Jones, Davis's film combined epic-scale stuntwork—most notably in the train crash and the dam sequence—with an intensely focused human conflict in which Gerard and Kimble seemed to represent two halves of the same, obsessively driven soul.

As it opened in August that year, few could find fault anywhere. "This is a home run," raved Janet Maslin in the *New York Times*, as she praised Davis's "sensational" direction and Harrison and Jones's "steely perfection . . . Mr. Ford succeeds in making his character deeply sympathetic from the film's opening frames. This actor's wary intelligence is no surprise but he projects it with particular grace in this spare, visceral story," she went on.

And: "Ford's performance is in another league from David Janssen's sleepwalk through the sixties series," wrote Quentin Curtis in the *Independent on Sunday* as the film opened to almost universal acclaim in the United Kingdom. In a summer of stiff competition from Clint Eastwood's *In the Line of Fire* and Tom Cruise's *The Firm*, *The Fugitive* was—aptly enough—the runaway box-office success, raking in $180 million in the United States alone.

The success surprised its star. "We had a lot of problems doing it, and I was concerned about the final product," Harrison told the CNN talk-show host Larry King. "I didn't think *The Fugitive* would do as well as it did." Tommy Lee Jones's Gerard would go on to collect him a Best Supporting Actor Oscar the following spring. Harrison would be nominated for a Best Actor Golden Globe, but would once more miss out.

24

THE RYAN GAME

On a baking hot day at Disneyland, the argument between two browbeaten parents was hardly untypical. Along with hundreds of others, the well-heeled couple had been waiting on endless lines with their young son. By now even the high-pitched platitudes of Mickey Mouse and friends couldn't calm their infant's fraying nerves.

"*No!*" the father insisted from behind his dark glasses.

"Why not?" the child's exasperated mother protested in return.

To judge by his expression, Melissa Mathison might have been asking her husband to pose nude for *Playgirl*. To Harrison Ford, however, her suggestion that he use his fame to cut in line was just as unthinkable!

On that occasion, in 1993, Melissa eventually persuaded Harrison to slip himself, her, and Malcolm out of the logjam and discreetly drop his name at the head of the long line. For a long time afterward she thought she had "violated something very important in his sense of ethics," Melissa told the author David Halberstam.

"For her, the issue was getting a little boy out of a long line on a hot day. For Ford, his very integrity was at stake," Halberstam later wrote.

In applying the self-made rules which now ran his life, Harrison was as intransigent as ever. "The only reasonable place to be a movie star is on the set when you can use it to control your own destiny," ran his argument. "And that is its *only* use."

On this, and so many other matters Hollywood, Harrison's was the voice in the wilderness. With a new administration in the White House, the celebrity endorsement of politics had reached its zenith in America. As far as Harrison was concerned, name-dropping at Disneyland represented the thin edge of the same wedge he now saw extending all the way into Washington.

Bill and Hillary Clinton were once house guests in Wyoming; Hillary, like Harrison, is a graduate of Maine East. But the idea of joining Barbra Streisand, Goldie Hawn, and Sally Field at Clinton's inauguration in 1992 was utterly unthinkable to him.

"I'm sick to *death* of celebrity spokesmen for causes," he raged. "Critical issues are being decided on the basis of who you like the best. It's Who has the prettiest team? Vote for your favorite star. It's complete bull. Drives me *nuts*."

His anger explained the near secrecy with which he handled his huge contributions to charity. He had for years given away generous tranches of his multi-million-dollar paychecks. As hard as he had worked to help worthy causes, he had worked even harder to keep his role quiet.

Sometimes his philanthropy was far from altruistic, for many of his donations reflect the passions that fire his life away from moviemaking. He was for some time, for instance, a board member of the nonpolitical Conservation International—an environmental group working on a variety of "bio-diversity" projects in thirty or so overseas countries.

Harrison's hard-won dollars financed conservation in regions as remote as Madagascar and the Amazon rain forest. At board meetings he fought to make sure his money went to the less fashionable, unpublicized ventures in each region. "He's very interested in having the organization focused on priorities and not getting distracted by the flavor of the day," said Peter Seligman, CI's chairman.

It was during the organization's bid to create a two-million-acre biosphere reserve in the Chaco Rey region of Colombia that he had first allowed Seligman to bend the rules on the use of his famous name. "After negotiations with the minister of economic development, the gentleman turned to me and said, 'Do you think you can get Harrison Ford's autograph? It's for my son,' " Seligman reported. Harrison obliged only when he was sure the deal was struck. "Harrison understands what he can do for the environment and he does it."

Over the years he has also made substantial donations or lent his name to charities from the Save the Children Foundation and the American Cancer Society to the Will Rogers Foundation and the Archaeological Advisory Group projects from Alaska to North Carolina. In almost every case, however, he has played down the significance of his work.

Publicly, for instance, his contribution to the Lancaster Farmland Trust, an organization dedicated to preserving the countryside around the Amish heartland where *Witness* had been filmed, ran to no more than a plea for the preservation of "a special place. . . . This is too important a part of America to lose by default," he wrote in a letter of support used to raise funds in the early 1990s. Privately, his financial muscle helped guarantee the nonprofit trust's survival in a difficult period.

Only those nearest and dearest to him can persuade him to raise his profile any higher than the patrons' list on his charities' letterheads. In 1992 he appeared on a CNBC chat show with longtime lawyer friend Gerry Spence to talk about his work in alleviating homelessness in Santa Cruz, California. He had become involved in the project through Willard while his own son was studying in the city. On another occasion he spent the Saturday before Christmas serving punch to the homeless at the Los Angeles Mission.

In summer 1993, Harrison had little choice but to use the unreasonable force of his celebrity. If he had not, a young Tibetan Buddhist might have been executed for associating with westerners like him.

Evidence of the growing influence of Buddhism began to seep into Harrison's conversations with journalists at the beginning of the 1990s. The simplicity of its doctrines seemed to have struck a chord. Along its path to inner peace he had found a commodity that, for him at least, had seemed just as elusive—happiness.

"Happiness is something you have to learn to be open to, and I never have gone to a psychiatrist," he explained in 1990. "All the money spent on my education boils down to what the Buddha said: 'Work out your salvation with diligence.'"

In 1992 a documentary maker, Vanessa Boeye, had been the first to discover the depth of his interest. Boeye approached him to narrate a documentary about the treacherous journey undertaken by the Dalai Lama's emissary, Khamtruel Rinpoche, to the isolated Buddhist kingdom of Mustang, high in the Himalayas.

"We liked his voice," said Boeye. "He immediately agreed to get involved because he sympathizes with the Tibetan cause." His help did Boeye's film no end of good. A brief run of her film, *Mustang: The Hidden Kingdom*, sold out in Los Angeles and was shown around the world on television.

Melissa's interest had, if anything, been even more intensely aroused by Buddhist philosophy. After meeting the Dalai Lama, the spiritual Tibetan head exiled from his homeland since the Chinese invasion of 1950, she had grown fascinated by the story of the life of the religion's holiest figure. In 1992, Harrison had traveled with Melissa to Tibet as she began working, with the blessing of the Lama, on *Kundun*, an idea for a screenplay based on his life as a boy. (Kundun was the Lama's childhood nickname.)

In stark contrast to the high profile adopted by Richard Gere, Susan Sarandon, and Tim Robbins, Harrison and Melissa succeeded in keeping secret their visits to Tibet and Dharamsala, the Lama's northern Indian retreat. There may have been a commercial edge, however, to their clandestine behavior. Hollywood's growing interest in all things Buddhist had already spawned Bernardo Bertolucci's *Little Buddha* with Keanu Reeves, and Melissa feared that any leak about her screenplay might inspire imitators or competitors. Yet there was no doubting the impact made on both of them by the repression they saw on their visit to Tibet.

The "thick feeling of fear" they felt immediately was symbolized by the nervousness of Tibetans to even mention the Lama's name for fear of punishment by the Chinese. One evening Harrison and Melissa coaxed a woman they had befriended to sing a song. "While she was singing, even though we were in a room, among friends, with closed doors, she kept looking over one shoulder and then another as she sang and was very happy to have finished her song," Melissa said later. The song, unbeknown to Harrison and Melissa, had included several mentions of the Lama. "That's the level of fear that exists." "This is what they've done to us—they've made us fear one another," Harrison and Melissa were regularly told during their visit.

Their guide throughout their visit to Tibet had been a forty-seven-year-old from Lhasa, Gendun Rinchen. Rinchen, one of the most popular guides with Europeans and Americans in the Tibetan capital, had touched both Harrison and Melissa with his sincerity and humor as he helped them pick their way through Lhasa and its famous Barkor Square and the Himalayas beyond. Melissa later recounted a touching scene when, after meeting them at the airport, Rinchen had taken them to a typical Tibetan village. "A bunch of little kids came running up to the car, and Rinchen pulled out a tissue and started wiping all their noses," said Melissa. "Not only was it just an automatic gesture of compassion on his part, but he also wanted them to look their best in front of the foreigners. He wanted us to witness the dignity that they had."

To their amazement, in May of the following year, news filtered back that Rinchen had been arrested and faced the death penalty. Rinchen's "crime" had been to write a letter, listing the names of political prisoners being held under Chinese rule. He had intended to pass the letter to a member of a visiting European Commission party, investigating human rights abuses in Lhasa, but had been arrested two days beforehand.

Alerted to the situation by Amnesty International, Harrison and Melissa immediately offered support for protests and a letter-writing campaign. Melissa penned an op-ed piece on Rinchen's plight, published in the *New York Times*. From their living room in Jackson Hole they chose the BBC's influential World Service to drive home their fears for Rinchen's welfare. It was a measure of the anxiety they felt that Harrison took time in the week he was admitted to hospital in June 1993 to make the broadcast.

During his time with the guide, Harrison explained, Rinchen's political agitation extended no further than talking about the lack of human rights in Tibet. "That the Tibetan people themselves had no right to assemble, had no right to publish, had no right to travel, were basically kept away from foreign visitors as much as possible. Those kind of things concerned him," he told the BBC's John Tidmarsh.

Since his visit, Harrison argued, the extent of the repression in Lhasa was less obviously apparent. It was Harrison's understanding that Rinchen did not want the EC visitors, one of the most important delegations to have visited Tibet, to leave without a true picture of the human rights situation. "The machine-gun-toting soldiers on the rooftops in the Barkor have been replaced with security cameras," he said. "The policemen by and large are now plainclothes policemen, and he was afraid they would leave without having a sense of what was really going on."

Harrison explained the gravity of the situation. "As far as Amnesty International knows, only one Tibetan has been charged with this crime before," he said. "We're very concerned that he might face the death penalty for stealing state secrets."

The authorities in Lhasa were left in no doubt about Rinchen's high-profile support when a visiting American senator, Max Baucus, pressed Tibet's second most senior official, Deputy Secretary Rak Dhi to release him and other political prisoners in a visit later that August. At the time, the Chinese authorities defended their decision, claiming Rinchen "coaxed people to overthrow our present system" and had "stolen many confidential materials for a long time." By January 1994, however, continued lobbying secured Rinchen's release after eight months in a prison cell. When he fled the country and traveled to America and Washington the following year, Harrison and Melissa were among those there to welcome him.

The Hollywood career on which Joaquim De Almeida embarked in the early 1990s owed more to his rakish Latino looks than his estimable work for European art-house directors like the Italian Taviani brothers. One smitten American writer compared the seductive glaze of the rugged Portuguese star's eyes to "Vaselined coffee beans."

It was, coincidentally, in a converted coffee factory in the Mexican town of Coatepec that the sensitive star of the European school of filmmaking received his one and only master class at the Harrison Ford academy of action-hero acting. Neither tutor nor pupil found it an enjoyable experience.

In March 1994, Coatepec was doubling as Colombia during filming of *Clear and Present Danger*, the second of the Jack Ryan movies Harrison had signed to make three years earlier. The coffee house was staging a climactic fight between Ryan and Felix Cortez, the drug-trading villain of the piece, played by De Almeida. The latter, a newcomer to the sort of big-budget stuntwork that was second nature to Harrison, had spent much of the day frustratedly watching his double, Tom Elliott, trade blows with the actor he had waited months to work alongside. Throughout, Harrison and Phillip Noyce, the Australian director, had demanded more and more takes to make the slugging match look more authentic. "The thing with Harrison is that he is so used to it that he gets so intense. He would shout, 'No, no, no, that's no good. That wasn't a buy, let's do it again,' " said De Almeida. "He does it all. He has incredible experience."

Impatient to get in on the action, De Almeida had been working hard with stunt coordinator Dick Ziker and Elliott. Harrison, however, had grave doubts when he stepped into Elliott's place for a choreographed fight scene. "Let's try it," he said, nodding toward De Almeida, still to be convinced.

The scene required Harrison to ambush De Almeida, kick a gun out of his hand and then throw a series of whooshing punches past his face. De Almeida would then parry his blows and launch a sidekick at his attacker.

In his runthrough with Ziker and Elliott, De Almeida had been taught to land his kick harmlessly on his opponent's left thigh.

With most of the set watching on, De Almeida safely negotiated the first part of the exchange. The gasps were audible, however, as his kick connected squarely with the most delicate region between Harrison's splayed legs. "Christ, right in the goodies!" someone was heard to whisper.

For a second Harrison was doubled up in agony. A beat later he drew his fist back ready to land a haymaker. As De Almeida looked helplessly on, he saw the thunder slowly drain from his star's face. Opening a finger from his fist and pointing at his assailant Harrison growled: "That's exactly why you're not doing the shot!"

His reaction was not untypical. He had never suffered fools gladly, no matter how impeccable their acting credentials might have looked elsewhere. In the heat of that Mexican moment, however, his outburst may have had more to do with the fact that *Clear and Present Danger* was proving the most problematic shoot of his career so far. What is more, De Almeida's misplaced foot had been the latest in a series of shots to land woundingly below the waist.

First published in 1989, Clancy's novel had sold more than six million copies to become comfortably the biggest seller of its year. Its labyrinthine plot weaved its conspiratorial way from the White House, to the CIA, to the drug barons of Colombia. From the opening day of shooting on November 3, 1993, the film adaptation came complete with its own complexities—problems political, logistical, even seismological!

First, inevitably, there was Tom Clancy himself. *Clear and Present Danger* was his most popular book, and with his customary force he had left Paramount and Mace Neufeld in no doubt that he expected it to be the best film adaptation yet. A first script, by the author's friend John Milius, had pleased Clancy but left the reassembled *Patriot Games* team of Neufeld, Noyce, and Paramount cold. Faithful to a 700-page novel in which the hero does not appear until page 300, the script left Noyce protesting that there was no place for Harrison in the film. "There was a place, but the audience would have rioted."

It needed a seven-figure fee to entice *Patriot Games* co-screenwriter Donald Stewart back into the fold. After Clancy mauled his adaptation—"if you shoot this script, *Sliver* will look like *Citizen Kane*," he said in one of his many faxed memos—he, like Harrison, wondered whether it was worth the pain. "First things first," Clancy continued in another memo. "*Clear and Present Danger* was the No. 1 bestselling novel of the 1980s. One might conclude that the novel's basic story-line had some quality to it. Why, then, has nearly every aspect of the book been tossed away?"

Still weary of Clancy's griping since *Patriot Games*, Harrison spelled out the simplicity of the situation during the shoot. "You do things when you are typing that you would never do if you had to fucking stand there and deliver," he raged in his most heated outburst against the interfering author. "It's inevitable that a book changes in bringing it to the screen. It's generally accepted by those professionals that have had some experience with the process. And if one doesn't want to submit to the process, the simple expedient is not to sell your stuff."

Clancy was not the only unhappy party. Phillip Noyce had to allay fears within the Pentagon that the script presented the armed forces as irresponsibly gung ho. Stewart's screenplay revolved around a secret CIA plot, authorized by the president of the United States, in which a rogue ex-navy SEAL wages war against the Colombian drug cartels in retaliation for their assassination of an American businessman. Jack Ryan, cast as a by-the-book Boy Scout in the story, intervenes to stop the illegal hostilities and then rescue a group of stranded U.S. servicemen in Colombia.

Neufeld and Noyce were relying on the Pentagon for a variety of military hardware, from an aircraft carrier to Black Hawk helicopters. Noyce and Stewart had to agree to a series of script changes before they got clearance—more than a week after principal photography had started in Los Angeles.

More problems piled up when the production switched to Mexico. The government there was unwilling to issue permits for much of its explosives and weaponry. A brief but bloody revolution had broken out in the state of Chiapas in the south of the country just a week before. The permits came through only forty-eight hours before filming was due to begin.

To cap it all, footage that had made it back to the safety of Los Angeles was then destroyed in the earthquake of early 1994! "After shooting two films in a series, you would think the third would be easier," said a deflated Neufeld on the set at the time. "But it hasn't."

As on *Patriot Games*, Noyce, Neufeld, and writer Stewart never found Harrison anywhere other than in the thick of the war zone action. Shooting began without a satisfactory "third act." As a result the script was being amended and updated throughout, with daily story meetings involving Stewart, Noyce, Neufeld, and Harrison. Steven Zaillian, the hot young writer of *Schindler's List*, was also hired to strengthen Ryan's role.

Harrison's major beef was with the ending. In the book Ryan confronts the president over his illegal war in the privacy of the Oval Office, threatening to go public if it is not called off. He encouraged Zaillian to write an ending which had Ryan going to Congress, where he publicly blew the lid off the scandal. He thought the ambiguous "will he or won't he?" ending of the book was "insufficient entertainment."

Clancy and Milius, both right-wing Reaganites, hated the idea and called it "ridiculous. . . . Anyone in this day and age who thinks that Congress is an honorable organization is a fool," Milius moaned.

Many adjectives were attached to Harrison during shooting—perfectionist, pedant, pain-in-the-ass. Fool was not among them, however. He sniffed out false notes like some cinematic truffle hound. His attention could switch from the biggest issues to the most minuscule of details.

For instance, in Mexico City during an elaborate shoot-out sequence, in which Ryan is ambushed on a visit to Colombia, Harrison spotted that the shirt and tie he had been given by costume head Bernie Pollack did not exactly match those he had been wearing as he was seen leaving to board the plane in America. The originals had been held up in customs.

"Bernie Pollack had got a striped shirt that was almost identical but could not find a tie to match," said Mace Neufeld. "I said, 'No one is going to see it.' Harrison said: 'Well, I will know it!' "

The crisis was averted when a crew member cut through the red tape and produced the right shirt and tie. "We were going to send someone to New York!" admitted Neufeld. "The truth is that no one would have seen it."

There were those who appreciated Harrison's unerring eye for detail, particularly the embattled, on-set screenwriter Stewart, who once more found his star suggesting lines that improved on his own: "He knows the right thing to say and do. He's got this quality that, if it doesn't ring right, he doesn't seem able to say it or do it. So in a story meeting, he just gives you a better gesture, and nine times out of ten, a better line."

It was Harrison, for instance, who saw the need to go against his usual deconstructionist instincts and add new lines in the run-up to the film's hijack scene. As the script stood, there was little to suggest any friendship between Ryan and a colleague who would be killed in the attack. Harrison suggested Stewart insert extracts of day-to-day dialogue to establish a relationship between the two men. His instincts, justified when the scene was shot, were that Ryan—and the audience—would feel a greater sense of outrage at the death.

Pragmatism, however, was soon holding sway over such perfectionism. As the production slipped behind schedule and panic-filled memos from Paramount joined those of Clancy's in the fax tray, the arguments between the normally passive Noyce and his persnickity star became heated.

During filming, Noyce kept his comments confined to the diplomatic. "It was more stressful. We had less of a script this time, so we had more to argue about," he smiled before going on to compare his relationship with Harrison to a marriage, polite the first time around, less so the second.

It was probably little consolation to Noyce that he was far from alone. Even as shooting had begun on *Clear and Present Danger*, another director had seen his film consigned to a dustbin by Harrison's "point of view." The hapless Japanese commercial director was ordered to reshoot the cellular-phone Harrison had made months earlier with another cameraman. According to reports, Harrison, not averse to the odd mega-yen payday promoting products like Kirin beer, was not happy with the lighting.

By the time filming had ended in the spring of 1994, the Australian Philip Noyce's comments on Harrison's attitude problem had become much blunter.

"Anal," was the word that stood out as he described his star's fretful behavior to the *Sydney Morning Herald*. He amplified on it later in London. "He is morally brave, doggedly obsessive, detail-oriented. Harrison can be a bloody pain," he complained.

Harrison attempted to put a more positive spin on their differences in the weeks that followed. "We try to meld our energies together, that's the ambition, for him to keep his strong point of view and for me to keep my strong point of view and for us to end up with something twice as strong," he said. "We usually come to an accommodation. But directors have a point of view and I have a point of view about what I do too."

In the workshop and on the movie set, precision was everything to Harrison. In less defensive moments he was able to admit he even worried himself with his obsession with life's finer details. At home it manifested itself in an orderliness and everything-has-its-place attitude that could drive Melissa and everyone else crazy.

Visitors to the ranch would express awe at the array of carpentry tools on display and the orderliness with which they were laid out, according to size and shape, function and form. "It was as if a carpenter had died and gone to heaven," one visitor observed.

Many found Harrison's insistence on order dangerously close to obsessional. When Bruce Newman, a Los Angeles journalist, visited him at Jackson Hole in the run-up to the release of *Clear and Present Danger*, like many others he could not help but notice Harrison's compulsive need for order—even on the edge of the wilderness. As Newman sat down with his interviewee in the beautiful log cabin he had built in a glade of blue spruce trees, Harrison spotted that the hideaway's few pieces of furniture had been rearranged. Before he could settle to speak to him, Harrison stalked the room, repositioning pieces exactly as he wanted them. "I have to go around and put everything back where it belongs," he told his visitor, with an embarrassed shrug. "People move things three or four inches and it drives me crazy."

As ever, he made light of his foibles with doses of self-deprecatory humor. "I'm the kind of guy who straightens the piles out on his desk," he admitted once. He would make lists of "things to do" everywhere, even on the back of his hand. One day, he joked, he would write himself a note to "drop dead."

Visitors to his homes in Los Angeles and New York witnessed the same phenomenon there. It was Mike Nichols, staying at his Los Angeles home for a few months, who voiced a thought that had worked its way into the minds of many. Exquisitely spartan, without "a single piece of chintz or bullshit," the home reminded the director of a mansion built by Shakers. Nichols was struck by how the house was governed by the same tasteful, minimalist principles that its owner applied to his work. "The house becomes a metaphor—everything works perfectly," Nichols said.

Such perfectionism was, of course, simply an extension of his indomitability, his need for control. It is one of the greatest ironies of all that Harrison, with his perfectionist's eye and his hatred of a job done badly, subjects himself to the process of filmmaking at all. As he puts it: "There are a thousand ways to fuck up a movie."

By now, his perfectionism had become the driving force within every movie he made. He refused to take the executive-producer credit that he could rightfully have claimed on both the Clancy films and *The Fugitive* as well. Yet as far as some were concerned, he was often effectively the director—although the idea of officially directing held little or no interest. "I like to work intensely for a period of time and then finish and go back to something resembling real life. If you direct, you're looking at two years instead of five or six months. Enough is enough."

Maybe it was shot during a few spare hours during the filming of *Clear and Present Danger*; perhaps it was done as a favor to a friend. Whatever his motivation, Harrison Ford made a very brief unbilled cameo appearance during the closing credits of Barry Levinson's 1994 film, *Jimmy Hollywood*. Ford plays himself playing the role of Jimmy Hollywood in a fictional movie being made based upon Jimmy's life. The scenes are bright spots in a rather disappointing film, as "the real" Jimmy, played by Joe Pesci, watches Ford enact the events of his life, then stops the action, lays a hand on Ford's shoulder and tells him, "That's not the way it happened. Do it like this."

Jimmy Hollywood can hardly be considered a Harrison Ford film, but diehard fans may want to rent the video and fast-forward to the end to catch Ford's appearance.

Talk of trouble on the *Clear and Present Danger* project transpired long before shooting finally ended. Talking to interviewers in Mexico in January, Harrison made no secret of his impatience with Tom Clancy in particular. He pulled up short of declaring open war, but intimated that if the author wanted to start one, he was more than ready to oblige.

Harrison's clout within Hollywood was now sufficient to intimidate anyone. For those who had not seen him in more than twenty years, the contrast between professional hawk and personal dove they witnessed at Skywalker Ranch that year was all the more fascinating.

Harrison and Melissa had traveled to Marin County to celebrate George Lucas's fiftieth birthday on May 14. The event was a reunion for many of those whose lives had been touched by his reclusive genius. As three hundred people joined Lucas for lunch, senior members of the gathering began making impromptu speeches. Candy Clark saw a look of horror spread over Harrison Ford's face.

"I watched him as they were going round the table. All the big boys got up and said these wonderful things—Scorsese, Spielberg, and then

Robert Zemeckis. As it got closer to Harrison he just turned red—he freaked," she said. "It was stage-fright—he is just so shy. He said something and then when he sat down he took a big gulp out of his wine."

The transformation from the fearsome hell-raiser of the *Graffiti* set was unmistakable. To Clark he seemed a calmer, more contented shadow of the scary character she had avoided at all costs in Petaluma. "Even his eye shape has changed," she claimed. "He used to have edges at the top of his eyes—his eyes would be squared off. Now they are more relaxed, softer edged. . . . Success did him a lot of good. It really made him blossom; it made him a lot happier. It calmed him down and opened him up and took off the edge, brought out the humor."

Harrison's aversion to such events remained as ferocious as ever. "I am better off in ones and twos," he admitted.

Even on the rare occasions Melissa could winkle him out, she often regretted the effort. Their friend Arnold Glimcher and his wife saw them at the Museum of the Moving Image night in honor of Mike Nichols, held in New York in March 1990, while Harrison was in the city making *Working Girl*. "Harrison had to come, and he was in excruciating pain," Glimcher said.

At least he had been given prior warning weeks before Lucas's birthday. At Bally's Hotel in Las Vegas, when he collected the "Box-Office Star of the Century" award from the National Association of Theater Owners, Lucas, an even scarcer face at such gatherings, traveled to Las Vegas to present his friend with the award.

Like each of its studio rivals, Paramount, under its new owners, Viacom, used the occasion to wheel out its heavy guns. *Clear and Present Danger* was among its prime products for the coming summer, as was *Star Trek: Generations* and *Forrest Gump*. William Shatner and Patrick Stewart and Tom Hanks joined Harrison in performing the hard sell.

Throughout the convention, however, Lucas, Harrison, and the Paramount brass kept their own counsel on the project that would have put the broadest smile on the theater owners' faces. With Spielberg, the duo had set the wheels in motion for a fourth Indiana Jones film. Jeb Stuart, who had impressed Harrison on *The Fugitive*, was already working on a first draft, and a provisional date of early 1996 had been set for shooting to begin. However, shooting continues to be postponed because of schedule conflicts and rewrites.

The prospect of another Jack Ryan film had been the last thing on anyone's mind. Nothing heals Hollywood wounds quite like the soothing sound of cash registers, however, and as *Clear and Present Danger* opened to the best figures posted by any of the Ryan movies—$28.8 million in its first five days—and surged on to top *The Hunt for Red October*, the combatants made maneuvers worthy of the United Nations.

With Paramount still sitting on film rights to the Jack Ryan character for the next four years, Neufeld opened negotiations for a new Clancy book. The mega-seller *The Sum of All Fears*, in which Middle Eastern terrorists blow up the Superbowl, and *Debt of Honor*, in which Ryan confronts a Japanese industrialist intent on conquering America, were the likeliest candidates. So too, he made it clear, were Ryan scripts written by someone other than Clancy—if the author continued to be so difficult to deal with.

While Clancy rattled on about having more control next time, the series' coproducer, whose office wall is plastered with copies of Clancy's high-combustion communications to "Mr. Neufeld," hinted he was man enough to bury the hatchet if his nemesis was. "If Rabin and Arafat could shake hands, Clancy and Neufeld could," he joked.

But Harrison was in no hurry to reenter the fray. It had taken him eight years to complete the Indiana Jones trilogy. This time he might take even longer, he hinted. As if to bait Clancy even more, he suggested that he wait until he was sixty before playing the thirtysomething hero once more!

If he was in the mood for one last, laconic laugh at Tom Clancy, however, he needed to look no further than that year's *Forbes* Top 40. While Clancy had slipped to twenty-seventh in the table, falling behind archrivals Michael Crichton, Stephen King, and John Grisham, Harrison had leapt to the very top of the Hollywood heap. His tenth-place ranking and his annual earnings of $27 million—$44 million over two years—dwarfed anything anyone else had earned in acting. The lion's share of his millions had come courtesy of salary and his 11.5 percent profit-share from *Clear and Present Danger*.

His second outing as Ryan enriched his reputation even more than his bank balance. Critics and audiences alike began to acknowledge that somewhere along the path from *Patriot Games* to *The Fugitive* and *Clear and Present Danger*, he had evolved a new presence. It was partly that his maturing features seemed somehow more comfortable on-screen than ever before; stillness—a quality absent amid the action of his earlier films—had suddenly become one of the most powerful weapons in his acting armory. He had also acquired something rare among modern actors; he had become the focus of his films.

"This is the mark of a true Film Star," wrote Julie Burchill in the *Sunday Times*. "The screen seems more alive when it's filled with Ford doing boring things like buying an airplane ticket or talking on the phone than it does during the explosions and chases. He *is* the action."

The message to Tom Clancy was unequivocal. "Ford's wary intelligence does wonders for a potentially one-dimensional character. Jack's heroism on screen has much broader appeal than it does on the page," Janet Maslin wrote in the *New York Times*. Christopher Tookey in the *Daily Mail* spelled it out even more plainly. "Ford is more than a box-office attraction, he is one of the finest screen actors of our time. The movie—and Mr. Clancy—is lucky to have him."

That summer, Harrison responded to the praise with a characteristic, nervous shrug. "Practice makes perfect they say, but I don't know about this perfect part."

25

DYING IS EASY

reg Kinnear's taste for tongue-in-cheek mischief had, by 1994,
G earned him his own late-night chat show on NBC-TV and
whispered promises of prime-time greatness à la David Let-
terman and Jay Leno.

When Scott Rudin asked the suavely handsome ex-journalist to
audition for a movie role, Kinnear assumed the producer had either
gone mad or else been confused by a misleading item on his résumé.
He broke the news to Rudin that he had merely *covered* the premiere
of *Hollywood Chainsaw Hookers* for an entertainment cable channel. He
had not, he was sorry to say, appeared in it! (Nor in any other movie
for that matter.)

By January 1995, as he stood under the arc-lights, watched over by
the magisterial figure of Sydney Pollack and a hundred or so techni-
cians, the comedian's well of witty one-liners had begun to run dry. It
was left to Harrison Ford to deliver the line that silenced quick-fire
Kinnear.

Kinnear had not been the only one astonished when Rudin and
Pollack cast him in the prestige project on Paramount's books for the
winter of 1995—a remake of Billy Wilder's *Sabrina*.

He arrived for an early costume test chewing gum ferociously in an
attempt to calm his nerves.

"It's okay to chew gum, isn't it?" he asked Harrison as he took his mark alongside him under the lights.

"Sure," the actor drawled in reply, impeccable in a tuxedo, seemingly unflappable as he waited for the cameras to roll. "No problem."

No sooner had the set been quieted down and Pollack called, "Action," than Harrison's mood was transformed and his face consumed by dark clouds.

"Are you chewing gum?" he barked at Kinnear, before spinning on his burnished heels to address Pollack. "Sydney, I can't work with this guy!"

The sly smile that released Kinnear from his agony seemed to take an eternity in forming.

Arch, at times as arid as the Atacama Desert, Harrison's humor was as familiar a part of his offscreen personality as his facial scar was on it. "I don't know if it's wry or dry or a combination of wry dryness, but it always takes me off guard," said Bonnie Bedelia, often on the receiving end during the making of *Presumed Innocent*.

One day, finishing off in makeup, Bedelia was convinced something had been missed in her preparation. Who better to ask than the Great Perfectionist?

"He was reading the *New York Times* and I turned to him and I said: 'Harrison?' He glanced up over the top of his paper and I said: 'Look at me. Do I look finished to you?' I was ready to walk on the set and I didn't feel right. Something was wrong and I couldn't figure out what it was," she said. "He just looked me quickly up and down and he said, without missing a beat: 'Well, you could have been taller.' "

His wit was never better served than when the sensitive subject of money was involved. On the set of *Regarding Henry* he joined in a ludicrous bet, organized by writer Jeffrey Abrams. "I was arguing with a grip that there were peanuts in plain M&Ms," grinned Abrams. "I'm saying there is and this guy is saying, 'No way.' Harrison walks by and hears this. He says, 'Bullshit.' "

As a crowd gathered Abrams began taking bets. "One guy says, 'I bet you $20', then another says, 'I bet you $100.' And then Harrison says, "I bet you $1,000.' " Eventually, with almost $3,000 riding on his claim,

Abrams got a runner sent out to buy a packet of the sweets. "Sure enough, in the ingredients list there are peanuts."

By the next day, virtually everyone had paid his debt, except Harrison. Abrams assumed the star did not want to make a public show of his fortune and had overlooked it. "I'm thinking, 'Will he pay up? Probably not.' "

During the first major break in filming, however, Harrison appeared hauling a huge burlap bag acquired from a local bank. "He had it filled with $1,000—in pennies!"

As Han Solo and Indiana Jones, Harrison had worn his highly tuned irony on his sleeve. But with the exception of *Working Girl* and the odd, almost subliminal moment in *Regarding Henry*, his humor had been given little room to breathe since. It had certainly been kept on ice in the Tom Clancy movies!

The appeal of *Sabrina*, a script developed by Rudin and screenwriter Barbara Benedek for Paramount, lay in its lightness. An updated version of Billy Wilder's 1954 classic, in which Humphrey Bogart and William Holden formed a lustrous love triangle with Audrey Hepburn, its story revolved around two wealthy brothers, one a dour, driven industrialist, another a dashing playboy, who compete for the love of Sabrina, the ugly-duckling daughter of the family's chauffeur.

Harrison had never seen the original. After arranging a screening, he was sure of three things. He could not fail to improve on Bogart's by-the-numbers performance. "I felt as uncomfortable watching [him] as I think he was being there." The casting of the extraordinary Hepburn's successor as Sabrina would be a key to the film's success. And it needed Sydney Pollack to direct.

When, with the enthusiastic support of Paramount chairman Sherry Lansing, Harrison and Rudin approached their *Presumed Innocent* producer, he expressed serious doubts, however.

"My initial reaction was that it was a silly idea," Pollack said. "It took me a long time to convince myself that there was any point at all in trying to remake this film. Then I got a telephone call from Harrison."

In a lengthy conversation, Harrison outlined his ideas for modernizing the film. Linus, the older brother he intended playing, would become the myopic mastermind of a fiber-optics company, a shark in the mold of Barry Diller and Mike Ovitz, the kings of the new multi-media Hollywood. In his drive to make millions, Linus had sacrificed his personal happiness. While his brother, David, would remain a layabout lothario, fond of slipping into the bushes with a bottle of champagne, two glasses, and a roguish smile, Sabrina would also be a thoroughly modern woman, a naive young girl who blossoms into a *Vogue* photographer. The story would center on the threat Sabrina poses to a billion-dollar marriage between David and the daughter of a company Linus is set to get his corporate teeth into. In an ultimate act of business one-upmanship, Linus would trick Sabrina into falling in love with him instead.

"Harrison was quite convincing, so I went back and ran the original picture," said Pollack. "I was charmed by it, but I did feel that it was very much a picture of America in the 1950s. Very much part of that last decade of innocence and optimism before things started to change in the 1960s."

Pollack's agonizings were, if anything, more legendary than Harrison's. Not even his most successful films, *They Shoot Horses, Don't They?*, *Out of Africa*, and *Tootsie*, were projects he accepted quickly. His biggest fear was following in Wilder's footsteps. "People are very unforgiving of remakes," he protested. "I said no two or three times." Each refusal only served to strengthen Harrison's resolve. "What changed my mind was thinking seriously about working with him. He has very few opportunities to do a love story," he said.

Eventually Pollack buckled. As Harrison leaned on him, he said: "Well, what the hell, let's do it."

Pollack's enthusiasm was heightened by the interest Tom Cruise, the star of his last film, *The Firm*, was showing in the role of David Larrabee. Yet the casting of Sabrina remained the crucial element in the film. Pollack looked at "hundreds" of possibles, both established and unknown names, testing Harrison with many of them. An early candidate, Winona Ryder, one of the few women willing to risk comparisons with Hepburn, faded from the running after rumors—dismissed as "bullshit" by Harrison—that Melissa had warned him she was too young to play opposite him. Both Pollack and Harrison agreed that if there was a flaw in Ryder, it was rather that she was too close to Hepburn in looks and spirit. A more serious contender was the

English Royal Ballet's charismatic star Darcey Bussell. Juliette Binoche was also tested with Harrison.

Pollack had also looked at the most talked about young actress in Hollywood, the English star Julia Ormond, and seen "nothing that made me think she could play this character." Fate, however, conspired to have her test with Harrison during a spell in London away from the Welsh set where she was working on *First Knight* with Sean Connery and Richard Gere.

Pollack tested the two together in a key scene in which Linus realizes the damage he is wreaking within Sabrina's fragile psyche. "The scene I tested was the long scene in which he tells her that he is lying to her. When she says, 'You have made me so happy,' she glowed, and I could see Harrison beginning to get physically ill," said Pollack. "In some way she made that turn possible. Harrison, as tough and mean as he was, could not continue the charade. It was such a pivotal moment for me," said Pollack.

By late autumn, Pollack had cast Ormond. By then, Cruise had dropped out. Greg Kinnear, reassured that he would "never get the part" when he auditioned in August, received the phone call breaking the news that he had been cast as David Larrabee hours before he taped an edition of his TV show. He had absolutely no idea of what he said on the show. "I must send Tom Cruise some flowers," he would keep babbling for much of the next year.

Shooting began in the spring, on locations at Glen Cove, Long Island, Martha's Vineyard, and Paris.

After the script traumas of *Clear and Present Danger*, Harrison wanted no script conferences, no line-by-line warfare with his director. "I just didn't want that this time," he said on the set. "I wanted to be directed."

He was happy to entrust the film to the sagacious old hand. "Sydney's like an old wine; he's been around for a while. Well made to start with, and aging well."

Pollack was not spared glimpses of his star's persnickity side entirely, however. Ties were once more a major factor. Harrison insisted that Linus have one hundred of them, identical in every detail. "The idea is that Linus has one hundred polka-dot ties so that it gives him five minutes less he has to spend worrying about something that is other than money," Pollack said—with an arch of an eyebrow—later.

As the shoot wore on, Harrison turned from Kinnear's tormentor into his teacher. The newcomer's background had given him a jaundiced view of Hollywood. "I am very wary of big stars," Kinnear admitted. "I didn't know if he would be in the trailer asking for all-green jelly beans. But he is a solid guy, always prepared, incredibly professional. He did not really sit me down and say, 'Look, kid, it's like this.' I learned by example from him."

Ormond overcame initial nerves—heightened by Pollack's request that she cut off her pre-Raphaelite curls, a "major part of her femininity"—to join in Harrison's lighthearted approach. "Harrison loves jokes," she said. She was glad she was spared Kinnear's indoctrination, however. "I'd have probably had an apoplectic fit and left."

In Paris, Harrison was even able to see the funny side when a newspaper ran a picture showing him in a romantic clinch with his leading lady. It turned out that the photo, run complete with a tale involving Melissa hotfooting it to Paris to play "the avenging wife," was from a scene in the movie!

Harrison had not been linked with any of his leading ladies since the distant days of *Hanover Street* and Lesley-Anne Down. Away from work he had remained one hundred percent immune from the gossip-mongering of Hollywood and beyond. Despite his inescapable attractions, he claimed it was a rarity when he was treated to the kind of propositioning that was meat and drink to peers like Jack Nicholson. "Temptation is a two-way street," he argued. "It rarely crops up unless one seeks it. There's a stink people carry when they are looking for sexual adventure. It is not on me, though."

Melissa took the Ormond story with the pinch of salt it deserved. "Harrison doesn't attract that kind of innuendo much," she said, laughing it off. There was more than a hint of the danger that lurked ahead if he did stray, however. "He's lucky!"

Ormond, already falsely bedded down with Brad Pitt during filming of *Legends of the Fall*, simply added the rumor to her résumé. "Now, you tell me, if Harrison Ford was having an affair with someone, would he take them to a very public bridge in Paris and suck face with them? I mean, get real," she later said bemusedly. "I don't know what kind of sex lives journalists have, but with the rest of the world, let me tell you, there's genitalia involved."

She did not deny his appeal, however. Beneath the gravitas and good humor, Ormond found Harrison's underlying insecurity as fascinating as it was baffling. "I don't think Harrison appreciates how much people think of him."

Even to those who had known him over time, the depth of his diffidence could still surprise. During filming on *Clear and Present Danger*, Sir Anthony Hopkins, interviewed on *The Today Show*, had cited Harrison as, in his opinion, the best screen actor in America. "Harrison was really embarrassed by that," Mace Neufeld recalled. When it was mentioned, he grimaced and begged the producer: "Don't say that to anybody."

He had, over the years, accepted a few select plaudits. Before his "Star of the Century" award, he had accepted UCLA's Spencer Tracy Award, recognition of his now untouchable reputation as modern cinema's heir to the great Everyman. He had even broken his boycott of the Oscars, acting as a presenter at the 1994 awards at which Steven Spielberg's drought finally ended with a shower of alloy-plated statuettes for *Schindler's List*. Yet in his mind Harrison maintained an instinctive skepticism about Hollywood and all its hyperbole. There was, as ever, a kind of logic to it. By never having been fashionable, his argument went, he had avoided becoming *un*fashionable.

"When they put that much passion into ordaining you a superstar," he said once, "then every law of physics of the situation demands that they put an equal amount of energy into dragging your ass down again when they're done with you."

At the Larrabee mansion, on the twenty-acre Salutation Estate built by a grandson of J. Pierpont Morgan on Long Island Sound, preparations were underway for a glittering ball. When a piece of the set crashed on to the crowded ballroom floor, Harrison defused any panic by striding out on to the set, arms raised like some president saved from an assassin's bullet, his face puffed up with mock pomposity and announcing: "I'm all right." The 150-strong cast of extras dissolved into laughter.

The laughter was muted back at Paramount, however. Hopes of having Indiana Jones back on the road later in the year were dashed when the second draft of the new script was returned to writer Jeb Stuart for more work. The storyline of *Indiana Jones and the Lost Continent*, conceived originally by George Lucas, seemed promising enough. Indiana stumbles across the Lost World of Atlantis just as early nuclear tests are about to destroy it forever. There had already been talk of Sandra Bullock, Hollywood's new *femme du jour* thanks to the summer hit *Speed*, playing Indiana's love interest.

Given that *The Last Crusade* had needed five drafts before it was accepted by Spielberg, Lucas, and Harrison, the news was hardly unpredictable. Yet the ripple effect was tantamount to a minor nuclear explosion, as every hero script in town suddenly descended on Pat McQueeney's desk. Arnold Kopelson wasted little time in offering him a sequel to *The Fugitive* and a new draft of *The Iron Horseman*, an idea for a railroad western Harrison had been interested in for some time. Harrison also considered, then rejected, *Daylight*—a film with Rob Cohen which Sylvester Stallone eventually picked up. Talks got underway for him to play Travis McGee, John D. MacDonald's detective, and he was also connected with a new adaptation of Sinclair Lewis's *Dodsworth*, set to be directed by Broadway producer Marty Richards and adapted by Alfred Uhry, writer of the Oscar-festooned *Driving Miss Daisy*. William Wyler's version of the literary evergreen, originally starring Walter Huston as the American businessman Dodsworth, whose life is changed when he takes his wife on a tour of Europe, was nominated for six Oscars in 1936.

Sixty years on, as *Sabrina* was released, Harrison's interest in remakes of admired Golden Age classics was suddenly on the wane. Reaction to *Sabrina* only served to confirm what its star had been muttering during his publicity interviews: "The old canard that dying is easy but comedy is hard is true."

In America and Europe, critics and audiences found it difficult to warm to Harrison's performance, and the film in general. Adjectives like "gruff," "dull," and "cold" were common currency.

Most reflected the simple truth. Harrison and Julia Ormond did not generate either the heat or the magic necessary to fire the modern fairy tale. Without that central spark, the film remained a slow-burning ember. Harrison's performance was, at times, as uncomfortable as any he had yet given. Some wondered whether he had been ill. "Ford is slow, ponderous and self-consciously 'the money' in the movie, in every sense," wrote Alexander Walker. "And for some reason he doesn't look very well either."

While it performed adequately at the box office, *Sabrina* failed to remove the fundamental doubts Sydney Pollack had expressed at the very beginning. Even when Harrison picked up a nomination at the Golden Globe Awards for Best Actor in a comedy role—where he was beaten by John Travolta for *Get Shorty*—one word, for most, summed up the enterprise: Why? It was to become a question Harrison would find himself asking far too frequently over the coming months.

26

TROUBLES

y early 1996, the ruffled, Robert Redfordesque features of Brad
Pitt had seemingly graced the cover of every glamour magazine
from Tokyo to Timbuktu. In the wake of *Interview With the Vampire* with Tom Cruise and *Seven* with Morgan Freeman, the thirty-two-year-old—out of Oklahoma via *Dallas*, the TV series—was in the grip
of "the big Wombassa."

It is doubtful whether his cherubic image graced the well-polished
furniture at the Ford family household in Manhattan, however. For
both Harrison and Melissa, Pitt had become a rather ugly thorn in
their sides.

As 1995 drew to a close, Harrison had agreed to Melissa's suggestion
that they spend an entire year living in New York. The logic was overwhelming both personally and professionally. Malcolm, now eight, and
Georgia, five, were enrolled full-time at private schools in the city.
And after years of hard work, *Kundun*, Melissa's Dalai Lama script, was
ready to go before the cameras with New York's most celebrated filmmaking citizen, Martin Scorsese, as director.

Harrison was less than comfortable about relocating himself. Early
on during his exile, he took the unusual step of inviting a journalist,
Trip Gabriel of the *New York Times*, into the apartment on Central
Park West.

Sitting in his living room, surrounded by an exquisite collection of early American furniture and a few prized pieces of his art collection, he seemed to Gabriel a restless, slightly lost soul.

Throughout he played nervously with a Wyatt Earp mustache he had grown "as an experiment." Midway through the conversation he insisted on moving from one room to another because he disliked the acoustics in his dining room. Every nuance of his body language suggested he had been disconnected from something central to his very existence.

Harrison had grown to enjoy elements of his life in America's most cosmopolitan city. He and Melissa were not short of friends, from Mike Nichols and his newsreader wife, Diane Sawyer, to Arnold Glimcher. But he made no secret of the fact he found Central Park and the city's great museums a poor substitute for the openness of the Midwest and the natural wonders of his land beneath the Grand Tetons. There was disappointed laughter in his voice as he explained to Gabriel how Malcolm and Georgia had grown bored with the sight of herds of elk wandering in their back garden in Jackson, yet pleaded to be taken to the Museum of Natural History where they would "stand with their noses pressed to the glass looking at a stuffed elk."

It was obvious to his visitor that Harrison viewed the coming year with a profound kind of dread. "There's always some project to get involved in back there," he sighed. "I find it hard to find things to do here."

It was Mike Nichols who best summed up the importance Jackson Hole played in his friend's complex yet simple life. "Very successful actors pay an enormous price in shame for doing something that is not quite serious enough, that isn't quite manly. It is why they drink and do drugs. It's why they womanize," he said once. "Harrison's rigor and practicality, his living with and for his family and staying out of any and all social life—his carpenter's approach to acting—have somehow preserved him from the restlessness and self-dissatisfaction." In New York the restlessness and self-dissatisfaction were seeping into his life once more.

At first Harrison and Melissa had been ecstatic when Martin Scorsese agreed to direct *Kundun* in August of 1995. Fascinated by pre–War Tibet since seeing rare footage on television years earlier, Scorsese was effusive about bringing Melissa's work to life in northern India, where location scouting was already advanced. "This is a story of indomitable will and fervent religious commitment set against a physical backdrop and compelling world politics," his press release to *Variety* announced.

Their elation was short-lived, however. Almost immediately after Scorsese made his announcement, Tristar confirmed that it was also going ahead with *Seven Years in Tibet*, an adaptation of the book of the same name by Heinrich Harrer, an Austrian climber and skier who befriended and became a tutor to the Dalai Lama after escaping from an Indian prisoner-of-war camp. Harrer's memoir told the story of his seven years with the Buddhist leader and his flight to India during the Chinese invasion of 1950. The French director Jean-Jacques Annaud had been signed to direct. The role of Harrer had been snapped up by Brad Pitt.

As the race to get the first Lama movie on screen began, Melissa and Harrison, who were by now effectively acting as the film's coproducers, took solace in their personal friendship with the Dalai Lama. Both had become increasingly active in supporting the Tibetan cause. Melissa had been installed on the board of the Washington-based International Campaign for Tibet.

In September, 1995—in an echo of his scene at the end of *Clear and Present Danger*—Harrison had even appeared before the Senate's East Asian and Pacific Affairs Subcommittee. With the Clinton administration building bridges with China, he made a measured speech asking that the diplomats remember the "courageous people of Tibet." "As an American who cares deeply about justice, freedom, and democracy, I can tell you that this is a cause that touches at the core of our own values." He went on to urge the Clinton administration to appoint a special envoy to Tibet and to meet with the Dalai Lama during a visit to Washington the following week. Both he and Melissa appeared at the Dalai Lama's side in the capital at a dinner in his honor days later. By October, however, their "special relationship" with Dharamsala was strained. Naive to the ways of Hollywood, the Dalai Lama had also given *Seven Years in Tibet* his blessing. Suddenly caught in the middle of what seemed a baffling contest, he let it be known that he thought there was room for two films about his life.

"I have read Melissa Mathison's script. It is very good, very moving. Those people have been very supportive and sympathetic," he said of

Mr. and Mrs. Harrison Ford. Yet he thought Harrer's book "beautiful and good," too. Melissa and Harrison were said to have been "furious" at the development.

By the spring of 1996, however, the crisis had taken another turn. The Indian government refused to allow either film to shoot in Dharamsala or anywhere else on the subcontinent. Official sources in New Delhi explained that with ongoing border disputes with the Chinese, it did not want to offend its powerful neighbor.

Anaud had opted to shoot his film in Argentina. Now Scorsese and Melissa were forced to move their film to Morocco. Soon Disney, to whom they had switched the project after initial interest from Universal, was fending off pressure from the Chinese government to drop the film altogether.

It had been in 1995, as Melissa watched her long-cherished project begin its descent into trouble, that her husband had fielded a phone call from the producer Larry Gordon. Ironically Gordon was calling on behalf of the actor who—albeit indirectly—had been causing his wife such anguish.

The Devil's Own, the story of a young IRA terrorist who finds himself befriending a middle-aged, New York cop during an arms-buying visit to America, had been Brad Pitt's pet project for more than four years. With Gordon as producer, Pitt was finally free to play the film's lead, Irish gunman Frankie McGuire.

Like Pitt and Lisa Henson, copresident of Columbia who had agreed to make the movie, Gordon saw writer Kevin Jarre's oblique story as a dark exploration of "how men relate to each other." With an IRA ceasefire in the wind, the timing could not have been more propitious.

Keen to flex his newly developed Hollywood muscles, Pitt had originally wanted Bryan Singer, hot off the stylish *The Usual Suspects*, and Gene Hackman or Sean Connery for the role of Tom O'Meara, the cop. As *Seven* invested him with even more power, he indulged his fantasies and floated the idea of hiring Harrison Ford for the role.

At the time Pitt admitted he regarded Harrison with something akin to awe. "He comes from this place of integrity and common sense which I think was instilled in me as a kid, and it's something I always look up to when I see it," he explained.

Pitt asked Gordon to pass the script on to Pat McQueeney, who

soon found her client expressing interest. If nothing else, with shooting due to go ahead in New York early in 1996, it seemed a perfect
means of avoiding boredom during the exile from Wyoming.

Division set in within a troubled Columbia hierarchy almost immediately. Harrison agreed to take on the role of O'Meara, but Lisa
Henson was among those who argued that Pitt alone would deliver
the audience they needed. More important, he would do so at a price
they could afford. She feared the original $30 million budget might
spiral out of control if one of Hollywood's more demanding (and high-
est-paid) professionals climbed aboard.

As far as Columbia's embattled chairman, Mark Canton, was concerned, however, the casting was a coup. Desperate to deliver a hit to
the studio's increasingly disillusioned Japanese owner, Sony, Canton
had already gambled on a collection of star vehicles, from *Mary Reilly*
with Julia Roberts to *The Cable Guy* with the newly installed "King of
Comedy" Jim Carrey. To Canton the idea of Harrison Ford and Brad
Pitt together was simply irresistible.

Almost immediately what had begun life as an exercise in fantasy
casting started transforming itself into something rather darker. As Lisa
Henson and others had feared, the budget began to expand exponen-
tially. Pitt's salary had been set at $9 million, with Larry Gordon's fixed
at $1.5 million. By the time Pat McQueeney had negotiated a $20 million payment for her client, however, the principals' salary bill had
been tripled—with a director's fee yet to be added. Soon that had taken
the figure to $35.5 million. Both Harrison and Pitt submitted lists of
favored directors. Only Alan J. Pakula appeared on both men's sub-
missions. His signature cost an additional $5 million.

By the time both Harrison and Pakula had been provided with the
rewritten scripts each had demanded as part of their deals, the danger
signals were visible. Vincent Patrick, writer of *The Pope of Greenwich
Village*, and David Aaron Cohen, author of *V.I. Warshawski*, had submitted new drafts that left Kevin Jarre's original script barely recognizable.

As far as Patrick was concerned, his job was clear. What had been
a "one star" vehicle now demanded room for a new—and rather heavyweight—passenger. "Equal action heroes," was the phrase he used later.
"Supporting two stars was what this was about."

Harrison, Pitt, and Pakula disagreed wildly on which version should form the basis of their movie. As a shooting date loomed into view, it became clear that the script would have to evolve as the production progressed. For Harrison it was a wearisome but far from unfamiliar process. For Pitt, however, it looked like the beginning of the end of a project he felt personally protective toward. "I think he panicked because of all the script changes," Pakula explained later.

As Pitt's disillusionment deepened, his agents let Columbia know he wanted to withdraw. Inside the studio those who foresaw nothing but trouble ahead counseled Canton and his senior executives to accept this decision and let the film fall apart. Instead, Columbia's response was the threat of a $63 million lawsuit.

In turmoil over what to do, Pitt turned to Harrison for advice. In the apartment overlooking Central Park, he offered what seemed like sound, sagacious reassurance. "Harrison told me, 'Look we're here now. It's our only chance to do this. Let's just figure it out,' " Pitt confided afterward. After his meeting Pitt agreed to go ahead with the movie. Neither he nor Harrison would "figure out" *The Devil's Own*, however.

Shooting began in Belfast and New York in January 1996. Pitt had spent time in Northern Ireland from where he had returned with a credible Ulster accent and what he later described as "a certain understanding" of the troubles. "The responsibility was on my head to represent this faction of people whose lives have been governed and whose families have been scarred by this war," he declared afterward. His aim, he went on, was to avoid "trivializing" the situation and to keep faith with the friends he had made in Ireland, "or I would be doing them a great injustice."

If it was clear that Pitt's allegiance lay broadly with the Republican movement, it was instantly obvious that Harrison's rested elsewhere. "Baldly, it was an apology for the IRA. I refused to be part of that," he said later. Early disagreements centered on the politics. Yet to many on the set, the confrontations they were soon witnessing boiled down to ego. "There were two big stars, both of them wanting to be the star of this movie," said one Sony executive.

Some saw it as a sign that Harrison was feeling vulnerable at the prospect of being overshadowed by a younger star. "It's the first time Harrison has ever had reason to be threatened," said another executive. Others felt that the paranoia was coming from Pitt, who was worried by the closeness Pakula and Harrison had clearly developed in their previous collaboration on *Presumed Innocent.*

Publicly at least, Pakula tried to remain neutral. Privately he was haunted by the ghosts of *All the President's Men,* where the cool and urbane Robert Redford had locked horns with the impulsive and occasionally neurotic Dustin Hoffman. Often Redford would call *his* alter ego, Bob Woodward, to support his position in an argument. Immediately Hoffman would call Carl Bernstein for support of his opinion. "It was a tempestuous process. Each one saw the story very differently," he recalled. "The process was very frightening to Brad, more so than to Harrison, who has worked on several films where you write as you go along." Pitt's main gripe, according to Pakula, was that the film was transforming itself into *Patriot Games II.*

In an effort to bolster his character's credibility Pitt brought in pro-Republican Irish writer Terry George, who had worked on *In the Name of the Father* with Daniel Day-Lewis and directed his own film, *Some Mother's Son,* with Helen Mirren. At one stage no fewer than four writers appeared to be contributing often-conflicting ideas. As the two stars' view of the direction the movie should take diverged further and further, it was inevitable that word of the tensions would leak out. New York's tabloid press seized on the rumors and counterrumors with glee.

Soon the confrontation between the leading man of one generation and his heir apparent from the next had become a remake of *All About Eve.* "It made for good reading," Pakula said afterward.

First, stories circulated that the two actors were not speaking to each other off the set. Harrison and Pitt remained locked up in their trailers until they were required. When illicit photographs of the two fighting in a New York street emerged, the feud stories intensified even further. According to some, the blows exchanged in one particular fight scene were utterly real.

Tensions were helped little by events elsewhere. Much of Columbia's enthusiasm for the project stemmed from the relative stability in Ulster. Early in 1996 the fragile, yearlong peace ended with the death of two men in an IRA blast at London's Canary Wharf. The air of desperation that returned to Belfast spread across the Atlantic.

Frequently mornings would be lost because Pakula and his leading men would be locked in script meetings. The shooting schedule was well past the midway point, and yet the film had no agreed "final act." At a cost of another $1 million, rewrite expert Robert Mark Kamen was brought in to break the deadlock. In his long career Kamen had not come across a situation quite like it. "We were flying blind," he admitted later. While Harrison shot his scenes, the writer worked on scenes with Pitt. When Pitt was called before the cameras, the situation was reversed. At the end of each day the writer would move on to working on Pakula's version.

As the shoot stretched on beyond its deadline and the budget swelled ever larger, wise old heads at Columbia shook their heads. "They had three different scripts," one production insider confided later. "They were making Brad Pitt's movie, Harrison Ford's movie, and Alan Pakula's movie."

By the time the shoot had finally come to an end in the early summer of 1996, the budget had ballooned toward the $90 million mark. Inevitably, heated questions were now being asked back at Columbia. To many inside and outside the studio, Mark Canton's insistence that the film be finished looked like a crazed blend of prayer, pride, and self-preservatory panic. By now the film's problems were so well publicized it had become a case study in how a dream project could transform itself into a nightmare. One producer who worked for the studio admitted "amazement." "Everyone was willing to gracefully walk away from the movie, and the studio held it together," he told *Premiere* magazine as it analyzed Hollywood's new cause célèbre. He claimed Canton was "too embarrassed" to close the film down. "It was Mark Canton's way of buying the continuation of his job. And we all knew it," added another studio insider. Of all the reputations tarnished by *The Devil's Own*, none suffered as severely as Canton's. By now it was clear his "star vehicle" policy had failed dismally. Both *Mary Reilly* and *The Cable Guy*, along with his De Niro film, *The Fan*, had bombed. To his Japanese employers, *The Devil's Own* was the final straw. Before Pakula had turned in a final cut, Canton was gone, replaced by former United Artists chief John Calley.

* * *

For all his public disdain of political celebrities, Harrison found the invitation he and Melissa received from the White House in August 1996 utterly irresistible.

Bill and Hillary Clinton had included the Fords on the guest list for a celebration to mark the President's fiftieth birthday. The fact the event was taking place in Jackson Hole, where the President was holidaying nearby with his wife and daughter, Chelsea, was enticing enough. After the troubles of *The Devil's Own*, the simplicity of the Midwestern life had never seemed so appealing to Harrison. However, the Clintons' invitation provided a professional opportunity simply too good to be missed.

By now Harrison was already immersed in another project, *Air Force One*. Based on a script by Andrew Marlowe, *Air Force One* revolved around the hijacking of the presidential airplane by a group of Kazakhstani terrorists. Harrison had been offered the role of U.S. President James Marshall, a Vietnam Air Force veteran suddenly confronted with the most important mission of his life.

Harrison had liked the script immediately. Its clear, uncompli-cated—not to mention uncontentious—story line offered a perfect antidote to the trials of his previous film. The addition of the laconic Wolfgang Petersen, the German whose direction of the compelling U-Boat drama *Das Boot* (1981) had paved the way to Hollywood success with hits like *In the Line of Fire* (1992) with Clint Eastwood and John Malkovich, had added even further to its appeal. Columbia's willing-ness to pay him $20 million of the $85 million budget—plus an addi-tional fifteen percent of the gross—did little to dampen his enthusiasm.

On August 19, Harrison took his seat next to the President at the lavish party. It was not long before the conversation had turned to his own forthcoming occupancy of the Oval Office.

Clinton, perhaps sensing a public relations opportunity of his own, happily agreed to allow Harrison and Petersen access to the real Air Force One while he was in Wyoming. "A big, wonderful hotel room," Petesen gushed after seeing the high-tech interior of the most famous and best-equipped private airplane in the world.

Clinton's guided tour helped both Harrison and the director add important details to a character central to the film. Boeing, manufac-turers of the aircraft, had already agreed to allow Petersen's design team access to the original's blueprints. A former Pentagon aide had also been enlisted as a consultant.

Ultimately the plane built on a soundstage at Culver City was roomier than the prototype. In most respects, however, it represented the most authentic depiction of the plane yet seen on film.

Visitors to the Culver City set found Harrison relieved to be free of the tensions of *The Devil's Own*. He drew playful parallels between the film he was now working on and Petersen's previous claustrophobic masterpiece, *Das Boot*. "It's a tube movie," Harrison smiled to one interviewer. "Wolfgang is one of the great tube-moviemakers."

His mood had been further improved by the addition to the cast of Glenn Close as the vice president. Harrison and Petersen had been told originally she was unavailable. It had been at the President's birthday party that Harrison had found Close among the guests and approached her directly. Her schedule was suddenly clear.

As ever, Harrison approached his fight scenes with a realism bordering on the reckless. Harrison encouraged Gary Oldman—recruited to extend his seemingly limitless range of unhinged psychopaths, this time as the leader of the hijackers—to hold nothing back in their scenes together. "It was fun knocking Indiana Jones around," laughed the Englishman afterward. Harrison sustained a rotor cuff injury during one of the fights. His willingness to put himself through physical pain once more surprised many.

"There's no vanity there. He does it flat-out all the time," said Wendy Crewson, Marshall's first lady.

"Harrison doesn't care if he has all sorts of black marks on his body," added Petersen. "When his face was really red and swollen, I'd just push back close-ups a few days."

As he threw himself into the role, Harrison may have imagined he had rid himself of the problems of *The Devil's Own*. He was mistaken.

Having tested his first cut on audiences, Alan Pakula had resigned himself to having to shoot a new ending. Pakula's strength remained mood rather than machismo. Even he conceded that the film's finale— in which O'Meara hunts down McGuire after discovering the truth about his mission to America—needed more of the latter.

Midway through the shoot of *Air Force One* Harrison was forced to return to New York. For Pitt, set to begin work on *Seven Years in Tibet* in Argentina, however, Pakula's summons was even more inconvenient. Jean-Jacques Annaud had to put back production as his star returned to the role he now wished he had never undertaken.

Pitt's fears that the film had transformed itself into *Patriot Games II* were vindicated in at least one sense. Just as three years earlier, this time Harrison was called back to reshoot the new, more dramatic climax—once more a to-the-death showdown with his nemesis, once more a scene filmed aboard a violently pitching fishing boat.

The rematch provided the cannier conspiracy theorists with a field day. Soon the New York newstands were displaying headlines suggesting Pitt had been "kidnapped" by Harrison in an effort to buy more time for Melissa, Martin Scorsese, and *Kundun*. As far as Pitt was concerned the story seemed the most fantastical yet. "How ridiculous," he laughed later when asked about what was clearly a coincidence. Perhaps wisely, no one dared ask Harrison his views on the hypothesis.

Perhaps in preparation for the spiritual journey he was about to take with Jean-Jacques Annaud, Pitt left the set of *Devil's Own* in a surprisingly placatory mood. He had even sent Pakula a first edition of *Finnegan's Wake*, signed by James Joyce, as a peace offering. His sense of inner peace and enlightenment dissipated as soon as he returned from Argentina, however.

After seeing Pakula's final cut, at the end of January 1997, Pitt unburdened himself to *Newsweek* magazine in one of the more colorful outbursts in recent movie history. Pitt all but disowned a movie he now described variously as "ridiculous" and "dogshit." "We had no script," he complained. "Well, we had a great script, but it got tossed for various reasons." One quote would be recycled a thousand times around the world over the coming months. His collaboration with Alan J. Pakula and Harrison Ford represented "the most irresponsible bit of filmmaking—if you can even call it that—that I've ever seen."

For the second time, Columbia threatened Pitt with legal action. By March, he had been persuaded to write to *Newsweek* explaining that it was only the shoot that had been "irresponsible"—"he likes the film a great deal," Pakula added on his behalf later—and was pressured into appearing on the interview circuit to promote the film.

"I put together a bunch of thoughts which led to some confusion" became his rather lame lament.

Wary of the negativity already attached to the film and its subject, Harrison undertook his own publicity chores with an equal degree of relish. He retreated into his shell even more than normal during his interviews. Whenever asked directly about Pitt, he responded robotically. "Working with Brad was fine," he said time and again. "The tabloids reported this battle of two egos and it never was that. I really enjoyed working with him."

Questions about the film's treatment of the troubles seemed even more like unexploded hand grenades. "I didn't want to make an apology or an argument for the IRA," he replied defensively. "I just wanted to be seen wrestling with the question."

His caution had never been so well placed. The film was released to derision. If the creative tension he had brought to the rewriting process had somehow improved both *The Fugitive* and *Clear and Present Danger*, it had not worked a third time. The fault lay not in the performance. A scene in which O'Meara gets drunk and opens himself up to McGuire after watching his partner, played by Ruben Blades, gun down an unarmed criminal was among the most nakedly emotional and touching he had played in years. Yet even within an often ill-informed America, what praise there was for both Harrison's and Pitt's performances was drowned out by the sound of insult and outrage at the film's ham-fisted attempt to deal with the greatest political conundrum of our age. Whatever moral and narrative structure may have existed at the outset had clearly been reduced to rubble by the internal warfare that had raged on the set. On the first front, Pitt's character represented a politically naive and hopelessly simplistic vision of a coldhearted yet somehow pitiable killer. On the second, the promise issued by Pitt's Frankie not once but twice in the film, "Don't look for happy endings, it's not an American story, it's an Irish one," was willfully broken by a contrived and formulaic ending that had Hollywood written all over it. Michael Medved of the *New York Post* led the assault, labeling the film "an eloquent apology for murderous terrorism." "No amount of acting excellence can cover this movie's devilish attempt to rationalize and ultimately to glamorize the most deadly sort of political violence," Medved wrote. "Brad Pitt plays the cutest, cud-dliest coldblooded killer you've ever met."

"There is a slapdash atmosphere to the proceedings," wrote Bob Thomas of the Associated Press. "What might have shed light on the troubles becomes another exercise in violence."

Harrison had undergone the experience before with *Patriot Games*. Yet by the time the film was finally released in the United Kingdom—after the May 1 general election—*The Devil's Own* had become the year's bête noire. "The politics are those of a Beverly Hills kinder-garten," wrote Christopher Tookey of the *Daily Mail*, the country's barometer of middlebrow sensibility. "Even if Northern Ireland peace negotiations were progressing smoothly, this Hollywood glamorization of an IRA assassin would be crass and unhelpful."

When, days after its opening, Princess Diana snuck her underage son Prince Harry, just twelve, into a screening of the R-rated film at her local Kensington cinema, the negativity reached critical mass. Less than a week after the IRA murder of two policemen had dealt the peace process another blow, the decision led the former head of the Conservative Northern Ireland Committee, Andrew Hunter MP, to denounce the film as "sickening" and Diana's decision to take her sons—whose father's mentor, Lord Mountbatten, had, after all, been murdered by the IRA—"irresponsible."

"Underage Storm as Diana Takes Harry to IRA Film," foamed the *Daily Mail*. An embarrassed Diana was forced to make a public apol-ogy for the mistake. Even Pat McQueeney was dragged into the con-troversy. Bombarded by calls from Fleet Street, she asked Harrison for his thoughts. "He says it is none of his business as he is not the mother or the father," she told the tabloid *Daily Mirror*, which then somehow construed this as tacit support of Diana.

Even the high wattage of George Clooney and Arnold Schwarzeneg-ger—in London to launch *Batman & Robin*—was overshadowed by the controversy. Yet the film's newfound notoriety did little to liven up *The Devil's Own's* box office. After taking in a promising £700,000 ($450,000) in its first weekend, its receipts fell away as dramatically as in America.

It was left to Alan Pakula to deliver the film's epitaph. Asked why Harrison and Pitt had asked him to direct their first—and probably last—movie together, the bearded patrician shrugged, then grimaced: "Maybe they know I like to take a lot of punishment!"

For Brad Pitt, the film's failure marked the beginning of the rockiest period in his career so far. The breakup of his long-term relationship with Gwyneth Paltrow did little to ease the pain of what was a severe personal disappointment. For Harrison, however, the troubles were rather quickly forgotten.

Melissa was by now nearing the end of the road with *Kundun*, set for a Christmas 1997 release by Disney chief Michael Eisner despite renewed Chinese pressure for its suppression. Ahead of Harrison were three potential projects: an *African Queen*–style adventure, *Six Days, Seven Nights*, another outing as Jack Ryan in Lee and Janet Scott Batchler's adaptation of Tom Clancy's *Cardinal of the Kremlin*, and a thriller set in Sarajevo, *Age of Aquarius*. Still looming on the horizon was Indy IV.

Harrison, more than anyone, was keen to find a script he could approve of. "It's a problem," he explained. "Let's say I go to the hardware store and buy screws. I don't want to talk about whether I'm going to do *Indiana Jones IV*. I do talk about it, but then I forget what kind of screws I went there for." Yet he knew the risks of a premature yes. "Might as well have the hat on my fucking head, because in twenty minutes you're gonna have a release date."

It had been Wolfgang Petersen and his finished cut of *Air Force One* that had done most to erase the unpleasantness of *The Devil's Own*, however. The film had shaped itself into what Harrison by now recognized as a surefire hit.

Petersen's ability as a director of carefully choreographed tension had rarely been better illustrated. As if to confirm the opinion of those who believed Harrison should have taken on the role two years earlier in *The American President* (which went to Michael Douglas), his portrayal of the U.S. commander in chief exuded a perfect blend of dignity and authority, determination and heroism. It had been a charismatic cocktail Petersen had been able to take advantage of. "If it was Bill Clinton up there, he'd be in trouble," Petersen said afterward. "But this is Harrison Ford. He pulls if off."

If Harrison had been sheepish in his support for *The Devil's Own*, he

was now galvanized by the scent of a new hit. In May he had personally approached Jonathan Dolgen, head of Viacom, Paramount's parent
company, in an effort to avoid opening James Cameron's *Titanic* on
the same weekend. With Cameron's film already deep in trouble,
Dolgen's decision may already have been made. Yet it spoke volumes
for Harrison's power—and his willingness to wield it—when
Paramount rescheduled *Titanic* for December.

His approach to publicity was equally aggressive. Harrison even
agreed to ham it up in a beard as his boyhood hero Abe Lincoln on
the cover of the heavyweight *George* magazine, as well as a cover story
in *People* magazine and appearances on the late-night talk shows.

His energetic approach paid dividends on the weekend of July 25 as
Air Force One took advantage of the lack of competition in spectacular fashion. Its opening box office figures were remarkable even by the
Harrison Ford standard. A gross of $37.1 million dislodged the
summer's previously undisputed champion, Barry Sonnenfeld's sci-fi
spoof, *Men in Black*, from America's number one spot. Statistically it
represented a triple triumph: the best-ever opening weekend for a film
released so relatively late in the summer, i.e. after July 4; the highest
for a R-rated movie, eclipsing the $36.3 million made by Tom Cruise's
Interview With the Vampire three years earlier; and, most significant for
Harrison at least, the strongest opening any of his movies had *ever*
enjoyed. The film's performance did not wane in its second week
either, adding another $25.7 million.

Its reviews were no less impressive. Peter Travers of *Rolling Stone*
wrote of Petersen, "You don't stay glued to the screen because a hack
director has strung together a few workable formulas. [This] is gripping, nail-biting, edge-of-your-seat entertainment because you are in
the hands of a master craftsman." And of the film's star, Travers said,
"What a relief to see this underrated actor back in gear after *Sabrina*
and *The Devil's Own*, two rare flops in the Ford canon. His wit is dry—
acerbic but never campy." Owen Gleiberman wrote in his A-rated
Entertainment Weekly review, "Harrison Ford as the President of the
United States is such a perfect piece of casting that it's once a fantasy
and a joke: The joke is how perfect the fantasy is."

Harrison had never been one for baseball analogies. After the dual
disappointments of *Sabrina* and *The Devil's Own*, however, no one had

been more aware of the potential danger of a third successive strike. It made the success of *Air Force One* one of his sweeter home runs. Arriving as it did twelve days after he turned fifty-five, it also represented one of the more agreeable birthday presents even Harrison had received. With 15 percent of the gross guaranteed, he was on course to—at worst—double his $20 million fee. In truth, however, he took greater pleasure in simply breathing the air back in Jackson Hole, where he spent the occasion with Melissa and his children.

"Being normal is a kind of victory," Harrison Ford is apt to say. Nowhere is he guaranteed that triumph as surely as he is among the spruce and the cottonwood, the elk, and the osprey, watching the Snake River run through his property outside Jackson Hole. His life in Wyoming is, of course, an idyll entrenched in the pioneer past of America. It is the dream of Eden that sustained his ancestors on their journeys across the seas. His are the roots dreamt of by the displaced and the disowned, the impoverished, and the insecure, who formed his own—and America's—family tree.

It was in his grandparents' days, as vaudeville gave way to cinema and radio, that American entertainment gave shape to another enduring dream. It has maintained the myth of the heroic man of action close to its heart ever since.

Today, at the end of cinema's first century, Harrison Ford stands alone as the heir to Henry Fonda and John Wayne, to James Stewart and Gary Cooper. He embodies the spirit of the man who ends the fights that others start, the avenger who rights the wrongs that others do. He is, more than any actor alive, the quiet outsider at the heart of American mythology.

It has been in his life as it has been in his art—from schoolyard Sisyphus to fraternity misfit, from studio reject to Hollywood exile. Peace was all he asked in the junior high school playground. Peace remains all he craves today.

He has faith that he will one day find it. Heaven help whoever denies him then.

"If I die and I ain't peaceful, then I'm really gonna be pissed off . . ."

Author's Note and Acknowledgments

The sardonic smile was never far from his lips when I met Harrison Ford in San Francisco in June 1994. It was there, amid the opulence of the Ritz Carlton Hotel, that I interviewed him prior to the release of *Clear and Present Danger*. He used the smile first to dismiss the Star of the Century award he had been given a few weeks earlier. "It was just their way of saying thanks for selling so much popcorn," he told me. When the subject turned to Tom Clancy's well-worn whine that—at the age of fifty-two—Ford was too advanced in years to play his thirtysomething hero Jack Ryan, the grimace reformed itself and he sighed: "I'm too old to answer that question."

Days earlier, in Los Angeles, another of Hollywood's reigning heavyweights, Arnold Schwarzenegger, had told me of the sleepless nights he had been given by the burden of carrying the $100 million-budgeted *True Lies*, opening at the same time. "My films cost half as much, so I get half as worried," Ford replied when I wondered how he coped with the burden of his films' megamillion expense. "The great discovery about meeting the man who made Indiana Jones flesh," I wrote at the time, "is that he owns a sense of humor as dry as the Dead Sea Scrolls."

There were other discoveries. It was then, for instance, he confirmed for the first time that a fourth Indiana Jones film was in the cards. He also intimated that he might soon consider retiring. "I often think about quitting and doing something else," he told me. (Elsewhere he admitted: "My fantasy would be tinkling the ivories by myself on late wintry nights, just mumbling the blues.") "But then I think it will take me thirty years to learn how to do that. And then I will probably drop dead in the middle of it without having gotten good enough to satisfy myself. I guess I'll just muddle on."

Throughout the interview, I was struck by the gulf that separated him from the other front-rank film stars I have met in similar circumstances over the years. He is not—like Stallone and Schwarzenegger—a prisoner of his physique. Look into his eyes and you see he is not a hostage to the pathological ambition of Cruise or, to a lesser extent, Costner. He was, as the clippings I had read en route warned, wary, intensely intelligent, and meticulous in his use of language. Yet as he sat on the edge of a period French sofa, sipped from a cup of bitumen-black coffee, the sleeves of his powder-blue shirt rolled up ready for work, he exuded the common appeal that remains the bedrock of his phenomenal success.

It was in San Francisco that the idea for this biography began to percolate away. Sifting through an unsatisfying collection of clippings, I was struck by how little is known about Ford, and his early years in particular. Soon after I returned to London an embryonic outline solidified into something firmer.

Early on I wrote to him asking for any cooperation he might be willing to give. Initially, his agent, Patricia McQueeney, was enthusiastic about assisting me. She agreed that a comprehensive biography of the most succesful box-office star in cinema history was long overdue and offered to approach friends like Steven Spielberg to arrange interviews. She also agreed to see me on one of my visits to Los Angeles. Her offer did not sound like the sort of hollow Hollywood promise I have spent years listening to as a journalist. I set off to conduct my research in Chicago and the Midwest cautiously but genuinely optimistic.

It was during a phone call intended to arrange a lunch with Patricia on my arrival in Los Angeles that she passed on the news that her client had vetoed her involvement. "He doesn't want to be seen to be pushing himself forward," she explained, seemingly as curious as I about what exactly that meant. Over the course of my remaining travels, it was rare to find the hand of Ford or McQueeney actively at work to obstruct me. There were, of course, a few who insisted on checking with them before speaking with me. Generally, they then declined to cooperate. More commonly, people were happy to acknowledge their association with a man who seems to have been genuinely well liked throughout his life. As ever, I hope I lived up to their trust in this book.

In the end, then, this is an unauthorized biography. It is, more than likely, the only kind of biography that will ever be written about Harrison Ford. He has no memoirs to contribute to the world. He doesn't keep a diary, write letters, "haven't even sent a postcard." Nor is he a candidate for a psychiatrist's-couch confessional. He says, "I'm not willing to gift-box myself and say; 'This is the puzzle, no piece missing.' "

While I have succeeded in assembling much new material and have talked to many people who have not spoken publicly about him before, this is not "the puzzle, no piece missing." What it is, however, is the most detailed chronicle of the life and work of Harrison Ford yet attempted.

"I owe a lot of it to luck," Harrison Ford told me when I met him in San Francisco, repeating once more the mantra he uses to sum up his success. As a biographer I must acknowledge that same debt. In the time it has taken me to compile this book I have been lucky enough to meet and enjoy the company of a wonderfully disparate group of people. I cannot hope to acknowledge them all here, yet I cannot let the opportunity pass to thank some of those individuals who made my journey such a memorable one personally:

In Chicago I am indebted to Doug Harrison at Maine East High School, not just for allowing me to roam through his school's records but for assisting in the fiddly photographic arrangements that followed. He also supplied me with names to set me off on the hunt for fellow members of the Class of 1960. Of all "Harry" Ford's former classmates, I must single out Dennis Zetek. His industry on my behalf, not to mention his convivial barroom company, was an enormous boon. Elsewhere in the Windy City I must also thank Michael Wilmington of the *Chicago Tribune* for his urbane company and Bill Haljum for his insightful—and witty—offerings from the Ripon days. Others who were helpful there include Dorothy Densler, Chuck Schaden, Frank Hren, Anne Zetek, Jim Coomer, Cathy Coomer, Betty Lalik, and Grace Fair. I would also like to thank H. Clark Dean for his diligent genealogical research on my behalf.

I will never forget my visit to Ripon, Wisconsin, and the college of which that small city is so justifiably proud. Nor will I forget the kindness and efficiency of Loren Boone, Jeanette Kruger, and Sharon Reber in the college relations office. Special thanks must go to Irv Ott and Robert "Spud" Hannaford for taking time out of their college schedules to see me during my snowbound stay. It was in Ripon that I became aware of the reverence in which Professor William Tyree was held by all who had encountered him. Months later, during a long, amusing, and often inspiring evening at the University Arms in Cambridge, I learned why Harrison Ford, like so many others, have awarded him such a special place in their affections. It was an honor to spend time talking with him.

Elsewhere in Wisconsin I was appreciative of the help provided by David Lagerman at the *Milwaukee Sentinel/Journal* and Dori Sutton at the Barrett Memorial Library in Williams Bay for her research into Harrison Ford's season with the Belfry Players in 1964. It was Dori who was also instrumental in putting me in contact with William Fucik, the director whose influence on Harrison proved greater than I suspected. During my conversation with him in Newport Beach, he modestly asked me to demote his role within Harrison Ford's story to that of a minor player. I hope he can forgive me for making the decision not to accommodate him.

Around America so many others connected with the Harry Ford of those distant high school, college, and early acting days were helpful. Particular thanks must go to Bill Russell, Stuart Shakman, Marilyn Spiegel, Nancy Moses, Trudie Swanson, and Larry Clapper, Nancy Prellwitz, John Hibbard, Don Schober, Bill Per Lee, Marie Lee Matthis, Lester Schwartz, and Mike Cuthbert.

In Laguna Beach thanks are due to Doug Rowe for his invitation to visit and talk to him and his help in contacting Doris Shields and Marthella Randall at the town's splendid new playhouse.

In Los Angeles it was a pleasure to share an affable lunch with Fred Roos, who as well as decanting his memories, helped me contact others who had known his "protégé" during the dark days of the 1960s and early 1970s in Hollywood. Walter Beakel, a wise old Hollywood head now living in Santa Fe, New Mexico, was an illuminating guide to the early days of Columbia and Universal, as were Harrison Ford's fellow "studio fodder" actors Don Stroud and Paul Petersen. Candy Clark had some telling memories of *American Graffiti* and was also helpful in nudging me toward other sources.

In Los Angeles I am particularly grateful to Todd Coleman, a thorough and thoughtful journalist who was kind enough to allow me to use the thirty hours or so of interview material he amassed while writing a tribute to Harrison Ford for the *Hollywood Reporter*.

In New York I was grateful for the help of Rob La Franca of *Forbes* Magazines and Dudley Freeman and his excellent agency. In Paris the encyclopedic knowledge of my colleague Tony Crawley proved priceless. Tony too was generous in allowing me access to the extensive interviews he conducted with Ford in the early years of his fame, when he seemed to be eternally at his side. Tony was also instrumental in connecting me with Agnes Varda, another whose memories of the Harrison Ford of the barren 1960s added much to my understanding of his anger with Old Hollywood.

In the United Kingdom, where Harrison Ford was to lay down the foundations for his fame, many of his old *Star Wars* colleagues were helpful to me. Dave Prowse in particular put me in contact with the still tight-knit band of brothers who shared that adventure "long ago, in a galaxy far, far away." Kenny Baker, Peter Mayhew, Jeremy Bulloch, and Warwick Davis were all generous with their time, as were crew members Tony Waye and Ronnie Taylor.

Once more I owe much to friends and family for their support. This time my parents supplied much more than words of encouragement. The makeshift office in which I spent the weeks around the New Year of 1996 was an oasis of calm at a time of high anxiety. *Diolch*. Thanks, too, to Tina, Graham, and Penny for their understanding.

Of the friends who proved their worth once more—Steve and Fiona, Bart and Martyn "Thunderbird Hire" Palmer—I can add the names of new allies, Pauline and Paul, Lesley and Steve, Geoff (cuts-R-us) Sutton, Toni, Brian, Jay, Fiona (thanks for the translations), Zoe and Uncle Pat Hill. Specific thanks must, however, go to journalist and biographer Daphne Lockyer, now a full-fledged member of the madman-in-the-attic club. Her wicked wisdom, often dispensed while she was struggling with her own book, lifted the gloom more often than she knows.

For the second time I have benefited from the cool assurance of my editor Helen Gummer. The experience of producing this book was entirely different from my previous one. Helen, however, remained loyal, incisive, and encouraging—often in difficult circumstances. I am fortunate to count her as a friend.

I hope I can now count Mike Lewis at Carol Publishing in New York in the same category. During the editing of this American edition, it was my good fortune to benefit from Mike's general wisdom and specialist Harrison Ford knowledge. I look forward to working with him again.

Finally I owe an indescribable debt of gratitude to Cilene Soares. No one suffered more in the face of my deadline, no one offered such unconditional support. I cannot dedicate this book to anyone other than her.

Notes

This book draws on more than one hundred interviews, the majority of which were conducted by the author between June 1994 and July 1996. Original material within this book also includes more than thirty interviews conducted by the American writer Todd Coleman of the *Hollywood Reporter* in early 1994 during the compilation of a special tribute to Harrison Ford. It also draws on a series of interviews Ford conducted with the English journalist and author Tony Crawley in *Films Illustrated, Starburst,* and *Cinema* magazines during the early years of his fame and the author's own interview with Harrison Ford in San Francisco in June 1994.

Prologue

The award of the Star of the Century honor and the NATO convention was widely covered in the Hollywood trade press and was discussed when the author interviewed Ford. This account is based primarily on that conversation and assorted reports of the event, particularly in the *Hollywood Reporter* of March 11, 1994.

Chapters 1 and 2: "Steerage to Suburbia" and "Boy Least Likely to Succeed"

It was Harrison Ford himself who first revealed details of the playground persecution he endured as a young boy. Earliest references to it appeared in *Time* magazine on May 28, 1989, and then in syndicated newspapers across America. This account of his beatings combines his own recollections of the events at that time with the corroborative memories of his Meltzer classmates Dennis Zetek and Marilyn Spiegel.

The Ford family history has, until now, remained largely undisclosed. The account here was constructed in collaboration with the Chicago genealogist H. Clark Dean. Information is based on the following genealogical documents:

State of New York, Certificate and Record of Birth No 57150, for John Ford, registered November 26, 1906.

State of New Jersey, Certificate and Record of Birth for Dora Nidelman, registered Octobe: 9, 1917.

Volume 203 of the Fourteenth Census of the United States, 1920, Kings County, Brooklyn, Enumeration District, 1492, covering Stratford Avenue, Brooklyn.

Cook County Illinois, Marriage Certificate/License No: 1718401-0, February 3, 1942.

Affidavit for Marriage License submitted by John Ford, January 30, 1942.

Cook County, Illinois, Birth Certificate No 32898, for Harrison Ford registered July 27, 1942.

The description of the radio and advertising industries of the 1940s and 1950s draws on sources that include Dorothy Densler at DDB Needham (formerly Needham, Louis, Brorby) in Chicago; a profile of Maurice Needham and his agency in *Radio Annual and Television Yearbook, 1956*; David Halberstam's excellent portrayal of the advertising boom in his book *The Fifties*; and authoratative background provided by the eminent radio historian Chuck Schaden to whom I spoke in Chicago.

The sections on his suburban childhood in Morton Grove and Park Ridge have been informed by author interviews conducted in Chicago with Dennis Zetek and elsewhere in America with Marilyn Spiegel, Nancy Moses, Bill Russell, Jim Coomer, Trudie Swanson, and Larry Clapper. Details of day-to-day life at Maine East High School were also drawn from editions of the *Lens* between 1956 and 1960 viewed at the school in the spring of 1995.

Other references in this section are:

"It was a rough life and my father is unwilling to talk about it" interview with Lawrence Grobel, *Playboy*, September 1993.

"I think it's Yiddish for 'son of Harry.' Even though I wasn't son of Harry" interview with Bruce Newman, *Los Angeles Times Calendar*, August 14, 1994.

"being told that I had a little brother" interview with Jeffrey Abrams in *Weekend Guardian*, August 17, 1991.

"The family joke is that there were different milkmen" Terence Ford interview, *People* magazine, February 10, 1992.

"Our three-year age difference prevented any rivalry" interview, *People* magazine, February 10, 1992.

"Carver invented 101 uses for peanuts. I guess that is kind of unusual" interview by Montgomery Shephard, 1989.

"He didn't go home at night and tell his wife how uncooperative the coal was" interview by Brian D. Johnson, *Maclean's*, July 15, 1991.

"He seemed to have a more interesting career than most other guys' dads" Ian Brodie, *Family Weekly*, May 20, 1984.

"He turned out to be short and unconventional looking" Sky King story quoted in *Time*, by Elaine Dudka and Denise Worrell and Jane Walker in *Time*, May 29, 1989.

"A lot of what he did was in opposition to his father" quoted in Georgina Howell interview, *Sunday Times* magazine, August 8, 1993.

"They might have sensed an underlying arrogance that they didn't want to blossom" interview with Bruce Newman, *Los Angeles Times Calendar*, August 14, 1994.

"I got even by getting on better with the girls" interview with Cindy Pearlman, *Chicago Sun Times*, July 31, 1994.

"My parents came through the Depression" interview David Lewin, *You* magazine, January 4, 1987.

"planks of personality" interview Gordon Thomas, *Western Mail*, September 15, 1989.

"probably the most heroic thing I've ever done" *Playboy*, April 1988, interview with Bill Zehme.

Class of 1960 graduation, report in the *Park Ridge Advocate*, June 9, 1960.

Chapters 3 and 4: "Fish Out of Water" and "Ladykiller"

This account of Harrison's college days draws together interviews and correspondence conducted at Ripon College itself in the spring of 1995 and later in both Britain and America with the following: Bill Haljum, Irv Ott, Bill Per Lee, Nancy Hohnbach Prellwitz, Mary Lee Franke Matthis, John Hibbard, Don Schober, William Tyree, Robert "Spud" Hannaford, and Lester Schwartz. Historical background on the college itself came courtesy of the official history of Ripon, *Ripon College: A History*, by Robert Ashley and George H. Miller. Other details relating to matters including the *Mug*, the controversy surrounding *Threepenny Opera*, and reviews from the Ripon College Days newspaper were gleaned from files at the Ripon office of college relations.

Other sources were:

"I think a personal favor may have been called in" *Chicago Tribune*, 1990.

"I didn't fit in—nor did I want to" interview with David Halberstam, *Vanity Fair*, July 1993.

"some sort of depression" interview with Duane Byrge in *Hollywood Reporter Tribune*, March 1994.

"I would sleep for four or five days at a time" interview David Halberstam, *Vanity Fair*, July 1993.

"there was an option to NOT grow up" interview with Martha Frankel in *Movies USA*, May 1992.

Death of Hortense Marquardt, *Milwaukee Sentinel Journal*, February 17, 1958.

Death of Charles Marquardt, *Milwaukee Sentinel Journal*, December 3, 1961.

"a fake mustache and a half pound of talcum powder in my hair" and "that's when I caught the illness" interview in *Elle*, February 1988, by Nancy Mills.

"not taken lightly" interview with Ian Brodie, *Family Weekly*, May 20, 1984.

Chapter 5: "The Bathtub Baritone"

This chapter draws on interviews conducted by the author with William Fucik, Mike Cuthbert, Michael Wilmington, Robert Hannaford, Bill Russell, Nancy Hohnbach, and Bill Per Lee.

Details of Harrison and Mary Marquardt's Milwaukee wedding were confirmed by State of Wisconsin Certificate of Marriage, No: 64/010694, registered June 30, 1964.

Other references include:

"scientifically provable" interview with Stephanie Mansfield, in *GQ*, June 1994.

"announce to people what I was going to do with my life," "discouragement was always something I was happy to have" interview with Bruce Newman, *Los Angeles Times Calendar*, August 14, 1994.

"It was easier to be poor in California" Tony Crawley, interview *Films Illustrated*, April 1978.

Chapter 6: "California Dreaming"

This chapter draws heavily on author interviews with Doug Rowe, Marthella Randall, and Doris Shields in Laguna Beach, William Fucik in Newport Beach, and Ian Bernard in northern California.

Other references are:

"I just stood there until somebody finally stopped" account of car crash based on numerous interviews primarily *Vanity Fair*, James Kaplan, August 1990 and *US* magazine, August 20, 1990 by Jerry Lazar.

"nobody said any more to me than 'A large pie with cheese and pepperoni' " *Sunday Telegraph*, June 1989.

"When I was very young I thought myself a maverick" interview by Gini Sikes, *Mademoiselle*, February 1988.

Chapter 7: "You Ain't Got It, Kid"

Harrison Ford's own accounts of his early days at Columbia, particularly those given to Tony Crawley, provided a foundation for this chapter. Its construction owes most, however, to author interviews with Walter Beakel, Bill

Haljum, Paul Petersen, and Agnes Varda, whose film biography of her husband, *L'Univers de Jacques Demy*, was also helpful.

Other references are:

"define me by my mistakes" Stephen Fay, *Sunday Times* magazine, May 1985.

"I came into a business that was completely fucked" interview with Stephanie Mansfield, in GQ, June 1994.

rent was "$75 a month" from *Rolling Stone*, June 5, 1981, "Harrison Ford: The Man With the Whip."

"Harrison was my only friend" Paul Winfield interviewed by Sarah Gristwood in *Sunday Express* magazine, September 1991.

"Any substance that altered my mind, I took" interview Terence Ford, *People* magazine, February 10, 1992.

"I was sure that the most important thing for an actor was to hold on to was what was individual about himself" *Playboy*, April 1988, Bill Zehme.

"I had no future in this business" Harrison quoted in interview with Agnes Varda in *L'Univers de Jacques Demy*.

Chapter 8: "Universal Soldier"

This chapter is largely based on author interviews with William Tyree, Walter Beakel, Fred Roos, Paul Petersen, and Don Stroud.

Additional sources:

"I did it on the basis of a moral conviction which I still have" Gini Sikes, *Mademoiselle*, February 1988.

"I don't know what they thought" interview Christine Appleyard, *Daily Mirror*, January 12, 1987.

"I have a constant level of stress that is not either necessary or completely healthy" interview Stephanie Mansfield, GQ, June 1994.

"He was a hippie producer, I guess" interview *Playboy*, April 1988.

"I went and bought a tarantula" in Georgina Howell interview, *Sunday Times* magazine, August 8, 1993.

"I couldn't keep up with those guys. It was too much" MTV, *The Big Picture*, summer 1989.

"Everybody in Hollywood was taking acid and smoking dope and here I was acting like a baby actor getting nowhere" interview Tony Crawley, *Films Illustrated*, April 1978.

"If you think you're going nowhere and you stop, then you're not going nowhere anymore" interview Susan Squire, *Family Weekly*, August 2, 1981.

Chapter 9: "Misfit, Outcast, Orphan"

This chapter is based primarily on author interviews with Fred Roos, Walter Beakel, Doug Rowe, Bill Haljum, and Candy Clark; Todd Coleman's lengthy interviews with Patricia McQueeney, Cindy Williams, and George Lucas; and Tony Crawley's early interviews with Harrison Ford.

Additional sources include:

"I'll build you two tables for $200" David Halberstam interview with Ford in *Vanity Fair*, July 1993.

"It gave me my balls back" interview Tony Crawley, *Cinema*, winter 1981.

"You could always tell he was going to be a star. There was always something different about him and he had a special quality for a young actor—something powerful and forceful" Joan Didion quoted by James Kaplan, *Vanity Fair*, August 1990.

"If I'd been in the company of priests I would have behaved differently" interview with Virginia Campbell, *Movieline*, December 1995.

"I lost all my front teeth" interview Mal Vincent, *Norfolk Virginian Pilot*, August 9 1993.

"When I cry, I cry alone" interview David Lewin, *You* magazine, January 4, 1987.

Chapter 10: "A Cowboy in a Starship"

The story of Harrison's casting, subsequent performance, and doubts about Han Solo relies mainly on author interviews with Fred Roos, Walter Beakel, and Doug Rowe in America; Anthony Waye, David Prowse, Peter Mayhew, and Kenny Baker in England; and George Lucas's recollections to Todd Coleman. The acres of newsprint devoted to the making of *Star Wars* added the background on Lucas's struggle to create the story and the film, with *Time* magazine's major analysis of the phenomenon on May 30, 1977, and Dale Pollock's book *Skywalking* the best sources. Tony Crawley's series of interviews with Ford between 1978 and 1982 were also particularly useful. Other sources were:

"I felt about as big as a pea" quoted in *City Limits*, interview with Dave Pirie, September 10, 1982.

"She goaded me on" interview *US* magazine, June 20, 1983.

"I got paid less for the part of Han Solo" interview Jan Etherington, *TV Times*, October 16, 1982.

"Boring Wood" quoted in *Ritz* magazine, February 1982.

"He was delightfully down to earth" interview with Virginia Campbell in *Movieline*, December 1995.

"This carpenter stud" Carrie Fisher quoted in *Vanity Fair* interview by James Kaplan, August 1990.

"I knew he was going to be a star—someone of the order of Tracy or Bogart" Fisher quoted in *Daily Variety*, March 4, 1994 by David Kronke.

Chapter 11: "Patricia, This Is a Miracle"

Key interviews for this chapter were provided by Fred Roos, Doug Rowe, Walter Beakel, Patricia McQueeney, and Henry Winkler. The majority of Harrison Ford's quotes from the period came from interviews with Tony Crawley. Other sources are:

"Harrison Ford Left These" Sally Kellerman quoted in *Screen International*, September 18, 1982 by Peter Noble.

"He's doing it on purpose" quoted in interview with Roderick Mann in *Los Angeles Times Calendar*, September 6, 1981.

"I was lost" and "I did it for money" criticism of *Force Ten From Navarone* in interview with Ralph Applebaum, *Films*, September 1981.

"It's difficult to pull them out of school for a length of time at this stage in their lives" interview with Mike Munn, *Photoplay*, April 1978.

Chapter 12: "The Bloom Off the Rose"

Interviewees who shone revealing light on the period that led to Harrison's marital breakdown and the beginnings of his relationship with Melissa Mathison included Fred Roos, Walter Beakel, Doug Rowe, Bill Russell, William Tyree, and Mace Neufeld. Other references and sources include:

"monomaniacal attitude" and the account of how Hyams persuaded Harrison to film *Hanover Street* is from an article by Bart Mills in the *Los Angeles Times Calendar* section on May 28, 1978.

"I agreed to do it expecting that the script" quoted in interview with Roderick Mann in *Los Angeles Times Calendar*, September 6, 1981.

"the bloom was sort of off the rose" Carrie Fisher quoted by James Kaplan in *Vanity Fair*, August 1990.

"Do you want me to say it's not true?" *People* magazine, August 14, 1978.

The profile of Melissa Mathison draws on interviews with Fred Roos and a number of interviews and profiles published, primarily in the *Los Angeles Times* on July 24, 1982, the *New York Times* on February 12, 1982, *Vanity Fair* in August 1990, and the *Los Angeles Times Calendar* section on July 9, 1995.

"We went wild in amusement parks at night to get away," Carrie Fisher, *People*, August 14, 1978.

"divorced to each other for the rest of our lives" Ian Brodie, *Family Weekly*, May 20, 1984.

"mutual and generous" interview Tom Seligson, *Parade*, December 25, 1988.

"It had just gone its course" Carrie Fisher quoted in *Vanity Fair*, August 1990.

"Mary and I were dragged apart more and more," *US* magazine, June 20, 1983.

"Success and I will never forgive it for that" interview with Douglas Thompson, *For Women*, April 30 1989.

Chapter 13: "Enslaved to the Empire"

Interviews with Patricia McQueeney, Peter Mayhew, Dave Prowse, and Fred Roos were helpful as were many of the major articles on the making of *The Empire Strikes Back*, particularly in *Rolling Stone* on July 24, 1980, and publicist Alan Arnold's journal *Once Upon a Galaxy*. Other sources are:

"Harrison was constantly calling me on it," Irvin Kershner quoted in *Cinescape* magazine, January 1996.

"I keep saying that if fifty people tell me they like it, then I may change my mind" quoted in interview with Roderick Mann in *Los Angeles Times Calendar*, September 6, 1981.

"Everything became modularized, everything had to be built in two foot dimensions" interview David Ansen, *Newsweek*, June 15, 1981.

"If somebody put $3,000 in my hand when I was a carpenter it felt like real money" Danae Brook, *Evening News*, February 2, 1978.

"We just spent four months working the garden" interview with Ralph Applebaum, *Films*, September 1981.

Chapter 14: "The Whip Hand"

The account of the genesis of *Raiders of the Lost Ark* and Harrison's casting as Indy is based on interviews with George Lucas, Howard Kazanjian, Fred Roos, and Pat McQueeney and a variety of other sources, many of whom have referred to the beachside birth of the film and its place in the forming of the "New Hollywood." These include *A Deal to Remember* by Ben Stein in *New West* magazine in February 1981, *Newsweek*, June 15, 1981, Dale Pollock's *Skywalker*, John Baxter's *Steven Spielberg*, and Michael Pye and Linda Myles's *The Movie Brats*.

The section on the making of *Raiders of the Lost Ark* draws on sources that include interviews with Lucas, Kazanjian, and McQueeney; books by Derek Taylor, John Baxter, Dale Pollock, Aljean Harmetz, and Douglas Brode; extended interviews with cast and crew in *American Cinematographer* in November 1981, *Newsweek* on June 15, 1981; and Tony Crawley's interviews with Harrison Ford at the annual Deauville film festival in the early 1980s.

Other sources include:

"He's a very tough bargainer" Anne Spielberg quoted in the *New Yorker*, March 21, 1994.

"almost as innovative" quoted in *Los Angeles Herald Examiner*, 1981.

"It's a strange thing . . ." interview with Tony Crawley, *Starburst*, 1982.

"A lot of people thought it was a big phoney ball" and other quotes from Randall from a special edition of *American Cinematographer*, November 1981.

"He looks at actors as part of the scenery" Karen Allen quoted in Baxter.

"Steven would say: 'What are you going to do this time, Harrison?' " Bill Hootkins quoted in Baxter.

"She sets a good example. She's a happy person" interview Jeanne Wolff, *Redbook*.

"The amazing thing about Harrison" Spielberg quoted by Joan Goodman in *The Times*, May 18, 1985.

"HARRISON 'STAR WARS' FORD AND TOP HOLLYWOOD SCRIPT WRITER TO MARRY," *National Enquirer*, October 7, 1980, by Malcom Boyes.

"Melissa isn't very thrilled about it though" interview James Verniere, *Arts Weekly*, July 14, 1982.

"We specialize in what we call 'meals in minutes,' " interview Susan Squire, *Family Weekly*, August 2, 1981.

"Oh, no, not another space pilot" interview James Verniere, *Arts Weekly*, July 14, 1982.

"What a beard that guy has. He completely tore my face up" Sean Young interviewed by Ivor Davis in *Daily Express*, August 4, 1982.

"He's one of the sexiest men I've ever met" Sean Young quoted in *People* magazine, 1982.

"Night filming . . . drives everybody a little whacko after a while" interview David Pirie, *City Limits*, September 10, 1982.

"I know he was ready to kill Ridley" quoted in *Premiere* by Steve Oney, March 1988.

Chapter 15: "A Freed Man"

The account of Harrison's appearance at the Deauville Festival is based on articles and interviews by Tony Crawley and others at the time. Melissa's involvement in *E.T.* draws on published interviews with her and from Spielberg biographies by Brode and Baxter. The making of *Return of the Jedi* draws on the author's interviews with Peter Mayhew, Kenny Baker, and David Prowse and major articles on the filming, in particularly *Time*, May 23, 1983, and the *New York Times* on July 11, 1982. Other quoted references are:

"I think—I like to think—I'm a fun dad" interview George Haddad Garcia, *Photoplay*, May 1982.

"I'm a late bloomer. I resisted maturity because I had to learn to do my job, which takes a long time" interview David Lewin, *US* magazine, October 13, 1981.

"I don't feel great about the divorce, but maybe I was hard to live with" interview George Haddad Garcia, *Photoplay*, May 1982.

"I respond to a sort of barometric pressure" Lewin, *US* magazine, October 13, 1981.

"I was definitely not Mr. Sweetness and Light" interview Tom Seligson, *Parade*, December 25, 1988.

"In my youthful ignorance my need not to be dominated was greater than my sense of responsibility" interview Andrew Duncan, *Radio Times*, January 1996.

"It's the teens, the kids who have given me this success" interview George Haddad Garcia, *Photoplay*, May 1982.

"I get all the pleasure of Harrison's kids" interview Melissa with Mike Bygrave, *You Magazine*, 1982.

"I was immediately sold on the story but not on any sort of sci-fi level," Mathison interviewed in *Los Angeles Times*, July 24, 1982.

"I'm good at how they talk because it's how I talk, basically" Melissa in *Los Angeles Times*, July 24, 1982.

"He doesn't suffer fools gladly. If you don't know what you're going to do on the day he gets a little confused and upset" Richard Marquand on Ford in *Starburst*, June 1983.

Chapter 16: "New Beginnings"

The account of Harrison and Melissa's low-key wedding is drawn from numerous reports of the event at the time, including *Time*, *Cosmopolitan*, and the *National Enquirer*. The making of *Temple of Doom* is drawn from a variety of sources, primarily interviews with Ford and Vic Armstrong by Glenn Collins of the *New York Times*, reprinted in the *International Herald Tribune* and *Los Angeles Herald Examiner* in May 1984. The detailed account of his operation is drawn from a report by Ian Brodie in the May 20, 1984, edition of *Family Weekly*. Named author interviewees in this chapter include Fred Roos. Other sources include:

"We all have big changes in our lives that are more or less a second chance" interview with Sarah Gristwood in *Sunday Express Magazine*, September 1991.

"that ugly little fuck" quoted in *City Limits*, interview with Dave Pirie, September 10, 1982.

"I don't get crazy anymore" interview Jeanne Wolf, *Redbook*.

"I don't need a rubber stamp to continually check against" and preceding quote from *Hollywood Reporter Tribute Issue* interview with Duane Byrge, *Hollywood Reporter Special Tribute*, March 1994.

"Melissa and I have mutual respect for and tolerance of each other's foibles and failures" interview in *Milwaukee Sentinel*, July 25, 1990, by Glenn Plaskin.

"Was that scene really dogshit?" interview with Gini Sikes in *Mademoiselle*, February 1988.

"I know just how far back to lean to get out of the picture" Melissa in *Los Angeles Times*, July 24, 1982.

"nonsense" Ridley Scott quoted in *Starburst*, November 1982.

"more a pawn than a partner" and "could have been more than a cult picture" interview with Virginia Campbell, *Movieline*, December 1995.

"Eendeana Zhones, Eendeana Zhones" John Gregory Dunne quoted in *Vanity Fair*, July 1993.

"Both were playing movies I was in" interview with Virginia Campbell, in *Movieline*, December 1995.

"If people know too much about me" interview *New York Newsday*, July 4, 1982.

"Unlike most actors, he is without the need to seduce or charm everyone he meets" Susanna Moore quoted in *New York Times* interview by Trip Gabriel, December 10, 1995.

The account of Harrison's run in with David Litchfield and *Ritz* magazine is taken from the magzine at the time, February 1982.

"He was in incomprehensible pain" and other quotes from George Lucas in *Daily Variety*, March 4, 1994 by David Kronke.

"Is this the way you run your movies" and the anecdote about Barbra Streisand, Carrie Fisher, and Irvin Kershner's appearance on the *Temple of Doom* set comes from an interview with Pat Roach in *Starlog* of June 1988.

Chapter 17: "Bookwork"

Todd Coleman's interviews with Patricia McQueeney and Peter Weir provided the backbone of this chapter. Further references include:

"I wanted to be like those directors in the forties who took assignments from their studios and got on with them" Peter Weir in *American Cinematographer*, April 1986, by Robert S. Birchard.

"I never went back" Kelly McGillis quoted in *Chicago Tribune*, April 5, 1985.

"It's much more fun to watch the tension and anticipation than it is to watch people *shtup!*" *Movieline* interview, Virginia Campbell, December 1995.

"He's planting a crop, or building a bookshelf in Wyoming" Spielberg quoted by James Kaplan in *Vanity Fair*, August 1990.

"I sit and stare at the walls or I walk around and bump into the front and the back of my trailer," he told the American writer Joan Goodman in June 1982, the *Times*.

"Occasionally I rose to protest, but moviemaking is a collaborative effort, and while my attitude was noted, it did not prevail," Sellers *Harrison Ford*, page 166.

Peter Weir's account of the *Witness* test screening comes from an interview with *Screen International* published on June 22, 1985.

Chapter 18: "A Lion in a Cage"

The account of the making of *The Mosquito Coast* is drawn from the numerous interviews and articles written during shooting in Belize, primarily Paul Theroux's article for *Vanity Fair* in December 1986, Guy Martin's piece for *Esquire* in October 1986, and Allan Hunter's for *Films and Filming* magazine in February 1987. These were supplemented by interviews with Peter Weir, Pat McQueeney, and Fred Roos. Additional sources include:

"We're living in a disposable, replaceable, jerry-built world" interview with Bill Zehme, *Playboy*, April 1988.

"You know it's all made from ears and ass parts" interview with Bruce Newman in the *Los Angeles Times Calendar* section, August 14, 1994.

"It just absorbs, digests, and shits out personalities just like yesterday's prunes" interview with Steve Oney in *Premiere*, March 1988.

"It was almost Mother and Allie" Peter Weir, interviewed in the *Chicago Sun Times*, December 1986

"I went absolutely to pieces when I met Harrison Ford" Helen Mirren, *Los Angeles Times*, October 1986.

"It's like trying to fill a big room with an accordion band or a large orchestra where you can bring up the violins and tinkle the bass" interview with Allan Hunter, *Films and Filming*, February 1987.

"I wanted *not* to have control of the situation" interview with *Chicago Tribune*, Gene Siskel, December 14, 1986.

"She works anywhere she can, in the back of the car if she has to" interview with Ian Brodie, *Family Weekly*, 1984.

"I was with a monster agency once" interview with Duane Byrge, *Hollywood Reporter*, March 1994.

"I do keep score" interview with Stephanie Mansfield, in *GQ*, June 1994.

Chapter 19: "Mildly Disturbed"

The account of the making of *Frantic* is drawn from location reports and interviews written at the time, primarily in Premiere, in April 1988, and the *New York Post* on March 9, 1988. The section on *Working Girl* relies on interviews with Patricia McQueeney and Mike Nichols and assorted articles at the time. Details on the house at Jackson Hole have been assembled from the observations of a number of visitors, including Mike Nichols, Jim Harrison, and journalists including Duane Byrge of the *Hollywood Reporter*, James Kaplan of *Vanity Fair*, and Bruce Newman of the *Los Angeles Times*. Other sources include:

"don't even try to interview me" Phillip Wuntch, *New York Times*, February 12, 1982.

"My whole life I've been horrified to have my picture taken" interview with Melissa Mathison, *Los Angeles Times*, July 24, 1982.

"I'm always worried about her," he would come to explain. "That pretty much defines my reality" *Premiere*, Steve Oney, March 1988.

"I have always tried to do different things. It seems to me the logical ambition of an actor" interview Bob Thomas, Associated Press, in *Oshkosh Northwestern*, January 3, 1987.

"The role of an actor is to serve as a mirror" interview with *Chicago Tribune*, Gene Siskel, December 14, 1986.

"At forty-four I can only hope that the old adage that having children keeps you young is true" is from an interview with Baz Bamigboye, *Daily Mail*, January 1987.

"He's remarkably self-possessed" interview Jeanne Wolf, *Redbook*.

"When it's over, I need to patch up everything and get my life back on its feet again" interview with Natalie Gittelson, *McCall's* magazine, June 1991.

"To imagine how terrible someone would feel if his wife were kidnapped wasn't hard" interview with Gini Sikes, *Mademoiselle*, February 1988.

"In terms of details, people don't build houses like that" Jim Harrison quoted in *Vanity Fair*, August 1990.

"Taking that amount of anxiety and pent-up frustration around with you all the time is difficult. It affected me internally" interview by Josey Berlin, *New York Post*, January 2, 1989.

"Fish out of water sometimes die from a lack of something to breathe" interview with Virginia Campbell, *Movieline*, December 1995.

"I get it, this is about real Staten Island girls" profile of Nichols by Joan Juliet Buck in *Vanity Fair*.

Chapter 20: "Never Say Never"

The account of the making of *Indiana Jones and the Last Crusade* was compiled from a variety of sources including biographies by Baxter and Andrew Yule. The description of day-to-day life on the Wyoming ranch draws on a number of interviews Ford has given on his routine there. The section on his rejection of Ripon's honorary degree is based on the author's interview with William Tyree.

Fran Horneff and Jake Steinfeld quotes appeared in the *New York Daily News* on June 5, 1989.

"a creaky old bag of bones" interview with Gerald Clarke, *Time*, February 25, 1985.

"I never play socially" interview with Virginia Campbell, in *Movieline*, December 1995.

"My first reaction was he's not old enough. Then I forgot, I'm too old" interview with Stephen Schaefer in the *Boston Herald*, May 21, 1989.

"If he hits you he hits you" Kevork Malikyan quoted in John Baxter's biography of Spielberg.

Indiana Jones "could kill him" story ran in the *Globe* on January 10, 1989.

"Well we all agreed it was stupid, but we all agreed it would work and it does" interview with Rod Lurie in *New York Daily News*, May 22, 1989.

"I can't play opposite someone called Doody" in Baxter's *Spielberg*.

"I was bound to have fun playing a gruff, Victorian Scottish father" Connery interview by Elaine Dudka, Denise Worrell and Jane Walker in *Time*, May 29, 1989.

"Back to the banal tasks where I belong"—see below.

"I'll fix a fence, repair a piece of equipment or plough the driveway if there's snow. There's always plenty of work to do" both quotes from Tom Seligson, *Parade*, December 25, 1988 .

"Being normal," he would often say, "is a kind of victory" *Elle*, Nancy Mills, February 1988.

"That's none of your ****ing business" interview with Tim Willis, *You Magazine*, August 28, 1988.

"Never say never again" interview with Rod Lurie, *New York Daily News* on May 22, 1989.

"Them that stuck it out was them that won" interview with David Lewin in *US* magazine, October 13, 1981.

"Why don't they invite all the flunkies" interview with Virginia Campbell, *Movieline*, December 1995.

Chapter 21: "Legal Tender"

The account of the legal battle over *E.T.* is drawn from reports in the Hollywood trade press in the first week of March 1989. Author interviews with Fred Roos and Walter Beakel, and Todd Coleman interviews with Bonnie Bedelia, Jeffrey Abrams, and Patricia McQueeney supplemented other sources for the sections on *Presumed Innocent* and *Regarding Henry*. Lengthy on-location pieces on the filming of *Presumed Innocent* in *Premiere* in August 1990 and *Regarding Henry* in *Premiere* in July 1991 were helpful in providing background. Other references are:

"Not the royalty you fear because they can tax you, but the royalty you love because they will make your lives better" Spielberg in *Time*, May 29, 1989.

"Vanity is Fair," "US, as opposed to them," and "Peephole" Lawrence Grobel, *Playboy* interview 1993.

Details of the *News of the World* libel victory came from reports in the *Daily Telegraph* and the *Scotsman* on September 28, 1990.

"Maybe Henry Fonda as he was forty years ago" Pakula interview with Kirsty McNeill, *City Limits*, October 4, 1990.

"He is very quick to make negative decisions. A positive one takes a lot longer" Earl McGrath quoted in Georgina Howell interview, *Sunday Times* magazine, August 8, 1993.

"At the risk of sounding patronizing, Harrison . . ." Pakula in *City Limits*, October 4, 1990.

"What happened in that take is what happened to Harrison" and preceding quotes are from an interview with Jane Adams of *Today* newspaper, on September 20, 1990.

"I don't regret those choices that I didn't make that went on to be big successes for someone else" *Hollywood Reporter Tribute*, March 1994.

"Most scripts I read I don't get past page 20, because they don't have any ambition or any focus or any skill" profile by Simon Banner, *Times Saturday Review*, August 31, 1991.

"I know that moment when you go in to apologize to your kid and you end up hectoring him" interview with Kevin O'Sullivan, *People* magazine, September 8, 1991.

"Girls are different . . ." interview Natalie Gittelson, *McCall's*, June 1991.

"I like your work" interview with Jeffrey Abrams in *Weekend Guardian*, August 17–18, 1991.

"That was the one time I was absolutely befuddled" interview *Entertainment Weekly*, July 12, 1992.

"I'd just as soon people knew as little about me as possible for a variety of reasons" interview in *US* magazine, August 20, 1990 by Jerry Lazar.

Chapter 22: "Who Wants to Be a Hundredaire?"

The account of the making of *Patriot Games* draws on interviews with Mace Neufeld and Bob Rehme, Donald Stewart and Philip Noyce, as well as major articles in *Premiere* in June 1992 and *Empire* in October 1992. Other sources:

"So you're saying you're a hundredaire?" Jeffrey Abrams interview *Weekend Guardian*, August 17–18, 1991.

"I am never far from saying 'oh, wow—how did this come to pass?' " interview David Lewin, *You Magazine*, January 4, 1987.

"It's none of their goddam business" Gerald Clarke, *Time*, February 25, 1985.

"No one is worth these amounts—except to someone else who has the potential to make even more from engaging us" interview with Andrew Duncan, *Radio Times*, January 1996.

"I don't *need* to make the money. You don't *have* to keep your price up" interview, Corinna Honan, *Daily Mail*, September 4, 1992.

Chapter 23: "Running Home"

Much of the account of the making of *The Fugitive* is based on interviews with Arnold Kopelson conducted by the author in London in 1993 and Todd Coleman in Los Angeles in 1994. Additional interviews with Jeb Stuart, Andrew Davis, Patricia McQueeney, and Peter Robb-King were conducted by Todd Coleman.

Other sources:

"Some of our elderly patients didn't recognize him" Dr McKinsey interviewed in *Entertainment Weekly* by Cindy Pearlman, April 23, 1993.

"I think there is such a thing" and following quotes in *Chicago Tribune*, 1990.

"I didn't know the streets anymore, I was really lost" interview Cindy Pearlman, *Chicago Sun Times*, December 17, 1995.

"I wanted to know the minutiae" *Time Out*, Steve Grant, September 22, 1993.

"He didn't even go home to sleep" report in *Globe*, August 3, 1993.

"They knew me when I was just a poor carpenter and a bad actor" Rod Lurie, *New York Daily News*, May 22, 1989.

"I really want to preserve it for my kids—to let them know this is what's dear to me rather than a pile of money in the middle of the floor" interview in *Premiere*, March 1988, Steve Oney.

"I realize that what's most sustaining is having kids" *USA Today*, June 5, 1992 by Tom Green.

"It's no accident that he plays a lot of heroes" Carrie Fisher, quoted in *Time* by Gerald Clarke, February 25, 1985.

"I'm a lot happier it's not Terence Costner or Terence Belushi" Terence Ford interviewed in *People*, February 10, 1982.

"When producer's hear they that I am Harrison Ford's brother they think they are going to get Indiana Jones on the cheap" interview with Martin Dunn in the *Sun*, July 20, 1989.

"Occasionally, he'll ask me what I think about something, and I'll tell him" Harrison interview by Jerry Lazar, *US* magazine, August 20, 1990.

"Harrison was the one who forced me to keep going" interview the *Sun*, July 20, 1989.

"If this truck is found, please return to Richard Kimble" *National Enquirer*, August 31, 1993.

"I didn't think *The Fugitive* would do as well as it did" Larry King column, *USA Today*, January 2, 1996.

Chapter 24: "The Ryan Game"

The account of the making of *Clear and Present Danger* is based on the author's own interviews with Harrison Ford, Joaquim De Almeida, Mace Neufeld, and others at the Ritz Carlton Hotel in San Francisco in June 1994. Additional interviews by Todd Coleman with Donald Stewart, Mace Neufeld, and Philip Noyce were also helpful, as were articles in *Entertainment Weekly* (on the ongoing complaints of Tom Clancy), *Premiere*, and elsewhere. Comments from Candy Clark are from an author interview.

The opening account of the Disneyland scene comes from comments made to author David Halberstam, referred to in his *Vanity Fair* profile of Ford, while details of Harrison's charity work and his involvement in Buddhism are derived from sources including a March 4, 1994, *Daily Variety* article on his involvement with Conservation International, a report on his support of Amish territory in the *Lancaster* (*Pennsylvania*) *New Era*, April 9, 1990, by Ed Klimuska, the transcript of the BBC World Service interview with John Tidmarsh, correspondence between Harrison and U.S. Senator Max Baucus, and Gendun Rinchen's testimony to the East Asian and Pacific Affairs Subcommittee of the Senate Foreign Relations Commitee on September 7, 1995.

Other sources:

"And that is its *only* use" interview David Halberstam, *Vanity Fair*, July 1993.

"I'm sick to *death* of celebrity spokesmen for causes. Drives me nuts" interview by Corinna Honan, *Daily Mail*, September 4, 1992.

quotes from Peter Seligman in March 4, 1994 edition of *Daily Variety*, report by Jerry Roberts.

"Work out your salvation with diligence" interview with Natalie Gittelson, *McCall's*, June 1991.

"Mustang, The Hidden Kingdom," from *Hello!* magazine, 1994.

The "thick feeling of fear" and subsequent quotes from Harrison and Melissa on the Rinchen issue are from a transcript of the BBC World Service, *Outlook* program on June 16, 1993.

"That's exactly why you're not doing the goddamn shot!" interview with Randy Wayne White, *Premiere*, September 1994.

"You do things when you are typing that you would never do if you had to fucking stand there and deliver" interview *Entertainment Weekly*, August 19, 1994.

"anal" Noyce in *Sydney Morning Herald*, August 20, 1994.

"made him look terrible" story about Japanese advert in the *Star*, November 2, 1993.

"straightens all the piles" interview in *Chicago Sun Times*, by Richard Roeper, July 15, 1990.

"The house becomes a metaphor" Mike Nichols in *Vanity Fair*, August 1990.

"If you direct you're looking at two years instead of five or six months. Enough is enough" interview Virginia Campbell, *Movieline*, December 1995.

"I am better off in ones and twos" David Lewis, *US* magazine, October 13, 1981.

"Harrison had to come, and he was in excruciating pain" Glimcher quoted in *Vanity Fair*, August 1990.

"If Rabin and Arafat could shake hands, Clancy and Neufeld could" Neufeld quoted, *Entertainment Weekly*, August 19, 1994.

Chapter 25: "Dying Is Easy"

The account of the making of *Sabrina* is drawn from interviews given by Sydney Pollack and Greg Kinnear during an interview-press conference at the Dorchester in London attended by the author in January 1996. Other primary sources include a lengthy article on the making of the movie in *Premiere* in November 1995. Also:

"Temptation is a two-way street" and following quotes are from an interview with Shaun Usher in the *Daily Mail* on September 24, 1990.

"Harrison doesn't attract that kind of innuendo much" in *Entertainment Weekly*, August 11, 1995.

"Now, you tell me, if Harrison Ford was having an affair with someone" Julia Ormond interviewed by Peter Richmond in *GQ*, May 1996.

"I don't think Harrison appreciates how much people think of him" Julia Ormond in *OK* magazine, January 1996.

"Drag your ass back down again" quote in interview by Brian D. Johnson, *Maclean's*, July 15, 1991.

"The old canard that dying is easy but comedy is hard is true" *New York Times*, Trip Gabriel, December 1995.

Chapter 26: "Troubles"

The account of the making of *The Devil's Own* is drawn from the wide variety of trade newspaper and magazine articles that covered the controversy during 1996 and 1997. Particularly helpful were *Film Review*; June 1997; *Newsweek*, January 28; 1997; *Premiere*, January 1997; *Sunday Times* (London), January 19, 1997. The making of *Air Force One* was drawn from an equally disparate collection of articles and interviews, including *Vogue*, March 1997; *Premiere*, July 1997; The New York *Daily News*, July 1997; and *Entertainment Weekly*, May 1997. Other sources include:

"There's always some project to get involved in back there" *New York Times*, Trip Gabriel, December 1995.

"Very successful actors pay an enormous price in shame" Mike Nichols in *Vanity Fair*, James Kaplan, August 1990.

The announcement of Scorsese's involvement in *Kundun* was made in *Variety* on August 14, 1995.

"Furious" and the *Seven Days in Tibet v. Kundun* row was the subject of a *Sunday Times* feature on October 15, 1995.

"Harrison told me: 'Look we're here now' " and "The responsibility was on my head" interview with Lesley O'Toole, *The Guardian*, June 13, 1997.

"Baldly it was an apology for the IRA. I refused to be part of that" interview by James Delingpole, *Daily Telegraph Magazine*, June 14, 1997.

"The process was very frightening to Brad" Pakula interviewed by Demetrios Matheou, *Premiere*, May 1997.

"Wolfgang is one of the great tube-movie makers" *Air Force One* location report, *Premiere*, February 1997.

"Working with Brad was fine" interview with Lesley O'Toole, *The Guardian*, June 13, 1997.

"I just wanted to be seen wrestling with the question" interview, *Neon* magazine, June 1997.

"Underage Storm as Diana Takes Harry to IRA Film," *Daily Mail*, June 23, 1997.

"He says it is none of his business as he is not the mother or the father" Pat McQueeney, *The Mirror*, June 24, 1997.

"Maybe they know I like to take a lot of punishment!" Pakula interviewed by Demetrios Matheou, *Premiere*, May 1997.

"Let's say I go to the hardware store and buy screws. I don't want to talk about whether I'm going to do *Indiana Jones IV*" interview with Cindy Pearlman, *Chicago Sun Times*, December 17, 1995.

"Might as well have the hat on my fucking head" interview with Stephanie Mansfield, in GQ magazine, June 1994.

"If I die and I ain't peaceful" interview with Stephanie Mansfield, in GQ magazine, June 1994.

Bibliography

Arnold, Alan. *Once Upon a Galaxy: A Journal of the Making of the Empire Strikes Back*. Ballantine, 1980.

Ashley, Robert, and Miller, George H. *Ripon College: A History*. Ripon College Press, 1990.

Barabas, SuzAnne Barabas, and Barabas, Gabor. *Gunsmoke: A Complete History*. McFarland, 1990.

Baxter, John. *Steven Spielberg: The Unauthorized Biography*. HarperCollins, 1996.

Brode, Douglas. *The Films of Steven Spielberg*, Citadel, New York, 1995.

Brooks, Tim, and Marsh, Earle. *The Complete Directory to Prime Time Network and Cable TV Shows*. Ballantine, 1979.

Cooke, Alistair. *America*. BBC Books, 1973.

Eisner, Joel, and Krinsky, David. *Television Comedy Series—An Episodic Guide to 153 TV Sitcoms in Syndication*. McFarland, 1984.

Evans, Bob. *The Kid Stays in the Picture*. Aurum, 1994.

Farber, David. *The Age of Great Dreams: America in the 1960s*. Hill and Wang, 1994.

Gelmis, Joseph. *The Film Director as Superstar*. Doubleday, 1970.

Gianakos, Larry James. *Television Drama Series Programming: A Comprehensive Chronicle 1959–1975*. Scarecrow Press, 1978.

Gilbert, Martin. *Jewish History Atlas*. Weidenfeld and Nicolson, 1969.

Goodwin, Michael, and Wise, Naomi. *On the Edge: The Life and Times of Francis Coppola*. Morrow, New York, 1989.

Halberstam, David. *The Fifties*. Ballantine, 1993.

Harmetz, Aljean. *Rolling Breaks and Other Movie Business*. Knopf, 1983.

Hirschhorn, Clive. *The Columbia Story*. 1989.

Holden, Anthony. *The Oscars: The Secret History of Hollywood's Academy Awards*. Little, Brown, 1993.

Kirchner, Walther. *Russian History*. HarperCollins, 1991.

Laurie, Joe, Jr. *Vaudeville: From the Honky Tonks to the Palace*. Holt, 1953.

Lentz, Harris M., III. *Science Fiction, Horror and Fantasy Film and Television Credits*. McFarland, 1983.

Marill, Alvin H. *Movies Made for Television*. Zoetrope, New York, 1986.

McGilligan, Patrick. *Jack's Life*. Random House, 1994.

Pilato, Herbie J. *The Kung Fu Book of Caine*. Tuttle, 1993.

Parish, James Robert, and Terrace, Vincent. *The Complete Actors' Television Credits, 1948–1988*. Scarecrow Press, 1989.

Perry, Jeb H. *Universal Television*. Scarecrow Press, 1983.

Phillips, Julia. *You'll Never Eat Lunch in This Town Again*. Mandarin, 1991.

Pollock, Dale. *Skywalking: The Life and Films of George Lucas*. Harmony Books, New York, 1983.

Pye, Michael, and Myles, Linda. *The Movie Brats: How the Film Generation Took Over Hollywood*. Faber & Faber, 1979.

Schnedler, Jack. *Chicago*. Compass, 1993.

Schrader, Paul. *Schrader on Schrader and Other Writings*, edited by Kevin Jackson. Faber & Faber, London, 1990.

Sellers, Robert. *Harrison Ford*. Hale, 1992.

Taylor, Derek. *The Making of Raiders of the Lost Ark*. Ballantine, 1981.

Thomas, Bob. *King Cohn*. Bantam, New York, 1978.

Wiley, Mason, and Bona, Damien. *Inside Oscar: The Unofficial Story of the Academy Awards*. Ballantine, 1988.

Yule, Andrew. *Sean Connery: From 007 to Hollywood Icon*. Donald Fine, New York, 1992.

Credits

THEATER, 1964 to 1965

Take Her, She's Mine
The Belfry Theater, Williams Bay, Wisconsin. Summer 1964.
DIRECTOR: William Fucik.
CAST: Ray Sager, Fred DiMaio, Eleanor Ferris, Marian Carroll, Nancy Schuyler, Connie Platts, Jeff Jacobs, Michael Wilmington.

Little Mary Sunshine
The Belfry Theater, Williams Bay, Wisconsin. Summer 1964.
DIRECTOR: William Fucik. Choreography/Music: Ann Rich Burghoff, Mike Cuthbert.
CAST: Raymond Sager, Fred Di Maio.

Night of the Iguana
The Belfry Theater, Williams Bay, Wisconsin. Summer 1964.
ROLE: Reverend T. Lawrence Shannon.
DIRECTOR: William Fucik.
CAST: Raymond Sager, Fred Di Maio, Shirley Kehoe, Lois Blakesley, Joan Madden, Sherman Swanson.

Dark of the Moon
The Belfry Theater, Williams Bay, Wisconsin. Summer 1964.
DIRECTOR: William Fucik.
CAST: Raymond Sager, Fred Di Maio, Eleanor Ferris, Frances Dee, Fred Clausen, Edna Wilmington.

Damn Yankees
The Belfry Theater, Williams Bay, Wisconsin. Summer 1964.
ROLE: Joe Hardy.
DIRECTOR: William Fucik. Choreography/Music: Ann Rich Burghoff, Mike Cuthbert.
CAST: Raymond Sager, Fred Di Maio, Linda Girard, Shirley McNeil, Shirley Hayes, Arlene Robbins.

Sunday in New York
The Belfry Theater, Williams Bay, Wisconsin. Summer 1964.
DIRECTOR: William Fucik.
CAST: Raymond Sager, Fred Di Maio.

John Brown's Body
Laguna Beach Playhouse, March, 1965.
ROLE: Clay Wingate.
DIRECTOR: Doug Rowe. Musical Arrangement: Ian Bernard.
CAST: Rowe, Marthella Randall, Denise Ulm, Bob Wentz, Ed Brown.

TELEVISION, 1967–1977

EPISODIC APPEARANCES

The Virginian
BROADCAST: NBC. (February 1, 1967)
EPISODE: The Modoc Kid.
CAST: James Drury, Doug McClure—guest John Saxon.

Ironside
BROADCAST: NBC. (December 7, 1967)
EPISODE: The Past Is Prologue.
CAST: Raymond Burr, Don Galloway, Barbara Anderson, Johnny Seven—
guests, Victor Jory, Jill Donahue, Jean Inness.

My Friend Tony
BROADCAST: NBC. (February 16, 1969)
EPISODE: The Hazing.
CAST: James Whitmore, Enzo Cerusico—guests, Steve Franken, Tom Fielding.

Love, American Style
BROADCAST: ABC. (November 24, 1969)
EPISODE: Love and the Former Marriage.
CAST: Carl Betz, Dana Wynter, Elliott Reid, Jenny Sullivan.

Dan August
BROADCAST: ABC. (March 11, 1971)
EPISODE: The Manufactured Man.
CAST: Burt Reynolds, Norman Fell, Ned Romero, Richard Anderson, Ena
Hartmann—guests Peter Brown, David Soul, Mickey Rooney, Keith Andes,
Barney Phillips, Billy Dee Williams.

Gunsmoke
BROADCAST: CBS. (November 20, 1972)
EPISODE: The Sodbusters. ROLE: Print.
CAST: James Arness—guests Morgan Woodward, Alex Cord, Katherine
Justice, Leif Garrett, Dawn Lyn, Robert Viharo, Richard Bull, Joe di Reda.

Gunsmoke
BROADCAST: CBS. (February 5, 1973)
EPISODE: Whelan's Men. ROLE: Hobey.
CAST: James Arness, Amanda Blake—guests Robert Burr, William Bramley, Noble Willingham, Frank Ramirez, Gerald McRaney, Bobby Hall.

Kung Fu
BROADCAST: ABC. (February 21, 1974)
EPISODE: Crossties.
CAST: David Carradine—guests Barry Sullivan, Andy Robinson, Denver Pyle, John Anderson, Dennis Fimple.

Petrocelli
BROADCAST: NBC. (October 2, 1974)
EPISODE: Edge of Evil.
CAST: Barry Newman, Susan Howard, Albert Salmi, David Huddleston—guests William Shatner, Susan Oliver, Lynn Carlin, Dana Elcar, Morgan Paull, Glenn Corbett.

TELEVISION FILMS/PILOTS/MOVIES OF THE WEEK

The Intruders
BROADCAST: NBC. (November 10, 1970)
ROLE: Carl.
DIRECTOR: William A. Graham. Producer: Bert Granet (executive), James Duff McAdams. Writer: Dean E. Riesner from a story by William Douglas Lansford.
CAST: Anne Francis, Don Murray, Edmond O'Brien, John Saxon, Shelly Novack, Dean Stanton, Zalman King, Stuart Margolin, Gene Evans, Edward Andrews.

Judgment: The Court Martial of Lt. William Calley
BROADCAST: ABC. (January 12, 1975)
DIRECTOR/PRODUCER: Stanley Kramer. Writer: Henry Denker.
CAST: Tony Musante, Richard Basehart, Bo Hopkins, G. D. Spradlin, Bill Lucking, Linda Haynes, Olive Clark, Ben Plazza, Leon Russom, Fredd Wayne.

James A. Michener's "Dynasty"
BROADCAST: NBC. (March 13, 1976)
ROLE: Mark Blackwood.
DIRECTOR: Lee Philips. Producer: David Paradine. Writer: Sidney Carroll from a story by James A. Michener.
CAST: Sarah Miles, Stacy Keach, Harris Yulin, Amy Irving, Granville Van Dusen, Charles Weldon, Gerrit Graham.

The Possessed
BROADCAST: NBC. (May 1, 1977)
ROLE: Paul Winjam.
DIRECTOR: Jerry Thorpe. Producer: Philip Mandelker. Writer: John Sacret
Young.
CAST: James Farentino, Joan Hackett, Claudette Nevins, Eugene Roche, Ann
Dusenberry, Diana Scarwid, Dinah Manoff, Carol Jones, P. J. Soles.

FEATURE FILMS, 1967 TO THE PRESENT DAY

Dead Heat on a Merry-Go-Round
Columbia. (1967)
ROLE: Bellboy.
DIRECTOR/WRITER: Bernard Girard. Producer: Carter de Haven.
Cast: James Coburn, Camilla Sparv, Aldo Ray, Nina Wayne, Severn Darden,
Todd Armstrong, Rose Marie, Robert Webber.

A Time for Killing/The Long Ride Home (UK title)
Columbia/Sage Western. (1967)
ROLE: Lieutenant Shaffer.
DIRECTOR: Phil Karlson. Producer: Harry Joe Brown. Writer: Halsted Welles
from a novel by Nelson and Shirley Wolford.
CAST: Glenn Ford, George Hamilton, Inger Stevens, Max Baer, Paul Petersen,
Todd Armstrong.

Luv
Columbia/Jalem. (1967)
ROLE: Hippie.
DIRECTOR: Clive Donner. Producer: Martin Manulis. Writer: Elliott Baker from
a play by Murray Shisgal.
CAST: Jack Lemmon, Peter Falk, Elaine May, Nina Wayne, Severn Darden,
Paul Hartman, Eddie Mayehoff.

Journey to Shiloh
Universal. (1967)
ROLE: Willie Bill Bearden.
DIRECTOR: William Hale. Producer: Howard Christie. Writer: Gene Coon
based on a novel by Will Henry.
CAST: James Caan, Michael Sarrazin, Brenda Scott, Paul Petersen, Don
Stroud, Jan Michael Vincent, John Doucetter, Noah Beery.

Zabriskie Point
MGM/Carlo Ponti. (1969)
ROLE: Airport worker.

DIRECTOR: Michelangelo Antonioni. Producer: Carlo Ponti. Writer: Antonioni, Fred Gardner, Sam Shepard, Tonino Guerra, Clare Peploe.
CAST: Mark Frechette, Daria Halprin, Rod Taylor, Paul Fix, G. D. Spradlin, Bill Garaway, Kathleen Cleaver, Open Theater of Joe Chaikin.

Getting Straight
Columbia/The Organization. (1970)
ROLE: Jake.
DIRECTOR/PRODUCER: Richard Rush. Writer: Robert Kaufman based on a novel by Ken Kolb.
CAST: Elliott Gould, Candice Bergen, Robert F. Lyons, Jeff Corey, Max Julien, Cecil Kellaway, John Lormer, Leonard Stone, William Bramley, Jenny Sullivan.

American Graffiti
Universal/Lucasfilm. (1973)
ROLE: Bob Falfa.
DIRECTOR/WRITER: George Lucas. Producer: Francis Coppola/Gary Kurtz.
CAST: Richard Dreyfuss, Candy Clark, Ron Howard, Paul Le Mat, Charlie Martin Smith, Cindy Williams, Mackenzie Philips.

The Conversation
Paramount/Coppola. (1974)
ROLE: Martin Stett.
DIRECTOR/PRODUCER/WRITER: Francis Coppola.
CAST: Gene Hackman, Frederic Forrest, John Cazale, Allen Garfield, Cindy Williams.

Star Wars
Twentieth Century Fox/Lucasfilm. (1977)
ROLE: Han Solo.
DIRECTOR/WRITER: George Lucas. Producer: Gary Kurtz.
CAST: Sir Alec Guinness, Mark Hamill, Carrie Fisher, Peter Cushing, David Prowse, Anthony Daniels, Kenny Baker, Peter Mayhew.

Heroes
Universal. (1977)
ROLE: Kenny.
DIRECTOR: Jeremy Paul Kagan. Producer: David Foster, Lawrence Turman. Writer: James Carabatsos, David Freeman (uncredited).
CAST: Henry Winkler, Sally Field, Val Avery.

Force Ten From Navarone
Columbia/AIP/Guy Hamilton. (1978)
ROLE: Barnsby.

DIRECTOR: Guy Hamilton. Producer: Oliver A. Unger. Writer: Robin Chapman from a novel by Alistair MacLean.
CAST: Robert Shaw, Carl Weathers, Franco Nero, Edward Fox, Barbara Bach, Richard Kiel.

Hanover Street
Columbia. (1979)
ROLE: David Halloran.
DIRECTOR/WRITER: Peter Hyams. Producer: Paul N. Lazarus III.
CAST: Lesley-Anne Down, Christopher Plummer, Alec McCowen, Max Wall, Michael Sacks, Richard Masur.

The Frisco Kid
Warner. (1979)
ROLE: Tommy.
DIRECTOR: Robert Aldrich. Producer: Mace Neufeld. Writer: Michael Elias, Frank Shaw.
CAST: Gene Wilder, Ramon Bieri, Penny Peyser, Leo Fuchs, Val Bisoglio, William Smith, George Ralph Di Cenzo, Beege Barkett, Shay Duffin.

Apocalypse Now
Omni Zoetrope. (1979)
ROLE: Colonel Lucas.
DIRECTOR/PRODUCER: Francis Coppola. Writer: Coppola, John Milius.
CAST: Marlon Brando, Martin Sheen, Robert Duvall, Frederic Forrest, Dennis Hopper, Larry Fishburne, Sam Bottoms.

The Empire Strikes Back
Twentieth Century Fox/Lucasfilm. (1980)
ROLE: Han Solo.
DIRECTOR: Irvin Kershner. Producer: Gary Kurtz. Writer: Leigh Brackett, Lawrence Kasdan from a story by George Lucas.
CAST: Sir Alec Guinness, Carrie Fisher, Mark Hamill, Billy Dee Williams, Anthony Daniels, David Prowse, Kenny Baker, Peter Mayhew.

Raiders of the Lost Ark
Paramount/Lucasfilm. (1981)
ROLE: Indiana Jones.
DIRECTOR: Steven Spielberg. Producer: Frank Marshall. Writer: Lawrence Kasdan.
CAST: John Rhys Davies, Karen Allen, Ronald Lacey, Paul Freeman, Denholm Elliott, Alfred Molina.

Blade Runner
Warner/The Ladd Company/Blade Runner Partnership. (1982)

ROLE: Rick Deckard.
DIRECTOR: Ridley Scott. Producer: Scott, Michael Deeley. Writer: Hampton Fancher, David Peoples from a novel by Philip K. Dick.
CAST: Rutger Hauer, Sean Young, Edward James Olmos, Darryl Hannah, M. Emmet Walsh.

Return of the Jedi
Twentieth Century Fox/Lucasfilm. (1983)
ROLE: Han Solo.
DIRECTOR: Richard Marquand. Producer: Howard Kazanjian. Writer: Lawrence Kasdan, George Lucas.
CAST: Carrie Fisher, Mark Hamill, Anthony Daniels, Billy Dee Williams, David Prowse, Kenny Baker, Peter Mayhew.

Indiana Jones and the Temple of Doom
Paramount/Lucasfilm. (1984)
ROLE: Indiana Jones.
DIRECTOR: Steven Spielberg. Producer: Robert Watts. Writer: Willard Huyck, Gloria Katz from a story by George Lucas.
CAST: Kate Capshaw, David Yip, Denholm Elliott, Philip Stone, Ke Huy Quan, Amrish Puri, Roshan Seth, Dan Aykroyd, Roy Chiao.

Witness
Paramount/Edward Feldman. (1985)
ROLE: John Book.
DIRECTOR: Peter Weir. Producer: Edward Feldman. Writer:
W. Earl Wallace, William Kelley.
CAST: Kelly McGillis, Danny Glover, Lukas Haas, Alexander Godunov, Jan Rubes, Josef Sommer, Patti LuPone, Viggo Mortensen.

The Mosquito Coast
Saul Zaentz/Jerome Hellman. (1986)
ROLE: Allie Fox.
DIRECTOR: Peter Weir. Producer: Zaentz/Hellman. Writer: Paul Schrader from a novel by Paul Theroux.
CAST: Helen Mirren, River Phoenix, Jadrien Steele, Andre Gregory.

Frantic
Warner/Mount. (1988)
ROLE: Richard Walker.
DIRECTOR: Roman Polanski. Producer: Thom Mount, Tim Hampton. Writer: Polanski, Gerard Brach.
CAST: Emmanuelle Seigner, Betty Buckley, Alexandra Stewart, John Mahoney, Gerard Klein.

Working Girl
Twentieth Century Fox. (1988)
ROLE: Jack Trainer.
DIRECTOR: Mike Nichols. Producer: Douglas Wick. Writer: Kevin Wade.
CAST: Melanie Griffith, Sigourney Weaver, Joan Cusack, Alec Baldwin, Oliver Platt, Olympia Dukakis, Nora Dunn, James Lally, Philip Bosco.

Indiana Jones and the Last Crusade
UIP/Paramount/Lucasfilm. (1989)
ROLE: Indiana Jones.
DIRECTOR: Steven Spielberg. Producer: Robert Watts. Writer: Jeffrey Boam from a story by George Lucas.
CAST: Sean Connery, Alison Doody, Julian Glover, John Rhys-Davies, Denholm Elliott, River Phoenix, Kevork Malikyan, Richard Young, Michael Byrne, Alexei Sayle, Robert Eddison.

Presumed Innocent
Warner/Mirage. (1990)
ROLE: Rusty Sabich.
DIRECTOR: Alan J. Pakula. Producer: Sydney Pollack, Mark Rosenberg. Writer: Pakula, Frank Pierson from a novel by Scott Turow.
CAST: Greta Scacchi, Bonnie Bedelia, Brian Dennehy, Raul Julia, Paul Winfield, John Spencer, Sab Shimono, Joe Grifasi, Jesse Bradford.

Regarding Henry
UIP/Paramount. (1991)
ROLE: Henry Turner.
DIRECTOR: Mike Nichols. Producer: Scott Rudin, Mike Nichols. Writer: Jeffrey Abrams.
CAST: Annette Bening, Bill Nunn, Mikki Allen, Donald Moffat, Aida Linares, Bruce Altman, Elizabeth Wilson, Robin Bartlett, Rebecca Miller.

Patriot Games
Paramount/Neufeld-Rehme. (1992)
ROLE: Jack Ryan.
DIRECTOR: Phillip Noyce. Producer: Mace Neufeld, Robert Rehme. Writer: W. Peter Iliff, Donald Stewart from a novel by Tom Clancy.
CAST: Anne Archer, Sean Bean, James Earl Jones, James Fox, Patrick Bergin, Thora Birch, Samuel L. Jackson, Richard Harris, Polly Walker.

The Fugitive
Warner/Barish/Kopelson. (1993)
ROLE: Dr Richard Kimble.
DIRECTOR: Andrew Davis. Producer: Arnold Kopelson. Writer: Jeb Stuart and David Twohy based on characters created by Roy Huggins.

CAST: Tommy Lee Jones, Jeroen Krabbe, Sela Ward, Joe Pantoliano, Andreas Katsulas.

Clear And Present Danger
Paramount/Neufeld-Rehme. (1994)
ROLE: Jack Ryan.
DIRECTOR: Philip Noyce. Producer: Mace Neufeld, Robert Rehme. Writer: Donald Stewart, Steven Zaillian and John Milius from a novel by Tom Clancy.
CAST: Anne Archer, Willem Dafoe, James Earl Jones, Henry Czerny, Joaquim De Almeida, Donald Moffat, Harrus Yulin, Thora Birch, Miguel Sandoval.

Sabrina
UIP/Paramount/Mirage. (1995)
ROLE: Linus Larrabee.
DIRECTOR: Sydney Pollack. Producer: Pollack, Scott Rudin. Writer: Barbara Benedek, David Rayfiel.
CAST: Julia Ormond, Greg Kinnear.

The Devil's Own
Columbia TriStar/Lawrence Gordon. (1996)
ROLE: Tom O'Meara.
DIRECTOR: Alan J Pakula. Producer: Gordon, Robert F Colesberry. Writer: David Aaron Cohen, Vincent Patrick, Kevin Jarre.
CAST: Brad Pitt, Margaret Colin, Ruben Blades, Treat Williams, Natascha McElhone.

Air Force One
Beacon Pictures. (1997)
ROLE: President James Marshall.
DIRECTOR: Wolfgang Petersen. Writer: Andrew Marlowe.
CAST: Gary Oldman, Glenn Close, Wendy Crewson.

Index

HF = Harrison Ford. Films/plays in which he took part are indicated by HF